NW08001047 Create €15 00

Cornelius Cardew

A Reader

Edited by Edwin Prévost

WITHDRAWN

D1418741

Cornelius Cardew Reader – edited by Edwin Prévost © 2006

Copyright for all texts written by Cornelius Cardew reside in Horace Cardew.
Copyright for all other texts and illustrations reside with the respective authors
and publishers.

All rights reserved. No part of this publication may be reproduced,
stored in a retrieval system or transmitted in any form or by any other means,
without permission of the publishers.

First published in 2006 by:
Copula – an imprint of Matchless Recordings and Publishing
2 Shetlock's Cottages, Matching Tye, near Harlow, Essex CM17 OQR, UK

British Library Cataloguing in Publication Data

Cornelius Cardew: A Reader
Cardew, Cornelius and others

ISBN 0-9525492-2-0

Cover design: Ian Walters
Typography: Maureen Asser at Wildcat, email wildcat1@ntlworld.com
Printed by: Antony Rowe Ltd. Bumper's Farm, Chippenham, Wiltshire SN14 6LH, UK

Acknowledgements

Thanks are due in particular to the authors of the commentaries on Cardew's work who have been generous and positive in their responses to this publishing suggestion. Others have helped in the search for various sources and materials to assist publication. Most notably Harry Gilonis, John Lely, Michael Parsons, Jean Prévost, John Tilbury and Seymour Wright.

Acknowledgement is also due to the following for their kind permission (mostly freely given) to reprint articles and musical examples:

Contact Magazine, Financial Times, Leonardo Music Journal, The London Magazine, Matchless Recordings, The Musical Times, MusikTexte – Zeitshrift für neue Musik Köln, New Departures, New Statesman, Oxford University Press, Peters Edition Limited.

A number of magazines which had published Cardew's early writings no longer exist. Attempts were made to find the publishers to seek their formal permissions. In the light of our failure to acquire the conventional consent we ask for their forbearance.

NEWMAN UNIVERSITY
COLLEGE
BARTLEY GREEN
BIRMINGHAM B32 3NT

CLASS 780.92
BARCODE 01400185
AUTHOR CAR

Contents

Items in chronological order.

Editor's note: This Reader includes most of Cornelius Cardew's published writings. Many were published in newspapers and periodicals. Others appeared in books. We have also included a number of Cardew's lectures and talks. These have been mostly drawn from his notes. We decided to treat the different types of material by using different fonts. Some of these are close to the fonts used in the original (e.g. *Treatise Handbook*). In treating the various texts herein there were numerous typographical and stylistic inconsistencies throughout. Where possible, and for the sake of clarity, these have been corrected and unified.

Commentaries

Introduction
Michael Parsons

Cornelius Cardew (1936-1981) was one of the most adventurous and innovative musicians of his generation, a composer who questioned the very foundations of musical activity, extended its boundaries in unprecedented directions and enquired deeply into its social meaning and relevance. His passionate and untiring quest for wider social significance led him eventually to become a political activist. From 1972 he criticised and rejected his own previous musical life as a form of 'bourgeois individualism'. He joined a revolutionary Marxist-Leninist party and for the rest of his life he dedicated himself to political work, taking part in the anti-Fascist struggles in the East End of London and in the defence of racially threatened immigrant communities, campaigning in support of Irish Republicanism and in opposition to all forms of US, British and Soviet imperialism. At the height of his commitment to this political activity he died tragically at the age of 45, killed in a hit-and-run incident near his home in East London.

From an early age Cardew was exposed to an unusually wide range of cultural influences. His father, the potter Michael Cardew, was a pioneering artist and craftsman whose work reflected a deep involvement with African and Far-Eastern traditions; his mother was also an artist and teacher. He grew up in an unconventional atmosphere of libertarian bohemianism, and by the time he became a pupil in the choir school of Canterbury Cathedral, he was already a rebel and a dissident in relation to the prevalent values inculcated by an English public school education. As a student at the Royal Academy of Music (1953-57) he attracted attention as an outstandingly gifted pianist and composer, responsive to the most recent developments in European avant garde music. He espoused the principles of serialism in a number of early works, including two string trios and three piano sonatas; his complete assurance and technical mastery of this style of writing is evident in the virtuosity of his *Third Piano Sonata* (1957-58). He went to Germany to study with Stockhausen in 1957, and worked as his assistant on the composition of *Carré* (1959-60). During his time in Germany he came into contact with John Cage and David Tudor, whose ideas posed a challenge to the serial orthodoxy of the European avant garde, introducing the concept of indeterminacy and the liberation of sounds from compositional control through the use of chance methods.

Cardew returned to England in 1961 and took a course in graphic design. At the same time he studied the philosophical writings on logic and language of Wittgenstein, and undertook a thorough re-examination of the implications of musical notation. All this influenced the development of his music in the 1960s, in particular that of his 193 page graphic score *Treatise* (1963-67) (the title of which refers to Wittgenstein's early work *Tractatus Logico-Philosophicus*). He became increasingly dissatisfied with accepted conventions of composition, notation and performance. His search for new, more socially accountable ways of making music led him in 1966 to join the free improvisation group AMM, and this was followed by the composition of *The Great Learning* (1968-70), based on Ezra Pound's translation of the Confucian text, and the formation of the Scratch Orchestra in 1969. It was in response to the crisis which arose in the evolution of the Scratch Orchestra in 1971-72 that he engaged in a radical reconsideration of all his work up to this time, and came to adopt a Marxist-Leninist position which determined the direction of his later work.

This volume brings together a diverse collection of Cardew's essays, articles and writings from different stages in his career, together with related contributions by other writers dealing with various aspects of his music. His writing reflects developments and changes in the direction of his thinking from the late 1950s to the end of his life. The diametrically opposed views expressed in his earlier and later writing will be immediately evident, and this can of course be attributed to the change in perspective which accompanied his conversion to Marxism in the early 1970s. Even before this, however, Cardew's earlier development had been fraught with contradictions: it was characterised by a series of reversals, renunciations and changes of emphasis. This questioning attitude was inherent in his work from the start; he was, as Roger Smalley wrote in 1967, 'continually probing and developing the very nature of music' [1]. A remark he made while working on his *Octet 61* is typical: 'In this research it is always necessary to sacrifice trusted concepts'. Throughout this period, along with his challenges to established authority, musical and otherwise, it is possible to detect a streak of self-subversion, a critical intelligence which refuses to rest on any fixed assumptions. Cardew's trajectory had nothing in common with the conventional career structure of a composer who builds up a consistent body of work, fulfiling the expectations of those who provide him with incentives and commissions. Nevertheless, as John Tilbury observes, there is an underlying thread of humanism running through his work, providing continuity, even if it appears in very different and sometimes contradictory forms.

The earliest article in this collection, *The Unity of Musical Space* (1959), with its elaborate system of sub-clauses and its pseudo-technical jargon, may be read as a reaction to Stockhausen's theoretical writing. (Cardew had recently translated Stockhausen's essay '...how time passes...' for the English edition of the periodical Die Reihe.) At this time Cardew was already distancing himself from the total determinism of integral serialism, and it is not difficult to detect in this article, with its ironic reference to 'a tempered scale of sleeping hours', an element of parody of Stockhausen's thinking. In *Notation-Interpretation* (1959-61) on the other hand, Cardew's detailed examination of notation and rules for its interpretation is clearly indebted to his reading of Wittgenstein. In the development of the ideas which can be traced here and in the working notes to *Treatise* one finds a close parallel with the shift in Wittgenstein's ideas about language, from the 'picture theory' of the *Tractatus* to the use-related account in the later *Philosophical Investigations*. The idea of notation as a precise isomorphic description of an abstract sound structure, implicit in the integral serial music of the 1950s, is consistent with the pictorial theory of the *Tractatus* in which language is treated as a way of depicting the world; whereas the performer-related view of notation to which Cardew was drawn in the 1960s corresponds with Wittgenstein's later understanding of language in terms of rules for its use and forms of behaviour associated with it: 'how it meshes with life'. In other words Cardew, like Wittgenstein in his later work, became increasingly concerned with the activity of interpretation, rather than with the notion of a literal, fixed meaning for each sign.

The working notes to *Treatise* reveal Cardew thinking about graphic notation in a variety of different ways, often reconsidering his previous assumptions: at first, 'the sound should be a picture of the score'; later, the score 'seems not representational'. Elsewhere it is considered as 'a statement about a way of making music'. Sometimes it functions as a ground-plan or blueprint for conventionally notated pieces, such as *Bun No. 2* (1964) or *Volo Solo* (1965). At other times it seems to be regarded independently of any musical realisation, as a visual substitute for music or as 'a document from the sphere of activity in which music is written'. In the early stages of composition it is noted that the score should not be 'an arbitrary jumping-off point for improvisation', whereas later on 'an improvisatory character is essential to the piece'. In the light of his changing experience Cardew continually questions and re-examines his attitude to the work-in-progress; both the method and the style of writing are reminiscent of Wittgenstein.

In his article on the visual aspects of *Treatise*, Brian Dennis draws attention to further parallels with Wittgenstein's thinking. Cardew's method of self-interrogation and his debt to Wittgenstein remain strongly evident in the two important essays which are included in the *Treatise Handbook*: 'On the Role of the Instructions in the Interpretation of Indeterminate Music' (1965) and 'Towards an Ethic of Improvisation' (1968). In the later essay he describes his experience of free improvisation and draws attention to 'virtues a musician can develop'. His participation in playing with AMM was crucial at this stage: in free improvisation he discovered a medium in which notation as such is no longer relevant. The performer's authority is internalised, and the ethical dimension inherent in music as a freely chosen form of social activity takes precedence over the previous concern with rules and instructions. After his intensive and critical investigation of musical notation, Cardew at least for a while abandoned it altogether.

There remains however a degree of ambivalence. Cardew is clearly aware that he has made another sacrifice, and that in abandoning notation he has given up 'a system of formal guidelines' which can lead the composer and performer into 'uncharted regions'. In treating notation primarily as a stimulus to the performer, rather than as a representation of a fixed musical structure, Cardew had in fact already undermined one of the basic foundations of the Western musical tradition. Now he goes further and questions the entire concept of the need for music to have a formal identity, an 'outside-time' structure distinct from its performance. In free improvisation there is no such external structure to be distinguished from the real-time process of performance: 'the search is conducted in the medium of sound and the musician himself is at the heart of the experiment'.

The graphic score of *Treatise* is still a visual composition with a distinct formal identity, even if it is without fixed reference to any particular musical realisation. A further attempt to influence performers in a non-prescriptive way, without specifying what sounds they should make, can be seen in the curious verbal score *The Tiger's Mind* written in 1967 as 'an experiment in the direction of guided improvisation'. This takes the form of a poetic drama, giving performers a choice of roles and intended to create awareness of possible relationships which can be brought into play in free improvisation. It was written 'with AMM musicians in mind'; however, as Eddie Prévost observes, 'the very notion of directed play within AMM (was) an obvious contradiction'. For experienced improvising musicians there is no need of any such external stimulus. The potential educative value of such work for aspiring improvisers is nevertheless acknowledged.

The relationship between prescriptive rules and spontaneous impulses is again a central concern in *The Great Learning* (1968-70). Here Cardew returns to the selective use of musical notation, together with graphic and verbal indications of various kinds, as a way of identifying specific rhythmic and melodic components in the variable structure of the work as a whole. John Tilbury has drawn attention to the dualism inherent in Cardew's life and work as a key to understanding his motivations and achievements:[2] on the one hand 'the desire and respect for purity, dogma and asceticism' which initially attracted him to the discipline of serialism, to the logic of Wittgenstein's *Tractatus* and later to Marxism, and on the other hand 'the spontaneous and libertarian actions' which led him to indeterminacy and free improvisation. Both tendencies are evident in *The Great Learning* a work involving an exceptional degree of creative tension between extremes of control and freedom, discipline and spontaneity. In the early Chinese philosophical texts upon which it is based, in the contrast between the Confucian codification of rules for social behaviour and the Taoist celebration of intuition and spontaneity, Cardew discovered an inspirational vehicle for the expression of this dualism of opposites.

The formation of the Scratch Orchestra in 1969 may be seen as the culmination of Cardew's search for a group of performers, 'musical innocents' as he called them, who could respond to his ideas without preconceptions. This was his most far-reaching experiment in social music-making: to seek out players who had not been conditioned by the discipline of a formal musical education and to give them the freedom to respond to his proposals in ways that could not be controlled or foreseen. *The Draft Constitution* which Cardew wrote for the Scratch Orchestra has sometimes been interpreted as a kind of open-ended 'composition', in which he set out to encourage and stimulate but not to limit the orchestra's activities. It includes its own inherent subversion clause: 'The word music and its derivatives are here not understood to refer exclusively to sound and related phenomena (hearing, etc.). What they do refer to is flexible and depends entirely on the members of the Scratch Orchestra'. *The Draft Constitution* thus acted as a catalyst for the orchestra's heterogeneous experimental activities. It was this permissive approach which eventually opened the way for a current of political activity to emerge.

The circumstances which led to the formation of an ideological group within the orchestra are referred to in the Introduction to *Scratch Music*. This group was set up in the summer of 1971 to study the writings of Marx and Engels, Lenin and Mao Tsetung. Cardew was at first reluctant to embrace the new political agenda proposed by some of his colleagues. In June 1971, in answer to a question about political ideas within the orchestra, he had replied: 'It is not in the structure of the orchestra to serve a political aim' [3]. During the next few months, however, his interest in Chinese affairs acquired a new dimension: it was redirected from Confucianism to the thought of Mao Tsetung, which he now adopted with the enthusiasm of a new convert.

Until this time Cardew had shown little interest in politics; he had no previous experience of thinking in political terms, no wider perspective within which to evaluate the relevance of Mao's ideas in a Western context. He transposed them into the discussion of avant garde and experimental music without taking into account cultural differences between China and the West, and used them to justify his polemical attacks on Cage and Stockhausen. In relying upon Mao's prescriptive and utilitarian attitude to culture and taking his thought as a model of Marxism as such, Cardew ignored important features of the theoretical and philosophical basis of Western Marxism. He appealed to Marx's 11th Thesis on Feuerbach[4], taking it out of its original context and interpreting it as a call to give up theorising and resort to direct political action. He tried to understand complex issues in terms of polarised opposites, such as progressive/reactionary, individual/collective, for/against the interests of the working class. Some may take this as an example of 'crude thinking', which Brecht considered necessary in times of political confrontation as an antidote to academic sophistry and prevarication. Others will have strong reservations about the use of this oversimplified terminology, with its hectoring didacticism, its reliance on catchphrases, slogans and generalisations and its tendency to argue from foregone conclusions. In the series of essays which Cardew collected and published under the title *Stockhausen Serves Imperialism*, much of the writing reflects a reductive form of socio-economic determinism and reveals little awareness of crucial dialectical aspects of the relation between culture and society. In his enthusiasm for revolutionary change, he ignored the significance of Western Marxist theory in the domain of culture and politics, in the writings of Gramsci, Lukacs, Adorno, Marcuse and others. Much of this he would probably have denounced as 'revisionism' or 'armchair Marxism'. His refusal to take account of theoretical work of this kind suggests that he chose to regard Marxism as a fixed and self-justifying doctrine, rather than as a developing tradition of argument and analysis, subject like any other to critical examination and renewal.

Cardew's indiscriminate repudiation in the 1970s of avant garde and experimental music, including his own, can be seen as a direct result of these theoretical limitations. Under the influence of Mao's utilitarian view of culture, he renounced the spirit of open enquiry which had characterised his earlier work and suppressed the questioning intelligence that had previously been so evident. In his essay 'On Criticism' he went to the opposite extreme, claiming to speak for 'the vast majority of music lovers' in asserting that 'modern music (with very few exceptions) is footling, unwholesome, sensational, frustrating, offensive and depressing'. In sharp contradiction to his political stance, he now appears to identify with the most conservative element in the 'class audience' for classical music, those who seek in it satisfaction, comfort and reassurance. He refuses to acknowledge that what is disturbing and unsettling in modern music may have a significant critical dimension. He can see only that it is 'degenerate', that it 'reflects the decay' of bourgeois society. In resorting to such Zhdanovite rhetoric and relying on the 'reflection' theory of artistic production, he ignored the fact that Western Marxist theorists have proposed a very different account of aesthetic value, in which radical and innovative works are not merely 'reflections' of social conditions, but expressions of resistance which refuse to be assimilated into the falsified reality of the dominant culture. According to this interpretation, the political significance of music lies not in subservience to an external agenda, but in the critical re-examination of its own materials and processes of engagement. It is through the ways in which these are re-evaluated and transformed that music can implicitly affect our experience and understanding of social conditions, and so contribute to changes in consciousness which are the necessary precursors and catalysts of social change. In contrast, the functional approach adopted by Cardew in his later writing can all too easily become associated with a repressive dogmatism which rejects all technical, formal and aesthetic innovation and denies the value of independent artistic discovery.

Many would argue that a work such as *The Great Learning* is inherently political in the way it breaks down traditional hierarchical structures and explores new musical and social processes. Several articles in this collection attest to its vitality, freshness and inspirational value. Cardew's criticisms of the work and his reasons for repudiating it in 1974 were largely external to the music; they were directed primarily at the historical origins of the Confucian text and at Ezra Pound's translation. Following Mao Tsetung's principle of the subordination of artistic to political criteria, he refused to admit any distinction between musical and ideological content. Under the influence of criticism expressed in the Campaign against Confucius, an opportunistic move in the current power struggle within the Chinese leadership, Cardew evidently lost sight of the work's expression of ethical principles such as self-discipline, responsibility and mutual respect which had originally inspired him. He now treated these principles as if their value were determined exclusively by their aristocratic origins, and ignored the extent to which they are reinterpreted in the musical context of the work.

There can be no doubt about Cardew's sincerity and total commitment to his belief in the cause of revolutionary socialism. It is clear that the politically inspired writing of his later years represents an integral part of his life and work. It can hardly be denied, however, that it presents serious difficulties, not only for those who are primarily interested in his music, but also for those who are concerned to understand the wider social and political implications of the position he adopted. It is hard to avoid the impression that Cardew's ethical idealism became entrenched in prescriptive tendencies which bear little resemblance to his previous libertarian impulses. His interpretation of Marxism in these writings is schematic, anachronistic and oversimplified; it contains errors, distortions and misconceptions, some of which he acknowledged. His writing relies all too often on rhetoric and invective rather than on reasoned argument. Much of it is uncritically dependent on Mao Tsetung, whose influence he later repudiated[5]. It is based on preconceptions which fail to take into account the specific political, economic, cultural and educational conditions of post-War Western society; it lacks any real engagement with the question of mass media and the commercial production and dissemination of music. It deals with complex problems by reducing them to clichés and platitudes; in the absence of any deeper analysis, phrases such as 'the people's benefit' or 'the interests of the working class' remain empty formulas which are never given substance in terms of what they might actually mean in a contemporary Western situation.

Given such reservations, the question inevitably arises: what is the value of republishing these politically motivated writings, 30 years after they originally appeared?

The answer must be that, however flawed, they are an essential part of Cardew's legacy. They represent a bold and courageous attempt to deal with the contentious issue of the artist's political commitment. They are vital evidence of the progress of his ideas, of his struggle and self-education, a document of the times he lived through. The questions he raised and the problems he faced were real enough, and they remain in urgent need of theoretical and practical attention. It is important to try to understand the direction of Cardew's life and work as a whole, however contradictory it may seem; the availability of these writings will make it possible to reassess its wider significance. It will be instructive to compare his work with that of other composers who have taken up radical positions: Eisler, Nono, Henze, Lachenmann, Xenakis, Rzewski, for example, and many others who have searched and are still searching for different ways of expressing social and political commitment in musical terms.

In his book *Recollections of Wittgenstein*[6], Rush Rhees, who was a student of Wittgenstein's in Cambridge, recalls a conversation with him which took place in 1945. He had mentioned to Wittgenstein that he was thinking of joining the Revolutionary Communist Party (not the same party that Cardew was later to become a member of). He relates Wittgenstein's response as follows:

"When you are a member of a party you have to be prepared to act and speak as the party has decided. You will be trying to convince other people... If you are in the habit of trying one way, then turning back on your tracks like this and trying another, you will be no use as a party member. Perhaps the party line will change. But meanwhile what you say must be what the party has agreed to say. You keep along that road.

Whereas in doing philosophy you have got to be ready *constantly* to change the direction in which you are moving. At some point you see that there must be something wrong with the whole way you have been tackling the difficulty. You have to be able to give up those central notions which have seemed to be what you must keep if you are to think at all. Go back and start from scratch. And if you are thinking as a philosopher you cannot treat the ideas of communism differently from others.

Some people speak of philosophy as a way of living. Working as a member of a communist party is also a way of living."

These remarks of Wittgenstein anticipate with prophetic accuracy the implications of Cardew's change of allegiance in the 1970s. His early work, like that of Wittgenstein himself, was characterised by constant changes of direction and the giving up of central notions. Following the path he chose to take as a result of his switch to political commitment, he was no longer able to afford the luxury of 'thinking as a philosopher'.

Notes

1. Roger Smalley: 'Unconventional Conventions' (review of Cardew: *Four Works*), *The Musical Times*, November 1967, p.1030.

2. John Tilbury: essay in programme booklet, Cornelius Cardew Memorial Concert, Queen Elizabeth Hall, London, 16 May 1982, p.8.

3. Interview with Hannah Boenisch, June 1971 (unpublished).

4. 'The philosophers have only *interpreted* the world, in various ways; the point, however, is to *change* it'. 'Karl Marx, Theses on Feuerbach XI;' *Marx and Engels: Selected Works*, Vol. II, p.405, Foreign Languages Publishing House, Moscow 1958.

5. By the end of 1978 the Communist Party of England (Marxist-Leninist) had renounced its adherence to Maoism. Its allegiance was transferred to the Albanian communist leader Enver Hoxha, who was regarded as representing the 'correct' (i.e. Stalinist) line of Marxism-Leninism. The party was re-formed in 1979 as the Communist Party of Britain (Marxist-Leninist), with Cardew as one of its founding members. This change of allegiance is reflected in Cardew's later writing.

6. *Recollections of Wittgenstein*, ed. Rush Rhees, Oxford University Press 1984, p.208.

Unity of Musical Space
New Departures – 1959

musical space the unity of musical space the unity of musical space the

Already in the waltz from his opus 23 Schoenberg derived all the harmony and melody from a single series of twelve notes in a chosen order. But the potential energy required to convert such a unique idea into a general system was not yet available. In formulating the expression "the unity of musical space" he supplied this, in that he intended it as a formal concept (A)–

A: Webern approached a nullification of this concept by seeking to make one or more of the projections implied by it, or parts of them, identical with or similar to the original form. This search is… (a) …

a : …unnecessary because all the forms are already present in the original. This, when inverted, for example, is repeated. The thought that the whole world has been turned upside down in the process need not worry us : the difference between a world and a tone-row is only quantitative; a stable world with an inverted tone-row in it, and a stable tone-row with an inverted world round it are equivalent phenomena. Each (world, tone-row, I, others) must achieve his own reality, which is stability relative to a frame of reference which, seen from the outside, need by no means be, and very rarely is, itself stable. Our title, a constellation of words, signified a thematic reality for Schoenberg, has been interpretatively reduced by Karlheinz Stockhausen to a physical fact (X), and will become, I fancy, in any sense an economic necessity in a world which has very little time to think.

X : See 'Die Reihe' No. 3 : " … how time passes … " (Universal Edition, London) where the correspondence between rhythm and pitch is demonstrated.

unity of musical space the unity of musical space the unity of musical space

complementary to the melodic-harmonic one described above – which would justify the projection of one chosen direction or order into three others, namely inversion, retrograde-inversion and retrograde. These were called "mirror forms" of the original. For this concept to expand, its "mirror" must reflect not only the elementary

A Continued:) … a symptom of the literal treatment of physical things by so many mystics. This dichotomy is shocking for the more normal mortal who attempts to include his total life-potential in any creative act. That is not to say that Webern did not achieve just this in almost every work, but that it limited him, though perhaps this very restriction generated a creative energy far greater than he would otherwise have achieved. Such remarks, however, are in the nature not of a precept but of an evaluation, and cast no light on the development of a compositional method. But in his literal treatment of the word 'mirror' (b), Webern tapped a potentially enormous reservoir, which he had not the equipment to exploit.

b : Whole cells, and groups of cells were reflected (inverted or reversed) in toto, but still only an angles of 180°

material of the twelve notes, but complete sounds, and constellations of these; not only must it reflect them, it must project them at various angles, magnify, filter, diffuse, and otherwise distort and change them (B).

B. Of the space in which these things can take place we will take two(c) dimensions and write them on to the two time-axes (X) of duration-cms –x– and frequency-cms –y–. The y-axis is a tempered scale, or, differently expressed, a projection of a logarithmic curve onto a straight. To reproduce the same situation on the x-axis would produce an accelerando (d) over the whole piece(e).

d : No cause for distress, for the following reasons :
    1. consideration of the number of articulation possibilities.
    2. insurance of a constant basic experiential time, corresponding to a constant interval in the frequency scale.
    3. exhilaration brought about by displacement, corresponding to transportation in pitch.
    All these can help to destroy the accelerative character of x-axial curvature.

e : The relationship between clock and experiential time is in any case problematic (Y), as the latter is constantly subjected to a combination of contracting and

Y : If we take a paradigm the case where the axis is not a curve, but has a constant divergence from the straight of an angle of approximately 48°, and postulate that the opening of a certain event carries an expectancy factor of 8 minutes, after 4 minutes clock-time the expectancy will already be down to 2 minutes, and at 5' it will be 30", and at 5' 12", 7.5" and the whole thing will finish before 5' 20" have elapsed. But the human body does not function by clockwork, and the listener will probably be convinced that he has heard something lasting 8 minutes.

B Continued:) Important though the results (f) of the realisation that the two or more axes of musical space are curves are, they must not be taken into account when drawing on its graphical presentation, since the *constant* frequency-*relationships*, and not the *increasing* frequency-*differences*, are measured on the y-axis, and we have applied the same principle to the x-axis. The graphical presentation takes the form of a straight-line frame of reference, where points are defined by their coordinates, surfaces by the lengths and angular relationships of their sides, curves by their equations, and the surfaces enclosed by these by their differentials.

e Continued :) expanding tensions, difficult for a composer to control (C), but easy for him to influence (Z).

f :   1. only straight lines at an angle of 45° remain straight.
      2. all other straight lines become curves.
      3. curves complementary to axis-curve become straight lines.
      4. all other curves become higher degree curves.

C: To control these tensions the composer would have to compose not only music but menus for a considerable period before his concert, and a tempered scale of sleeping-hours, relative to age, weight, sex, etc. In the face of these difficulties some would prefer to extract, before a short piece, one tooth from each in the audience who possesses any, thus ensuring at least the dominating tendency in the majority's experiential time.

Z : As proof of the human susceptibility to influence, one has only to cite the ease with which some composers make 10 minutes seem like 2 hours. But no influence should be exclusive : time should not be made to fly, crawl, or stand still, but all these in varying degrees and successions.

Notation – Interpretation, etc.

TEMPO – Summer 1961

1 – What follows is notes, made at various stages and on a variety of topics. Few of these remarks make any pretence to completeness, and I have not attempted to fill in the gaps and 'cover' any particular field thoroughly. Few of these remarks follow on from one to the next, so they may be read at random.

Perhaps it will be helpful to imagine in what *rôles* the various remarks are made; whether as composer, listener, interpreter, critic, publicity man, or simply theoretician. I have discussed only those things which concern, or have concerned me directly (and this may be taken as an apology).

At the time (Spring 1959 to Spring 1960) it was easier, as will be readily appreciated, to write notes about what I was doing, than to write music. To write notes about what I am doing at the moment, on the other hand, seems much more difficult than simply to do it. Also, all through that time and right up to October 1960 (when it received its first performance) I was working practically continuously on *Carré* by Karlheinz Stockhausen, and the experience of writing someone else's music could hardly fail to result in a considerable sharpening of the critical faculty (I wrote very little music of my own in that time).

Some terms seem to require elucidation:

Indeterminacy. (Cage: 'pieces which are indeterminate as regards their performance'.) I would say that a piece is indeterminate when the player (or players) has an active hand in giving the piece a form.

Identity (of a piece of music). A senseless but useful concept. What is *essential* to a piece of music constitutes its identity. Of course, ideally speaking, everything about a piece is essential to it.

Time-space. Here, the spacing and length of the notes on the page, are put into a more or less direct relation to the timing and duration of the sounds. Earle Brown rationalized the process and has used it fairly extensively (*Music for Cello and Piano* is an example). Cage (*Winter Music, Music for Piano*), Bussotti and Stockhausen (*Zyklus*) also take advantage of it. The space can be measured or observed (depending on the instance), or the eye can travel along it at a constant or fluctuating pace (depending on the instance). The idea's attraction lies in the fact that it dispenses with any sort of symbolic time-notation.

2 – The notation of music is a creative (or synthetic) activity not to be confused with logical notation.

Notation and composition determine each other. Differentiate between creating a language in order to say *something* and evolving a language in which you can say anything.

A musical notation is a language which determines what you can say, what you want to say determines your language.

As a composer you have both aspects in your hand, but when you come to open your hand you find only one thing and it is not divisible.

3 – 'Time-space'. To place a dot in space is fun (e.g. in a drawing) because the time one does it in is free. But when placing a dot in time-space, there is no 'higher order' time in which to consider. The dimension which made drawing the dot a pleasure has now become space, and we know of no further dimension. Each point in time-space is 'seen' once only, irrevocably, and lo! one has either used it or not. Heavens, it is easy to use time-space, because music-writing takes paper-space, and it's no problem to give it the name 'time'. Something of course results. But what? 'Do you hear what I'm seeing?'.

For the view that time-space is a profitable speculation, one could argue that it is 'exciting' to treat time as if it were space; one reaches 'impossible' situations, and this is of course very interesting, stimulating, exciting: 'Groping for the ungraspable is the most satisfying of modern pastimes', where the satisfaction lies in the fact that satisfaction is impossible.   v '59

4 – Let us select five stages in the production of music:
(1) what is written.
(2) information gleaned by the player from (1).
(3) the player.
(4) the action to produce sound.
(5) the sound.

I suppose many people imagine that this last is the material for composition. But one cannot 'write' sound; the best one could do would be to 'sound' the sound, which would superannuate the interpreter (and however much we may complain, we would not be without him for worlds). So one must write, and (1) is what one writes. (2) depends to a large extent on (3), who has been part of the notation only in exceptional cases (*5 pieces for David Tudor* by Sylvano Bussotti is an example. The words *David Tudor* in the title are in no sense a dedication, but rather an instrumental indication, part of the notation). But even without notating the interpreter, one can do a little more here than merely hoping for 'the best' (see 30). Most notations deal mainly in (4): 'do what I tell you and the right sounds will come of their own accord', which is not true of course, but there is no one who is not reluctant to admit just how much he relies on (3). The attempt to describe (5) completely, resulted *originally* in electronic music (this has very little to do with electronic music today). v '59

5 – 'Musical interpretation' has become more and more a single term with less and less in common with the everyday meaning of the word 'interpret'. Cage has re-opened the expression and utilized its implications in such fields as structure, notation, performance. His word 'indeterminacy' is like a conviction: the relation between musical score and performance cannot be determined. If this is not realized, difficulties will always be encountered in composing, rehearsing and performing (not to mention listening). The indeterminacies of traditional notation became to such an extent accepted that it was forgotten that they existed, and of what sort they were. The results of this can be seen in much of the pointillist music of the 50s (Boulez, Berio, Goeyvaerts, Pousseur, Stockhausen, Van San, etc.). The music seemed to exclude all possibility of interpretation in any real sense; the utmost differentiation, refinement and exactitude were demanded of the players. Just because of this contradiction it is stimulating work, and sometimes rewarding to interpret this music, for any interpretation is forced to transcend the rigidity of the compositional procedure, and music results (but the feeling is almost unavoidable that one is misrepresenting the composer!).

Now Cage is aware of the dangers of working within a traditional system whose functioning has become subconscious. And he is aware of the indeterminacy of the relations between compositional idea, notation, performance and audition. But whereas most European composers work on the reduction of the indeterminacy to a minimum, Cage sets out to *use* it. Consequent on this comes the fundamental difference in thinking about the 'identity' of a piece of music. For instance: constituting the identity of a European piece are, e.g., the tones that occur in it and their characteristics (pitch, loudness, length, etc. in Boulez for example), or the themes that occur in it, their implications (harmonic and melodic) and modifications, etc., etc. On the other hand, constituting the identity of e.g. *Winter Music* is the fact *that there should be* more or less complex eruptions into silence, and that these should come from one or more pianos. This being the unmistakable identity of the piece, there is room for free interpenetration at all points in the process (composition, notation, performance, audition). 'Mistaken identity' is excluded, and 'anything may happen'. (Cage has opened the gate into a field.) iii '60

6 – There can be no indeterminacy in the notation itself – that would mean a sort of blurred sign (as in Bussotti) – but only in the rules for its interpretation (as in Cage's piano concerto: • means *soft* or short). x '59

7 – One point is, that every sign should be active (compare the bar lines in Feldman and Boulez). Here are openings for indeterminacy, or freedom for the player: he must decide which signs he will give activity to, or allow to act. The composer can bring this about in a variety of ways: by overloading the player with so many rules that they begin to contradict each other; or by using the same sign in a variety of contexts where it *cannot* mean the same (paradoxical notation); or by giving no rules whatever and obliging the player to seek out just such rules as he needs or as will make sense of the notation. (This last is very important, and often seems the case with Feldman.) All these are psychological obscurities directed at the player in the hope of waking him up.

The whole question of determinacy is liable to melt into thin air under scrutiny. Take the sign '–' (written over a note): in 4 different systems of notation (starting with the most determinate), it means (1) 5" secs., (2) long, (3) a length of time, and (4) what you will. This sort of 'absolute' indeterminacy (but note that in (4) your decision in one case will determine other cases) has been attempted by Bussotti (but even his picture is still e.g. read from left to right). In the case of Bussotti it is important to remember that you are dealing with a drawing, not with writing, that you therefore *require* neither dictionary nor rules for its interpretation. But in a notation, as in writing, fluctuations of typography or handwriting should not prejudice its determinacy. An indeterminacy here would be the case where you ask 'is that an A or an 0 ?', or in music 'is that a line or a dot?' (it's no answer to say 'it's a mark, anyway'! That would again make it into a drawing).

'I can't read it, but it looks great.' Drawings *suggest* their own interpretation. In how far your 'notation plus rules' determines the sound, is a matter of your system's completeness (illusory: a system can be closed but not complete). x '59

8 – Suppose the player to behave as follows: he reads the notation and makes himself a picture of the sound (in his mind – the hypothetically imagined sound). He then attempts to reproduce this picture in sound; he plays, and then listens to the sound he has made; he compares it with the picture of the sound he had in his mind beforehand, and he may make a few changes, reducing the most glaring discrepancies, releasing wrong notes quickly, reducing the notes he finds too loud, etc., etc.

What I am looking for is a notation (way of writing a text) where fidelity to this text is *possible*. Perhaps a notation of the way in which instruments 'actually are played'. This leads to the question: what actions *are* actually involved in playing? And here the concept of the 'hypothetically imagined sound' becomes dubious: – on what basis does the player imagine the sound? On the basis of his understanding of the notation? But the process of imagining cannot be included in the notation!

Let us exclude 'imagining' from the realm of the player's 'actual action', and excluding this, we must also exclude the post-natal corrective – the comparison of the actual with the hypothetically imagined sound. In many cases we do not imagine the sound on the basis of the notation, but on the basis of our previous experience, i.e. (too) while practising the piece, and therefore the 'imagined' sound has no particular claim to correctness at all, and therefore a comparison of the actual sound with it has no sense whatever. The sound is imagined on the basis of your experimentally performing actions in rehearsal, which puts you in the difficult position of having to adapt your 'hypothetically imagined sound' to new conditions. The sound I make at home is not the same as the sound I make in the concert hall – *cannot* be the same and therefore *should not* be attempted.

vii '59

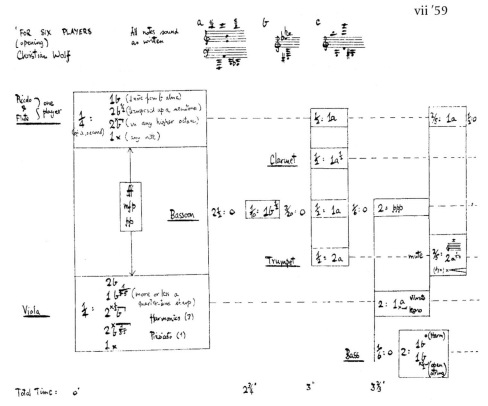

9 – Such a notation as Wolff's *6 players* is no longer a notation that one can *read*. It is more like material for composition – it must be translated into a notation. This in connection with the frequent 'impossible' situations in the piece, as – imaginary example: – viola must play nine tones, amongst which two pizzicato and two harmonics, in half a second. One interpretation of this – and it is a fundamental interpretation; one that requires a notation if the piece is to be brought to performance – is to have the player play as many notes as he can in half a second, while the remainder he is free to distribute over the whole of the rest of the piece. In this interpretation we have taken the time ($\frac{1}{2}$") as binding. Now imagine three such events in succession, lasting respectively $\frac{1}{2}$", $2\frac{1}{3}$", $\frac{2}{3}$"; in another interpretation these do not add up to $3\frac{1}{2}$", because we can take the *events* as binding (see note 11). Thus the 9 tones in the first $\frac{1}{2}$" form an indivisible agglomeration of sound, which the player must *aim* to achieve in half a second (he won't succeed). For this too a notation must be sought, and this presents a serious problem because it often happens in the piece that two or more players must reach the same point at the same time. One then attempts to fit a conductor into this picture, etc., etc.   v '60

10 – Here one is seeking a notation for a pre-existing situation, so one's problems are largely logical, and the difficulty is to see the situation clearly.

Wolff's notation could be called an experimental notation (as could 'time-space'). One reason why one could call it experimental is that what can happen to the signs is not predetermined in the signs themselves (it is as though his signs were pre-symbolic). Thus you may find yourself having to play $3\frac{1}{2}$ tones in 0 seconds (! !). (Christian would frown faintly, and then smile a solution.)

11 – One can establish a hierarchy among the rules and make general decisions about which rule takes precedence (where two rules seem mutually exclusive). Alternatively one can decide for each particular situation which rules are binding. (This applies particularly to Wolff and Feldman. Wolff's 'instructions' consist largely of suggestions.)

12 – One is often warned about the dangers in giving a new meaning to an old sign. I find, however, that it is reassuring to be familiar with the sign, even though not with its meaning. The old meaning forms a sort of magnetic pole which tugs the new interpretation out of the square (and incidentally, detracts from the banality of so-called 'new meanings'). Apart from this, I feel that things which are difficult to understand should be said in such a way that at least they are easy to read;

otherwise the difficulty encountered in reading prevents you from even starting to understand. (But beware of separating 'reading' and 'understanding' completely.)

Another point is that a familiar sign is much more easily recognized (identified), and consequently one does not have to waste time comparing the sign with a model in order to be sure that you are interpreting the right sign. The musician's eye is trained to recognize the difference between ♪ and ♪, but not that between e.g. 0 and *0* (meaning, for example, that the note is ♮ or #), although there is a more significant difference between these. It is misguided (I find, at least, that 'it doesn't do you any good') to insist on such 'improvements' on the grounds that they present a more economical transmission of 'information' because to a musician they patently don't. If the composer's intention is to disorientate the musician, then of course by all means.

Such a composer would be a composer of human rather than musical situations (there is much to be discussed here; too much). This means devising a human notation rather than a musical one; that is to say, placing more emphasis on the human aspect of notations. The Americans (Cage, Wolff, Brown, Feldman) have long been this way inclined, and the prime example is the young American LaMonte Young, whose *Poem* may be familiar to some. LaMonte dispenses with musical notation altogether and 'writes' his pieces in the language of everyday.

13 – A notation should be directed to a large extent towards the people who read it, rather than towards the sounds they will make.   v '60

14 – Imagine a piece of music with the title 'about music'. Any performance of this would then have the title 'music'.

15 – The only criterion for a sound is: 'was the player expecting (intending) to make it?' (see note 8). If not, it was a mistake, and makes a different *sort* of claim to beauty. As a mistake, it comes under criteria for action: mistakes are the only truly spontaneous actions we are capable of.   x '59

16 – Compare 'that seems natural' with 'that seems logical' with 'there is a sort of severe logic in it' meaning it's not natural but it's 'right'. 'Ugly' sounds (cf: James) get beauty through their logical positioning. Form, temporal logic, memory, expectation: these form an agenda to ignore which gives you generality at the expense of intensity.   x '59

17 – Imagine a notation with the following point of departure: interesting actions

have interesting, nice-and-easy-to-write notations, whereas boring ones have boring, difficult-or-impossible-to-write notations. (Russell's idea – that complexes must be designated by complex signs – would have to go by the board here.)

18 – Concerning some non-musical durations; durations not carrying a change. One such is 'the length of a breath' – it *need* not carry a change, though of course it *can* – one uses the human frame for no other reason than that it is there. 'The length of a breath' can have no *musical* significance (here again – as in note 25 – it cannot really represent a duration, since it must allow for the most diverse human frames, including those which can breathe in through their noses while still blowing through their mouths, though in theory this is only a menace when the prescription is 'as long as possible').

Another such duration is the silence (or accidental noises) needed for the preparation of a sound (e.g. taking silent notes, making literal 'preparations', getting your fingers round a difficult chord, etc.), which makes no musical sense in the moment of its existence, and the reason for its duration becomes clear only afterwards, when the sound has manifested the effect of the preparation.

In both cases it is an acoustical change that is missing, and that is why I call them non-musical durations. However, this lack suits them very well to sustaining the impression of a time-structure. This 'feeling of structure' relies on the occurrence of things for *no immediately apparent reason*, and this 'feeling' seems to be all one can achieve in the way of time-structure, since perception as a whole (seeing the temporal structure of the piece laid out in front of you) cannot be the case in music (memory and expectation to be considered elsewhere).   ix '59

19 – Towards a music without structure! The 'feeling of structure' is not a very important *feeling*, I should say, and it is therefore fine if a note goes, say, flat or sharp at the end of a breath. It gives an apparent reason for stopping (the *real* reason, after all).   x '59

20 – Note found in the score of my *octet 1959*: 'control the registers here! Octaves seem to predominate', I misread this as 'control heightens here, octaves seem to predominate' and wondered at my own insight! The apparition of the unreasonable (octaves!) in the score, suggests that there are *hidden* reasons, and this too is the 'feeling of structure': seeking the sense in the apparently senseless. This note is followed by: 'how to make the form a necessity and not a form'. But this 'necessary form' (organic form) is the greatest hindrance to the 'feeling of structure'.   x '59

21 – Differentiate between 'not seeing the sense' and 'finding something senseless'. Having once found something sensible, it carries weight to declare it senseless. 'I refuse to call it senseless until I have seen the sense of it' is therefore a reasonable sentence.   iii '60

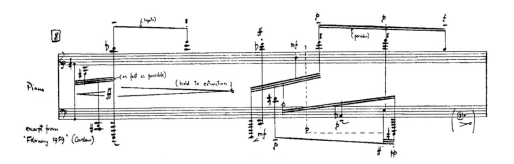

22 – One feature of this piece is the method used for controlling the length of tones: a tone is struck at a particular dynamic, and is released when it has reached another. So for example, the length of a tone is the time taken by this particular tone to make the diminuendo from *mf* to *pp*. Such tones are sometimes accompanied by a sign meaning e.g. 'relatively long', and it becomes clear that our interpretation of the signs *mf* and *pp* will also have to be relative, and we come up against the question: 'are the dynamics controlling the durations, or are the durations controlling the dynamics?'. Neither, for the player controls both, that is he controls their interaction. This is the real meaning of such signs as 'long', 'loud', etc.: their function is to put the player in a position where he is conscious of himself, of his own experience of 'long', 'loud', etc. He is conscious of what he is doing and of the capacities of the instrument at which he sits. The function of such signs is to bring the pianist to life. The piece is also so devised that the pianist can respond correctly (to the stimuli which are the signs) under any circumstances. These circumstances include size and quality of instrument, hall, pianist, audience, etc. (Actually various combinations of unfortunate circumstances have, at various times, made it almost impossible to keep the piece identifiable, but these were 'unreasonable circumstances'.)

I have heard people criticizing interpretations of music in a variety of ways, 'he played some wrong notes, but was faithful to the composer's intention', or 'he played correctly but seemed to miss the point'. Such criticism disturbs me (though I have often found it valid) because it implies that there is something behind the notation, something the composer meant but did not write. In my piece there is no intention separate from the notation; the intention is that the player should respond to the notation. He should not interpret in a particular way (e.g. how he imagines the composer intended) but should be engaged in the act of interpretation. (NOTE: what I really meant to say, was that the piece could be played correctly by a pianist having no previous acquaintance with western music. But such methods belong to logic. The animal doesn't exist anyway; in getting acquainted with the piano you get acquainted with western music.)

A wrong note in this piece is unambiguously a mistake, since the only indication of tempo is 'as fast as possible' (for some short groups), and only playing 'faster than possible' can result in a wrong note. It is clear that playing 'faster than possible' is a wrong interpretation of 'as fast as possible'; a wrong interpretation resulting perhaps from the consideration that the composer intended a particular speed when he wrote 'as fast as possible' (which cannot be the case: a particular *speed* is given by a metronome indication and note values). 'As fast as possible' does not even imply that you must give an *impression* of speed (e.g. by playing wrong notes), it is simply an incentive to action.

23 – The last word about 'as fast as possible'. It is impossible that the composer intends any particular speed by it, or any particular durations, so any speed will satisfy him. So instead of 'as fast as possible', write 'as fast as you like (not periodic)'.

'With that do you intend to say that the prescription "as fast as possible" has no further use?'.

'On the contrary; it is a very efficacious prescription when the effect desired is one of confusion'.   x '59

24 – Concerning the 'feeling of structure' in this piece. The notation ⌐⌐⌐ for durations (!) almost forces you towards an 'organic' structure, by suggesting that something should coincide with the end of the note. The ceasing of one note generates the attack of another (legato). The other notation used in the piece for durations (.,⸗,-,⌒) tends on the other hand to boost the 'feeling of structure'; for these signs say nothing about where – at what point *in the music* – the note should cease, and in consequence it seems to cease arbitrarily (arbitrariness is characteristic of the 'feeling of structure'). Sometimes the uses of the two types of sign 'overlap', and this as it were gives the player his second wind; he is again free to choose.

25 –The notation of indeterminate events is problematic. It is both a criticism

and an asset of *February 1959* that an indeterminacy could creep in without my noticing it. If you want to notate an indeterminate length (of time), the sign for it cannot have length (on paper); i.e. you must use a 'dot'-type sign.

Remember that all signs meaning 'long', 'medium', 'short', etc. are *only* incentives to the player; the situation you have composed must allow him to to find *any* length 'long' (i.e. he must be free in his experiencing of length), except where length is otherwise determined (e.g. by diminuendo in *February 1959*).   x '59

26 – 'Refrain' by Karlheinz Stockhausen is an example of the signs having length where the sounds have length, and, because in addition to this the various dynamics are given by the thickness of the line and the instruments involved (vibes, piano, celesta) all produce decaying sounds, it is almost impossible to avoid the feeling that you are looking at a picture of the sound and consequently interpreting it visually. Take an imaginary example: ▬▬▬ . Suppose this to represent a tone struck *mf* and held until you can only just hear it (*pppp*). Now at the point indicated in this sound another player is to enter, so he takes out his ruler and measures the thickness of the line at the point where he is supposed to enter (shown by arrow). He finds it has a thickness (.4 mm, say) corresponding to the level *ppp*. But what 'indicates'? Time and again in rehearsal I have played in this way, only to have Karlheinz shout 'wait! wait!'. 'I did wait – until it was *ppp*.' 'But look at that line! The time before your entry is about twice as long as the time after it, and his sound still has a long way to go before it reaches its minimum'. Really, one is tempted to say that some composers don't understand their own notations! Here the case is clear; the sound of a piano decays rapidly at first, and then much slower, so that if we postulate that *mf, mp, p, pp, ppp, pppp* are 6 evenly spaced dynamics, the sound takes longer to decay from *ppp* to *pppp* than it does from *mf* to *mp*. *Everybody* knows this, and Karlheinz in particular; but his notation has misled him – in his drawing of the sound he has used a straight line diminuendo, Thus, though the score has the appearance of a 'drawn' notation, it is actually a written one. This does not mean it is impossible to interpret, but merely that it is very difficult to interpret in the presence of the composer (composers always think they own their pieces). Actually this notation poses some very nice problems and could be very enlivening in the life of an interpreter.

27 – *Refrain* again. Measurement is part of the notation process (for the dynamics), but is not evident in the visual result, which means that the player has to go through the measuring process in reverse in order to find the sound. Thus,

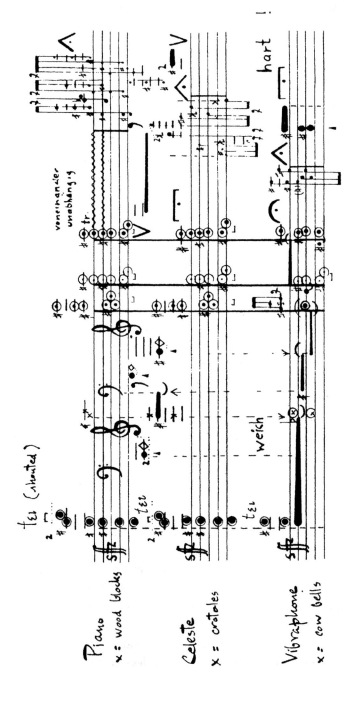

excerpt from 'Refrain' by Karlheinz Stockhausen

notes in circles are held through to next line.

ɣ = velar click (consult London University Phonetics Dept. also for "tɛι")

2... = octave higher.

composer (or his copyist) and interpreter have to make the same measurements at different stages. Very uneconomical (is this such a savage criticism?). A measurement once made should be made so as to stay made.   ii '60
(Cage, in his instruction for *Variations*: 'measure, or simply observe distances from points to lines'.)

28 – A musical notation that looks beautiful is not a beautiful notation, because it is not the function of a musical notation to look beautiful (functionalism).
   Any attempts in this direction (Bussotti) could be called 'aesthetic notations'. Notation for its own sake, but in a different sense from say, pure mathematics.
                                                                                    ii '60

29 – Russell: 'a perfect notation would be a substitute for thought'. Stockhausen: 'a perfect notation? Would that be one where you can immediately imagine 'how it sounds'? Then order me one right away. But because it will always be imperfect, we have to go on thinking through a lot of rubbish. When you read music, it's better to imagine music than to *think* all the time what the signs mean.
   But there is a limit to the music that can be drawn.   vii '59

30 – The question of the correctitude of a performance (to recapitulate). About a performance of a piece of classical music one person says 'he played correctly but failed to see the intention', and another 'he did not play all the notes but was faithful to the composer's intention'. Fidelity to the intention of the composer thus appears to be separate from fidelity to the notation. As much as to say, the composer does not notate what he intends! It is a personal success or failure of the interpreter, whether or not he can divine the intention behind the notation (for the view that this intention is expressed in the rules for the notation, see below).
   It comes to this; in classical music one can obey all the rules for the interpretation of the notation, and still not give a correct performance. Can we imagine a music where it is possible to give a correct performance merely by following these rules? These rules must be such that they can be obeyed under any circumstances; these may affect the result, but do not hinder the player's obedience to the rules. To make, too, rules which may be obeyed *differently* according to the circumstances. (I seem to be saying in fact that it is the rules here which are being interpreted and not the notation. And would one not find behind these rules an intention (not notated) as to how these rules were to be interpreted e.g. under certain circumstances, etc., etc. ....??).

I do not wish to write music which *anybody* can play as well as, say, David Tudor, but that somehow, as a result of the notation (plus the accompanying rules, plus the rules for the interpretation of the rules, plus… the NOTATION) it would never occur to anyone who had not the capacity to do it correctly to attempt the piece (just as no one but a genuine dilettante would independently have the idea to play Feldman. This 'independence' is an essential feature of my dilettante).

Here we are in a similar situation to that where things are left 'free', and then the composer tells the player afterwards that he played well or badly ('used' the freedom well or badly). If there exist criteria for making such a judgment, then there is no freedom. Playing a piece in which the dynamics are free, it should make no difference whatever to the piece (its identity) (its value) if I play *mp* continuously. viii '59

31 – 'Rules' and 'notation' are inextricably intermingled, and it is misleading to separate them. There never was a notation without rules – these describe the relationship between the notation and what is notated. The trouble in classical music is that so many of these rules are inexplicit – given by tradition, and obeyed to such an extent subconsciously that they would be difficult to formulate.

viii '59

32 – The notation should put the player on the right road. He can rise above the notation if he works through the notation. Interpreting according to the rules should lead him to the identity of the piece; this grasped, he may slough off the rules and interpret freely, secure in the fact that he knows what he is doing – he 'knows' the piece.

33 – A dilettante musician is one who has a weakness for music. He takes delight in doing it and consequently has a more than even chance of doing it properly. An amateur on the other hand, is incompetent and incapable of understanding. These definitions are of course irrespective of whether he practises music for bread or for love or both.

34 – 'Dynamics are free' does not mean that there are to be no dynamics, or one constant dynamic, but invites the player to ask himself 'what dynamic(s) for this sound?', thus bringing him into the situation of having to take care of the sound, putting it in his charge, making him responsible.

ii '60

Example 5

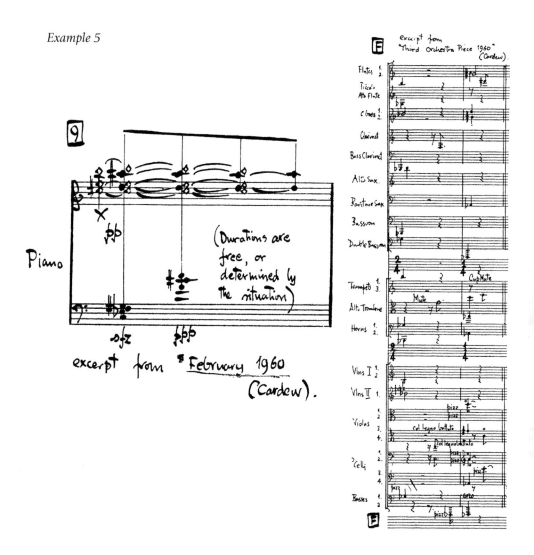

35 – Two instructions for the piano piece are: 'the duration of each "quaver" is free, or determined by the situation', and 'each "quaver" is one sound in a natural process of decay, therefore (!) the prescription "legato" should be observed wherever applicable'. This last is an example of an 'obscure' rule, designed to make it impossible to study the rules separately from the music (is this a telling victory?). The explanation of 'therefore': because if two sounds are separated, a different sound – where tones are tied – or a pause appears in the hiatus. (Rules which send the player packing back to the music.)

19

36 – The fact that the conductor is free should not suggest to him any vulgar images of spontaneity. The feeling of arbitrariness should be avoided (as far as possible). Real freedom lies in the recognition of one's responsibilities. (It is only in the score that the composer can talk to the conductor in this way – he is by nature shy and unassuming in rehearsal – so this too is part of his notation.)   xii '60

37 – The proper way, write something down, and then play it, without looking at what you have written. Just the two – writing and playing; no reading! You must remember what you wrote – then you will remember what is significant about it and with time leave out what is unmemorable and insignificant – and that is writing. And then you must play *with* it – that is, with what you remember. Playing is necessarily an elaboration; it is so concrete – things must be tied together, balanced, arranged, made to fit.

38 – Loudness is not necessarily an *important* characteristic of the sound, *ff, f, p, pp,* do not necessarily belong to the same class of sign. For instance: *ff* means 'everything you've got', *f* means 'louder than the context', *p* means 'with a "beautiful." quality', *pp* means 'extreme espressivo'. Naturally they are the same type of sign, but they do not form a class.

39 – Some rules for my *third orchestra piece 1960*: play each group over and over; refer back to groups (the example shows one group). ♩ is on the beat, ♪. is just after the beat, ♪ is between beats, ♪ is just before the beat. No beat should be twice as long or short or more than those on either side of it. No beat should be sub-divided. Each tone may be played or not, and generally speaking this is to be decided by the player on the spur of the moment. No tone *has* to be played, and from this it follows that a smaller orchestra may be used than that listed; but this should not be taken to extremes, it is a piece for orchestra (see Ex. 5).

Together with the freedom either to play or not to play, must come the freedom to do anything in between – almost to play, or almost not to play, to play, *more or less*, i.e. the freedom to play soft or loud, and short or long. However, I can suggest *f* or *p* (by the simple expedient of writing it in the score), or ⌢ ('longer') or ⁓ ('portato '), etc., just as I can 'suggest' that a particular tone should be played, by scoring it for five or six instruments.

One more rule: 'the conductor may make suggestions to the musicians (about dynamics, durations, who should play, "no pitches above middle C in this group", etc.), but after rather than before studying the score'. (I am not insulting the conductor, but rather guarding against far-out 'modern' interpretations.)

40 – The aura surrounding a modern score. The pre-publication history of a piece should be published along with the score. A modern score is such an enigmatic phenomenon, however detailed, or precise, or illuminating the instructions for playing it. It is difficult to focus on it; its features are so elusive. Juries leafing through a modern score say 'nothing seems to happen in it', forgetting that it consists of notes which must be read and heard. The modern score has a concentration that defies lecture.

A chronicle of the first performance, the experience gained from it, subsequent changes listed, different aspects shown by different performances as available, reactions of conductors and players – all this could help to bring the music into focus. And by surrounding the score with apparently *irrelevant* details – and I am not thinking of 'analysis' (as the construction methods of 'serial' scores used to be called), but, for example, of the circumstances in which it was written, or your financial status at the time, or the climate, etc., etc. (these are after all *also* reasons why the piece shows the features – or lack of feature – that it does) – it would be possible to give it a sort of approachable personality.

41 – The following example of Morton Feldman's work is so rich that I find myself unable to comment on it.

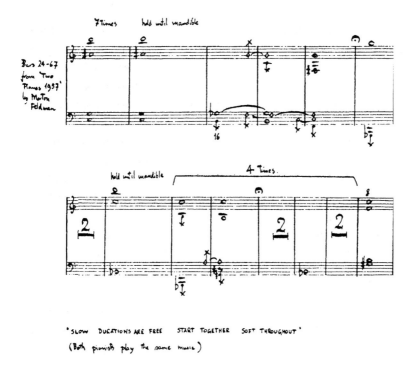

' SLOW   DURATIONS ARE FREE   START TOGETHER   SOFT THROUGHOUT '

(Both pianists play the same music)

42 – Availability of scores. All Cage's work may now be obtained through Peters' Edition (with some delay). His *Winter Music*, on the other hand, can be viewed immediately in the magazine New Departures 2/3 , obtainable from Otto Schmink, 57, Greek Street, W.1.

A selection of Bussotti's works has been published by Universal Edition (signed copies are more expensive), from whom Stockhausen's *Refrain* may also be obtained, if not now, then in the near future. *Carré* on the other hand – which is a work for 4 orchestras and 4 choruses under 4 conductors and lasts 35 minutes – is unlikely to be available for some time.

Isolated pieces by Wolff and Feldman have appeared in the American 'New Music Publications', which may be borrowed from the library of the American Information Service. Feldman's *Piano 3 Hands* may appear shortly in the Leeds magazine *Accent* together with my comment on it.

My *February 1959* appeared in *New Departures 1* which is now a collector's item, but *February 1960* is to be found amongst the *Darmstäder Beiträge zur neuen Musik 1960* which is obtainable, at a price, from Schott's Music Publishers.

London v. '61

[Editor's note: The illustration used in note 41, above, is a facsimile of Cardew's own hand. Copied c.1961 (presumably) from a draft version of *Two Pianos* (1957) as presented by Morton Feldman. There are differences to the later published version (1962). The printed version has no bar lines and varies in other minor ways.]

Report on Stockhausen's 'Carré' – Part 1
The Musical Times – October 1961

Stockhausen's *Carré* for four orchestras was performed in Hamburg on October last year (1960). In this article Cornelius Cardew describes his experiences while collaborating with the composer on its creation and execution.

The theoretical possibility or impossibility of collaboration in composing a musical score… Of what interest are such theoretical possibilities or impossibilities? Examine the reasons of the parties involved in any particular case of collaboration. But how many such cases are there? Well, imagine some.

When I was actually involved in the collaboration with Stockhausen on 'his' *Carré* (for four orchestras, four choruses, four conductors, four sides of the room) I spent some of the afternoons when work on it seemed pointless, thinking of possible or sensible forms that a collaboration could take. The idea that most took my fancy ran somewhat as follows: one, or each of the composers concerned would write some music of a casual nature (i.e. not completed or closed, but with casual indications of dynamics, instrumentation, notes, phrases, perhaps a few bars sketched) and post it – this was an important aspect – to his or her collaborators). All verbal comments would be avoided, except those usual in the notation of musical ideas (e.g. 'flute', 'crescendo', 'full orchestra without percussion' – and this last not necessarily supplemented by a list of the 'full' orchestra or of the omitted percussion).

On receipt of this material (which I romantically visualise as a dirty piece of manuscript paper), the other collaborator proceeds to comment upon it, musically. He may add, change, modify, oppose, protest, destroy, restrict. embroider, etc. He then sends the whole – the original material together with any supplementary sheets – back to the first composer. I felt that neither composer should keep the material for more than a couple of days at a time, and that the process could continue for as long as was necessary or desired. An end to the process could be formalised as follows: when one of the composers returns the material without having done anything to it, the other may take this as a sign that he is to complete the score, i.e. make a performable score of it. Or they may duplicate the material and each make a performable score, thus making two, or as many versions of the piece as there are collaborators.

I still find this idea feasible, and would embark on it with anyone who cared to collaborate with me, though I cannot answer for the results. And it is this which indicates the great merit of the idea, that it is *dilettante* and entered into with free love and acceptance of no matter what eventuality – like abandoning the project, or shooting your collaborators, or never finishing it… all of which are impossible when the work in question is a commission.

* * *

My collaboration with Karlheinz was, on the one hand, an expression of his altruistic desire to help me personally, and on the other, his solution of his problem of having more commitments than he could accomplish single handed. *Carré* was commissioned by Radio Hamburg, and was conceived during Karlheinz's long flights over North America while he was lecturing there. I had spent February and March at a loose end in England, writing *February 1959* in odd moments, and making my final comment on my studies in electronic music in an article called *the unity of musical space*; returned to Cologne in April with an open mind and a work hungry spirit; and found a whole heap of more or less hieroglyphic notes, including 101 snappy items of the same general form as Example 1 (which I have freely invented, no longer having access to any of the material of *Carré*). These I proceeded to realise, working daily chez Stockhausen from 3pm until dinnertime, aided, irritated, confused, encouraged, and sometimes even guided by his own eagle eye, or his voluminous notes, or his random narrations as he worked on his experiments for what later became *Kontakte* (for piano, percussion, and four track track tape).

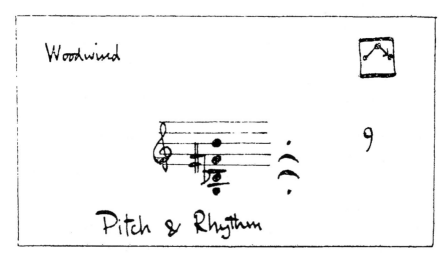

Example 1 The sign on the right shows the movement between the orchestras. 9 is one of 12 dynamic levels. Dot means this note staccato or very short, slur sign very long. Pitch and rhythm are the elements to be brought into play during this group.

At the end of three months or so, during which I also wrote my *Octet 1959* and learnt the guitar part of *Le Marteau sans Maitre*, a rough score had come into existence; I had an obscure idea of what the piece would be like, and Karlheinz's more whimsical notions about the piece had been abandoned, and all seemed set, when, on the eve of my return to England, Karlheinz sprang the idea of the 'insertions' (episodes outside the general run of the piece – at this stage they had very little in common with what they eventually became) which were to delay the completion of even the rough score until March 1960, when I finished the last page (containing 3,000 odd notes) of the last insertion (comprising ten or so such pages) in a sun filled library in Amsterdam.

The 'story' of this piece is longer and more harrowing than the 'story' of any other piece I have written. Which says something about its value. Like the Viennese painter who remarked – very pleased with himself – to a critic, 'Yes, a lot of work went into that picture.' 'Well isn't that just too bad,' was the reply, 'because none of it is ever going to come out again'.

* * *

The score of *Carré* is four scores, one for each orchestra. So the score *Carré 1* consists of the first orchestra written out in full, and above, reductions of the other three orchestras, each on two staves. Thus none of the scores can give a really detailed impression of the sound, and a total view of the piece is very difficult to achieve at all, except in performance. This was perhaps one of the reasons why the question cropped up as to whether or not the 101 groups like Example 1 could constitute a sort of score for publication. David Tudor was of the opinion that they could; so was I; but Karlheinz on the other hand would probably oppose the idea strongly. This score, if published, would be the score of a piece for four orchestras by Karlheinz Stockhausen and no mistake about it. For a performance, some would have to 'interpret' it (just as I did, with differences which we will mention later) into a proper performable score. If there were several such interpretations and performances, comparison of these would enable an earnest critic to distribute his blame between the composer (Stockhausen) and the realizer.

Let us look for manifestations of personality in the piece. There are doubtless many in the Basic Score (comprising the 101 groups as in Ex 1) which label it incontrovertibly STOCKHAUSEN, but these manifestations are in the Basic Score, and not necessarily in the Final Score. That is to say that were the realizer to approach the Basic Score with sufficient boldness, these manifestations could become insignificant – intentionally concealed, or unintentionally ignored. I, for one, would certainly now approach the task in this fearless spirit, and allow my imagination to act unconditionally on the material of the Basic Score. I would hazard the opinion that it is lack of faith in these manifestations that would lead Karlheinz to oppose the release of such a score. ('Release' is the right word: the score leaves your hands, and *anything* may happen to it. But then, you could reserve the right to veto performances, if you felt that way about it, and you could appoint executors in cases where you, personally, were not able to do so).

Cage, Wolff, Bussotti – to name but a few who do release basic scores, though of different sorts – do have this faith. 'But if there is a way you want it to be, write it that way' (as composers of indeterminate music who complain about performances of their pieces are often told), and I think Karlheinz does want his music to be a certain way, and it is as a result of this that he has constantly exerted his personality in coaching performances of his works (indeed performances in which he has had no hand have been exceptions; even the Glasgow performance of *Gruppen* was modeled on a tape-recording of a performance in which Stockhausen was the principal conductor); thus he had evaded the necessity of finding an adequate formalization of his ideas.

It is in this role – that of breathing down the performer's neck – that you find him exerting his personality in *Carré*; his advice to me while working on the Basic Score, his copious notes and hieroglyphics accompanying the Basic Score, his elucidations of the signs used in the Basic Score, there were the strongest manifestations of personality in the complex process which we loosely term *Carré*. And in fact I did work at the score all the time keeping his intentions in mind, though my own 'personality' tended more and more to interfere as the work progressed. The sections which were finally cut in the performance were either ones in which my personality conflicted with his – or seemed to – or ones which manifested virtually no personality at all (an unusually ideal state of affairs, and hard to come by, in my opinion), i.e. some sections near the beginning where I would not yet have conceived of interfering and where he had failed to manifest his intentions in such a way that I could appreciate and act upon them. But generally our personalities interacted freely, and with much friendly discussion.

* * *

Now something about the *musical* basis of the collaboration. When we met in April 1959 we discovered that we had both written cyclic pieces, i.e. pieces in which you can start anywhere (in his *Zyklus* for one percussion player, on any page; in my *February 1959*, with any group) and join the end to the beginning. Both pieces present a cyclic recurrence of elements: certain sounds or tones recur at regularly increasing or decreasing intervals, and then back – like a simple harmonic curve. In both pieces a number of these cycles overlap, and the form is characterised at any given point by whatever element is passing through its density peak at that moment. One major difference between the pieces was that he used a notation in which space corresponded to time, and he was thus able to plot the recurrence of elements as logarithmic series; whereas I wished to dispense with the measurement of time in this sense. I used neither a number of beats nor a number of seconds for measuring the recurrence of the elements, but a number of musical events. The length of the musical events was determined by the condition of the sounds themselves (e.g. a time would last as long as it took to decay from *f* to *mp*, etc.), combined with a few relative indications like long, short, etc. Thus, whereas his elements would recur after 3,2,1,2,3 units of *time*, mine would recur after 3,2,1,2,3 units of *music*, or musical elements. I had naively feared this was a new idea (as it may well have been a new idea to use it systematically), and so was overjoyed to find the whole of *Carré* laid out in this manner – each group like Ex. 1 can be considered a musical event in this sense.

But instead of being cyclic, the recurrence of elements in *Carré* was generally straight-line, so that any element (each sign in Ex. 1 can be considered one of a class of elements) would occur more and more frequently up to a climax (of this element), and any climax of this sort heralded a structural shift; a new element would be introduced and perhaps this new element would start at its maximum frequency of occurrence, and thereafter decrease in frequency until it faded out altogether. (I am giving no indication of the actual structure of the piece – only of the type of structure). So this aspect of the piece afforded me personally considerable interest, irrespective of the shaping of the individual musical events in themselves.

* * *

The instrumentation. The selection and distribution of the instruments had me slightly worried. First, it was irritating to have to write for an instrument that one has never consciously heard, like the cymbalom (Hungarian dance music, Stravinsky's *Renard*); one has constantly to refer to a diagrammatic picture of the instrument to find out what is playable and what is not. Second, Stockhausen's insistence on equal numbers of brass and wind instruments (four brass and four wind in each orchestra); I prefer a more conventional balance. And then the choice of wind instruments; instruments like E flat clarinet and double bassoon were vetoed as unnecessary – and it is true, the whole piece does unfold within a space of 4½ octaves, with only occasional excursions, for which Karlheinz was not responsible. But I felt that instruments of extreme timbre and range could have helped to rectify the unbalance caused by equal numbers of brass and wind. Later, I came to enjoy the limitations involved in using only instruments with fairly centrally placed ranges, especially in their extreme and characteristic registers; but that was after I had worked off any disappointment on the instrumentation (piccolo, alto flute, oboe, E flat clarinet, bass clarinet, double bassoon, violin, double bass) of my own *Octet 1959*.

With the brass, Karlheinz was more liberal; a high F trumpet, bass trumpet, alto trombone and tuba were all featured. The strings lacked all initiative: a 2-2-2-2 combination was used in each orchestra – no basses, and this was, I think, one of the causes of a certain lack of orchestral bulk which prevented the four conductors from sustaining the necessary rapport, so widely separated in such a large hall; a slight wrongness of scale which kept each orchestra distinctly a chamber orchestra, but within a situation that definitely required a really big 'orchestra.' An orchestra which can provide 16 brass (6 were horns), 8 percussion players and, among the wind, 3 saxophones and 3 clarinets, can surely boast more than 32 strings! The 8 percussionists were my greatest worry, since I have but little penchant for the sounds. In the rough score, I sketched their parts vaguely, simply, mechanically and minimally, assuring myself that Karlheinz would brush them up when he came to correct the final score. This he never did, or only in a very few cases, and so the percussion parts retained their simplicity, and were finally completely appropriate and unobtrusive almost all the time (they play incessantly).

Piano, harp, cymbalom and vibraphone completed the orchestra – he referred to them as 'attack instruments', and they were used chiefly to colour the entries of other instruments, and only occasionally achieved independence – and had all else been equal, these would have been sufficient to characterise the four sides of the hall, aurally. But all else was not equal; the four orchestras were not identical, but they were not *significantly* differentiated. And it would have been so easy to have made them either the one or the other.

One word about the clapping, finger snapping, tongue clicking, phonetic mouthing chorus (2-2-2-2 in each orchestra): I wrote their notes and Karlheinz their nonsense, later laboriously copied according to the rules laid down by the International Phonetic Association. They were one of the liveliest features of the general sound, and sang beautifully at the performance.

* * *

The notation. Stockhausen's original idea for the notation was to have lines of twelve different thicknesses, representing twelve different loudness levels. These lines were to be prolonged in correspondence to the durations of the sounds, and would wander about over the stave in cases of *glissando*, and get thicker and thinner in the event of a dynamic change (*cres. dim.* etc.). Thus, the three essential aspects of any sound – pitch, loudness, duration – would be welded into a single sign with three corresponding features – placing on the stave for pitch, thickness for loudness, length for durations. The weightiest objection to this was the fact that were we to choose twelve *appreciable* differentiations of thickness, the stave would have to be so large that the height of the total score would have come to something like four yards. And the incredible labour involved, even were one to develop such long arms: using the Graphos pen – which dries up if you dream even for two seconds (and it would take you longer than that to walk round to the other end of the score) – constantly changing between twelve different sized nibs.

In the rough score I used the numbers 1-12 for the dynamics, and these were reduced in the final score to *pp, p, f, ff*, much to my relief. (Even after reaching this decision, the decision to write the four scores separately was still a forced one). The prolongation of the lines was retained, to accommodate the frequent *glissandi*. Where fast passages were required, these were written as quavers, with sundry commas, dots, and short lines to indicate the rhythmic profile (Example 2). The rapport between conductors and players, and the timing (no metrics and no stopwatches) were laid out generally as follows:

Most significant changes in the sound were to be brought about by a sign from the conductor. To avoid the confusion that would result if all these signs were down beats, they were grouped in 2,3,4 or 5, making up 'bars' with beats of irregular length. These irregular beats were written as relative lengths on the page; thus the first beat could be short (1 cm say), the second long (say 8 cm), the third somewhere between the two (say 3.5 cm), the fourth a little longer than the second (say 9 cm), and so on.

Each group was thus divided into irregular lengths, and over the whole group was written a time (say 24") decided on by Karlheinz and myself empirically, by mentally 'hearing' the group a few times, timing it each time, and taking the mean time of the various times we had timed it. The conductor can repeat this process: he can interpret the varying lengths by eye, and check his time against a stopwatch, and if he finds he has taken too long, he can 'correct' his timing. But we decided on these numbers (times) *after* writing the music, so I could never really regard them as binding (they were not composed), and I personally would have liked the conductors to have felt free to ignore them in all cases except those where they actually found they had to refer to them in order to get an idea of what the music was about.

I found this sort of notation – anti-beat, with no metrical drive – almost ideal for the conception of *Carré*; as we have already mentioned, Karlheinz conceived the piece in the hours spent flying over the USA during his lecture tour there. Sounds 'at peace', which last and last and do not change, or change suddenly and briefly – this was the general idea, or one of them. I enjoyed this general idea very much, and in actual fact, while composing, I would often write 'a sound' and gaze out of the window at the summer afternoon gardens 'listening' to it for 10 to 20 minutes, and not just the 12" or whatever it might be that was actually audible in the concert hall.

* * *

Conducting procedure. Each conductor stood with his back to the wall, and where two or more of them had a beat in common, they were to agree on this by looking at each other. The musicians received signs with which they were perfectly familiar, namely a 1st, 2nd, 3rd, 4th beat of the bar; and every sign was accompanied by an acoustical occurrence – a change in the sound; so there were no empty beats. A synchronized attack is one of the problems presented by the absence of a pulse; how can several instruments enter together when they have no reliable and common means of predicting the advent of the next beat? This was easily solved by prefacing each beat with a short up-beat of a constant length.

Report on Stockhausen's 'Carré' – Part 2
The Musical Times – November 1961

In part 1 of this article, which appeared last month, Cornelius Cardew described the conception, planning and composition of Stockhausen's *Carré* for four orchestras. This month he deals with the 'insertions' (added episodes outside the general run of the piece), and the way the work was brought to performance.

Let us now talk about the 'insertions', for it is these that constitute the exceptions to the temporal concept and technique outlined last month. In the insertions, Stockhausen intended that 'space' should emancipate itself; and the sounds' movements in space should be their chief feature. Our main problem – chiefly because it was the most predictable one – was that the sounds would always proceed by jerks around the room, for between each orchestra there was a considerable space.

The problem has also cropped up in the course of Karlheinz's work on *Kontakte*, and he found a sort of 'ideal' solution which did not actually produce very satisfactory results in the 'laboratory experiment' performed by him at the Cologne radio station. This experiment consisted in mounting a revolving loudspeaker in the centre, and placing four microphones, each recording on one track of the four track tape recorder, around it. The 'signal' (sound) was then relayed through the loudspeaker, which mechanically spun at various speeds. He had calculated that the signal would be constantly 'audible' to all four microphones, but would achieve 'presence' only when the speaker was directly opposite the microphone. Thus the dynamic curves and intensity levels of the rising and setting sounds (in the land of perpetual sound, for at no point is the sound inaudible to any microphone) – which would be impossible to plot synthetically – could be recorded directly. As I said, the results were none too satisfactory, though some were usable.

* * *

This may be a similar case to that proposed by Norbert Wiener (I quote from hearsay), where 'a Man' is recorded – cell structure, electronic impulses, everything you can think of, all fed into a computer, which records and stores the 'information' in a fraction of a second, and can transmit it in the form of radio waves. Thousands of miles away, the converse machine collects this 'information' from the ether, and recovers it into 'a Man.' (I forget what happens to the original man; perhaps the machine actually 'takes him apart' for the purpose of recording him). 'Cell structure, electronic impulses, everything you can think of…', but who can think of everything? And I find myself posing the same question with regard to Karlheinz's experiment.

The movement of sounds in space is largely a psychological phenomenon; the problem is to create the illusion that the sound source is moving – easy for the stereo record engineers, harder with live performers. I found this illusion most successfully accomplished by careful music blending, in cases where similar (in timbre and notes and dynamics) sounds were painstakingly handed over from one orchestra to another. Your attention 'wanders' across the intervening space in the time when both orchestras are playing the same sound. But in the insertions it was intended that the listener should be caught up in a sort of hair-raising sound spin. Insertion 69X, for example (since these insertions were *outside* the general run of the piece, 'extras', I called them X, and indeed some of them are almost unsuitable for kids under 16), is laid out as follows:

A soprano D (a ninth above middle C) is passed around the four orchestras at the rate of 12 changes per minute – each chorus sustains it for five seconds plus one second after the next chorus has taken it up. Simultaneously, the strings and woodwind revolve in the opposite direction at the rate of 60 changes per minute. This is an agitated flimmer, *f* as opposed to the *pp* soprano D, and moves over the pitch range, sometimes haunting the high spots and sometimes the medium or low, or distributed over the whole range but with a density emphasis moving from high to low. Soon all the percussive instruments (harp, piano, vibes, cymbalom) enter simultaneously with an extremely sharp *ff* chord, and the flimmer becomes a murmur and this dies away.

* * *

There are a number of interferences like this, and each initiates some significant change in the excited flimmer of strings and wind: they reverse their direction and turn clockwise instead of anti-clockwise, or they double their speed to 120 per minute, or they all cluster into the high register, etc. In the end the revolutions lose momentum, become hesitant, proceed by jerks, and the flimmer is relegated to the beginnings of the sounds only, and finally just the sopranos are left. The D ceases to revolve, and the orchestra in which it has 'landed' proves to be the site of the quiet brass chord – sustained under the sopranos – that introduces the next group of the piece proper. Throughout this drama the cymbalom (in the third orchestra – behind the audience, as I had imagined) plays a virtuosic cadenza come rain come shine.

It can easily be seen that such an event lends itself ideally to a metrical notation; the revolutions are regular, and each orchestra plays one 'beat' out of four, and this is actually the way it was conducted – in 4/4, and 4/8 when the speed is doubled. But instead of using note values, all the music was written as 'breaks', articulated as in Ex. 2, which had to be approximately fitted into metrical schemata. This makes for an agitated, unprofiled sound, forming a perfect contrast to the rest of the music, which though non-metrical, gives a completely 'measured' impression.

The same is true of Insertion 82X, which is laid out on much a grander scale. Here the orchestras enter one after the other and play ferocious cascades in which everybody takes part, descending from their highest to their lowest registers. This too revolves, but with much more overlap, so that the first orchestra has reached its low register just when the fourth orchestra is starting its descent. An intensification process leads to each orchestra in turn having blocked chords, while the others continue their melodic cascades. This ceases abruptly, and discovers a *pp* finely differentiated whisper from the strings. This is a technique that crops up quite a few times. Stockhausen calls them 'windows' – the sound is opened – the barrage or screen taken down – and exposes the view beyond; this view can then also be 'opened' and something shown behind that again.

82X is written in much the same way as 69X, but the musical content is different. The group presents a gradual transition from the melodic type of articulation to a chordal texture. This transitional process goes through all sorts of spins, in different directions and at various speeds, until finally space becomes submerged in a chaotic chordal chopping. It seems to be something other than sound that emerges from this total immersion in *fortissimo* attacks at the rate of about 60 chords per second. This stops abruptly leaving the four choruses alone, *pianissimo* – one listens with a sort of drugged passivity and relief – who wander around in close harmony for a while before the next group begins.

* * *

I say 'relief' speaking for myself alone; one of the beauties of the piece – leave aside the insertions – is that virtually nothing can go seriously wrong; all is relaxed and beautiful, and each musician is free to devote his attention to the production of a good sound. But in the insertions, the slightest lapse of attentiveness can have disastrous results; embarrassing gaps appear in the 'spin' – and these are very noticeable – or you hear one player after all the others have stopped, and because there is such a row going on, you can be sure that he is playing in a most slap-dash manner, without any of the distinction which could make such an exposed mistake worth listening to.

But there are doubtless many who would have preferred the whole piece to have been like these insertions, and indeed one can imagine that the memory of them is the only thing a great many people took home after the concert. For the insertions are certainly the most 'sensational' aspects of the piece – and they are furthermore what one would expect of a new piece by Stockhausen for four orchestras, so they would be accompanied by a certain experience of fulfillment. And it is a romantic therapy for the modern luxurious listener to be dragged round the city walls by the ears, by proxy.

I came to Hamburg for the start of the rehearsals (ten days before the performance) in some obscurely fabricated supervisional role. Such a performance is inescapably unsupervised, and if I achieved nothing in shaping the performance, I certainly did not achieve less than Karlheinz (except in his role of conductor, of course) unless his somewhat drastic last minute cuts can be considered an achievement in this direction. This cutting session, with only one day of rehearsals to go, was the nearest thing to a Hollywood 'story conference' that I have ever experienced.

Michael Gielen, Andrej Markowski, Mauricio Kagel and the composer – the four conductors – sat, score in laps, armed with thick blue pencils, murmuring the occasional futile objections to Karlheinz's imperious "cut…, cut…," the while imbibing Scotch (it is Karlheinz's irrepressible habit to lavish his total fee on expensive meals and drink for all and sundry before and after a performance) and strong Russian (Hamburg) tea by turns, while David Tudor and I – the passive participants of this conference, for we had no scores and nothing but 'cut…, cut…,' to tell us what was going on – got quietly stoned each in his way, David on tea alone. I went home to bed murmuring histrionically phrases like 'there go the piece's last chances of coherence', and 'so much the less music,' and I was gratified the next day when musicians were heard to sigh and say such things as "but we played that bit so beautifully," referring to some particularly poignant cut.

* * *

Indeed, the majority of the musicians showed a remarkable amount of good will. They soon came to terms with the unconventional aspects of the notation (there was a near panic when it turned out that the parts for one orchestra were almost illegible and that some of the parts were missing. The staff copyists at the radio had never seen anything like it, and finally Stockhausen and I had to do most of the fresh copying) and rehearsals progressed smoothly through all possible combinations of instruments: strings alone, brass and wind, brass and strings, wind and percussion, etc. The most successful rehearsals were those just before the four orchestras met. Each orchestra on its own – a chamber orchestra of 26 or so players – rehearsed in turn in the (relatively small) concert halls at the radio, and it was marvellous to hear every detail of the individual scores played with great clarity, confidence and precision. Balance was perfect, and all the players so attuned to one another that the most remarkable blended sounds were produced without any sensation of strain. It was when we moved to the big hall of the 'Planten & Blomen' that the real difficulties began.

It was a sort of exhibition hall – a large square hangar, fitted up with a multitude of loudspeakers (for the first half of the concert was to consist of electronic music) and four cubicles for the separate recording of the four orchestras, and a fifth where they were to be mixed. My job was supposed to be flitting among these cubicles adjusting the balance of the four microphones for each orchestra, and then the balance of the four orchestras together in the fifth cubicle, meanwhile running out into the main hall every few seconds to give detailed instructions as to who was too loud and too soft, and too early and too late, among 108 musicians, who were – to increase the difficulty – invisible and unreachable from the cubicles – and all this carrying a heavy armful of four full scores each opened at the right page. But what happens when you want to turn a page…?

I gradually realized that the piece was leading its own life and that the best thing to do was to sit back and listen. The chief difficulty was this: when one orchestra was playing – however quietly – its conductor could hardly hear anything of what the other three orchestras were doing. Consequently, each conductor was constantly requiring the other three to give more; particularly, they were concerned about 'signals' from the other orchestras, cues for the entries of their respective orchestras. So yelled consultations would ensue (which were trying for nerves, throats and lungs) despite the individual microphones and loudspeakers at each conductor's elbow, by means of which they could converse normally over the long distances involved. Somehow this was a psychological impracticability: the yells persisted, the conductors too, and the result was that the balance of each orchestra individually (this was the only balance that mattered; the balance of the four orchestras was uncontrollable and irrelevant since the audience was spread over the whole of the enclosed space) went to pieces in many cases.

Another difficulty – and this was also a difficulty with *Gruppen* – was that when four conductors have constantly to refer to one another, and watch each other for cues, and make beats come together, they have that amount less time to concentrate on the performance of their orchestras; the playing is apt to revert to its original shape of untidiness. Couple this with the fact that there is a time lag in a hall of that size, and that the conductors were the most widely separated people in the whole hall, and the reader may imagine something of the depressing process that set in as soon as all the orchestras started to rehearse together. The piece started to fall apart even before one had put it together, and it would have required great presence of mind (and courage) to avert this disaster by the sweet and reasonable method of each orchestra quietly getting on with its own business, and letting the total impression take care of itself.

* * *

The thing that makes coherent performances of the monumental works of the past possible is the unshakable conviction of the validity of the composer's indications. This enables the conductor to rest assured that if he unpacks the piece with sufficient care and respect, the present will be discovered inside, intact. With *Carré*, it seemed that not even Karlheinz was convinced of the validity of the indications in the score, and was therefore more inclined to lay down the piece like a law; and arbitrary law, easily disfigurable by heavy-handedness. I do not pretend that it would have been easy to let the piece play itself – to *assist* (a complex and imponderable mingling of active and passive functions) at its birth or self-demonstration or what you will – but I think it would have been rewarding. The described situation led 'naturally' to the cuts, and also to a frequent embarrassed hasting away with groups, getting them over with, a 'now for heaven's sake let's get on with the story' sort of feeling. Many groups – even where there were no cuts – were reduced to less than half their planned lengths, so very little (or let's say much less than I would have liked) remained of the perfect stillness of the original conception. There was very little of the air of hours of flying high above the North American clouds, which the programme note had been so kind as to mention. I am of course offering only my own personal and prejudiced and exaggerated impression when I say that the life of the piece was *nurtured* up to the point when each orchestra was rehearsing separately, in the concert hall and rehearsal rooms of the radio, but that thereafter it was *bullied* into an atavistic maturity, realizing only a fraction of its musical potential.

* * *

The audience finally sat in four triangles, backing onto the four orchestras and facing towards the centre, so that the places in the score where I had actually imagined the sounds as in front of, or behind, or on either side of the listener, or sounds which were to move from behind the listener to his right hand side, etc. went by the board except for one quarter of the audience. But this fades to irrelevance when one remembers that theoretically – equally irrelevant – there is only one ideal spot for the listener, i.e. equidistant from each orchestra – and actually no one sat there because it was occupied by the control panel for the electronic music in the first half of the concert. As I mentioned, the concert was broadcast on VHF, and consequently reached only a small public of interested listeners who lived within a distance of thirty miles or so of Hamburg Radio. In spite of a formal request that the audience should remain quiet for the announcer to announce the end of the broadcast, he was unable to do so – prolonged cheers, cat calls, boos and clapping drowned him almost completely – and I believe the closing announcements had to be broadcast from a studio. I sat in a cubicle and bit my nails.

The American School of John Cage

[A radio programme on Earle Brown, Morton Feldman and Christian Wolff – broadcast on WestDeutsche Rundfunk on 27th December 1962 – transcribed from Cardew's note books]

Christian Wolff, Earle Brown and Morton Feldman, lumped together as the three most significant pupils, friends, of John Cage. Yet how different they are, and how different from their teacher. One could say that they had received the perfect education from their teacher, that education whose sole visible result is certain freedom of thought, rather than the adoption of a particular way of thinking. Free thinking leads to honesty and truth, but also to isolation. If the distance between Wolff, Brown and Feldman is greater than that between Stockhausen, Boulez and Nono it is because their minds are livelier, their conclusions more far-reaching and, furthermore, arrived at with greater frankness. The three Europeans are certainly more ambitious, their concepts larger, their forms more extended and their sense of direction more consciously developed. But they lack perspicuity, or far-sightedness; they are avowed revolutionaries and therefore concerned with what they reject. History, on the other hand, is the arrival and assimilation of elements from outside, ideas God knows whence. The Indians certainly didn't know where Columbus came from and the Europeans certainly did not realize that their most valuable contribution to Indian Culture was the horse which the Indians were later to use in defending themselves against the proverbial cowboys.

However that may be, our position in Europe is now the reverse, and having so long been in the habit of exporting ideas and other manifestations of culture, and exporting them about by force, we are now on the receiving end, and very difficult we find it to assimilate the ideas that come to us from America and other places which are now virtually on our doorstep. Never mind, perhaps it will turn out thus: that the more passionately we reject these ideas, the more powerful they will be in us when we finally do assimilate them, as of course we must, and on our own terms so to speak.

For the moment I would like to propose that the music of these composers springs from states of mind, as of being, a certain attitude of mind embedded in a particular atmosphere. What goes on in this atmosphere, the decisions taken in it, and conclusions reached in it, in a word the logic of any activity within this atmosphere, remains completely obscure to us if we cannot enter into the same atmosphere. If the performance is good, it may be our stubbornness or unresponsiveness that prevents us entering the atmosphere, or it may be that the atmosphere is insufficiently projected by the composer. And if the performance is bad, the atmosphere is imperfectly purveyed – most goods will get damaged in transit if the transportation is unsuitable – and we are not to blame. Of course even a history book represents an attitude of mind embedded in an atmosphere. We do not breathe nothingness, but air, and what a senseless [mouthing] speech would seem, if our ears were attuned only, say, to bombardment by particles of steel. I am merely saying that it is the solution in which it takes place that evokes sense of an action, the solution, the atmosphere, the context.

In water, the fish communicates, it lives, and it may be that often the music of Wolff, Brown and Feldman is out of water in our European concert halls. But we must find water in which they can live, which seems impossible since until we find it we cannot understand what they are saying. Right now I am trying to synthesize some of that water, and you will presently hear the music.

How did I come to appreciate this music in the first place? I was lucky enough to have some personal contact with David Tudor when he played some of it, and I could appreciate the spirit in which he performed. I have a fundamental conviction that every honest utterance makes sense, and his attitude to the works was enough to convince me of their honesty. How serious all this sounds. It is too general. I have to be a little more matter of fact and critical. It would be wrong to pretend that these works are great masterpieces of art, or even that they represent wholly honest utterances. But (even) in everyday life, which of our utterances can be said to be wholly honest or dishonest? We live in a muddle of half-truths, partial concealment, evasions, privacy, shame, pride (which are said to be the same), pretences, ambitions. It takes the very extremes of deprivation, exhaustion, delirium to make honest men of us, or even men who desire the truth, the truth has become so much a last resort for us, somewhat like religion. But back to earth, compare the composer who has arrived at a point where really any note will do, so long as it is one single note – simply writes the figure 1, realizing that perhaps in the performance there may be valid reasons for the player to choose one or another note, compare him with the composer who reasons "well, since any note will do, it doesn't matter which one I write, so I'll write this one" thus evading the responsibility of writing what he heard, which was no particular note, and denying the performer the possibility of choosing spontaneously, which might have served, by his hesitancy, or air of decision, or of seeking, to create the right atmosphere for the piece. No, when we are exceptionally tired, we do not lack the energy to decide on important questions, what we lack is the energy to deal with the myriad trivial decisions with which we fill our lives.

Tiredness reveals art, also provides susceptibility to strange influences. As in Proust, a work of art is the only [mirror] where we see through another's eyes. The complete expression of a different point of view (the artist's own).

Amplify "state of being".

Investigate how much is heard by composers of indeterminate music. Wolff – Form as Vorgang like Stockhausen, but different. Earle and his instruments. Feldman and his image.

It is when we are exceptionally tired – mentally exhausted – that we have enough courage not to try to cover up the truth, to evade the issue. What we are tired of, after all, are the countless trivial decisions that fill our lives and our music, of deciding which note, when – were we to see clearly – it really doesn't matter which note. Tiredness frees our minds of their mechanism, their superficial critical faculty. When we are tired we are in a position to be affected by – for example – great art. It is the weary man who perceives the truth. Whether he then still has the energy to express it, is another matter. When we appreciate a great work of art, what is happening is that we are looking through someone else's eyes, we are briefly – or if we are lucky – permanently endowed with another man's understanding, his perception of the truth, his understanding of the world. The great artist has found expression for his view, for his understanding, he has succeeded in making it plain. He is not communicating with anyone in particular, he is simply communicating, he is not giving you a message, he is merely finding expression for himself. This is what is universal in art, it is available to all, not addressed to a particular section of the community. A masterpiece of art is a complete picture, existing on its own. (I think this attitude of mine is partially attributable to Proust).

The idea of indeterminate music – where some details (sometimes a great many) are left to a performer or an editor, conductor, or what have you, where the composer gives, in fact, an incomplete picture – poses a large number of problems. Mozart, to pick an example out of the blue, had a sharp vision, a sharp eye, a sharp mind – and sharp ears. So does Picasso. But there are other modern minds to whom the truth is a blur, and if it were not a blur it would not be the truth. The philosopher Wittgenstein holds – as I understand him – that the truth is not an explanation, but lies away, somewhere, in an indescribable region, which can however be apprehended by us simply by a scrutiny of the various concrete facts, all of which lie plainly exposed to our eyes. The paintings of Mark Rothko – a post-war American – symbolize a transition between the sharpness of Mozart and the blur of John Cage. There are definite areas of very definite colour – sharply perceived; but there is no discrete relation between these areas, since the edges are blurred. One could perhaps say that this is definitely a red patch on a brown ground, but it is impossible to say, or see, exactly how the red patch lies on the brown ground. Whether in front or behind, or [shining] through or at an angle etc. (This situation leads easily to the fashionable modern philosophy that sure enough when you do this then that happens, but this does not necessarily mean anything). These are random examples considered cursorily.

The industrial revolution and progress in science and in the means of transportation from one country to another have brought us into contact with things that we do not understand. They have also, conveniently, given us the idea that these things are definitely understandable. (In Mozart's time the truth was something spiritual but definite, in our time the truth is something material but vague). This conception of the truth is blurred; however transitory it may be, it produces the only honest utterances of our time. Again we have got the general.

By some association of ideas (which I am unable to demonstrate to you, for which you may blame me, but you must also blame our time) I would like to speak a little about the composer's faculty of hearing what he writes. Mozart, as I said, had sharp ears. So does Morton Feldman, as I hope you will agree when I play you his *Last Pieces* at the end of this programme. But Feldman has written many pieces where the actual notes are not specified. A pupil of his – Michael von Biel – once asked him how, remembering the importance that Feldman attached to the actual notes that he does write – he obviously hears all of them very [acutely] – he accounts for the occasions where he doesn't specify any notes. Feldman replied that in this case he had heard all the available notes. So that it did not constitute a gap in his hearing of notes, but a blur. The same applies to Christian Wolff when he indicates for instance four notes from 'a' ('a' being a set of pitches given at the outset) one of them transposed up or down an octave, two of which are pizzicato, and one of them pianissimo. This provides an inexhaustible field of possibilities, but nevertheless a limited one, one that you can grasp. In the same way one can write a set of notes without specifying their durations, tempo, loudness, instrumentation etc. and still be able to hear them, without having to hear every possible version of them separately, i.e. however they are played, one will be able to recognize them. (Incidentally, this can be considered in relation to dode-caphonic music: one could refer each note to its place in the serial grid, but it is by no means necessary to do so). (Another bracket, this is perhaps abstraction in music – when the ancients abstracted whiteness from all the different objects that are white, perhaps they had – though they would hotly have denied indulging anything so sensual – a visual image of a white blur). The composer accepts (John Cage designates this courageous, others naive) all the possible versions within the field as being equally valid. The performer then chooses what he will play, and if he's anything of an interpreter he will express himself in his choice, himself and thus also, his conception of the piece. If the interpreter feels himself in a quandary as to what to play then he had better refrain from performing the piece until he is no longer in a quandary (similarly the com-poser who is in a quandary as to what to write). Christian Wolff's recent pieces can be seen as a series of blurs, of varying kind and density – indeed it may happen that you reach a spot where there is no blur at all – only one possibility – and even then the interpreter is, as ever, faced with the imponderable problem of exactly how to play it.

Earle Brown wrote a series of sheets of music under the general heading *Folio*, in which he takes this idea to extremes. As a natural consequence of a piece consisting of nothing but a series of blurs, he made a single mark on a piece of white paper, and this mark meant "anything". This is revealing about the character of Earle Brown as a composer – a cast of mind which is very apt to see necessity where there is none. Once, in the instruction concerning the performance of an orchestral piece of mine, having specified that certain notes could either be played or not, I went on to remark that "together with the freedom either to play or not to play a note, must come the freedom to play more or less, i.e. softer or louder, longer or shorter." But where is the must? I was immediately asked. Where indeed; obviously it is conceivable that a note should be played either loud and long or not at all. But the must remained, for it soon became clear to me that it was not a logical must, but an aesthetic must. For aesthetic reasons, reasons concerned with the music itself I felt it necessary that there should be available a whole gamut of possibilities between the presence of a note and its absence. This whole gamut was not available for every note; some were marked soft, others short, and beyond these there was a sign for the borderline case between presence and absence i.e. a sign meaning extremely soft and extremely short.

To return to Earle Brown – it is clear that total blur is not the logical conclusion of a tendency towards blurred shapes. The *reductio ad absurdum* is the solution of the man for whom the world is senseless. The example I have quoted from Brown's *Folio* indicates to me that the blurred world is senseless to him. And indeed he has abandoned indeterminacy in the sense in which we have considered it hitherto. But logical extremes have retained their fascination for Earle. Indeterminacy pokes its nose into his music again when he works with the theoretical possibilities of instruments. Indeterminacy obtains in the discrepancy between theoretical and practical possibility. This has become a conscious factor in his work; he knows and loves instruments (whether he does instrumentalists is debatable), he himself plays several, and while working for Capitol as a recording engineer he once recorded himself playing all the instruments in a piece. The instrument is for him a concrete object, even more than it is a sound. When he writes a particularly difficult passage for an instrument he certainly has a sound in mind, but more important is perhaps the fingering. The indeterminacy – what he cannot hear – is the subsidiary sounds that the anguished performer will produce in the attempt to execute the impossible. Curiously enough, however anguished the performer, the texture of the music is such that whatever sounds he produces will not sound anguished – they are the natural product of the difficulty of execution. Earle Brown's musicianship is of the highest professional standard, and his ear has benefited from the years of training in the recording studio. And, though he may courageously and magnanimously accept the sounds born of human weakness, perhaps he dreams of the day when the musician will be born who can actually make the sounds (and the fingerings) that he has written.

Perhaps on that day his work will present to us a complete picture – and it will be one of indescribable subtlety and diversity. So far, performances of his works have been marred by a certain crudity, an atmosphere of imperfection and dissatisfaction (this is often expressed by the musicians, not only a dissatisfaction with the composer, but with themselves, for their insufficiency), and yet there are hints of the richness and depth that will perhaps remain hidden forever in the score. The work of Earle Brown's that you will hear after this talk is *Pentathus* for 10 instruments, played by members of the *Die Reihe Ensemble*, Vienna, conducted by Kurt Schwertsik. This score is written in the traditional notation throughout.

The piece by Christian Wolff that you will hear is also notated in the traditional manner, and it is an earlier work than those pieces that I described earlier as being a series of blurs of different shapes and sizes. It is a work for prepared piano. Perhaps I should say a few words about the prepared piano, since it is not often nowadays that one has the chance to hear it, even [much] about it. A piano is prepared by placing objects – rubbers, screws, coins and any oddments of any material – inside the piano amongst the strings, lying on them, jabbed between them, connecting them with the soundboard. These objects change the sound that the string makes when the appropriate key is played. John Cage, a real pupil of Henry Cowell who used tone clusters, and also wrote pieces to be played directly on the strings of the piano, invented the prepared piano in the late 1930s and for a long time he was the only person engaged in its development. Presumably – it is unusual to hear his works for prepared piano – he was engaged in discovering new preparations, i.e. new materials to stick in the piano, and new ways of sticking them in. The crowning glory and culmination of this voyage of discovery must surely be Cage's *Piano Concerto*, (not the one that has been performed several times recently in Europe but an earlier one), the piano for which takes six hours to prepare. I have not heard this work, but David Tudor tells me that the piano produces an alarming variety of sounds, including some very sharp bangs produced by inserting screws between the strings in the near side of the bridge.

Apparently it is also alarming to play because some of the preparations are inserted very delicately, and it only requires an attack on the key that is slightly too forceful, to send the preparation flying; it might lean over and disturb neighbouring strings and their preparations, or fall through with a clatter onto the soundboard, or even down into the action of the piano. I think Stockhausen was the first to discern the convincing ratification of the prepared piano when he remarked that the composer is creating a unique instrumentation for his piece, rather than using a ready-made range of sounds laid down by the traditional structure of the instrument or a traditional combination of instruments, e.g. a string quartet.

However, I think it is characteristic of great works of classical music that they embody a fresh appreciation of the ready-made medium; one has the feeling that the composer is indeed discovering the medium for himself, or rather, discovering in the medium the perfect embodiment of his new conception, however common the medium concerned may be, e.g. a piece for solo piano. And of course, nothing can possibly be gained by forcing oneself to invent a unique medium for one's piece. More recently Cage moved away from the preparation of the piano in advance, and turned to manual manipulation inside the piano, e.g. plucking the strings and muting them with a finger while attacking the key with the other hand. This has the advantage that we can modify the sound of any note at anytime, and also that we can get a variety of sounds from one key, e.g. by damping the string at different points, etc.

Christian Wolff was the heir apparent to the prepared piano. The first work he wrote after becoming a student of Cage was his *Four Pieces for Prepared Piano*. Written in 1951 this is his only published work, and he was, I believe, 17 years old when he wrote it. His previous music teacher had realised that she had nothing further to teach him, and had sent him to Cage, who had begun by analysing Webern's works with him. These pieces are among the most perfect examples of writing for the prepared piano. Nine strings are prepared, and each of the four pieces uses a different selection from these together with a limited number of unaltered tones. The spacing of the sounds is reminiscent of Webern, each sound is given plenty of room to breathe, and the structure is executed with perfect economy: the changes of sound introduced in each piece are very telling, and yet the four pieces cohere perfectly. In these pieces each of the sounds is very carefully "heard" by the composer – the preparations are described in detail – e.g. a screw with a loose nut two inches from the bridge for one note; and for another, two adjacent rubber wedges as close as possible to the dampers. His more recent pieces (the ones I described as a series of blurs of different shapes and sizes) still contain preparations, but not in the same precise way. Y and Z, for instance, may designate two preparations of different materials (i.e. one of wood and one paper, or one metal and one rubber) placed on any string. The preparation may also be moved in the course of the piece, so that it will have a different pitch at its second occurrence than it did at its first.

The piece that you will hear at the end of this talk is entitled simply *For Prepared Piano* and it was written sometime after the *Four Pieces For Prepared Piano* that I have described and sometime before the recent pieces of which I have spoken. As in the earlier piece, the preparations are described in detail and remain where they are (with luck) throughout the piece. The formal concept of the piece is such, however, that at the beginning of the piece one hears almost exclusively prepared sounds, and these are subsequently eliminated by gradual degrees, until finally one hears almost exclusively the natural sounds of the piano. The composition of the piece is, however, imperfect since the dynamics required tend to uproot the preparations, which has the double effect: a) of leaving natural sounds where a prepared sound was intended, and b) making prepared sounds where natural sounds were intended (for the uprooted preparation is free to roll around on the unprepared strings). This is however an unintentional indeterminacy, and the formal concept (that of a gradual transition from alien to familiar sounds) seems to have a lot in common with Stockhausen's *Form as Process*. The form of Stockhausen's *Kreuzspiel*, for example, consists of the process by which each of the elements exchange their positions; what was high at the start, is low at the end, and what was low at the start is high at the end, and the point where they cross (*Kreuzspiel*) signalises some important structural shift. The form of his *Kontrapunkte* is based on similar procedures: the beginning is characterised by rapid fluctuations over the whole range (of timbre, pitch, loudness, duration, etc. etc.) in which, in the nature of things, the extreme areas are necessarily prominent; and the end is characterised by a [minimum] of change within a narrow medium range (all instruments have dropped out except the piano, the dynamics tend to stick within the range *pp – mf*, the pitches [gambol] around in the lower register, showing only a vague (though insistent) profile towards middle C, and the motion has become a constant interplay of the various groupings of semiquavers, either simple or dotted, or as triplets or quintuplets.

Stockhausen's detractors can dismiss both these forms, that of *Kreuzspiel* by saying that nothing is accomplished by turning an 'x' back to front, its form remains the same, and that of *Kontrapunkte* by saying that the piece is just a long petering out, from the complex and varied sounds of the opening to the uniformity of the close. And this is also a criticism that can be levelled at Wolff's piece. It equates interesting with unusual, the sounds become less interesting the fewer preparations that are heard, and consequently the piece becomes more and more boring as it progresses. This criticism is a manifestation of a fallacy that is becoming more and more widespread (ever wider spread), and that is that unfamiliar things are more interesting than familiar things. The argument being that familiarity with an object exhausts the object, we learn all there is to know about it and it holds nothing further for us. Nothing could be more mistaken. The less we know about an object, the more primitive the concepts by means of which we try to grasp it. Take for instance flight; when people first started making aeroplanes, they made complex structures of wood and canvas, perhaps they thought it would be something like sailing, but lightness was the primary consideration. But as the sensation of flight became more familiar, would-be fliers became aware of the real problems of aerodynamics and concentrated their attention on design and the disposition of weight and surface. What happens in Christian's piece is somewhat similar. The sensual intoxication of unusual sounds is progressively denied the listener, and as the sounds become more usual, so the listener is invited to penetrate more deeply into them. In this way something unfamiliar is brought home.

Morton Feldman's *Last Pieces*, with which this programme will end show some divergence from the normal notation. Each piece looks like series of chords all written as crotchets without tails. There are occasional pause signs, grace notes and arpeggio markings, but the overall appearance of the pieces on paper is uniform. Their headings differ, however, the first piece being marked "slow, soft, durations are free," the second "fast, soft, durations are free," the third "very slow, soft, durations are free," and the last "very fast, soft as possible, durations are free for each hand." And yet, after playing these pieces for some time, I find myself thinking that they are, after all, all the same. If you like, each piece represents a different aspect of the same sound. I will say a few words later on about their differences, for the moment I would like to concentrate on this sameness.

When I remarked earlier that this music was written out of a state of being, it was chiefly Morton Feldman that I had in mind. Feldman has written a great deal of music that is very much all of a piece. (Leaving aside his experiments with graph notation as he calls it, which seems to spring from some other place in his character, and to be executed by some other faculty. It is perfectly conceivable that a composer should be engaged in two widely divergent lines of investigation, and this is, I think, the case with Feldman, though recently I believe he has tried to bring his graph music more in line with the others).

Almost all his music is slow and soft. Only at first sight is this a limitation; I see it rather as a narrow door, to whose dimensions one has to adapt oneself (as in *Alice in Wonderland*) before one can pass through it into the State of Being that is expressed in Feldman's music. Only when one has become accustomed to the dimness of the light, can one begin to perceive the richness and variety of colour which is the material of the music. When one has passed through the narrow door and got accustomed to the dim light, one realises the range of his imagination and the significant differences that distinguish one piece from another. Since differences of dynamics and tempo have been almost entirely banished, the significant events in the music must be of a melodic or harmonic nature – melodic and harmonic understood in the most abstract sense, as meaning simply the succession or superposition of tones. These two aspects provide the mountains and the hills in the music, the rivers and seas, the wind and the rain, all the features of the landscape are created in these terms. And yet the slowness and softness, for all they are invariable (I am speaking now of a large number of his pieces including *Music for Four Pianos, Two Pianos* 1957, *Piano Three Hands, Piano Four Hands, Music for Horn and Cello* and others. *The Last Pieces* represent a new departure which I shall deal with separately), are a significant condition for the music. They are its medium, through which everything that occurs is seen. They are in a sense the eyes of the observer. Of course, having decided that tempo and dynamics should be invariable (I do not suggest that Feldman decided on this, I think rather, that he came to it) one could thus decide that all the pieces should be loud and fast, or loud and slow, or soft and fast, and it is worth investigating why Feldman's music is, in fact, soft and slow. You will have to take my word for it that he does not write it slow with the intention of enervating his audience with worry about when the next sound will come. Rather he sees the sounds as reverberating endlessly, never getting lost, changing their resonances as they die away, or rather do not die away, but recede from our ears. And soft, because softness is more compelling, because an insidious invasion of our senses is more effective than a frontal attack, because our ears must strain to catch the music, they must become more sensitive before they can perceive the world of sound in which Feldman's music takes place, and it would not do to batter them into insensibility. The music's state of being is soft and slow, and until we accept this, the music will never reveal itself to us.

In the *Last Pieces* the impunity of tempo has been relaxed; each piece has its own tempo: slow, fast, very slow, very fast. This means that in each of the pieces the sounds are plumbed to a different depth. The same sound, or the same sort of sound, taken at four different levels. In the first piece we absorb the sound, we are immersed in it. There is ample time to follow every change of chord, we can study its relation to the sound that preceded it. Indeed our perception of each sound is irrevocably coloured by the preceding sound, especially where this continues to sound (durations are free). In the second piece we are suddenly confronted with motion, swept along by the sounds unable to catch them, hold them, we become intoxicated with what seems, by contrast, to be a wild and unpredictable flight. There are several brief rests, and occasionally the pedal will catch some note and prolong it (durations are free), often the chords are so thick that, though soft, they have a percussive effect, and the analytical aspect of our appreciation is blotted out entirely. This piece is over very quickly and there is a breathless feeling of recovering our balance during the third piece (very slow). Sometimes it seems that one re-enacts the whole of the second piece in each of the spaces in the third. The chords last so long that our appreciation of them as being part of a context is almost entirely lost. In this piece one feels almost that the remark durations are free is addressed to the notes themselves rather than to the pianist, as if to say, hold out as long as you can, there is no hurry, nothing is coming to cut you off. This is the deepest level to which the sounds are penetrated. The chords are allowed to speak for themselves – exhaustively. The overtones of the component notes in a chord are given ample time to argue things out amongst themselves, sometimes the pedal will interfere, sometimes not. The balancing of the notes within a chord becomes uneven, since in the attempt to play softly the imperfections in the instrument become apparent; nothing now escapes the ear, which is led down and down, deeper and deeper into the wide world contained in each chord.

The fourth piece is so fast that one can no longer play as softly as one might wish (this explains why, whereas the other pieces are marked soft, this one is marked soft as possible, i.e. as softly as the tempo allows). The hands should get carried away by their own momentum, they are no longer tied together (durations are free for each hand), but rush on independently. There are pauses in which they can be reunited, but in between they run ahead sometimes out of control, like a fish that breaks the surface, it doesn't know much about flying! And that's true, this piece seems to break through into a fresh element. Isolated high notes describe a broken line way up in the sky, some notes splash through in a forte, the grace notes flicker by, and all feeling of security, even the sense of direction, that was retained in the other fast piece, is lost in this brilliant rediscovery of the dynamic element in music.

The words are pale and wan, I realise that they can inspire no faith, but the musical images are fresh and vital, and I see Feldman as the first composer to break free from the dogma and dreary theorizing that has enshrouded new music for so long.

Feldman has evolved a language that is capable of expressing his ideas in all their freshness and intensity, it is not a synthetic language dictated by any lame need to justify atonal music or the serial idea or any other theoretical concept, such as that the twelve notes have equal rights, or that noise is as important as notes, etc. etc. Lastly, the performance of the *Last Pieces* leaves something to be desired; it is by myself, but there is unfortunately no tape available by David Tudor, who is probably the only pianist of transcendental virtue who could undertake a performance of it.

Autumn '60

– a lecture given to The Heretics Society, Cambridge

Transcribed from note books. Entry dated 5th September 1962.

What are the characteristics of this music we have just listened to? What emotions has it aroused? (It would be unjust to deny these, merely because it is a piece of contemporary music). What impressions does it create? These are the appropriate questions to ask with regard to this piece, and also about many other pieces of so-called indeterminate music, since they appeal directly to our sense of hearing. The sounds are generated directly and spontaneously by the musicians themselves. Thus we cannot ask– What plan is hidden behind these sounds? Or – What is the piece about? There is no by-passing of the sensual impression of the sounds themselves. What these sounds create in us, as listeners, should correspond in some measure to what the composer, me in this case, put into it, but this correspondence is hardly traceable: it exists like the sounds but it is beyond our faculty of delineation. If I put myself in your place as a listener, I would criticise this piece for its excessive melancholy. Sometimes this melancholy is acceptable, it has its own dignity, the dignity of some genuine Weltschmerz (like the crying of a baby), it is almost impossible to credit it to mere silliness, it is so often a genuine expression of suffering and malaise, though of course it depends on the baby, but I think the overall impression is rather lugubriously mournful (I wish to display the piece's ready accessibility to criticism, thereby giving countenance to the idea that where deserved, it is if not equally accessible, at least reasonably accessible to appreciation – criticism is always the easiest art). There are various things at the back of this lugubrious mournfulness, chief among them being the slowness and regularity of the music. I need hardly remind you that these are the invariable characteristics of funeral music. Now, as far as the score is concerned, the music is neither slow nor regular, so one of the things we have to investigate is where this slowness and regularity come from.

Perhaps this is the place to describe shortly how the piece is notated and brought to performance. Perhaps we shall find some indirect way by which the score can produce the impression of slowness and regularity. Here we go: each of any number of players, playing any instruments, receives a copy of the score, which consists of one stave containing all the details pertaining to the sounds to be made, underneath which is another stave, empty, for the musician to write in whatever he decides to play. For each beat there is a selection of indications, loud, soft, long, short, hold for 1, 2, 3 or 4 beats, pizz., mute, slide up or down, tremolo, instrument names, names of notes, to be observed. One beat may contain the indications viola, loud, staccato, mute, and each player must then try and observe all but two of these indications. So in this case the viola has several possibilities: he may play with the mute on, in which case he will not play loud, and not staccato, or if he doesn't use the mute, he can play loud or staccato but not both together. The rest of the strings and the brass also have the option of using mutes or not; those who do play muted, can play loud or staccato but not both, and those who don't use their mutes together with all the other instruments that haven't got mutes – woodwind, percussion, etc. – have no option but to play both loud and staccato. In this example each musician can play any note he chooses.

Each musician can enter anywhere before the next beat, and each musician is free not to play at all, if he considers his sound inappropriate. The piece consists of a chain of situations like this, each one different, divided into sections of varying length separated by silences. The conductor holds the whole thing together, and he also is free within broad limits; each beat is free in length i.e. the tempo can change with each beat, though of course it need not, and each beat can be conducted in a variety of ways; sharp and clear, giving the musicians the opportunity to enter together, or vague, so that there is no clear line between the beats. The conductor can also advise the players of what he would like them to do, e.g. play in a low register for a particular passage, or use this or that note, or ignore all glissando marks for some sections, or to play quietly, etc.

In all this there is no hint of a general slowness or regularity (to return to where we left off) so they must originate in the performance somehow or other. However, I do not believe that either the musician or the conductor are entirely to blame for this characteristic. I see it either as a necessary condition of our time, for which nothing is to blame, or if anything, it is the newness and unfamiliarity of the medium, which affects both the players and the listener, and a sort of transitional flavour that is, and has always been, attached to experiments of all kinds. But we will go into this later, as well as into the question as to how for such works can be called experiments; let us continue for the moment to seek causes for the feeling of melancholy. Perhaps some possible causes can be blamed on the composer, for instance the frequent occurrence of small glissandos. (These are sad by association with weeping and wailing and sobbing.)

But really the melancholy comes from hesitancies.

The transitional flavour.

The experiment.

Look for other possible sources of melancholy in the score. It is true that the little arrow pointing up or down does occur very frequently in the score. But this little arrow designates all possible glissandos – the exhilarating uprush of the piano keys, for example, as well as the stopping of the horn. The players are not altogether to blame for not seeing the range of possibilities straight away, the conductor is really more to blame, since his was the responsibility of studying, and knowing the score, and completely appreciating whatever it implies. But finally, here too the composer is to blame; it is a weakness that the sign should not occur in a context that would suggest the variety of interpretations that are possible; it is also a weakness to use the same sign so often that the players are sick of the sight of it and play the same sound every time. These weaknesses in the composition are by no means insurmountable in a performance, but they are certainly there. Just as certainly, the composer has helped to create the general air of melancholy by using the notes F, G♭, A♭, B♭, D♭ and these only. Each musician of course constantly has the opportunity of using one note he likes, but where there is a note indicated it is always one of these five in some register or another. And of course wherever a note is indicated several people will play it, and so one gets a mixture of attacks and durations and colours on the same note. So, despite all appearances to the contrary, these notes stick out, and have an important role to play. The dirge, the constant recurrence of a limited range of notes, was definitely a part of the composition.

The choice of notes is in my opinion the prime function of the composer, and the hard core of feeling that abides in the relations between notes will survive the most willful treatment of dynamics or tempo. The reasons for this fundamental belief of mine are many and various, first and foremost of course I have experienced the fact that tones have emotional content, and on the theoretical side one can deduce the experience *post facto* from the interaction of the overtones of the notes themselves. We assimilate the harmony or conflict of overtones subconsciously – we do not actually hear the overtones, but they are always present in what we hear – they take us unawares and give rise to those inexplicable and apparently spontaneous impressions that go to make up an emotional response.

So there we are, the emotional savour of the piece is inescapable, and no doubt it is sad. When we are happy we have subjugated the world, we ride on it or even escape from it into other spaces. But when we are still, and study the world itself and inhabit it, we are as though in a cave surrounded by the material of the world, which washes over us, and we are part of it, and it isn't sugar. Well, I haven't yet reached that happy state that I described, so the emotional savour of the piece is sad, and I have nothing against this. What I criticise is the exaggeration, the histrionic melancholy, or as I said before, the lugubrious mournfulness. Now is the time to talk about the origin of this exaggeration, and how I see it as a necessary condition of our time, and the wildly transitional context of music today.

The musicians in pieces like this are faced with a situation which they cannot grasp. They do not know what they are doing. So many factors are unknown, that there is a terrible feeling of insecurity. There is a great pattern inherent in lack of confidence. Hesitancy may be the expression in some cases of a great and natural delicacy, but here it springs from unknowing, uncertainty as to what is expected of one. This slows down one's reaction time, one hangs onto each beat as to a last refuge, and each changeover to the next seems like a perilous journey. This applies equally to the conductor – he does not know what sound to expect, and when it comes he strives to assimilate it, seeking in it the answer as to how to proceed. In the performance he is somewhat frantic with anxiety, whereas to us, calmly listening, each beat seems long and we are able to plumb the morbid tensions in each sound, before the next one takes its place. The thick succulent chords that hold on and on, notes get added, some disappear, various other changes occur, but the sound is prolonged, drained to the last drop, because the musicians are reluctant to abandon a context which they have managed to grasp. This is what gives it such a mournful character – these long fluctuating chords. So many of them are long that this gives them the semblance of regularity however unevenly spaced they may actually be in time. Thus the mournfulness that we experience when listening to it is our sympathetic response to the agony experienced in the performance. This is the present situation – a transitional state, as I have said. Soon our experiments will begin to show results, and these will be added to our fund of experience, and we will be better equipped to create true versions of experimental pieces. The fashion for complexity of sound will also subside as we emerge from this transitional time. It is a common illusion, especially in artistic circles, that the more complex the experiment, the more we will learn from it. In this way we pile up our confusion, burying ourselves in a mass of conflicting data. (In this piece, however, as I shall show later, the more musicians that are engaged in it, the simpler it will become). Soon too, there will be more musicians capable of grappling with problems such as those presented by this piece.

Now is the time to investigate what exactly is required of the musicians in this piece. The new thing that is required of them is the capacity to grasp the logic of their activity – the rules of the game. Only when the player has thoroughly assimilated the logical side, when it has become a second nature to him, will he be able to appreciate the music and poetry contained in the piece. What happens at the moment is that the players who are interested in the logic of the situation are so fascinated by it that they feel obliged to do something at once, to solve every sound, and to make themselves a very complex part, which blinds them to what everyone else is doing and so leaves them unaware of the musical result of their activity. When the rules of the game have been properly assimilated, the musician will realise that his contribution to the music need not be so ardent and continuous; his silence and the occasional flash of his imagination can be his most valuable contributions. He must digest the material thoroughly and become thoroughly acquainted with the range of possibilities at any given moment; only then can he acquire a genuine spontaneity of expression. A general consciousness of what he is doing will give the player greater freedom in his reaction to what the other players are doing, and thus the piece itself will acquire a lighter, freer, more uncomplicated quality.

This awareness is especially necessary in performances with a small number of musicians. When there are more musicians taking part in the performance, it is not quite so necessary (though of course it is still desirable) because the divergent interpretations of the individual musicians will begin to cancel each other out, and the aural image will take on a more general form. It was something approaching this general image that I heard while writing the piece. For each sound, for each set of signs, one is aware of a particular field of possibilities. It would be ridiculous to imagine that the composer 'hears' nothing while writing a piece like this; his head is full of sounds, all sorts of different sounds, all the sounds, in fact, that are possible within that particular situation. This is a very fascinating phenomenon for the composer, he is constantly checking his raving imagination against the material he has assembled, and the one modifies the other and *vice versa* until this general aural image gradually settles down like the leaves in a tea-cup after a storm. Now the more players there are engaged in the performance, the closer one gets to this aural sediment. One approaches a sort of synthesis of all possible interactions between the various signs. But as the general volume of sound increases, the conductor's job becomes more and more difficult, requires more resource and a much firmer and more sensitive hand.

Autumn '60 (Cologne)
Octet '61
Autumn '60 (Vienna)

Autumn '60 has been performed several times since it was written, in the autumn of 1960, and in a variety of different ways. It is as though the modern audience likes to hear things once and then throws them away like our paper handkerchiefs, our cardboard cups, our polythene wrappers etc. Pieces like this however can be made fresh each time, it is perpetually new for the listener as well as for the performer. And in consequence they get played several times. Pieces that are written in the conventional way seem to get played once or twice and then abandoned; that is, if they are lucky enough to get played at all – I have written a string quartet that is perfectly straightforward, and which will probably wait years before it is played. Which is ironical for in a way it is a much more personal expression than the pieces we have been discussing. But the modern audience does not want to hear profound utterances, it wants to be enlivened, and this demand for enlivenment has probably considerably intensified the craze for writing pieces that sound completely different each time you hear them. I am going to end this programme with a version of *Autumn '60* that I have not yet heard. It was played in Vienna, the conductor is again Kurt Schwertsik, and many of the players are the same as took part in the recording we heard at the beginning of this talk. But the performing procedure is completely different. For the performance in Vienna, the conductor wrote out many of the parts, and friends of his also did a couple each until all the required parts were written. These were given to the musicians, and they played them as best they could. In a way, this procedure runs counter to the basic idea of the piece which is that each musician should be responsible for his own part, as was the case in the recording made here in Cologne.

But this is a job which few musicians are willing to undertake with any degree of scrupulosity. It is stimulating, or should be, but it is not a stimulant that is calculated to agree with everyone's' stomach. Certainly the musicians are grateful when you relieve them of at least some of the responsibility. And it has its advantages; if, for instance,one writes out what notes the player is to play, this leaves him free to pay attention to when he will play them. But it is possible to go even further than this. For performances directed by Mauricio Kagel, I have had to write out a score, and since then I have added parts to his collection as they were required by him for performances with different instruments. This runs even more counter to the original idea, and I have noticed in these performances that the players have regained as often as not their usual attitude to contemporary music, i.e. "we play it, but don't blame us for what it sounds like" which is exactly the attitude which these pieces try to circumvent. But this stock of parts will be useful when, eventually, the work is attempted with an orchestra of reasonable size. The readymade parts can be distributed amongst those players who are the most unwilling or unable to make their own parts, while the rest make their own. Thus a reasonable proportion of the whole sound would be generated spontaneously, and some ill feeling avoided, which is as much as one can ask for.

There is one more point I would like to make about the freshness that one imagines will be characteristic of the piece if each time it is played it is different. When we admire the freshness of a great jazz musician's performance, – a musician whose recordings we have known and loved for years – what we are admiring is the new life that is given to something which is already present in us, namely through the thorough knowledge we have acquired from these recordings . This example is a good one; when a jazz musician records an improvised solo, there are many things that he does on the spur of the moment, and he would hard put to it to say exactly what he did play.

But the record remembers, and so do his fans – they get to know every quirk and squeak of a particular recording. One assimilates the material (a particular player's treatment of a melody, for example, and the sound he makes) and also the player's style. Then when one comes to hear him in a live concert, everything he plays seems familiar, and yet fresh; it has the vigour of spontaneity. This would have passed one by in many cases if one had not this familiarity acquired through the recordings.

One can also appreciate the difference when one hears the same melody played by someone else. It is not a prototype that one should get familiar with, this gives one very little. The knowledge of how something is written down, for example, is very little help. What is necessary is to capture the spontaneity, to come to grips with it at one's leisure. In short, it is a point of reference; a thorough acquaintance with one thing enhances one's enjoyment of 1000 other things, and particularly our enjoyment of the same thing in different guises. I am lucky enough to have a thorough acquaintance with the version of *Autumn '60* that you heard at the outset (which is probably why I am so critical of it) and I am therefore, even though, like you, I have not heard it before, in a better position to enjoy the performance that we are going to hear now. I have the advantage over you that I will recognise it. This is unfair, but it can't be helped, and in the future there will perhaps be opportunities for lovers of contemporary music to familiarise themselves with it on record. Until then, nothing is guaranteed, indeterminate music is not gilt-edged.

In re La Monte Young
New Departures – No. 4 1962

What if La Monte's pieces were the snide comments of the exhibitionist on the set-up that makes him possible? Troubadour in extremis, little that you can do that the New York avant garde (given that!) won't nod sagely as though they knew it already. *In Composition 1960 No. 6* he still does less and, in extremis, harps on the price (free) of participation (optional). Oh Audience, where is the composer who has not got one foot in you? And the other?

Poem reflects ordinary life in arbitrary snatches in the artificiality of arena. *Poem* is not printed here, though it is La Monte's most interesting piece to date, for the reason that it is simply a long and technical instruction manual. It consists of any number of performers performing any continuing activities for random but decided lengths of time within a total random but decided time. But the instruction manual is an interesting form of a piece of music: are many pieces detailed courses of instruction bringing a performer to the pitch of creating something? *Winter Music* could have been written in this form, but Cage chose to interpret it in twenty pages of manuscript, and really we are grateful.

Is a piece by La Monte an ill-intentioned but salutory insult, to be swallowed, digested, etc? And yet who should but feel sympathy for the spectacle of long-suffering humanity executing the same cluster six thousand one hundred and ninety-eight times 'for Henry Flynt'? X (any number) *For Henry Flynt*: does it exist? Play a large (both forearms) cluster (centrally placed, both black and white keys) on the piano at a regular rate (1-2 seconds per cluster) as loud as possible. A slight break between each cluster and the next. Tape available from *New Departures* for hire; proceeds to La Monte Young.

Does anything happen in La Monte's pieces? This is impossible to predict. Although bad performances are out, theoretically, I have experienced some. Is anything required of a performer besides an exhibitionistic bent? I find that I require all the resources I posses and often more to perform a piece by La Monte to my own satisfaction, let alone anyone else's. It is necessary to withdraw to an unusual distance and allow the piece to speak. (Does it say anything? Does what it says make sense? Sometimes I get a vague presentiment of sense. *Does this require faith?* Faith that all human activity makes sense, it is our understanding that is too small. Who is human until he has come to terms with insanity? Or am I being too sweeping. Confusion. I will not say a piece by La Monte is nonsense until I have understood it.) To withdraw and be under control requires a lot of performing experience. Too often an exhibitionist will mar the effect of the whole.

Or someone's inexperience will give him the appearance of exhibitionism.

The defence of the performer is far from La Monte's spirit: of course it is easy to be what you have spent your whole life becoming. But how does the audience know that the piano is being fed? A performer who cannot enter into the spirit of the thing will never convey same, in *any* music, and should not be pressed.

Do these pieces take us (have they power to move us) into uncharted areas of human experience of little usefulness? Who can determine the usefulness, beauty, reality of an area that is uncharted, indeed hitherto unsuspected? (Was it unsuspected?) Perhaps the music is devotional in character! Is it a secret language for some order of monks? Tudor told the following story: Toshi Ichiyanagi wanted to write a piece for La Monte and took his pen and a piece of card and drew on it up and down in a continuous line until the whole card was covered in scribbles with a general up and down motion. This he gave to La Monte. La Monte puzzled over the card and sought an interpretation. Eventually he hit on the following: he would take a piece of rough board and sandpaper it until it was clean. The sandpapering would follow the motion of the line, but keep on until the board was smooth. In the performance it took an unexpectedly long time to sand the board smooth. At one point a member of the audience shouted in protest 'Hey, La Monte, we know you're a genius.' But (sic) La Monte kept on. Sandpapering. Until the board was clean.

Composition 1960 #7
[Editorial note: In the original text the notation of *Composition 1960 #7* was placed here. However LaMonte Young denied us permission to reproduce it, suggesting that we gave it a verbal description, i.e:]

> The notation consists of a single fifth chord (B♮ below middle C and F# above middle C), in semibreves with open ties, with the instruction: 'to be held for a long time.'

Composition 1960 #3
Announce to the audience when the piece will begin and end and if there is a limit on duration. It may be of any duration.
Then announce that everyone may do whatever he wishes for the duration of the composition.

Piano Piece for David Tudor #1
Bring a bale of hay and a bucket of water onto the stage for the piano to eat
and drink. The performer may then feed the piano or leave it to eat by itself.
If the latter, it is over after the piano eats or decides not.

Composition 1960 #6
The performers (any number) sit on the stage watching and listening to the
audience in the same way the audience usually looks at and listens to performers.
If in an auditorium, the performers should be seated in rows or chairs or benches;
but if in a bar, for instance, the performers might have tables on stage and be
drinking as is the audience.

Composition 1960 #10
to Bob Morris
Draw a straight line
and follow it

Piano (Three Hands) – Morton Feldman

ACCENT – No. 4 Autumn 1962, Leeds College of Art and School of Architecture

1 – The player is confronted with a notation to which the conventional rules (need) not apply, and the composer has put nothing (2) in their place. It is necessary to find rules which make sense of the notation, or, if not rules, then a general understandIng (of the piece) on which to base one's decision in each case.

2 – Of the two rules given, one elucidates a sign which does not usually occur in the notation of music – at least not in the position in which it occurs here – (x), and the other explains that a conventional sign is not used in the conventional way (8-).

2b – The latter could be taken as an indication that all other conventional signs ARE used in the conventional way – or at least, in A conventional way.

3 – The nexus of one interpretation of this piece could be the selection of the following two rules, tending towards mutual exclusion.

i   quiet (4)

ii   tones written one above the other should be struck simultaneously (2b) (8).

If the sounds are to be played simultaneously, the player must exchange a signal with a degree of precision prejudicial to their reaching the dynamic level that Feldman would understand from 'quiet' (4). Vice versa, the quieter one plays, the less likelihood there is of chords coming together. The interaction of these two rules releases the possibility that music will occur (by rubbing two sticks together it is *possible* to make fire).

4 –'*As quiet as possible*' would indicate a reconciliation with the second rule and result in *mp*.

David Tudor: "play Feldman inwards" (i.e. to yourself, not to the back row.)

"utterly quiet": this is perhaps most decisive for the articulation of the sounds. This in the following ways:

If one plays so softly that nothing is audible, one is faced with two alternatives: leave it, or try again. If one chooses the latter it may happen that it sounds quite loud, since one is still trying to hold to the rule about chords sounding together. If it sounds quite loud the player is once more in a complex situation: should he leave it to take its natural course and perhaps let this affect the duration of the sound or should he decrease its loudness 'artificially' by releasing the key and then retaking it more or less immediately– depending on the register – without the string being struck again? If this operation is successful it releases more overtones while more or less damping the fundamental. This becomes an unforeseen feature of the sound. If this operation is unsuccessful one gets a very short duration, and generally speaking the duration should be long (6), so should one then try again? (7). If it is unsuccessful what then? (8)

4b – Indicating 'as soft as possible' in one of his piano pieces, Christian Wolff caters for three eventualities: too loud, too soft (i.e. inaudible), or success. The outcome in any performance is used to determine subsequent events.

5 – *First Apology*

When asked to write about contemporary music, I avoid the historical survey, i.e. who is alive and how? I prefer to spotlight one corner, sifting the dust, hoping that the greater the activity and the smaller the surface observed, the more is shown (about e.g. methods of observation?).

6 – 'Durations are long'
I deduce this from the rule 'slow' (9) (2b) together with the fact that there are no rests in the score. Problems appear in relation to this at Nos. 70–71 and 91 – 92, (10). In both cases the high note is tied over the bar line, while the low notes, whose natural durations are longer, should stop short before the bar line.

Here again there are two alternatives:
Either one considers the notation of the high note remaining alone as binding. In which case the lower notes must have short durations, or one considers the prescription 'durations are long' as binding, in which case a silence appears where the high note is held (7b)

7 – If one offers the rule 'every tone must be played, once only' this problem cancels out.

7b – It is possible to offer many rules, whose fields of operation are constantly overlapping. This problem is then one of the precedence: should one order the rules in a rigid (or even flexible) hierarchy, or select freely in each case?

8 – BUT IT IS NECESSARY TO REACH AN UNDERSTANDING OF THE SIGNS WHICH IS NEITHER NAIVE NOR PROFOUND. INTERPRETATION CONSISTS IN TAKING THE SIGNS AT THEIR FACE VALUE, the difficulty being to recognise the face value when you have found it.

9 – *The interpretation of absent signs*: for example; the lack of tempo indication, does not mean so much 'tempo is free', but rather 'you (the player) are responsible for the tempo.' If the player does not feel like taking this responsibility an alternative interpretation of this is that there is no tempo.

10 – Numbers referring to the score are obtained by counting semibreves from the beginning.

11 – Let us run over the bar lines and the pauses. (13) Should one articulate the bar lines by treating them, for example, as pedal indications? In any case they cannot be normal bar lines, since, in addition to the fact that they are long, durations are free and so all the paraphernalia of 'bars' (counting units, metric articulations etc.) becomes inapplicable. Cases like Nos. 61– 62 (10) forbid a *general* interpretation of them as silence. They can be interpreted as phrasing, but

I find it difficult to phrase always in threes, the same applies to the pedaling interpretation. One can think up something else (exercise for the imagination), or leave them uninterpreted, or interpret each separately, or sometimes one, sometimes the other.

11b – Some can be very easily interpreted, namely as vehicles for the pauses (Nos. 1, 2, 31-32, 34-35, 94-95) (10). These pauses sometimes apply to silence, sometimes to sound. If one interprets those that apply to sound as 'hold to extinction' one is as it were obliged to seek a sense for the sentence: 'Silence held extinction' (16 iii) and if one has decided to hold *all* sounds to extinction, what then? (8).

12 – *Places in a piece where ambiguities, superfluities, impossibilities or contradictions occur;* these are intimations that something special is required.

12b – Feldman is the one case where this seems a most dubious proposition.

13 *Second Apology*
To open one's mouth at all on the subject is to run over it. *Three Hands* is not a subject (like for example 'Guinea-pig').

14 – *'Durations are free'* only makes sense when combined with *'durations are long'*, as can bee seen from cases Nos. 61 – 62 (10). One free duration tied to another free duration equals one free duration. But: one long free duration tied to another long free duration equals one *very long* free duration.

15 – *The grace notes.* Firstly, who is to play them? They look as if they belong to the third hand but there is no x written above them. Secondly, they look so different from all the other notes (they are black), so do any of our general prescriptions apply to them? They would seem to be short, (but how short?): can they then also be loud (how loud?).

15b – The role played by grace notes in other pieces by Feldman can be of use here (but 21b).

16 – When all is said (and done), one is free; so there are no problems are there? *Freedom* (applying the word to the interpretation of music) results from being conscious, firstly, of the existence of alternatives, and secondly, that no choice or

decision amongst these alternatives can make the slightest value difference (cannot affect the 'Identity' of the piece).

So ... all these points and many others (22) constituting the field (17) of interpretation in this piece ... rather than solve them doctrinaire, before embarking on a performance, I prefer to reconsider them at each stage in every incident (this is an exaggeration). So that e.g. each pause demands a fresh assessment; not 'what does a pause sign mean (now and to all eternity)?' to which the answer could be a silence of five seconds or such like, but: 'what does this sign mean now?' According to circumstances, the answer can be:

i. 'wait until I have forgotten the foregoing pitch.'
ii 'wait until the audience (or my third hand) gets nervous.'
iii 'wait until the silence doesn't sound like silence any more.'
iv 'release all tones of the foregoing chord together.'
v   'wait for a sound from outside (town or country).'
vi 'wait until I feel like making the next sound.' (But for this I don't need the justification of a pause sign) (8).

17 – *Development of metaphor*; I'm sure that Feldman did not intend that one should plough this field, but rather that one should wander in it with one's ears open, and perhaps water it occasionally.

18 – *In the event of a performance*, neither these remarks nor the notation itself should be allowed to diminish your listening capacity. This could happen in the following way:

You hear a chord where all the tones are not struck together, and are tempted to gauge the extent of the so-called 'error', by comparing the sound with the notation. I find any such comparison misguided; there is only the most tenuous connection between the notation and the sounds (the pitch connection is perhaps (24) the most reliable). I am of the opinion that this connection cannot be discretely defined. I trust this will not be understood as a statement about my laziness, or the opposite, or indeed as anything in between, or suchlike.

18b – The notation does not attempt to approach the sound. (touch-me-not sounds, after all).

18c – IN THE NOTATION OF MUSIC YOU ARE DEALING PRIMARILY WITH PEOPLE. EVERYTHING ELSE IS SECONDARY.
Note in this connection the increasing importance of the 'rules'; these can be designed to 'make the player think', or to 'confuse' him or to 'amuse' him. You are trying to 'sell' the interpreter (prospective) on your piece.

19 – It might be asked whether it is not distracting to beset oneself with so many problems when one is playing a piece of music. But though it takes some time to list them, (anyway one has plenty of time) one is under no compulsion even to formulate them while playing the piece – we simply play.

19b – Does one play the piece poised in mid-air (sustained by the tension of being poised in mid-air) between the desire to act reasonably, and the desire to act unreasonably; or simply, between the desire to act and the desire to explain; or really, between the desire to create and the desire to analyse?

Finally it is necessary to come down to earth: this (tension) is not sustaining but stultifying – one must play, simply.

20 – Feldman: 'I make one sound, and then I move on to the next.'

21 – *First Appendix* – a selection of rules given by Feldman for other pieces.
'as soft as possible'
'slow'
'start together'
'durations are free'
'durations are free for each hand'

21b – Needless to say, the notations these rules apply to are sometimes very different from that of *Three Hands*.

22 – *Second Appendix* – idiosyncrasies.
Compare 38, 39, 42, 88, 89 etc. (positioning of notes on the staves and hands on the keyboard) (10) (23) (accidentals – 49, 19, 58 and if the last two seem 'natural' see 6–7, 52–53, 29–30 (24))
73–74 (is the 'b' or the 'a' supposed to resonate the silent note? and how?)
All these stimulate an interpretative imagination.
Others are mentioned in other parts of the text.

22b – Remark at last, that it is the dynamics which these idiosyncrasies affect chiefly. The dynamics reach a higher level of differentiation than any other aspect of the sounds. Rather it is chiefly the dynamics which these idiosyncrasies rivet our attention to.

No explicit provision is offered for the dynamics. (Go on from here).

23 – *It is not a reason we are looking for*; one reason for each quirk which would expose and point to one correct solution. Doubtless all that went into the making of the human being called Morton Feldman is behind these 'idiosyncrasies', but an intention? Improbable. It is the very lack of reason which sets them free (9b): floating points, catching at (and caught by) the interpretative imagination.

24 – Something else occurs to me. Is it not imaginable that the sign 16 – applies to *all* notes about or below it? This would indeed be a high flight of systematic thought, and would solve Nos. 29 –30 and 52–53 very satisfactorily. This hypothesis appeals also because the avoidance of leger-lines does not seem to be the sole function of the signs 8–, 16–; they seem rather to be an essential part of Feldman's way of thinking of intervals.
Note in this connection (compare Kagel's signs 8–, 15–, and Stockhausen's 2–, 4–, for one/two octaves higher) that Feldman's sign for three octaves higher is 32–.

25 – Earle Brown asks 'where does the third hand sit?'

Darmstadt 1964 – New Music has found its feet

The Financial Times – 31st July 1964

After the war Wolfgang Steinecke started a summer school in Darmstadt, the Internationale Ferienkurse für Neue Musik, for the propagation of the music that had been banned by the Nazis (Schoenberg, Berg and Webern). This school quickly became a centre for all the young composers who were trying to find a New Music. No one was excluded. Dr Steinecke died two years ago: today the programmes are chosen rather more carefully but tendentiously. This year's tendencies were nicely crystallised in the final concert last Friday evening, given by the Sudwestfunk Orchestra under the dry direction of Ernest Bour.

The concert began with Berg's *Three Orchestral Pieces, Op. 6*. This work is excessively complex both emotionally and orchestrally. Written at a decisive period in Berg's career (1912-14), it contains explicit references both back to Mahler and forward to his own masterpiece *Wozzeck*. In 1929 Berg revised the instrumentation of the piece and applied Schoenberg's principle of marking out the main and the subsidiary voices, the remainder being relegated to the accompaniment. Bour's interpretation exaggerated this tendency almost to the point of simplicity, with the results: (a) loss of richness, and, real power in sound, and (b) an inexplicable form (since a complex form cannot be made comprehensible by suppression of important details, that is, by being made simple). The general tendency that this represents, and which could be observed retrospectively in the *Ferienkursen* as a whole, is a desire for superficial clarity rather than depth and richness of expression.

After the interval came Bernd Alois Zimmerman's *Canto di Speranza* for cello and small orchestra. The tendency expressed in this work was nostalgia for the great composers of the past together with a complete absence of formal coherence. The piece contained not only unabsorbed references to past styles (for example, the exotic side of Bartok), but also a nostalgia for the 19th-century cult of the virtuoso. After the performance, the captious audience made it plain that they cared much less for the work than for the excellent soloist Siegfried Palm. (The same situation had occurred earlier when Bernhard Sebon interpreted a work for flute and electrical filter by Hans Heinrich Wiese: almost all factions in the audience unconditionally rejected the composition but greeted the performer with tumultuous applause.)

Other 'nostalgic' works during the Course: Maderna's *Dimensiono IV*, a hopelessly sentimental and episodic exchange between flute (three different sizes) and chamber ensemble; Lukas Foss's *Echoi* for four virtuosi, a sort of written out improvisation that used tonal material of extreme banality to unintentionally humourous effect; and Jacques Calonne's *Scolies* for chamber ensemble which culminated in an ineffectually constructed romantic climax.

The last work on the programme was Serocki's *Sinfonische Fresken* for large orchestra including quadruple winds, over 50 percussion instruments and a corresponding horde of strings. I was struck by the work's 'honesty' (a very English expression: an 'honest' man is one who does not try to camouflage his shortcomings; in fact by presenting them prominently he contrives to make them appear virtuous) and by the high craftsmanship of its execution (a modern work in which it is possible to really hear every single thing that is happening in the orchestra is a rare phenomenon – in fact it is rather suspicious). This is the music of Outer Space as Stan Kenton might conceive of it (but without Kenton's rhythm). Varèse is the father of this music of extraordinary, static sound effects, but Varèse's music generates great intensity, which suggests an intuition of hidden psychological drives. Serocki's piece on the other hand was pathetically obvious and not powerful at all – just very smoothly effective. Other works in this genre: Ligeti's *Aventures* in which the 'space' sounds are combined with a sort of social satirical vocal style, and the Spaniard Raxach's *Fluxion*, an effective piece of writing for chamber ensemble that left no after-image whatever on the mind.

In Darmstadt in the '50s it would have been impossible to criticise the compositions in this definite way because the performances then were such as to convey only clouded impressions of the works. This situation has now changed entirely. The performances by the International Chamber Ensemble under Maderna's direction were quite outstanding both as regards individual performance and ensemble work.

Although only a very few works (apart from those by Berg, Schoenberg and Webern) managed to escape the critical shroud (engendered by the tendencies outlined above) that encumbered my responses during the *Ferienkursen*, the following deserve to be mentioned: a significant performance by Else Stock of two parts of Boulez's *Third Piano Sonata*, Stockhausen's *Piano Pieces Nos. 7* and *8*, lovelessly performed by Aloys Kontarsky, Kagel's *Sonant* for harp, guitar, contrabass and skin instruments (percussion), Hans Helm's *Golem* (a Polemical attack on Heidegger for nine vocalists) an anachronistic performance of Earle Brown's *December 1952*, conducted by the composer, leaning heavily on experience gained from his recent *Available Forms* pieces, the Welshman Bernard Rands' polished *Espressioni IV* for two pianos, Dieter Schnebel's musicological entertainment *Glossolalie*. Milton Babbitt's sincere setting of Dylan Thomas's *Vision and Prayer* (the soprano Bethany Beardslee had to struggle against the over-loud electronic accompaniment).

Of the lecturers Milton Babbitt was well worth hearing. Under the heading *The Structure of Musical Systems* he moved from Schoenberg's *Fourth Quartet* to psycho acoustical perception problems of computer music in a series of 12 excellently delivered lectures. Pousseur spoke at equal length but in rather slower motion about the theoretical premises of Electronic Music, and interested students were invited to follow this up with a few days of practical work at the Munich Studio for Electronic Music. Yes, the Darmstadt Summer School has become an excellent Academy, and problems like Notation and Electronic Sound are competently handled in a rather academic way. What has got lost is the vital interest in new and serious experimental music.

Cage and Cunningham

The Musical Times – September 1964

Merce Cunningham's Dance Company of New York made their London debut at Sadler's Wells during the week beginning July 27th, and by public demand their season was extended at the Phoenix Theatre. Cunningham is choreographer of all the 15 works that were represented: John Cage is musical director, Robert Rauschenberg resident designer. The element of chance allowed in much of the music and choreography, and the chance interaction between them, provided questions basic not only to ballet: and Cornelius Cardew considers the significance for concert audiences of the Company's visit.

Most musicians must approach ballet with mixed feelings. Will the visual image divide – and detract from – the musical experience? Will the action on stage be a banally explicit interpretation – and hence a deformation – of the music's sense? And will the dance appropriate to itself the poise that should be the music's own? The public for ballet is therefore a different section of the population from that which goes to concerts of pure music – though naturally the two sections overlap. The existence of an expression like 'balletomania' is further evidence of the select quality of the ballet public.

The blurred but certain dividing line between the taste for ballet and the taste for music has now produced the following paradoxical situation. Pieces of music by John Cage, Morton Feldman, Toshi Ichiyanagi, Bo Nilsson, La Monte Young, Christian Wolff – all unwaveringly rejected or ignored by our more powerful pundits of musical taste (William Glock, Hans Keller, Peter Heyworth, etc.) – have slipped, without protest and with a high degree of acceptance from the ballet press, into the ears of the ballet public, and been *enjoyed*. The Merce Cunningham Dance Company's music was provided as usual by John Cage and David Tudor, with the admirable and willing assistance – at short notice – of nine English instrumentalists (Basil Tschaikov, Christopher Taylor, Denis Egan, Evan Watkins, Vera Kantrovitch, Elizabeth Watson, John Franka, Robert Meyer, Peter Greenham), and enthusiasts for Cage's work were able to hear repeated performances of his *Concert for Piano, Atlas Eclipticalis* (in combination with *Winter Music*) and *Duet for Cymbal*, as well as Feldman's graph piece *Ixion*, Wolff's *For Six or Seven Players*, La Monte Young's *Two Sounds*, Ichiyanagi's *Sapporo*, and many others which I unfortunately missed.

Cage's works represents unquestionably the most important development in musical composition since the war, and will exert more influence on the future evolutions and changes in composition and performance than the work of any European composers (including Boulez, who seems at present more concerned to absorb the influences of his French past). It is dubbed 'experimental' merely because it implies and demands a breakaway from conventional concert presentation, and sets about creating new modes of making music rather than a re-ordering of the emotional material of traditional music. The word 'experimental' should not be understood as implying any vagueness or tentativeness in Cage's musical thinking. The difficulties that his work presents to the ordinary music lover and professional musician are due to his new notion of the duration of a piece of music (many of his pieces can continue indefinitely), his acceptance of any sound as latent music (one of his pieces – *Variations IV* – consists of sounds made *outside* the theatre space and whatever sound sources happen to be discovered), and his involvement of the instrumentalist in the act of the music making in a completely new way (the performer in many of Cage's works has responsibilities towards the world of sound and that of human behaviour, rather than towards a musical tradition). Our recalcitrant English musical scene fancies it cannot afford to devote three hours broadcasting time to an experiment like *Atlas Eclipticalis*. Our valuable television time must be filled with worthy matters as education, documentation, entertainment, news, commentaries and advertising. With the result that we are well supplied with information, and are *au fait* with what is happening in the world today, but are starved of the vital contemporary cultural experiences.

Every one of Cunningham's dances throws up interesting and important points which deserve to be reviewed in detail. The same applies to Robert Rauschenberg's costumes and lighting (*Winterbranch*, for example, was danced on a dark stage populated with fingers of light and at one point an unidentifiable moving, twinkling spectre), and to David Tudor's extraordinary piano playing (his performance of Bo Nilsson's piano pieces on amplified piano was a *tour de force* not only of piano playing but of electronic engineering as well).

For the purposes of this article, however, I will try to describe only one of the dances in a general way: *Summerspace* to Morton Feldman's *Ixion*. This work, more than any of the others that I saw, was an almost perfect fusion of the diverse personalities at work in the company. Rauschenberg's backcloth was a brightly coloured unbroken speckled space of points, and his costumes all preserved the same motif. The music also was an almost unbroken stream of high, bubbling notes resolving only towards the end in quiet rows of chords. In both I felt a slight, reserved concession; in Rauschenberg the explicit use of paint and colour, and in Feldman the idea of constant animation and articulate form. The dance too, though generally made up of abstract patterns of movement, contained hints of animals, birds and leaves. The result was a wonderfully evocative 'summerspace' with a truly and beautifully seductive quality which robbed one of all sense of the weight of time and of the separateness of music, dance and painting.

Rome Letter – Nuova Consonanza
Financial Times – 25th May 1965

The selection of the title New Consonance for a series of avant garde concerts bespeaks an ironic, faintly self deprecatory attitude on the part of the organisers. And such an attitude does in fact exist: Franco Evangelisti, the prime instigator of this series and one of Italy's most virile composers, has ceased composing on the grounds that contemporary musical conceptions cannot be adequately realised until some means is devised for transforming 'brainwaves' (systems of minute electrical impulses, we are told) more or less directly, into sound.

This year the series comprised six concerts on six successive nights. The first four were conventional contemporary chamber music concerts, the sixth was shared between a drably staged theatrical score *The Emperor of Ice Cream* by Roger Reynolds, and a public discussion concerned chiefly with the unavailability of public money for the adequate presentation of new music. The fifth concert, with which we will be primarily concerned in this review, was shared by a specially formed experimental improvisation group, and a wildly intellectualised imitation *Happening* by Domenico Guaccero.

The glamour and the allure of the word 'improvisation' is something that few young composers can be immune to. It associates all too readily with images of self-expression and spontaneous utterance: it seems to offer escape from the impasse of notational complexity: its apparent implication that music is a manipulation of sounds is seductive. And then improvisation means 'Jazz.' It means the piano touch of Theolonius Monk, the polished ensemble of an MJQ: the perfect riding drive of a Charlie Parker, the pathos of a Miles Davis, all of which are objects of admiration, nostalgia and envy for many composers of the present generation.

The failure of this concert was in comprehending more than shallowly the forces at work in a jazz ensemble: solidarity, mutual support and invigoration there, the musicians played with a modest disclaiming air, as though each expected his neighbour to produce the life-giving sound, and hence denied any responsibility for its non-appearance, the conviction that any basic design can, if properly worked, be an inexhaustible mine of music (here the group hoped to safeguard themselves against 'influences' – as though that were possible or desirable – from jazz or elsewhere by refusing to use any basic designs): the straight sound, the unnotable earnest that the musician is playing himself, that he means what he says – a standard of integrity that most interpreters of contemporary music do not seem to regard as binding there, every sound was either intentionally deformed or imperfectly produced. In other words the attitude to the world of sound was wrong, for with the right attitude even the 'ugliest' sounds can have their place in music.

It might be thought unjustified to comment so exhaustively on the negative aspects of such an endeavour. On the contrary: for a musician every step taken in the wrong direction renders more pressing the desire to take steps in the right direction. The experience of vice intensifies the desire for virtue, and increases its value in the event of its attainment. Of the seven more or less experimental composers who made up the ensemble, all were more or less aware of the failure of this attempt, and finally realised that the decision to improvise is a big one, and the practice of improvisation a discipline that is arduous and worthwhile. Evangelisti himself was unfortunately prevented at the last moment from participating in the ensemble: had be been present the evening might have have taken an entirely different course: is any more direct transformation of 'brainwaves' into sound available to us than improvisation?

The large audience responded to this endeavour with sceptical indifference. It reserved its enthusiasm for Guaccero's sensational *Scenes of Power 2* in the second half of the programme. Atomic physics, Hitler, striptease, the prepared piano and capital punishment were some of the ingredients of the cultural political hash.

Audience 'participation' was induced by having simultaneous scenic activity both in the theatre's foyer and on the stage; the results were comparable to Tottenham Court Road tube station at 6pm during a bus strike. Meanwhile, Daniele Paris industriously and imperturbably conducted a small instrumental ensemble squashed into a tiny 'pit' in from of the stage, icing the whole with a pathetic veneer of provincial repertory ballet. Emerging into the orderly dissipation of the Via Veneto, I found my indifference crystallising into amusement – between these two poles that suck in and absorb whatever leisure moments we may have earned, where can music survive?

But tenuously it does survive. At least it was alive in 1950 when John Cage wrote the String Quartet (*Four Seasons*) that Italo Gomez and the Societa Cameristica Italiana performed – exquisitely – in one of the chamber concerts. It was alive in Christian Wolff's *Pieces For Prepared Piano* (1951) which were played in the following concert. Presumably it is still alive to this day – somewhere.

Composed Laughter
New Statesman – 10th December 1965

From the eager, almost querulous reception accorded Karlheinz Stockhausen at the ICA Gallery last Thursday it was obvious that his visit to this country was long overdue. After playing a half-hour fragment of his recent composition *Momente* (a recording made a few weeks ago in Cologne), he sat and suffered patiently a barrage of more or less specious questions under the glare and heat of too many BBC – TV arc lights for an hour and a half. His answers were concise and clear and spoke volumes for his experience and expertise in answering questions; but they did not give us any real insight into the processes at work in his music, and for this his questioners were only partly to blame.

However, his verbal reticence becomes comprehensible when taken in conjunction with the intimate expansiveness of the music. The work *Momente* is scored for soprano soloist, four choral groups of 12 singers each, four trumpets, four trombones and percussion. Before playing the tape Stockhausen gave a brief account of the multi-lingual text matter used in the piece. Excerpts from the *Song of Solomon* form the bulk of the comprehensible verbal singing, and he stated that, ideally, these should be translated into the language of the audience for any specific performance. Interwoven with this are extracts from personal letters, quotations from audience responses to other works by Stockhausen, 'nonsense' composed phonetically for specific situations, a whole range of unclassified vocal phenomena from laughter to tongue clicking, and in addition random quotations from literary and other sources in a variety of languages.

Obviously, such a work is a personal document in its own right; it is a composer speaking, and since even a composer may be a Whole Man, what he says is by no means exclusively musical. Stockhausen extracts the maximum suggestive power from every one of his sources, whether literary, erotic, associative (more or less esoteric), bestial, etc. No wonder then that he is reluctant to talk about it – such talk would really be enormously indiscreet: as indeed to say even such simple words as 'I love you' is indiscreet in the sense that what the words refer to is already itself explicit, potent and perfectly articulate. So *Momente* is potent and articulate and to talk about it is to use words in a kind of half-life condition; they dutifully, shamefacedly issue forth in response to questions asked.

One questioner remarked that under normal professional conditions this music (specifically *Momente*) is virtually impossible to perform. It is to Stockhausen's great credit that he transcends normal professional conditions. 'I would like very much to conduct the work for you,' he said, and his personal, almost manual control of the music was very evident on the tape. Almost throughout the piece the sound was inspired with a very particular, unmistakable internal vitality – under 'normal professional conditions' such vitality could not survive, and I can think of no more drastic indictment of normal professional conditions. Surely a pianist like Richter would be insulted if one were to refer to him: as a 'professional' pianist.

Another questioner wanted to know how Stockhausen had notated the soloist's high giggling laughter near the beginning of the piece. No, he did *not* tickle her on stage, but actually he might have done … perhaps in a rehearsal? Whatever it was, it was an excellent notation. Next question: was the laughter supposed to be funny or was it intended purely as a configuration of sounds? ('Mr Stockhausen, do you consider yourself a human being?') "Well, I compose the laughter, I don't know what people will do, when they listen to it, Perhaps they will think it funny and start to laugh too, perhaps they will like the sound of it, perhaps they will start wondering whether they are supposed to think it funny or just listen to it as sound."

The ICA Music Section laid on a concert of a few of Stockhausen's works two days after the General Forum that I have been describing. However, all the works in this concert date from the Fifties, a period when new music seems to have been in a very self devouring phase, obsessively concerned with internal problems of musical organisation. Not that the works are uninteresting: everything Stockhausen has written is on a level of intensity sufficient to penetrate all self-imposed barriers of esoteric thinking and technical complexity. But only in *Refrain* (composed in 1959) is there apparent the desire or the will for the music to radiate, to exert force, to compel an audience.

Stockhausen in London
The Musical Times – January 1966

The London lover of new music – proverbially starved – enjoyed a feast during the London Days of Contemporary Music organized by the ICA Music Section, Dec 2-5. Of the four evenings, two were devoted to Karlheinz Stockhausen: the first to him personally – a General Forum, with the composer answering questions, and the second to his music – a concert arranged by Roger Smalley containing chamber works written between 1954 and 1960.

Stockhausen, born 1928 in Cologne where he now runs the Studio for Electronic Music, has spread his theories, personally and music far and wide in the 15 years since he started composing. Only England has remained relatively uninterested in his work, fearing the difficulty and expense involved in presenting it on the scale that it requires in order to take root. At last the musical establishment took its courage in both hands and invited him for a personal visit, and it turned out that there exists a large demand for his music among ordinary music lovers and concert goers. All his appearances in London were sell-outs, including a lecture on electronic music at the German Cultural Institute, (in the provinces – Oxford, Cambridge, Glasgow – I understand he did not fare so well; he was booked to lecture on electronic music, simply because the professors involved did not realize that he wrote any other kind.)

The concert (Commonwealth Institute, Dec 4) showed that English musicians still lack the appropriate training and experience to approach his music satisfactorily. *Piano Pieces 5, 7* and *8* were played by Roger Smalley, who constructed the sounds correctly but failed to communicate a feeling of context and continuity. Yet his performance was the one that came closest to the clean vitality so necessary to Stockhausen's music of the fifties. *Zeitmasse* for 5 woodwinds, *Refrain* for three players and *Zyklus* for one percussionist all fell short in alertness and poise, lacking in any real precision, both technically and interpretationally.

These defects were somewhat compensated for by the tapes the composer brought with him. In the General Forum (ICA Gallery, Dec 2) he played a large section of *Momente*, a more recent work for soprano solo, four chorus groups, four trumpets, four trombones and percussion. The following evening at the German Cultural Institute he played *Mikrophonie 1* and *Mikrophonie 2*, both very recent compositions, to illustrate his lecture. These works are designed as an extension of electronic music; they represent an attempt to bring electronic music back into the concert hall.

Mikrophonie 1 employs a tam-tam of J. Arthur Rank proportions. This is scratched, rubbed, beaten and generally titivated ('excited' was the word Stockhausen used) in a variety of ways by two performers, while two other performers move directional microphones over the surface, sometimes close and sometimes further away, detecting, all manner of subtle 'microwaves' emanating from the excited instrument. Their findings are simultaneously processed and broadcast to the audience, through loudspeakers by two technicians who preside over amplifiers, filters and potentiometers. The results were extraordinary – noises that were sometimes almost human, but more often animal, were blended with sounds strictly electronic such as feedback and filter frequencies. In a way it is anomalous to listen to such music on tape. Tape is the medium of electronic music and hence essential to it, and it is the most accurate vehicle available for reproducing instrumental and vocal music. But in the case of *Mikrophonie 1* a large part of the experience must consist in the interplay between 'natural' and 'doctored' sounds, and this disappears if the work is heard on tape. In the case of *Mikrophonie 2* the anomaly is even more pronounced. Here, choral sounds are doctored in the manner described, but in addition pre-recorded tapes are fed into the performance, among other things excerpts from earlier music by Stockhausen (e.g. passages from the electronic piece *Gesang der Junglinge*).

Momente then was the most impressive experience of the London Days. The use of a sort of concertante voice part seemed to have a marvellously emancipating effect on the composer's imagination. With her unmistakably operatic overtones, the soloist breathed all kinds of exciting life into the score. "I am black, but comely." she sings, "because the sun hath looked upon me." The chorus applause with which the work sardonically opens has by this time thinned to a spasmodic crackle, into which the soloist lays the word *verbarnnt* – 'burned' – like a beautiful symbol of surrender and acceptance. And how telling it is that the German translation of the Bible says 'burned' where the English says 'looked upon'! It points up the world of difference between German and English performances of Stockhausen. Fire – that is exactly what the English performances lacked.

Inevitably, the other two concerts were anti-climactic. Young English composers were presented – cunning robins hoping to dart out from under the eagle's feathers after an easy trip to the empyrean – as well as some Americans, including the established Milton Babbitt, whose *Du*, song cycle for soprano and piano impressed by its sheer obliviousness of the potentialities of the vocal medium and music in general.

However, both concerts were saved; the first by an exhilarating and accomplished rendering of Webern's *Concerto op 24* by the Melos Ensemble. The slow movement could have borne a more Feldmanesque treatment; the sounds should be dwelt on to release their full emotional colour, not sacrificed to the inflexible crotchet movement – like First Species counterpoint – that the score seems to demand. But the last movement was like a piece of inspired slapstick by some artist of the calibre of Marcel Marceau.

What saved the other concert was a rich, idiosyncratic but perfectly articulate performance of Schoenberg's *String Trio* by the Oromonte String Trio (Perry Hart, Margaret Major, Bruno Schrecker). The musical establishment's restrictive practice with regard to the new music of today has borne fruit where the new music of yesterday (or the day before) is concerned; it has at least obliged a handful of instrumentalists to acquire a thorough familiarity with and understanding of a couple of pieces of music by Webern and Schoenberg.

Introduction to Four Works
Universal Edition – 1966

(The four works published in this edition were: *Autumn '60*, *Material for Harmony Instruments*, *Solo with Accompaniment* and *Memories of You*.)

It is not possible for a conductor to distribute parts for *Autumn '60* among orchestral musicians and then get up on the rostrum and conduct the piece. The very fact that the parts and the score are identical implies et al a higher degree of interest and involvement is demanded of the musicians. They have to acquaint themselves with the musical principles underlying the work; they have to investigate the range of possibilities opened up by the score. And finally they have to accept the responsibility for the part they play, for their musical contribution to the piece.

Nobody can be involved with this music in a merely professional capacity. These pieces stand to one another in a relation of mutual support and enrichment: experience gained from one is of vital importance in interpreting the others. In practical terms: any musician who has worked on *Autumn '60* (and no instrument is excluded from taking part in that piece) is in a position to tackle either part of *Solo with Accompaniment*; players of harmony instruments can also turn to *Material*, while all four pieces are available to pianists.

Even apart from these practical considerations, it seems that these pieces may be 'read' and enjoyed by people who do not play musical instruments. For such people it is of course a matter of little concern that the four pieces in this book are for different instrumental groupings. Educated music lovers buy full scores not only for the sake of taking them to concerts and 'following with the music', but also for the pleasure of actually reading the music, of experiencing a kind of imaginary prototype performance. It is well known that very often there is much more in a score than what is used in the production of a sounding performance, much more than what is communicated through a single performance.

Such speculations have a very specific relevance for the pieces in this volume. The musical potentialities of *Autumn '60* cannot be fully exploited in a single performance; a glance at the example on page 8 shows that the number of possible solutions for even a single beat far exceeds the number of musicians et al can be got together for a performance, and if all the possible solutions were presented simultaneously the result would in any case be an undifferentiated mass of sound. Thus the criterion of a good performance is not completeness (i.e. perfection), but rather the lucidity of its incompleteness. Any performance is a kind of documentary relic (more or less revealing) of the composer's conception. The music itself on the other hand lies in the score; the score is the composition, and as such has its own value apart from any particular interpretation.

Having stated that these notations exist in their own right, are even musically expressive in a certain sense, it is necessary to retreat from that position again and investigate the efficacy of the notations – how potent and economical is their stimulation of the instrumentalist and hence how well they are equipped for survival in a developing musical and cultural situation. A balance must be maintained between cogent explicitness (necessary to galvanise the player into action) and sufficient flexibility (in the symbols and the rules for their interpretation) to permit of evolution.

Their best guarantee for survival would be a completely self-contained, closed logical system for each piece. Such systems might be rediscovered even after a lapse of thousands of years in a state of preservation comparable to that of Egyptian mummies. But however beautifully preserved they would nevertheless be dead, their language and meaning forgotten. So these little systems – these pieces – are not self-contained; like seeds, they depend on the surrounding soil for nourishment, they are irremovably embedded in their environment, which is the musical situation today. And the mechanism of growth is built into them; the numbers in *Solo with Accompaniment* refer to qualities that can change with the changeable climate of music thinking, and obviously objects as yet uninvented can change the shape of *Memories of You*.

But beyond these growth mechanisms, the pieces also need camouflage to protect them from hostile forces in the early days of their life. One kind of protection is provided by the novelty and uniqueness of the notations: few musicians will take the trouble to decipher and learn the notations unless they have a positive interest in performing the works. But a more positive kind of camouflage is needed; something to persuade the watchful custodians of our musical garden that these tender young emergent plants bear more resemblance to flowers or vegetables than to weeds. So as seeds, besides containing a growth mechanism orientated towards the future, they also bear hereditary characteristics linking them with the past. So it will be found that the pitches given in *Autumn '60* – and in the nature of things these pitches will often predominate – are almost pentatonic. And in *Material*, although the pitches are seldom tonally associated, the rhythmic pulsation and the development of the rubato idea provide a similar handhold. *Solo with Accompaniment* and *Memories of You* are more aggressive, tougher, simpler in conception and consequently stand in less need of such camouflage. *Memories of You* even dispenses with the tempered scale, except insofar as this is represented symbolically by the presence of a grand piano.

Yoko Ono
The Financial Times – 29th September 1966

Yoko Ono – "born in bird year, who spent her childhood and adolescence collecting skies and seaweeds, and in late adolescence gave birth to a grapefruit and who is at present travelling as a private lecturer" (so says the programme) – is a name previously known to the writer only as the owner of a spacious loft in New York where some of the most experimental and spectacular events in new music were permitted to happen in the early sixties. In Yoko Ono's loft practically the total *oeuvre* of LaMonte Young was programmed for a single evening – however this 'Draw a straight line and follow it' being still incomplete after four hours, it was conceded that the rest of the programme would have to be postponed. This is of course all hearsay, and events 3,000 miles away are inevitably invested with legendary character to compensate for the absence of the actual experience.

Now Yoko Ono is in London, preceded by a friendly double spread in *Art and Artists*. Last night a small circle gathered to see her perform at the Africa Centre. Instead of a taxing evening of extended and experimental work, however, she gave what can only be described as a highly polished recital of her work conveniently broken down into short 'pieces' which were received by the majority of the audience with the kind of reverence usually given to concert pianists. In fact Yoko Ono is not a musician but a painter, which possibly accounts for her choice of this kind of format.

The character of the works was curiously moral and naive. Certain pieces definitely do you good: … 'Bag Piece' for instance, which is a kind of living sculpture. Yoko Ono and her husband disappear into a big black bag and move about inside it in a delicately erotic and tenderly suggestive way to the accompaniment of 'Bicycle Piece for Orchestra ' – a man riding a white bicycle around the auditorium as slowly and noiselessly as possible.

But my conviction of the uplifting quality of the work began to waver in the celebrated 'Cut Piece' which followed. It was impossible to disentangle the compulsion of the audience to cut and Yoko Ono's compulsion to *be* cut. In cutting off pieces of her clothing members of the audience show unmistakable signs of artistic striving, and she for her part is equally unmistakably striving towards a kind of nerveless detachment, so that all emotional interplay is precluded. As the piece progresses one becomes aware of another kind of nudity underneath the clothing of her skin, and this inner amorphous nude shape is visible only in her eyes, fixed unwinkingly on the audience.

The audience is critical to Yoko Ono's art, but the other participation pieces seemed like gratuitous games which could not take effect in the short time allotted to them. It is to be hoped that in her second concert (this evening at 7.45 at the Africa Centre, King Street, Covent Garden) she will be able to devote more time and intensity to this side of her activity.

Stockhausen's *Plus-Minus* and The Sounds of LaMonte Young
The London Magazine – April 1967

Conventionally, pieces of music are written for instruments, like clarinet and piano, or for orchestra, 'full' or 'chamber', or for voices in one combination or another. Some combinations of instruments have become titles: String Quartet, two violins, (viola and cello), Wind Quintet (flute, oboe, clarinet, bassoon, horn), Piano Trio (violin, cello and piano), these titles even implying often a specific form, so that the title 'String Quartet' really means (for classical music) 'piece in sonata form for string quartet'.

It is already rather alarming for some musicians to find a piece of music simply 'for instruments', that is for any number and combination of instruments (there now exist a number of such pieces, for example, Christian Wolff's *For One, Two or Three People*).

Now Karlheinz Stockhausen (born 1928), pioneer of serial and electronic music in Germany, has gone one step further: he has written a work 'for composers'. The title of the work is *Plus-Minus*. I have now been involved in 5 'compositions' (performances) of the piece, so I am in a position to give a 'survivor's account' of what actually is implied by the enigmatic superscription: 'for composers'.

The original aim of the piece was didactic: it was an exercise for the growing flock of Stockhausen's composition students in Cologne, Darmstadt, Pittsburgh and elsewhere. The basic score consists of seven large pages describing the formal evolution of the piece (which is variable insofar as the order of the seven pages is free) and seven pages of pitch material (chords and passages of notes) to be matched up with the seven formal pages at the discretion of the individual composers. The actual musical events consist of the pitch material given, mixed up in various ways with unpitched sounds (noises or 'Akzidentien', to use Stockhausen's own – invented – word). The resulting mixtures accumulate or disappear according to a complex procedure of addition and subtraction.

This brings us to the most interesting and problematical feature of the piece. When by process of subtraction an element 'disappears', it passes into a 'negative' stratum of sound, and in this negative sphere it has still to preserve its basic characteristics, but in a shadowy kind of way. When Frederic Rzewski and I were faced with the task of making the Création Mondiale in Rome two years ago, the selection of suitable and feasible negative sound sources was one of the most difficult problems we had to solve. Rzewski decided in favour of an electric organ of one kind or another, which of course allowed him perfectly to preserve the pitch characteristics of the equivalent positive sound, and I chose to use three transistor radios, tuned respectively to atmospherics, speech and music as being equivalent to the three categories of noise-sound mixture that were required by my version of the piece.

Next, we had to decide on certain general 'tendencies', these being again dependent on the add-subtract procedure or *Plus-Minus* principle. Rzewski, feeling the healthy composer's antagonism to pitch material provided by another composer (in this case Stockhausen), decided to use adding opportunities for the accumulation of 'Akzidentien' or noises, and subtracting opportunities for the elimination of the given pitch material. Further he attempted to bring each element as quickly as possible to the 13 position (13 repetitions of the same element), at which point Stockhausen decrees that the element in question reverts to its original 1 position but with a completely changed character and timbre. This new character and timbre Rzewski provided by inserting preparations in the piano (screws, pieces of cork, bolts, coins, etc.) hence completely distorting – and liberating himself from – the original pitch material as given by Stockhausen.

I, on the other hand, feeling the healthy composer's reluctance to compose another man's music, decided to bring all elements as quickly as possible into the negative sphere (transistor radios), and even in the positive sphere to strive for maximum simplicity by using every subtracting opportunity to eliminate 'Akzidentien'.

All set. We worked for weeks composing our versions and having come to the end of two pages (out of seven) we found that the piece was already running to 35 minutes' duration, a rather excessive length for a piece involving only two players. After four or five minutes flight over something that was quite recognizably Stockhausen country we found ourselves emerging into vast spaces of uncharted virgin steppe, a landscape of almost Wagnerian grandeur, and we experienced a feeling of elation (it must be remembered that this grew up only gradually through a number of very sticky rehearsals) and an invigorating sense of unlimited freedom. Around the 20 minute mark we found ourselves listening to quiet music on the radio while Rzewski coolly inserted his next set of preparations. At 25 minutes I was faced with a loud tremolo on a thunderous chord lasting over three minutes (an endurance test that demands fairly intensive athletic training). At 30 minutes we heard the news accompanied by drawn-out screeching 'Akzidentien'. Finally we were floating on a sea of quiet exotic resonances of incredible beauty, backed by an almost inaudible cluster proceeding mysteriously from the electric organ.

The effect on the audience was unbelievable. They were prostrated but not asleep. Finally it took them a few minutes to emerge from the state of deep trance that the piece had cast over them. Only the musicians in the audience were sceptical: 'mood music' they called it, 'Self-indulgent formalism', 'serialism gone to seed', etc. Rzewski's own comment after our three performances in Holland sums up the sense of wonder that the piece creates: 'It's incredible how such tripe can be so beautiful.'

The Sounds of LaMonte Young

For a whole half-hour it struggled through the poor loudspeaker of the tape recorder in a North London pub, drowning the television, driving away custom, boring its way into the minds of two aged and tenacious drinkers and the indulgent new barmaid and her baby. Truly, to locate the pulse of new music in London requires more than a monthly glance through the Bulletin of the Institute of Contemporary Arts.

The tape was a recording of a recent private performance by LaMonte Young in New York City. Many god-fearing musicians in this country will no doubt deny the existence of this composer, claiming complacently that he is a figment and a hoax foisted on the public by a snide BBC (the Third Programme's New Comment series once broadcast '62 for Henry Flynt', a composition by LaMonte Young that consists of repeated loud clusters played on the piano as uniformly and regularly as possible). But he is real.

LaMonte Young was born in America in 1936. Music he studied at Berkeley, California, under Leonard Stein (LaMonte sent the 'Henry Flynt' piece in response to a request from Stein for a piano piece to take on European tour – Stein did not play the work). In 1959 he came to Europe for the composition course given by Stockhausen at the Darmstadt Summer School of New Music. It was difficult for the two composers – both 'giants' of new music as it has turned out – to find a level of communication, but there must have been some important interchange of a non-verbal kind. Stockhausen's *Piano Piece IX* begins with 139 repetitions of the same chord progressing from maximum to minimum loudness – a weak, aesthetic version of the piece *For Henry Flynt* – and conversely the complex manipulations of random number tables that constitute the groundwork of LaMonte's early pieces surely owe something to the 'statistical field' theory that Stockhausen was elaborating at the time. My conjecture is that LaMonte was impressed by Stockhausen's ability to think schematically, and Stockhausen was impressed by LaMonte's ability to act (that is, write music) schematically. Subsequent developments have shown that the two 'giants' had at least one vital weakness in common: an enormous susceptibility to the seduction of pure sound.

LaMonte went back to America to continue his studies in Berkeley, and later in 1959 his first important compositions began to arrive in Europe: *Vision*, a composition for several instruments in which each sound is described with insistent precision, but where the duration and spacing of the sound within a total time of 11 minutes has to be worked out by the performance director with the aid of the random number book (alternatively the telephone directory). Finally he says that the musicians should be randomly placed throughout the auditorium and that all lights should be extinguished for the duration of the piece, the players having first provided themselves with luminous watches.

Then came *Poem*, probably the most widely performed of all LaMonte Young compositions. Originally, the piece was scored for 'tables, chairs, benches and other similar sound sources' (these objects were pushed or pulled across the floor according to determinations effected by the same method as in *Vision*), but then after some happy experiences at Berkeley the work developed into a kind of 'chamber opera' in which any activity, not necessarily even of a sounding variety, could constitute one strand in the complex weave of the composition, which could last minutes, or weeks, or aeons. In fact it was quickly realized that all being and happening from the very beginning of time had been nothing more nor less than a single gigantic performance of *Poem*. It seems to me that this realization provides the link between these complex early compositions and the utter simplicity and lyricism of the following set.

In 1960 he moved to New York and in the space of a couple of months produced a series of twenty or thirty verbal compositions ranging from the poetic 'Piano Piece for David Tudor: Some of them were very old grasshoppers' to the austere 'Composition for Bob Morris. Draw a straight line and follow it'. In a humourous moment John Cage wished to deny LaMonte's authorship of these compositions, claiming that they owed their power to the influence of a poetess associate of the composer's. A period of intensive performing activity followed the composition of these pieces. George Brecht, Toshi Ichiyanagi and many others contributed to the flood of similar compositions being written at that time. In collaboration with George Maciunas, LaMonte published a great Anthology of work of this kind. Thenceforth he wrote virtually nothing: the 'Henry Flynt' piece and a 'Death Chant' on the death of a friend's child are the only compositions known to me. Instead of composing he took to improvising long concerts with various associates: he started playing the sopranino saxophone seriously.

One further composition reached England in 1964 when the Merce Cunningham Dance Company was at Sadler's Wells and the Phoenix Theatre for a season. Cunningham had choreographed a composition called *Two Sounds*. The composer had provided two sounds in separate tapes, to be started at different points during the ballet. When the first sound starts you cannot imagine that any more horrible sound exists in the whole world. Then the second sound comes in and you have to admit you were wrong. That is the exaggerated account of the piece given by one of the managers of the dance company. Actually of course any two sounds could constitute the composition, even two very beautiful ones, if you can think of any (try playing a single note on the G-string of a Stradivarius for half an hour on end and see if it is still 'beautiful').

The one sound that I heard in the Islington pub was actually very beautiful, and got progressively more beautiful through the half-hour that the tape lasted. It took four people to produce it: LaMonte Young and his wife Marian Zazeela (voices), Tony Conrad (violin), and a three string viola drone provided by John Cale, a Welsh musician who was responsible for introducing the tape into this country. Both voices and instruments were amplified electronically to the point of virtual unrecognisability. Variations of timbre and texture were produced by tuning and intensity of the various partials of a single fundamental note. The result was rich enough to colour an evening, which is something, and indeed I can still hear that sound in my mind now, with its guttural tremors and the microphone slides back deep into LaMonte's throat.

What does it mean? One of the aged drinkers pointed over at us listeners and said well look at them; it obviously means something. And credit that old man's imagination in recognizing this, for it means something on a much more profound level and much more profusely than the 1,000 words of this article, to take a banal example. Like the chaotic and obsessive utterances of a schizophrenic, they may or may not mean something explicit to the professional analyst, yet even to us ordinary laymen they 'mean' that man's condition in a way that moves us more (or should) than merely artistic or intelligent attempts to shake the foundations of our complacent normality.

Sextet – The Tiger's Mind
by Cornelius Cardew

The Musical Times – June 1967
[later published by Hinrichsen/Peters Edition, London]

Daypiece

The tiger fights the mind that loves the circle that traps the tiger.
The circle is perfect and outside time. The wind blows dust in
tigers' eyes. Amy reflects, relaxes with her mind, which puts out
buds. (emulates the tree). Amy jumps through the circle and
comforts the tiger. The tiger sleeps in the tree. High wind. Amy
climbs the tree, which groans in the wind and succumbs.
The tiger burns.

Nightpiece

The tiger burns and sniffs the wind for news. He storms at the
circle; if inside to get out, if outside to get in. Amy sleeps while
the tiger hunts. She dreams of the wind, which then comes and
wakes her. The tree trips Amy in the dark and in her fall she
recognizes her mind. The mind, rocked by the wind tittering
in the leaves of the tree, and strangled by the circle, goes on the
nod. The circle is trying to teach its secrets to the tree. The tree
laughs at the mind and at the tiger fighting it.

Interpretation of this piece is to be viewed hopefully as a continuous process.

Initially the two texts given above should be regarded as limiting (i.e. play the given actions in the given order), the Daypiece and Nightpiece being used for performance on alternate occasions. All musicians should memorize the text to be used. Subsequently new actions and situations may be allowed to arise spontaneously, concurrent or interleaved with the given ones; also the succession of events may be altered, more or less at random (e.g. a performance of the Daypiece might open with the tiger asleep in the tree, or the mind loving the circle, or Amy's mind putting out buds, etc.). After additional experience it may be desirable to devise new texts involving the same six characters – the new texts should then be memorized as before. Finally it may be possible to play without a text, simply improvising actions and situations involving the six characters.

Initially the six characters may be played by six musicians, each one knowing which roles are allocated to the other players. Later, each musician may select his own role and allocate the other five roles without telling the other players (so that player A may select tree for himself and regard B as tiger, while B has selected tree also and regards A as circle – in this case we already have two aspects of tree present at once). Alternatively, each player may select his own role and allocate the other five in the course of play, as required by the performance of his own role. Logically, after this stage it is no longer so important that there be six players. When there are more than six players the characters may be duplicated or multiplied as often as necessary. However, Amy should never be duplicated (obviously it might happen that two players both regard themselves as Amy, but this is allowable as long as each one regards himself as the only Amy). When there are 12 or more players the roles should be allocated by a performance director and made common knowledge amongst the musicians (e.g. performers 1-6 are trees, 7 is Amy, 8 and 9 make up a circle, 10 is the wind and the rest are tigers). When there are less than six players, people or objects or sound sources outside the group may be used as dummies – without necessarily informing them of their role (for instance, if there are four players it might be convenient to take a sleeping onlooker – or an object in a sleeping position or a tape-recording of snoring – and place a tree-object in a position such that he becomes the tiger sleeping in the tree. He may sleep on for the duration of the performance. If he wakes he may still be regarded as the tiger, but the players should be prepared that he act not in accordance with the text. Alternatively a mechanical tiger may be devised – although it might seem more appropriate to devise mechanical minds, winds or circles). If there is only one player he should play the tiger.

The duration of the piece is not limited and it should preferably be performed on its own.

The following notes on the six characters are not limiting or definitive. They are intended primarily to encourage and assist prospective performers in the assumption of their roles. However, they do contain phrases that may be used in performance as additional material (e.g. Amy holding the tiger by the tail, the circle spinning, etc.) Individual performers may modify the given details and add new ones if they so desire (e.g. a zoologist performer may object to the view that the tiger's growling is instinctual, and might wish to add that the structure of his paws enables him to travel soundlessly over a particular kind of terrain. However, if our zoologist cannot accept tigers sleeping in trees he should choose a different role – at least until such time as the given texts have been discarded).

Amy is a person. She worships the tiger. She tags along holding him by the tail. Her mind is occupied with things close by. She comes to no harm in the wind, although it brings her intimations of things far away. However, in high winds she should avoid climbing trees.

The tiger is a beast; he likes to hunt. His face when he sights his prey is a silent explosion. In lean seasons he must conserve his strength and be on his guard against manginess. Movement is his language and Amy understands this language. His growling, etc., are merely his instinctual noises. His telecommunications system is based on the wind which brings him scents and sounds from far away. His hearing and sense of smell are very acute.

The tree is supposedly insensate. But it does respond to the stimuli of wind and sun, and is also subject to sickness. It can sustain severe damage and still repair itself. It is a haven for all kinds of life (animals, insects, plants) some of which are dependent on it parasitically. It keeps within itself a record of its age (seen as concentric circles). It is hard yet pliant. Dead trees may remain standing for centuries after their death. In life it expresses the circle of seasons in its flowering, its falling leaves, their changing colour, the rising sap, etc. Ironically, its seed is borne away on the wind which is a potentially dangerous enemy. Being unaware of the effect of its being, a tree may be beneficial, inimical or neutral in relation to others of its kind (e.g. it may be protecting a neighbouring tree from high winds at the same time as depriving it of vital sunlight. Having no mind of its own, the tree is a constant stimulus to the mind.

Wind is insubstantial: visible and audible only through the objects in its path. Wind is a persuasive image of freedom – blowing when and where it wants, now hot now cold, now hard now soft, now sweet now sour, frequently screaming, wailing, whimpering, groaning, but never suffering, always intact – but crack this image and behind it we find that wind is totally determined throughout its insubstantial being – on the one side by the atmospheric and geographical conditions that generate it and on the other by the form, size and substance of the obstacles in its path. Sometimes wind seems to vanish completely for days on end, but this is an illusion – he is ever-present.

The circle is an abstraction; the characteristic of myriads of things, the substance of none. It is a special case in the class of ellipses (the straight line is another), as the square is a special case in the class of rectangles (again the other extreme is the straight line). The faster it spins the less it appears to; when its spin reaches infinite velocity, the circle rests. It is a creation of the mind and at the same time a threat to it. In some inconceivably special situation the wind might cause the circle to acquire direction, enter time, become a wave.

The mind itself is never in danger, only its user. When the mind absorbs the threat of the circle, for instance, the owner may experience headache. If the owner relinquishes his mind in order to escape such effects, he is exposing himself to unknown hazards (from which the mind had previously protected him). If the mind is relinquished it lies dormant waiting for a new user. The mind is a nonentity – hard to recognise.

Sitting in the dark
The Musical Times – March 1968

At the suggestion of Michael Sargent of Focus Opera Group Cornelius Cardew has been working on a small opera book called' Schooltime Compositions', which will be performed at International Students' House on March 11 and 12 (one half-hour session each evening) under the titles' Dayschool' and' Nightschool'; operas by Ligeti and Kagel will also be given.

What distinguishes opera from other kinds of musical presentation? I have seen far too few operas for any answer of mine to carry weight. I see two possibilities: maximize the difference; minimize the difference.

You sit in the dark absorbed in action proceeding in a pool of light. Just like a classroom: children in the dark of ignorance focusing attention (erratically) on manipulations performed in the light of knowledge by the teacher. Hence Schooltime. Children go to Dayschool, grown-ups to Nightschool. We love in children their sagacity; what we love in grown-ups is a childlike quality.

The theatrical situation arouses disgust in me. The stage world is lit from one side only. A thin gaudy veneer is all that is necessary to reflect the light. A thin film of colour, like a flower child's cloak concealing decomposing undergarments and undernourished flesh. Actors glory in this artificiality; I prefer a beautiful body in rags. (I don't go into the case of a beautiful soul in a tattered body; I don't know why not.) Rags send the mind in search of an interior beauty. The senses leap ahead of the mind. They cultivate the mind; useless to try and cultivate the senses.

Moonlight etches the emotive black-and-white picture of things; twilight shows their multidimensional structure; daylight assaults the eye with the surfaces of things. Transient twilight brings the most peaceful feelings. The wind drops; the light is diffused, allowing things their own definition; scents are strong. Twilight is simultaneously source and goal.

Each of the *Schooltime Compositions* in the opera book is a matrix to draw out an interpreter's feelings about certain topics or materials. These pieces plus their interpreters are the characters in the opera. They undergo no dramatic development in the book; in performance they may. The pieces and their interpreters will be the same in both *Dayschool* and *Nightschool*. The different matrices grew around such things as words, melody, vocal sounds, triangles, pleasure, noise, working-to-rule, will and desire, keyboard. My plan is based on the translation of the word 'opera' into 'many people working'.

* * *

Let me explain. Simple equals rich; poverty comes from exhausting the possibilities. Any little thing can provide a matrix for expanding interpretation. A leaf or a sentence, or the sentence 'A leaf or a sentence' (imagine the veins as a lot of subjunctive clauses to the stalk). Actually, 'A leaf or a sentence' is not a sentence. As soon as you have a proper sentence (e.g. Burroughs 'My heart drink only desert words') the grammar itself forms a matrix – the different parts of speech occupying their respective positions and relating to the others in a variety of ways.

The Burroughs sentence is full of catches that require a mental leap to complete the sense (a sense): singular subject, plural verb suggests a plurality in the heart, a duplicity or multiplicity. Or view it as 'drinks' with the *s* deleted, and a pidgin language such as that of a man dying of exhaustion is suggested. This is over and above the simple metaphor of the heart's thirst, which is beautiful in itself. Etc., etc., through to the noun 'desert' used as an adjective (which is not uncommon), and the metaphor of drinking words (which is not uncommon either). Such analysis is pedantic; the sentence is not complex. Its meaning lies in your response to the simple pattern.

Some matrices serve as a measure of probity (cf La Monte Young's 'Draw a straight line and follow it'); others as a measure of virtuosity, courage, tenacity, alertness and so on. They point to the heart of some real matter, mental or material. The interpreter knows the general area of his potential action; he wishes or has talent to play, or sing, or construct, or illumine, or take exercise of one sort or another. He can draw out his interpretation in that direction. The interpreting route from matrix to action is what determines the condition he arrives in, the spirit in which he undertakes his action.

A musician's optimism – and now I am seeing that word in a new light: you live with the knowledge that at any time an (optimum) revelatory experience is possible; you have it in you but it is not under your control – stems from being wrapped up in a mystery. It may suit our momentary need to pretend we know the meaning of words like 'music'. 'musical', 'musicality' (I am keeping this consciously on a linguistic level), but in a musician's behaviour is expressed the knowledge that they are bottomless pits that not only defy definition and analysis but present no angle to them. Such words are like free electrons in a gas: as soon as a positively charged nucleus appears in their vicinity they zip into orbit and we assume that that's where they belong. Actually they are quite freely fungible. The occurrence of one constellation blinds us to the myriads that might have occurred; it gives us the present.

The explanatory second part of this article has been provided at the request of the Editor.

A Scratch Orchestra: draft constitution

The Musical Times – June 1969

Definition: A Scratch Orchestra is a large number of enthusiasts pooling their resources (not primarily material resources) and assembling for action (music-making, performance, edification).

Note: The word music and its derivatives are here not understood to refer exclusively to sound and related phenomena (hearing, etc.). What they do refer to is flexible and depends entirely on the members of the Scratch Orchestra.

The Scratch Orchestra intends to function in the public sphere, and this function will be expressed in the form of – for lack of a better word – concerts. In rotation (starting with the youngest) each member will have the option of designing a concert. If the option is taken up, all details of that concert are in the hands of that person or his delegates; if the option is waived the details of the concert will be determined by random methods, or by voting (a vote determines which of these two). The material of these concerts may be drawn, in part or wholly, from the basic repertory categories outlined below.

1. Scratch music

Each member of the orchestra provides himself with a notebook (or Scratchbook) in which he notates a number of accompaniments, performable continuously for indefinite periods. The number of accompaniments in each book should be equal to or greater than the current number of members of the orchestra. An accompaniment is defined as music that allows a solo (in the event of one occurring) to be appreciated as such. The notation may be accomplished using any means – verbal, graphic, musical, collage, etc. – and should be regarded as a period of training: never notate more than one accompaniment in a day. If many ideas arise in one day they may all be incorporated in one accompaniment. The last accompaniment in the list has the status of a solo and if used should only be used as such. On the addition of further items, was what previously a solo is relegated to the status of accompaniment, so that at any time each player has only one solo and that his most recent. The sole differentiation between a solo and an accompaniment is in the mode of playing.

The performance of this music can be entitled *Scratch Overture, Scratch Interlude* or *Scratch Finale* depending on its position in the concert.

2. Popular Classics

Only such works as are familiar to several members are eligible for this category. Particles of the selected works will be gathered in Appendix 1. A particle could be: a page of score, a page or more of an arrangement, a thematic analysis, a gramophone record, etc.

The technique of performance is as follows: a qualified member plays the given particle, while the remaining players join in as best they can, playing along, contributing whatever they can recall of the work in question, filing the gaps of memory with improvised variational material.

As is appropriate to the classics, avoid losing touch with the reading player (who may terminate the piece at his discretion), and strive to act concertedly rather than independently. These works should be programmed under their original titles.

3. Improvisation Rites

A selection of the rites in *Nature Study Notes* will be available in Appendix 2. Members should constantly bear in mind the possibility of contributing new rites. An improvisation rite is not a musical composition; it does not attempt to influence the music that will be played; at most it may establish a community of feeling, or a communal starting point, through ritual. Any suggested rite will be given a trial run and thereafter left to look after itself. Successful rites may well take on aspects of folklore, acquire nicknames, etc.

Free improvisation may also be indulged in from time to time.

4. Compositions

Appendix 3 will contain a list of compositions performable by the orchestra. Any compositions submitted by a member of the orchestra will be given a trial run in which all terms of the composition will be adhered to as closely as possible. Unless emphatically rejected, such compositions will probably remain as compositions in Appendix 3. If such a composition is repeatedly acclaimed it may qualify for inclusion in the Popular Classics, where it would be represented by a particle only, and adherence to the original terms of the composition would be waived.

5. Research Project

A fifth category may be evolved through the Research Project, an activity obligatory for all members of the Scratch Orchestra, to ensure its cultural expansion.

The Research Project. The universe is regarded from the viewpoint of travel. This means that an infinite of research vectors are regarded as hypothetically travellable. Travels may be undertaken in many dimensions, e.g. temporal, spatial, intellectual, spiritual, emotional. I imagine any vector will be found to impinge on all these dimensions at some point or other. For instance, if your research vector is the *Tiger*, you could be involved in time (since the tiger represents an evolving species), space (a trip to the zoo), intellect (the tiger's biology), spirit (the symbolic values acquired by the tiger) and emotion (your subjective relation to the animal).

The above is an intellectual structure, so for a start let's make the research vector a word or group of words rather than an object or an impression etc. A record of research is to be kept in the Scratchbook and this record may be made available to all.

Form time to time a journey will be proposed (Journey to Mars, Journey to the Court of Wu Ti, Journey to the Unconscious, Journey to West Ham, etc.). A discussion will suffice to provide a rough itinerary (e.g. embarkation at Cape Kennedy, type of vehicle to be used, number of hours in space, choice of landing site, return to earth or not, etc.).

Members whose vectors are relevant to this journey can pursue the relevance and consider the musical application of their research; members whose vectors are irrelevant (research on rocket fuels won't help with a journey to the Court of Wu Ti) can put themselves at the disposal of the others for the musical realization of their research.

A date can be fixed for the journey, which will take the form of a performance.

Conduct of research. Research should be through direct experience rather than academic; neglect no channels. The aim is: by direct contact, imagination, identification and study to get as close as possible to the object of your research. Avoid the mechanical accumulation of data: be constantly awake to the possibility of inventing new research techniques. The record in the Scratchbook should be a record of your activity rather than an accumulation of data. That means: the results of your research are in you, not in the book.

Example

Research vector	*Research record*
The Sun	29. vi. Looked up astronomical data in *EB* & made notes to accpt of dust motes (symbol of *EB*) and sunbeams.
	1-28. viii. Holiday in the Bahamas to expose myself to the sun.
	29. vii. Saw 'the Sun' as a collection of 6 letters and wrote out the 720 combinations of them.
	1. viii. Got interested in Sun's m or f. gender in different languages, and thence to historical personages regarded as the Sun (like Mao Tse-tung). Sought an astrological link between them.
Astrology	3. viii. Had my horoscope cast by Mme Jonesky of Gee's Court.
	etc.

(note that several vectors can run together)
(the facing page should be left blank for notes on eventual musical realizations).

Spare time activity for orchestra members: each member should work on the construction of a unique mechanical musical, electronic or other instrument.

APPENDICES

Appendix 1   *Popular Classics*
Particles from: Beethoven, *Pastoral Symphony*
Mozart, *Eine Kleine Nachtmusik*
Rachmaninov, *Second Piano Concerto*
J.S. Bach, *Sheep may safely graze*
Cage, *Piano Concert*
Brahms, *Requiem*
Schoenberg, *Pierrot Lunaire*
etc.
(blank pages for additions)

Appendix 2   *Improvisation Rites from the book 'Nature Study Notes'*
(two examples must suffice)
1 Initiation of the pulse
Continuation of the pulse
Deviation by means of accentuation, decoration, contradiction.

HOWARD SKEMPTON

14 All seated loosely in a circle, each player shall write or draw on each of the ten fingernails of the player on his left.

No action or sound should be made by a player after his fingernails have received this writing or drawing, other than music.

Closing rite: each player shall erase the marks from the fingernails of another player. Your participation in the music ceases when when the marks have been erased from your fingernails.

(Groups of two or more late-comers may use the same rite to join in an improvisation that is already in progress.)

RICHARD REASON

(blank page for additions)

Appendix 3   *List of compositions*
Lamonte Young, *Poem*
Von Biel, *World* II
Terry Riley, *in C*
Christopher Hobbs, *Voicepiece*
Stockhausen, *Aus den Sieben Tagen*
Wolff, *Play*
Cage, *Variation VI*
etc.
(blank pages for additions)

Appendix 4   *Special Projects and supplementary material*
(blank pages)

At the time of going to press the orchestra has 60 members. More are welcome. A meeting to confirm draft constitution and initiate training should precede the summer recess. Projected inaugural concert: November 1969.

Treatise Handbook

published by Edition Peters (Hinrichsen Edition Ltd), 1971

Contents:

[Editor's note: The following excludes Bun No. 2 (Chamber Orchestra) and Volo Solo]

Introduction

I wrote *Treatise* with the definite intention that it should stand entirely on its own, without any form of introduction or instruction to mislead prospective performers into the slavish practice of 'doing what they are told'. So it is with great reluctance – once having achieved, by some fluke, the 'cleanest' publication it were possible to imagine – that I have let myself be persuaded to collect these obscure and, where not obscure, uninteresting remarks into publishable form.

The temptations to explain why there is no explanation and offer instructions on how to cope with the lack of instructions hold no attraction. However, the years of work on *Treatise* have furnished me with a fund of experience obviously distinct from the experience embodied in the score itself. And this fund continues to accumulate, since my experience of and with the piece is by no means completed with the completion of the score; so some of the excreta of this fund may as well be made available to those who, because it's published, may shortly wish to be occupied with the score. Possibly some errors and misconceptions may thus be avoided.

To complete the information content of this handbook I must briefly outline the biography of the piece.

Early in 1963, on the basis of an elaborate scheme involving 67 elements, some musical, some graphic, I began sketching what I soon came to regard as my Treatise and pressed quite quickly ahead to what is now page 99. To start with my idea of what the piece was to be was so sketchy as to be completely inarticulate; later, in Buffalo in November 1966 I felt it necessary to completely re-compose the first 44 pages. In the summer of 1963 I put pages 45-51,57-62, 75-79 into fair copy, using a much larger format than the one I finally decided on. The apparent musicality of page 99 seemed a stumbling block that impeded my way for some time to come. My next decisive action on the piece was in December 1964 when I put seven separate pages into freehand fair copy using the format that the piece now appears in. These pages were 53, 64, 74, 89, 93, 96/7 (as one page), 99. I quickly decided against freehand drawing for the finished score. In Rome in the first months of 1965 I pushed ahead to page 143, putting it into fair copy as I went along, with the exception of the 'black pages' which I did not finalise until much later (?Feb. 1966). In England in the second half of 1965 I worked on redrawing in the new format the first passages I had copied out (45-51,57-62, 75-79) as well as reworking the intervening material and drawing it in fair copy. When I came to Buffalo in October 1966 I thus had the score complete and continuous from 45-143.

By this time the fluency of my draughtsmanship had increased and my conception of the piece was expanding. I re-appraised the schematic material that I had yet to compose and made substitutions for some of the elements that had not yet come into play. For instance: I had originally planned to work with solid black ellipsoids towards the end of the piece; now I substituted either the idea of melodic presentation or the tree form that features prominently towards the end (at this point I cannot remember which of these two took the place of the ellipsoids). I had become more and more strongly aware of the structure's adaptability to my desires since passages like 114-116 and 122-126, and especially from the experience of reworking 1-44. In the final 50 pages I exploited this adaptability to the full even to the point of activating the (originally passive and merely pause-counting) numbers. These last 50 pages were written in the early months of 1967 in Buffalo.

After this exposition it hardly seems necessary to excuse the fact that many of the verbal notes written while working on the piece at different stages are likely to be mutually contradictory. If they are not it is not my fault. I have made no attempt to clean them up with a view to consistency.

One item weighs against my general reluctance in connection with this handbook, and that is the opportunity to print *Volo Solo*, which I find a useful piece, full of sweet airs, and now I come to think of it that may be the reason European publishers have so consistently sneezed at it.

The analytical article that follows *Volo Solo* was written in Rome shortly after the completion of that piece.

Two years have elapsed since the foregoing was written. I have taken advantage of this delay in publication to include some new material, in particular the lecture on improvisation. Not that I now consider *Treatise* 'improvisatory' any more than I did while writing it. But it does seem (using hindsight) to have pointed in the direction of improvisation. A square musician (like myself) might use *Treatise* as a path to the ocean of spontaneity. Whether it will equip him for survival in that ocean is another question altogether. The lecture on improvisation represents an initial survey based on a thin veneer of experience.

9.2.70.

Treatise: Working Notes

6th Feb '63
A composer who hears sounds will try to find a notation for sounds. One who has ideas will find one that expresses his ideas, leaving their interpretation free, in confidence that his ideas have been accurately and concisely notated.

8th Feb '63
Notation is a way of making people move. If you lack others, like aggression or persuasion. The notation *should* do it. This is the most rewarding aspect of work on a notation. Trouble is: just as you find your sounds are too alien, intended 'for a different culture', you make the same discovery about your beautiful notation: no one is willing to understand it. No one moves.

14th March '63
I do not suggest that the art of composition is really a science of measurement and precision. I do think that any work demands precision of judgment, otherwise it will blow away. It is precision that illuminates (Confucius (Pound): "The sun's lance falling on the precise spot verbally"). This clarity is joy, however much it may suit our temperaments to continue rolling in the mud.

is all right if it is exactly what you want (although how interesting is it to want exactly that? Well, that depends on how badly you want it). But it is bad if it is a confession of failure. And that's the point; where is the difference located? Certainly not in the squiggle. Hence for you, dear listener, there is no difference whatever. (Which is why I can never turn to you for advice).

'63
(Written in the score) NB the sound should be a picture of the score, not vice versa.

'63
Interpreter! Remember that no meaning is as yet attached to the symbols. They are however to be interpreted in the context of their role in the whole. Distinguish symbols that enclose space (circle, etc.); those that have a characteristic feature. What symbols are for sounding and what for orientation. Example: the horizontal central bar is the main and most constant orientation; what happens where it ceases (or bends)? Do you go out of tune (e.g.)?

15th May '63

In connection with Frege's *Foundations of Arithmetic*: "Symbols are not empty simply because not meaning anything with which we can be acquainted". This reassurance is disqualified; he means it in the sense that one cannot be acquainted with – for example – 3. Frege would never have considered finishing the sentence with a full stop after 'anything'. If anybody *had* written it, intending a reference to some super-imagery or Jungian idea evoking a response only in the unconscious, Frege would have applied his sarcastic "Mysterious power of words devoid of thought" and his confident "No one will expect any sense to emerge from empty symbols".

May '63

The test: devote time not to writing on in the treatise, but studying it and trying to realise what exactly is at work in it. *How* does it keep my imagination at work? What actually am I manipulating in the way of material? Do I assume some material that is not explicit (e.g., real sounds)?

May '63

Intrapolation from the universal shapes of geometry, etc. to the idiosyncratic musical signs: a disturbing element is the signs that are not intrapolated in this way. *p f* 𝄞 𝄢 in particular. These pre-formed symbols have no place in (my) netz of stave lines. How to get rid of them is the problem, since they are important indices for many of the basic elements.

26th May '63

The dot-dash relationship of events and happenings. Events: something short, compact, homogeneous that we experience as complete (though we may only experience a part of it in fact) and as one thing. Happenings: something that continues, the end is not legible in the beginning. Two sets of parameters: event parameters and happening parameters.

14th June 63

Visual communications. How to develop a visual presentation through logic. How to show continuity in a diagram; in a series of stages, or by *reading* left to right, etc. In *Treatise*, the same problem: which lines are happening continuously, and which are instantaneous events; where to set the borderline? This should be solved. Otherwise work lapses into constant evasions. If one interpretation proves troublesome or unsatisfactory we slip into another; but this must be watched and conscious.

June '63

The grid. Like walking in a thick fog: suddenly we find a thread across the path, catch it and follow it – isn't it already an orientation, before we discover that it leads us up/down, to warmer/colder regions, in straight line or curve? The fact that we follow it makes it an orientation? But Frege: "being thought is a completely different thing from being true" (But Burroughs: "What do you mean is it true? It's only the latest bulletin").

Perhaps finally the merit of *Treatise* will depend on its geometrical resolution! However. it can certainly never be interesting as *geometry* (I have neither the ability nor the desire to make it so).

June '63
A concept, in Frege's sense, defines limits so that one can say with authority whether or not something falls under it. The signs of *Autumn '60* should be regarded in this way. If the sign for tremolo occurs it should be possible to hear off each musician separately and say 'tremolo' or 'not-tremolo' with confidence. Only with this sort of properly decisive interpretation of the signs, are the signs justified as the material of the piece. Otherwise the signs are merely an excuse (for self-expression and random improvisation).

Back to *Treatise*. In the case of *Treatise* a line or dot is certainly an immediate orientation as much as the thread in the fog. For immediately it stands in relation to the thick central stave line, which would correspond in some way to the track made by the man walking. This 'subject line' is essential; any other reference, such as page size, would be totally arbitrary. Note the disconcerting effect of broken staves in *Winter Music*.

19th July '63
Diagrammatic writing: the aim is to make it so that a sign can only follow appropriately after another sign. (This sentence expresses it badly. A sign that is inappropriate simply will not fit, physically – that is the aim.) In *Treatise* a sign has to be made appropriate to its context. Like words that exist as various parts of speech: according to its position in the grammar you have to select the appropriate form of the word.

July '63
Some principles, positive and negative, to govern interpretation. Remember that space does *not* correspond literally to time. The distance to the sun does not correspond irrevocably to x light-years or months. The time taken does not depend only on speed; it depends on the route. Perhaps when interpreting it will be possible to select some lines as 'time-lines'. Symbols or groups can then be grouped immediately and as a whole and placed in relation to some such time-line. Obviously a circle need not have the duration of its diameter. It may refer to something quite outside the flow of music or sound. It might correspond to some such mark as 'Tuba' or 'espressivo', i.e., as a determinant of running action.

Bear in mind that parts of the score may be devoid of direct musical relevance. (Like the composer David Tudor mentioned whose scores were interspersed with obscene poems for the interpreter to read – to himself). Whatever is seen in this way can be understood as 'influences' on the performance.

Just as the perfect geometrical forms are subjected in the score to destruction and distortion, corresponding perfect forms can be sought in sound (octaves and simultaneous attacks are two leads that spring to mind) and these destroyed or distorted. (E.g. a circle with an opening might be read as an open fifth with major and minor thirds trilling).

Thus, just as space does not correspond to time (despite the fact that the score is read from left to right, in fact here as in speech or writing) so the vertical space does not necessarily have a constant correspondence in pitch. A set of nine parallel lines at equal spacing may correspond in pitch to notes as diverse as the nine in Wolff's For Pianist 1, or to nine instruments of which two are brass, three are woodwind, four stringed, etc., etc.

And yet, where the score becomes fanciful or whimsical so too should the music?

The score must govern the music. It must have authority, and not merely be an arbitrary jumping off point for improvisation, with no internal consistency.

The numbers are included at the pauses for the reason that: any act or facet of the conception or composition of the score may have relevance for an interpretation. (In this sense Messiaen writes over a figure *battements du coeur* etc., because this was *in fact* the reference, and it *might* be of some help to an interpreter). It is the *fact* that there were 34 blank spaces before the first sign put in an appearance.

28th Sept '63
In the *Treatise* the score seems not representational. No rules of representation. Except the central line represents perhaps the performer or a single line of thought...

Somehow all these terms seem needy and not relevant. What is the relevant way of speaking about *Treatise*? What are the terms? Can one really say anything explicit about it?

Perhaps I should be more grammatical about writing the score; employ vertical and horizontal connectives ... To connect what? When I am tempted to use objects it is most unsatisfactory of all.

'An articulated network' describes better what I am working on. Not a discussion of (representing) objects. Work with your hands on the material (the netting); don't try and set up grammatical rules which you will only ignore in the next page.
    Concentrate on: the score must present something decisive and authoritative – almost dogmatic. Subtleties of design must be precise.

30th Sept '63

Reference. 'What is the reference of the network?' This is meaningless. Something – things – should be referable to the network.

'Make a sound; and then work on this sound with the aid of the Netz. *Let* the Netz work on the sound'. This *could* be a simple piece. But *Treatise* is not *this* simple piece.

Oct '63

Map projection analogy. Why am I not able to see why it is stupid to make a projection of a projection? Isn't it obvious that if one projection is not suitable, you should make another one, starting from scratch? By distorting the gridlines around Australia you can get any shape; by distorting the stave lines around a triad you can get any chord. Which is not interesting unless you have something particular in view (?). What do I have in view?

Blank – I give up ('Yes, my eyes are closed').

(What makes this live is the distortion of the 'any' chord. The way in which it has derived from the triad. 'Any chord' is nothing particular, but if it bears the marks of a distortion it has *that* character. This makes work on *Treatise* alive – the various interfering forces distorting and changing everything. The way the elements act on each other – it is like chemical processes: acid bites, circles roll and drag, and bend the stave lines of 'musical space'.)

However, if the grid lines are so distorted as to make Australia a perfect square, then in some way the shape of the grid-lines represents the shape of Australia – as though Australia could in some way be separated from its shape (Why should this be necessary?).

Fig 1

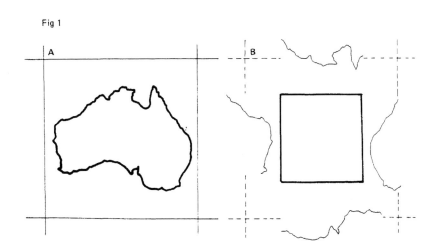

In similar fashion the dots of Cage's *Variations 1* are stretched by the determination lines into sound. The lines are a manipulation of musical space. How did he do it? Musical space was his material. How? Grid-lines are not material.

The altered grid-lines in B now present a disintegrated mirror image of the *outline* of Australia (enclosing no space). The space is **enclosed** by the square that Australia has become. To attempt this on a map of the world would present serious problems. It is only possible when concentrating on a single object (event). By treating certain grid-lines as the property of that object. (E.g. the line between Australia and New Guinea cannot mirror both coastlines.)

   It is impossible for me to abandon this piece (Rzewski's suggestion). As simply an arrangement of the 67 elements it is purely decorative. It must represent a true statement about a way of making music. Perhaps things will be made clearer by concentrating on the references of the elements. But …

These cannot refer until they exist in combination.

In Fig 2, A does not refer. Add 𝄞 (B) and it refers to a particular area of musical space. But suppose you do not add 𝄞 but a small rectangle (C). What is the reference now? My thought – and this is what I want.

But it seems to refer more to my eye and hand and pen (so what? these represent my thought). The various 'empty symbols' must be combined with *intention*, with something in view. Can I make empty symbols significant intuitively?

But Fig 2C is interesting. The rectangle now marks out a limited space for the insertion of a meaning index. A configuration waiting for sense (or life). E.g. either D or E (𝄞 placed at will within the rectangle), etc. etc. Like: the *Art of Fugue* makes no less sense for the fact that it is waiting for someone to write 'string quartet' or 'organ' at the front.

The conflicts in the composition arise from the non-homogeneity of the list of elements. (From this also arise the intuitive 'content' of the piece. Every day we have to create order in a non-homogeneous host of circumstances). This gives me a certain satisfaction – that the difficulties that I experience in writing the piece are of the same kind as those I experience in the flow of e.g., my emotional life.

Not quite right. I do not experience any difficulty at all in writing the piece, but in my attitude to what I have written and have still to write. As though it was a person I was living with, and was obliged to fathom to some extent for the sake of daily peace of mind, etc. No. It is not an obligation, it is my *desire* to fathom it out. "Love demands understanding".

Next point: whether or not the empty stave underneath is right. As being suggestive for beginners, it could be part of the score. But really the score itself is the empty stave on which the experienced performer should write.

Oct '63

Rzewski's first comment, that the score is ideal for measuring, is quite wrong. The score was drawn on a grid, and therefore measuring will produce uniform and boring results (it will just tell you what measurements were used in drawing the score) (which implies that at the moment I am thinking that the interpreter should not be concerned with analysis). A measurement is made once and for all. It is stupid to repeat the process – remember playing *Refrain* with Karlheinz constantly re-measuring the dynamics. If the proportions were judged by eye it would be different – and interpretative measurement could then be revealing. Well, generally speaking the angles in *Treatise* were drawn by eye (not measured, so far), so measurers can attach themselves to these.

Dec '63

A practical attempt. Take the enclosed spaces and divide them into the following categories: triangles, circles, circle derivatives (not very many), squares, square derivatives (horizontal and vertical rectangles), irregular enclosures. Musical categories can be matched up with these: triads, trills, irregular tremolos, periodicities, deviating periodicities, clusters that disintegrate in the direction of whatever shape is closest. Dynamics for all shapes can be determined thus: horizontal dimension gives the degree of loudness; vertical dimension gives the degree of dynamic contrast (this works well with most figures, especially circles, because the lower the dynamic the lower the contrast. Vertical rectangles will present problems, as they demand low dynamics with high degree of contrast).

(To a person who thinks the piece is a code to which the key is missing, what I am doing will look like providing a key. Actually I am simply interpreting. The piece is an abstract work of design, to which meanings have to be attached such that the design holds good).

Triangles (triads) generally occur with at least one side horizontal or vertical. If a triangle hangs from a horizontal we can call it top orientated, if it stands on a horizontal, bottom orientated; similarly with verticals: left orientated or right orientated. These orientation lines can define properties of the triads, as follows:

left-orientated – all three elements have equal dynamics,
top-orientated – all three elements have equal duration,
right-orientated – the three elements span two equal intervals,
bottom-orientated – all three elements are in the same register.

If a triangle has both a horizontal and a vertical side then the triad has two constants (two combinations of constants cannot occur: equal durations in the same register, and equal dynamics with equal intervals).

Every triangle can now be seen in relation to these orientation lines. They form a rectangle whose dimensions depend on the triangle. Triangles with two orientated sides or no orientated sides form complete rectangles; those with one orientated side form open-ended rectangles (see fig 3). The deviation of the sides of the triangle from the sides of the rectangle can then be used to determine the deviation from the constant of the various aspects of the triad. Depending on whether the angles are obtuse or acute these deviations can occur either outside or inside the rectangle. This distinction can be interpreted as indicating a deviation in the triad either at the point of attack or after the attack. (A deviation of duration at the point of attack could mean arpeggiation; deviation of register after the attack could mean that by means of harmonics the notes of a triad resonate in different registers after the attack, to take two slightly difficult cases). In the cases of double orientated and non orientated triangles it will be found that one side (in the former case the non orientated side, in the latter it can be anyone of the sides) has a double reference – it indicates a deviation from two constants. In the case of a single orientated triangle (open-ended rectangles) one aspect of the triad is undetermined (this makes it possible for the combinations to occur that were referred to as impossible above).

Fig 3

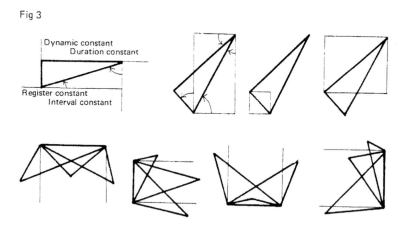

Dec '63
Colouring *Treatise*. Two quite different uses of colour: to clarify and to express.
Colouring *Treatise*, is one trying to clarify the notation, the design of the piece? Does it need clarification? What is there to explain? That such and such elements are combined in such and such ways?
Surely it is more as though one were trying to express the (subjective) effect that the design has on one. And one is trying to express this effect *back through* the design.

I should try and invent a concrete case: the design affects me in such and such a way, and I use it in such and such a way to express this affect that it has on me, etc., etc. The fact that this idea makes me feel tired is suspicious. Cannot the design simply stand on its own, and then I just choose to make music *besides*?

Because: psychologically the existence of the piece is fully explained by the situation of a composer who is not in a position to make music. The question to be put: 'If he cannot make music (circumstances do not allow) what *can* he make? The answer: *Treatise*.

What it is, is clear: the fusion of the graphic material of two professions. The difficult question is, what is our attitude to it? What are we to do with it? The only way to be rid of it is to finish it.

3rd Jan '64
Once you have written music – not just dreamed it but actually committed it to paper – and not great music by any means, you can never be the same again, even if you never write another note. Once you know what it is like to move in that sphere, you always want to return there. The *Treatise* is almost like a document or movie of that sphere – a travelogue of the land of composition. A real piece of music of course is *not* a document from the sphere of activity in which music is written, it is 'just' a piece of music, which all lovers of music can understand. *Treatise* tells *what it is like* to manipulate sounds in composition. Sounds-ideas; reading *Treatise* is a twilight experience where the two cannot be clearly distinguished.

26th June '64 (Florence)
Withdrawal symptoms. The notation is more important than the sound. Not the exactitude and success with which a notation notates a sound; but the musicalness of the notation in its notating.

28th June '64
Treatise. There is a great difference between: a) doing anything you like and at the same time reading the notations, and b) reading the notations and trying to translate them into action. Of course you can let the score work on previously given material, but you must have it work *actively*.

19th Sept '64
Bun for Orchestra: "...for all those who give up halfway, the fainthearted, the soft, those who comfort their souls with flummery *about* the soul and who feed it – because the intellect allegedly gives it stones instead of bread – on religious, philosophic and fictitious emotions, which are like buns soaked in milk". (Musil) This bun is a *stone* bun soaked in milk.

3rd Nov. '64
Making orchestra transcription of *Treatise* (for instance) is not undertaken for the

sake of public recognition, but simply surrendering to the vulgar desire to hear what I imagine. The technique of performance is losing its hold on me (I mean 'the way music is made' as a kind of philosophical enquiry). I remember with gratitude how a similar preoccupation with systems of notation relaxed its grip on me some time ago. Not that I lost interest; simply the threat of an obsession was removed.

5th Feb '65
Treatise. Watch for the laughs! (in re being with 7 Hungarians telling funny stories and finding that I knew where to laugh).

14th Feb '65
In work such as Bussotti's a merely profane interest is aroused (purely aesthetic?). Therefore, asked what all those squiggles in *Treatise* mean, I might reasonably answer: a) that it is very complicated to explain, and explanations are of dubious value, and b) that in any case it is secret.

21st Feb '65
Wittgenstein: "And if e.g. you play a game you hold by its rules. And it is an interesting fact that people set up rules for pleasure, and then hold by them".

11th March '65
Treatise: What is it? Well, it's a vertebrate...

22nd Nov '66
Performance advice. Divide the musicians into those involved in dot events (percussionists and pianists?) and those involved in line events. Dot events to be exclusively soft.

20th Jan '67
Reflection before a performance. A musical score is a logical construct inserted into the mess of potential sounds that permeate this planet and its atmosphere. That puts Beethoven and the rest in perspective!

Acknowledgements

Acknowledgements to those who gave me help and encouragement while working on *Treatise*.

Kurt Schwertsik ("Well, it's certainly a composition")

Giuseppe Chiari ("Il tuo *Treatise* e importantissimo")

Frederick Rzewski ("Why don't you just abandon it?")

Robin Page (for his continuous enthusiasm, waning only when the piece was complete)

Stella ("You must be a genius or something")

Andrew Porter

The Arts Council of Great Britain, for a grant to enable me to complete the composition

Ed Budowski, for his alacrity in publishing the work

Treatise: Résumé of pre-publication performances.

June '64
On the terrace of the Forte Belvedere, Florence (semi open air) pp 57 – 60 and 75 – 79 were played as two separate sections lasting 1½ and 4 minutes. Performers were Frederic Rzewski (noises from piano and other sources), Mauricio Kagel (reading aloud), Italo Gomez (cello), Sylvano Bussotti (percussion) and the composer (whistles).

The concert was organized by Giuseppe Chiari and the Gruppo Settanta. Rzewski played the central line (one of the few times the centre line has been interpreted) as continuous sound. At each break in the line he would start a new sound. This served as orientation for the other players, who with the exception of Kagel were also concerned with limited aspects of the score. Kagel insisted on his 'freedom'.

May '65
Pages 89-106 were performed at Walthamstow Forest Technical College (London). Duration 30 minutes approx. Other items in the programme were LaMonte Young's *Poem*, Michael von Biel's *World 2* and my own *Solo with Accompaniment*. Performers were John White (tuba), Roger Smalley (piano), John Tilbury (piano) David Bedford (accordion), Clem Adelman (saxophone) and the composer (guitar and conductor). On this occasion John White set the precedent for "perverse" interpretation by reading ascending lines as descending intervals. The concert was announced in the Financial Times with the following text by the composer:

EXPERIMENTAL MUSIC, by Cornelius Cardew

In Walthamstow tomorrow afternoon at 2.20 a concert of Experimental Music is to take place. It is the latest in a long straggling series of such concerts in this country. It is a sign that the seed of a new kind of musical life planted here by the American composer, John Cage, in 1956 is still growing, albeit in rather out-of-the-way places.

Generation Music 1 was the title given by John Tilbury and me to our first concert of Experimental Music at the Conway Hall in January, 1960. Since then we have continued to propagate this music with occasional encouragement from institutions (a concert at the Mermaid Theatre in 1961, part of a concert at the American Embassy in January 1964, under the auspices of the Park Lane Group and a concert at the ICA in December, 1964). Visitors from abroad have provided additional stimulus, for instance, the German composer Michael von Biel personally financed a Wigmore Hall concert in June, 1962.

This amount of concert experience has brought at least one fact to our attention, namely that this music is not really "concert music" and hence not readily digestible by the Concert public. The concert at the ICA included works by seven composers all radically different from one another and each of whom provided more food for listening and thought than could easily be assimilated in a single evening. The audience's neurotic response is thus explained: no sooner had they begun to get their teeth into one set of problems and sensations, then a completely different set would be set before them.

In many of these compositions no particular sounds are specified. And obviously where no sound is specified, any sound may occur: in other words, many of these pieces are capable of generating an unlimited amount of action within the field delimited by the composition, or along the lines laid down by the composition. This means that their best chance of creating understanding in an audience is to expand freely in an unlimited amount of time. And since different performances of the same piece can be very different in character (if different musicians are performing, for example) each piece should be performed a number of times.

The theatre situation seems the only possibility for giving an adequate representation of such pieces. For a start, a repertoire of 20 compositions could be booked for a two month season at a London theatre, each composition being given three performances spaced out over two months

In Walthamstow the situation is very different. The boardroom of the South West Essex Technical College and School of Art has been made available to John Tilbury, who holds a Liberal Studies lecturing post at the College, and endeavours to initiate day release carpenter's, plumbers' and joiners' apprentices into the mysteries of Experimental Music. His job is to de-solemnise the word music which is heartily abhorred by the majority of his students. To this end he has invited David Bedford (melodica and other sound producing media), John White (tuba), Roger Smalley (piano), Clem Adelman (tenor sax), and myself to play a program of works by Cage, von Biel, LaMonte Young and myself.

The general thesis of this programme is that music is not the same as sounds (a deep proposition that will probably never be fully clarified), that sounds (any sounds) become music if they are made or used by a musician, and that sounds are a feature of musical performance, but not a feature of musical composition. For example, my own work, *Treatise* is a continuous weaving and combining of a host of graphic elements (of which only a few are recognizably related to musical symbols) into a long visual composition, the meaning of which in terms of sounds is not specified in any way.

Any number of musicians using any media are free to participate in a "reading" of this score (it is written from left to right and "treats" of its graphic subject matter in exhaustive "arguments"), and each is free to interpret it in his own way. Any rigidity of interpretation is automatically thwarted by the confluence of different personalities.

I, as the composer, have no idea how the piece will sound in performance. And why should I? Our *Great Musical Heritage* is not in the immutable grooves of the thousands of gramophone records transmitting to us the great voices of the past. It is the enrichment of something primitive that we all carry around inside us: our living response to present experience.

Sept '65
pp 45 – 64,74, 89 –127 were performed at the Theatre Royal, Stratford (London). *Treatise* was the only musical item on the programme, which was organized by Mark Boyle for the Institute of Contemporary Arts. Duration was 40 minutes approx. Performers: John Tilbury (piano), the composer (cello), Kurt Schwertsik (horn), John Surman (saxophone), Keith Rowe (electric guitar). Peter Greenham conducted.

This was the first performance in which the pauses (numbers) were read as repeated chords. Briefly, the system is this: at each number each performer selects a note at random and plays it as softly as possible, repeating it as often as the number indicates and holding each repetition for a number of seconds corresponding to the number of repetitions. For example: 5 equals five repetitions of the same chord each lasting 5 seconds (the repetitions are coordinated by the conductor). The number 1 is regarded simply as a silence.

Three rehearsals preceded this performance, and Schwertsik made the ominous remark 'The more you say about it the more sense it makes'. Page 74 was coordinated in detail as a piece on its own, each of the five players associating himself with one of the lines of the five line system the page is based on. Thus the short line at the beginning rises from position 3 to position 2, and in the interpretation a phrase begun by musician 3 is completed by musician 2. Etc. Also in this performance the general principle was initiated of regarding distance away from the centre line as being indicative of loudness (the centre line representing silence).

Oct '65
A solo reading of pp 107 – 126 at Watford Institute of Technology (London). In the first half of the programme I played a solo version of Stockhausen's *Plus-Minus*, and I used the same instrumentarium for *Treatise*: piano, gong, three transistor radios. Duration approx. 20 minutes.

Here for the first time I regarded the five line system as a chord which progresses according to certain rules linked with angles made by the lines (see note for 4 trombones below). Small enclosed spaces connected with the five lines I interpreted as preparations inserted in the relevant strings of the piano. The gong was associated with squares in the score, and the radios with circles.

15th Jan '66
BBC recording of pp 107 – 126 for the series *Composer's Portrait*. Duration 20

minutes approx. This performance was largely based on the performance of October 65. Musicians taking part were John White (trombone), John Tilbury (piano), David Bedford (accordion), Keith Rowe (electric guitar), Peter Greenham (Hammond organ) and the composer (piano, gong and radios). The broadcast was preceded by the following text:

A composer's portrait is his Music. So I decided that this programme should consist mainly of music. Quite to what extent this music is mine is a point I will come back to in a minute. First I would like to say something about the piece itself, whose name is *Treatise* – T-R-E-A-T-I-S-E.

The idea of writing *Treatise* came to me at a time when I was working as a graphic designer in a publisher's office. While there I came to be occupied more and more with designing diagrams and charts and in the course of this work I became aware of the potential eloquence of simple black lines in a diagram. Thin, thick, curving, broken, and then the varying tones of grey made up of equally spaced parallel lines, and then the type numbers, words, short sentences like ornate, literary, art-nouveauish visual interlopers in the purely graphic context of the diagram. Recently, working on the performance we are going to do now, it has struck me that the use of a wireless set as a musical instrument is analogous to the appearance of type on a diagram. It is a pre-processed, fully fashioned element in amongst a whole lot of raw material.

Actually the score of *Treatise* does not contain any type. It is a score consisting entirely of lines and shapes – it contains no sounds, no directions to putative performers. It is still incomplete – about 80 pages exist, of which we will be playing a batch of 19. When it is finished it will be about 200 pages long – 200 pages of lines and shapes clustered around a strong, almost continuous central line, which can be imagined as the life-line of the reader, his centre, around which all manner of activity takes place. Some of the graphic material is actually musical in origin – for instance, the five line musical stave is constantly in evidence in all shapes and sizes but it is always ambiguous. Nevertheless, it is my contention that an instrumentalist who reads through 200 pages of such material will inevitably find himself forming musical associations, and these will form the basis of his interpretation.

Such associations belong of course to the musician who has them, and that is why I hesitated at the beginning to talk of the sounding music as *my* music. What I hope is that in playing this piece each musician will give of his *own* music– he will give it as his response to *my* music, which is the score itself.

This performance was re-broadcast on 8th. Feb. 1970, preceded by the following text:

I now regard *Treatise* as a transition between my early preoccupation with problems of music notation and my present concerns – improvisation and a musical life. It was a strenuous transition; I worked on the piece for five years, not knowing where it would lead, and came out of it more lost than when I went in, and desperately scanning the horizon for the next mountain range.

However I would have been a great deal loster if it hadn't been for the performance of January 1966, the tape of which you will hear in a minute. This was one of the first occasions on which I worked with Keith Rowe, who bore more or less the same relation to the electric guitar as David Tudor did to the piano (I put that in the past tense because by no stretch of the imagination could you now call them guitarist or pianist respectively).

Keith Rowe, together with Lou Gare, Eddie Prévost and Laurence Sheaff had at that time already begun their *AMM* weekly improvisation meetings, which I joined shortly after this. Joining *AMM* was the turning point, both in the composition of *Treatise* and in everything I have thought about music up to now. Before that, *Treatise* had been an elaborate attempt at graphic notation of music; after that time it became simply graphic music (which I can only define as a graphic score that produces in the reader, without any sound, something analogous to the experience of music), a network of nameless lines and spaces pursuing their own geometry untethered to themes and modulations, 12 note series and their transformations, the rules or laws of musical composition and all the other figments of the musicological imagination.

Up to the time of this performance, improvisation had always terrified me; I thought it must be something like composing, but accelerated a million times, a feat of which I knew I was incapable. With the *AMM* improvisers I discovered that anyone can play, me too, provided, as a Chinese musician of the 16th century put it, "the thoughts are serious, the mind peaceful and the will resolute", and what comes out in such play is vital and direct, rather than a translation or interpretation of intellect, attitude, notation, inspiration or what have you.

Well, scrutinise any point closely enough and you are liable to see it as a turning point, in relation to which everything else is either before or after – and this tells us something about the activity of scrutinising, but very little about music. Which is my devious way of saying that what you are going to hear is music, not a turning point, and the players of the music are John White, David Bedford, John Tilbury, Keith Rowe, Peter Greenham and myself. We played a section of about 20 pages occurring somewhere towards the middle of the 193 page score. These 20 pages were at that time the most recent instalment; the rest of the score was still to be written.

19th February '66
At the American Artists' Centre in Paris we performed pages 89-142 taking 40 minutes approx. Performers were John Tilbury, David Bedford and the composer. This was the first reading to include the 'black pages' (black areas were regarded as melody) and the first public performance that 'went astray' (disconcertingly Tilbury

was two pages behind most of the time). *Treatise* was preceded by *Volo Solo* on piano and prepared piano and followed by a simultaneous performance of works by George Brecht, Lamonte Young and Michael von Biel.

? February '66

Leeds, England. A reading by circa 15 art students plus Robin Page and the composer of pages 89 –129. A coloured and enlarged score was used (painted by the students during the preceding days) and the (student) conductor moved a baton continuously along it to keep everyone together. Duration 30 minutes approx. Also on the programme were compositions by Cage, George Brecht and LaMonte Young. The following note was written in May '66 to support my application to the Arts Council of Great Britain for a grant to forward me towards the completion of the piece:

Treatise is a graphic score, composed without reference to any system of rules governing the interpretation. It was begun in 1963 and is still incomplete; the hundred pages that are ready at present represent slightly over half the whole piece. The length of the score is the justification for the absence of an interpretative system; the graphic material is treated of in such an exhaustive manner that an interpretation (musical or otherwise) is able to emerge quasi unconsciously in the mind of the reader in the course of reading the score. Any number of musicians with any instruments can take part. Each musician plays from the score, reading it in terms of his individual instrument and inclination. A number of general decisions may be made in advance to hold the performance together, but an improvisatory character is essential to the piece. An appreciation or understanding of the piece in performance should grow in much the same way as the musicians' interpretation. Orientation is slow, in proportion to the length of the piece, but it is spontaneous, since no specific orientation is prescribed.

18th Sept '66

Warsaw Autumn Festival late night concert. We read pages 45 – 88 and took approximately one hour over it. Performers were John Tilbury and Zygmunt Krauze (pianos), David Bedford (accordion) and the composer (cello/conductor). All instruments except accordion were amplified.

Originally a trombone quartet from Sweden were to have taken part in this performance, and with this in mind I wrote the following provisional instruction sheet for them:

All play together wherever the 5 line musical stave appears (agree as to what constitutes an appearance). Each trombonist should appropriate one of the five lines as his particular domain (ideally there should be five trombones, or a way may be found whereby each of the four will interpret one of the four spaces between the lines). In the example below the top line is read by 1st trombone, 2nd line by 2nd

trombone, 4th line by 3rd trombone and bottom line by 4th trombone. Each
trombonist selects a particular note for the first occurrence of the stave. This note
may be articulated in any way, not necessarily as a single held duration
corresponding to the length of the line. Intervallic progression from the original note
can be derived as shown in Fig 4: A means perfect or augmented fourth up; B
means minor or major third up; C means minor or major second up; D means perfect
or augmented fourth down; E means minor or major third down; F means minor or
major second down.

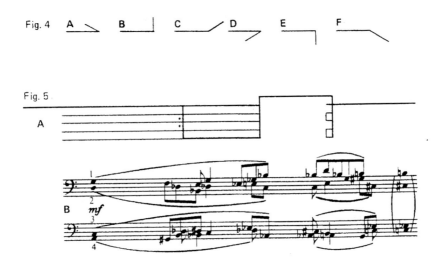

Fig 5 is an example: A is a passage from p 45 of the score: B is a possible realisation
of it. The chord at the beginning of B is arbitrarily selected, the chord in brackets at
the end is used for the commencement of the next occurrence of the 5 line stave.
Generally speaking dynamics should be governed by the spacing of the lines.

In Fig 6, A is soft, B is medium, C is loud. Naturally each trombonist may also select
other material in the piece to associate himself with. But at each occurrence of the 5
line stave the four players should function as a group.

116

17th Dec '66

Albright-Knox Art Gallery in Buffalo NY. Pages 1-20 were read, lasting 20 minutes approx. Performers were Carlos Alsina (Wurlitzer organ), Klaus von Wrochem (violin), Edward Burnham (percussion), Jan Williams (piano), Maryanne Amacher (half share of electric bass), Paul Zonn (clarinet), Jean Dupouy (viola), William Penn (trumpet), Andrew White (sax and electric bass), Makoto Michii (double bass) and the composer (radio/conductor).

The number 34 at the beginning was reduced to 17 and the performance began with 17 pianissimo chords each lasting 17 seconds. Each instrumentalist was concerned with particular configurations in the score. The five line system was interpreted as a progression of five note chords worked out by the composer, played by Alsina, Zonn, Von Wrochem, Michii, Dupouy. Conducting procedure: all instrumentalists besides following whatever beats were given (these were arranged beforehand) were supposed to turn pages in time with the conductor, who was sitting in front and has his score placed so that all could see which page was open. The following note was printed in the programme:

Treatise is a long continuous drawing – in form rather similar to a novel. But it is composed according to musical principles and is intended to serve as a score for musicians to play from. However, indications of sounds, noises and musical relationships do not figure in the score, which is purely graphic (rare exceptions occur when the signs used are *reminiscent* of musical notations – to the professional musician, these appear as lights in the fog, but for the fully indoctrinated reader, they pose knotty problems in musicology). The score does not specify the number or kind of instruments to be used, nor does it provide rules for the interpretation of the graphic material. Each player interprets the score according to his own acumen and sensibility. He may be guided by many things – by the internal structure of the score itself, by his personal experience of music making, by reference to the various traditions growing up around this and other indeterminate works, by the action of the other musicians working on the piece, and – failing these – by conversation with the composer during rehearsal. The general characteristic of the work is given by the title. *Treatise* is an exhaustive investigation or 'treatment' of a number of related topics.

20th Dec '66

Carnegie Recital Hall, New York City. Pages 144, duration 30 minutes approx. Same personnel, method and programme note as preceding performance. The initial number was again changed to 17.

16th Jan '67

Arts Council Drawing Room, London. Pages 107-116, duration 50 mins. Performers: John Tilbury and David Bedford (assisted by Francine Elliott). Performers used watches and allowed 5 minutes per page. The first half of the programme was devoted to *Solo with Accompaniment*.

15th Sept '67
Prague. Quax Ensemble led by Petr Kotik. Performance probably comprised pages
1– 44. Programme details follow:

Quax Ensemble Prague
Music Concert: Sunday, September 15th 1967
4 pm – 7:30 pm
Faculty of Law Student Building
17 October Street
Prague 1.

Performers: Petr Kotik, Jan Hyncica, Pavel Kendelik, Vaclav Zahradnik, Josef Vejvoda
Assistance: Jan Spaleny
Technical Direction: Jan Rendl

PROGRAM:
4:00–4:20 PM Karlheinz Stockhausen: *Plus-Minus*
4:30–5:10 PM Petr Kotik: *Contraband* [live electronic sound]
5:30–7.30 PM Cornelius Cardew: *Treatise*

Single admission: 10 kes,
Available in ticket counters.

8th April '67
Commonwealth Institute, London. Pages 1-193, duration 150 minutes approx.
Performers were Zygmunt Krauze, John Tilbury, David Bedford, John White, Egon
Mayer, John Surman, Lou Gare, Laurence Sheaff, Eddie Prévost, Keith Rowe, Robin
Page. The performance was directed by the composer. Programme note:

Treatise is a continuous graphic score of 193 pages to be read in sequence and from
left to right. It is comparable to a lengthy work of prose treating exhaustively of a
number of topics. In *Treatise* the topics are graphic elements, and an unspecified
number of performers is free to relate to these elements as each sees fit. There are
no rules governing this relationship. No player is told what to play; each has to find
this out for himself by reading the score. Probably this will be the only occasion on
which the work will be read through from beginning to end as a single performance.
In future – as in the past, at various stages of the work's incompletion – sections of it
will be performed, and performers will be free to interpret these sections in greater
detail than will be possible in the present reading. The function of the whole is to
establish the language so that each detail can become clear and explicit.

The work is played without a break; listeners requiring an interval should take one at
their discretion.

Conducting procedure was the same as for the performance of 17th Dec '66. But this time the 34 was left intact at the opening. The 34 repeated chords each lasting 34 seconds accounted for about 20 minutes of the performance. Again the various aspects of the graphic score were allocated to the various players, some of them working in pairs, Robin Page was to read the 'representational' elements in the score (those that are reminiscent of real life objects) as the basis for his visual interpretation, Rowe and Sheaff read straight lines, the former concentrating on horizontals, the latter on verticals. Mayer read freehand lines. And so on. This was a very strenuous performance; as John White remarked afterwards: "It was a music lesson". Only in the last two pages did the tension finally relax (at least in me). From amongst the various sustaining sounds music seemed to be issuing gently from some unspecifiable source. As though the duration of the performance had been devoted to clearing, ploughing and planting an expanse of desolate land, and only in the last few minutes did the first green shoots begin to show, I felt that with *Treatise* behind us we were at last in the land of music.

This was the first in a series of four concerts devoted to Experimental Music sponsored by the Arts Council of Great Britain and Michael White. The remaining concerts were devoted to Music for Four Pianos (Terry Riley, Earle Brown, Cage and Feldman); Experimental Works (LaMonte Young, George Brecht, Cage and Ichiyanagi) and Improvised Music (*AMM*).

19th May '67
York University (England). This performance was billed as a public rehearsal in the afternoon followed by a concert in the evening. We used the two stretches of approx. 2 hours each to read the entire score (with a break of one hour in the middle) Performers were Ranulf Glanville, Keith Rowe, Robin Page, John Tilbury, John White and the composer. Each player read the score in his own time, choosing his material independently of the others. The numbers were counted subjectively and generally soundlessly – no more repeated chords. No co-ordination was attempted.

For my own part (played on cello and amplified assorted circles) I decided that the most interesting things to interpret were those that had not been composed. Thus on the cello I read irregular enclosed spaces having 20 sides or more (10 sides or more if extending over 2 pages and 5 sides or more if extending over 3 pages or more): these I read as melodic phrases, curving sides as glissandi and distance away from the centre line indicating dynamics (pitches free). The amplified circles I used for black areas having 20 sides or more (10 or more if over 2 pages, etc. as before). In the pages where black areas occur I interpreted the bold central line as constituting a black area. For the numbers I used an abacus to count off environmental sounds. Material not relating to my own part I read as relating to the music being produced by the other musicians. This was a satisfying performance.

On the Role of the Instructions in the Interpretation of Indeterminate Music

The writing down of music is in process of disintegrating. In the past the notation of music was dependent on flexible conventions and a performer could use these to correct the tendencies of an aural tradition. In other words: by going back to study the notation of a piece a prospective interpreter could verify whether or not a certain popularisation by a famous virtuoso was justifiable. In the notation of music today two tendencies are apparent: 1) to so reduce the flexibility of the conventions that they become virtually inflexible (this means that and nothing else), and 2) to so increase the flexibility of the conventions that they in fact become non-conventional (this may mean this, that or the other, and not necessarily any of these). This is a simplification, and the examples I propose to discuss in this text are intended to show the complex situations that can arise with respect to pieces of music that are really delightfully simple and refreshingly primitive. (Everyone knows the anguish undergone by people who in the end come out with some gloriously simple remark like 'There is no other God but me' or *Cogito ergo sum*.

I propose to use my own *Volo Solo* as an example to demonstrate the 'normal' situation encountered in indeterminate music, i.e. that there are certain notations, and then certain instructions about how these notations are to be read or understood. My other example will be LaMonte Young's *X* (any integer) *for Henry Flynt*, a remarkable case of a piece that consists of no notations, and performing instructions that no one can agree upon.

Many pieces (*Volo Solo* is one) contain internal implications some of which (not all) the composer is aware of. These he describes in his instructions. But there may be other implications which require that certain instructions should be waived and others observed. Performers have to be careful to realise the exact nature of the notation apart from the instructions before venturing to shift the piece's emphasis onto another aspect. The tones of *Volo Solo* are the nucleus of the piece. The notion of performing excessively fast is a relative one: an amateur's fast will be relatively slow, therefore slowness is not something alien to the piece, therefore some virtuoso (he would also have to be something of a mental virtuoso) might decide to play it at a leisurely speed. Even at that speed he might manage to make the instrument 'break apart', although that again, being a subjective experience, is not necessarily binding. So, in this case, the notes represent a sort of base camp, the instructions pointing out one route (or group of routes) to the summit which is a performance. The instructions are the imposition of a system on a mass of raw material, and no system, however closed, perfect and complete, can lay claim to being the only one, since what a system really represents is a human interpretation and ordering of given facts or material.

The case of LaMonte Young's *X for Henry Flynt* is more difficult. What is the nucleus of that piece? What are the instructions? We may deduce that LaMonte's idea embraced the following categories and that he made decisions with regard to them (decisions are given in parentheses):

a) a sound (cluster, gong, bucket of bolts, …)
b) repetition of a sound (uniform)
c) a time interval (1-2 seconds)
d) an articulation of the time interval (a relatively short silence between sounds)
e) a dynamic (as loud as possible)
f) (not total duration of the piece, but) Number of sounds
g) a number of performers (one)

These categories and their interrelationships constitute the matrix of the piece. The decisions relating to b, c, d are expressly given by LaMonte. The decisions for a and f are definitely left open. e and g have been cursorily fixed, but without special mention. (g was altered by Rzewski, for example, in his performance in Rome with Hans Otte, and the piece was virtually destroyed). When we score the piece in this way it becomes apparent that everything may be altered (by altering the values in brackets) without altering the structure of the piece. Such alterations would produce a family of pieces. all 'topologically' identical. (Invent some). But when LaMonte insists on detail, he insists on his decisions for b, c, d. He *insists* on the variability of f, and *permits* the variability of a (This variability is from performance to performance, not within a single performance).

The foregoing analysis concerns itself with the internal structure of the piece. There are other angles. Let us for example take a frontal view: What is interesting about the piece in performance, from the audience's point of view?
1) its duration, and proportional to that:
2) the variation within the uniform repetition.
3) the stress imposed on the single performer and through him on the audience.
(Note that none of these form part of the compositional structure of the piece. These elements occur rather *in spite of* the instructions, although naturally they are the *result* of them. What the listener can hear and appreciate are the *errors* in the interpretation. If the piece were performed by a machine this interest would disappear and with it the composition. Truly this piece is gladiatorial; what the audience comes to witness is a rosy crucifixion).

Empirically then we can proscribe the 'area' of the piece (a subgroup of the family of topologically identical pieces): (Of course a different subgroup of that family might produce a different set of interesting and essential features in performance, e.g. with a large number of players the variation from uniformity is greater, but in the case of Rzewski's performance we have seen that this is just what diminished the interest of his performance. As in Homeopathy, perhaps the effect of the variation varies in inverse proportion to its magnitude.)

This 'area' then is:

a) one dense heavy decaying sound
b) repeated as uniformly and regularly as possible
c) at an interval of circa 1-2 seconds
d) with a short silence between each repetition
e) the sound is played as loud as possible
f) a relatively large number of times
g) by one performer.

Here we see that a, c, d, f are still free, but within fairly strict limits (and once the choices are made they must be adhered to uniformly), and b and e are relatively fixed (by 'as possible'), and g is fixed immutably (by the number 1).

Now we have to consider the internal implications in this piece of the words 'as possible', as they occur for instance in e: as loud as possible. Suppose the number of repetitions chosen is 3792, and the performer is in peak physical condition but has not played the piece before, and suppose also that he is playing it as a large cluster on the piano. The first cluster is very loud indeed, but after a certain number (say 600) he is physically exhausted and unable to control the movements of his arms beyond just letting them fall and then picking them up again with ever increasing difficulty. He is still playing 'as loud as possible' but the variation in the sound has risen steeply; it is in fact no longer loud in the absolute sense, and it is unrecognizably deformed. So now suppose the performer has rehearsed the piece beforehand and realises the strain that he will suffer in the course of it. For the sake of maintaining uniformity he decided to play the cluster moderately loud and thus keep the variation within homeopathic limits. Some listeners might prefer this latter attitude, finding the spectacle of iron reserve and endurance an edifying one, whereas the spectacle of the physical destruction of a man is a degrading one (even though it be only temporary). Others may prefer the former attitude, on the grounds that 'there is more happening', or that the spectacle of destruction is necessary for the fortification – or understanding – of the constructive instinct, or purely for sadistic reasons.

So much for the words 'as possible' in connection with loud. Let us now look at their implications as applied to 'uniformity and regularity.' What is the model for this uniformity? The first sound? Or does each sound become the model for the one succeeding it? If the former, the first sound has to be fixed in the mind as a mental ideal which all the remaining sounds are to approach as closely as possible. (In practice the first sound too is an attempt to approach a mental image that exists already before the piece began). If the latter method is chosen, constant care has to be taken to assimilate the various accidental variations as they occur. David Tudor has approached the piece in this way and tells how, on noticing that certain keys in the centre of the keyboard were not being depressed it became his task to make sure that these particular keys continued to be silent. This task of assimilating and maintaining accidental variations, if logically pursued, requires superhuman powers of concentration and technique. (It also presents the possibility that the piece might come to a 'natural end' before the decided number of repetitions has been accomplished). It must be remembered that although uniformity is demanded (as far as possible), what is *desired* is variation. It is simply this: that the variation that is desired is that which results from the human (not the superhuman) attempt at uniformity.

These same remarks can be applied to the prescription 'as regularly as possible', with the added difficulty that there are two kinds of regularity: subjective regularity and mechanical regularity, besides various other regularities that may be created by dependence on characteristics of the sound. For instance, the sound might be cut off each time when it reaches a certain dynamic level, and thus the time interval would vary in proportion to the variation in the loudness with which the cluster is played – which might be considerable, as we saw earlier.

What emerges from all this is that in the work of many composers (including Feldman, Wolff, Cage, myself, Rzewski, LaMonte Young and even Stockhausen if he himself happens to be absent) the interpretation of the instructions for a piece has a decisive influence on the performance. We have seen that to say that the instructions govern the performers' interpretation of the notations does not cover the case. Very often a performer's intuitive response to the notation influences to a large extent his interpretation of the instructions. In a lot of indeterminate music the would-be performer, bringing with him all his prejudices and virtues, intervenes in the composition of the piece, influences its identity in fact, at the moment when he first glances at the notation and jumps to a conclusion about what the piece is, what is its nature. Then he turns to the instructions, which on occasion may explain that certain notations do not for instance mean what many people might at first blush expect, and these he proceeds to interpret in relation to his preconceptions deriving from the notations themselves. This is often a good thing. Since very often the notations themselves are the determining factor in the method of composition of a piece, and hence in the piece's identity and structure. And the composer often provides his instructions as an interpretation of the piece, and not a binding one (as is clear in many of Cage's scores). Often, then, these instructions are limiting (at best) and misleading (at worst) and their interpretation is a matter of great importance for would-be performers. And the most important matter for the performer to decide is: which instructions are interpretative (an interpretation provided gratuitously by the composer) and which ones are essential to the piece, i.e. are actually notations in their own right, in which case they must naturally be respected. Ideally then, we should while composing strive to eliminate all mere interpretation, and concentrate on the notation itself, which should be as new and as fresh as possible (hence less likely to arouse preconceptions in the interpreter – though if you have a good interpreter isn't it likely that his preconceptions will be good too?) and should contain implicit in its internal structure, without any need of any instruction, all the implications necessary for a live interpretation.

At the outset I said of my *Volo Solo* that the instruction, 'as fast as physically possible' was an interpretative instruction, and that since an amateur's 'fast' is relatively slow, that 'speed' is not an essential of the work. But there is another instruction which says that the piece may be played by a 'virtuoso performer on any instrument', and if the piece is to be played only by virtuosi, i.e. people who are able to perform magic on their instrument, then it cannot be performed by an amateur, and this may lead us to conclude that speed is after all essential to the piece. But that is not the case – none of the instructions to the piece are essential, they are all interpretative, even the very title itself which might be taken to imply that it must be played by someone 'alone'. But no, I can very well imagine it being performed by several players. So none of the remarks that surround the piece are essential. In fact the most useful instructions are those which make it plain under what conditions the notation itself is not binding (i.e. when notes may be omitted, etc.).

At this point we may anticipate the probable end of the enquiry and assert – I repeat, this is only a probability – that what is implicit in the notation is this: that nothing whatever is binding, not even the well-tempered scale that I chose purely as a matter of convenience. I hope I have now made it clear that the writing down of music is in process of disintegrating. *Volo Solo* is evidence of the far advancement of this process at the present time, but I hope this will not prevent virtuosi and others all over the world from turning over its crumbling leaves during the short and precious duration of its half-life, on the off chance of deriving insight, edification or at least enjoyment from playing these notes that are not 'binding' (whatever that may mean), and perhaps even communicate something of this to a completely hypothetical and unlikely listener. It is a widely accepted doctrine – and I accept it myself with almost indecent alacrity since my survival depends on it – that even the meanest and most imperfect creature may be the unconscious bearer of a seed which, if by chance it fall on fertile ground, may take root and grow, and contribute, even if only infinitesimally, towards making Everything All Right.

12th February 1965

Towards an Ethic of Improvisation

I am trying to think of the various different kinds of virtue or strength that can be developed by the musician.

My chief difficulty in preparing this article lies in the fact that vice makes fascinating conversation, whereas virtue is viewed to best advantage in action. I therefore decide on an illustrative procedure.

Who can remain unmoved by the biography of Florence Nightingale in Encyclopaedia Britannica?

The career of Ludwig Wittgenstein the philosopher (brother of the famous left hand pianist who emigrated to America) – whose writings incidentally are full of musical insights – provides an equally stirring example:

He used a large inheritance to endow a literary prize. Studies in logic brought him to the publication of his *Tractatus Logico-Philosophicus* (1918) at the end of which he writes: "My propositions are elucidatory in this way: he who understands me finally recognizes them as senseless,..." and in the introduction: "... the truth of the thoughts communicated here seems to me unassailable and definitive. I am, therefore, of the opinion that the problems have in essentials been finally solved." Then, in the introduction to his second book *Philosophical Investigations* (1945) he writes: "Since beginning to occupy myself with philosophy again, sixteen years ago, I have been forced to recognize grave mistakes in what I wrote in that first book ... For more than one reason what I will publish here will have points of contact with what other people are writing today. – If my remarks do not bear a stamp which marks them as mine, – I do not wish to lay any further claim to them as my property."

"I make them public with doubtful feelings. It is not impossible that it should fall to the lot of this work, in its poverty and in the darkness of this time, to bring light into one brain or another – but, of course, it is not likely."

In his later writing Wittgenstein has abandoned theory, and all the glory that theory can bring on a philosopher (or musician), in favour of an illustrative technique. The following is one of his analogies:

"Do not be troubled by the fact that languages a. and b. consist only of orders. If you want to say that this shows them to be incomplete, ask yourself whether our language is complete; – whether it was so before the symbolism of chemistry and the notations of the infinitesimal calculus were incorporated in it; for these are, so to speak, suburbs of our language. (And how many houses or streets does it take before a town begins to be a town?) Our language can be seen as an ancient city: a maze of little streets and squares, of old and new houses, and of houses with additions from various periods; and this surrounded by a multitude of new boroughs with straight regular streets and uniform houses."

"It is easy to imagine a language consisting only of orders and reports in battle. – Or a language consisting only of questions and expressions for answering yes and no. And innumerable others. – And to imagine a language means to imagine a form of life."

A city analogy can also be used to illustrate the interpreter's relationship to the music he is playing. I once wrote: "Entering a city for the first time you view it at a particular time of day and year, under particular weather and light conditions. You see its surface and can form only theoretical ideas of how this surface was moulded. As you stay there over the years you see the light change in a million ways, you see the insides of houses – and having seen the inside of a house the outside will never look the same again. You get to know the inhabitants, maybe you marry one of them, eventually you are an inhabitant – a native yourself. You have become part of the city. If the city is attacked, *you* go to defend it; if it is under siege, *you* feel hunger – you are the city. When you play music, you *are* the music."

I can see clearly the incoherence of this analogy. Mechanically – comparing the real situation to one cogwheel and the analogy to another – it does not work. Nonetheless, in full conscience I soil my mouth with these incoherent words for the sake of what they bring about. At the words 'You are the music' something unexpected and mechanically real happens (purely by coincidence two teeth in the cogwheels meet up and mesh) the light changes and a new area of speculation opens based on the identity of the player and his music.

This kind of thing happens in improvisation. Two things running concurrently in haphazard fashion suddenly synchronise autonomously and sling you forcibly into a new phase. Rather like in the 6 day cycle race when you sling your partner into the next lap with a forcible handclasp. Yes, improvisation is a sport too, and a spectator sport, where the subtlest interplay on the physical level can throw into high relief some of the mystery of being alive.

Connected with this is the proposition that improvisation cannot be rehearsed. Training is substituted for rehearsal, and a certain moral discipline is an essential part of this training.

Written compositions are fired off into the future; even if never performed, the writing remains as a point of reference. Improvisation is in the present, its effect may live on in the souls of the participants, both active and passive (i.e. audience), but in its concrete form it is gone forever from the moment that it occurs, nor did it have any previous existence before the moment that it occurred, so neither is there any historical reference available.

Documents such as tape recordings of improvisation are essentially empty, as they preserve chiefly the form that something took and give at best an indistinct hint as to the feeling and cannot convey any sense of time and place.

At this point I had better define the kind of improvisation I wish to speak of. Obviously a recording of a jazz improvisation has some validity since its formal reference – the melody and harmony of a basic structure – is never far below the surface. This kind of validity vanishes when the improvisation has no formal limits. In 1965 I joined a group of four musicians in London who were giving weekly performances of what they called *AMM Music*, a very pure form of improvisation operating without any formal system or limitation. The four original members of *AMM* came from a jazz background; when I joined in I had no jazz experience whatever, yet there was no language problem. Sessions generally lasted about two hours with no formal breaks or interruptions, although there would sometimes occur extended periods of close to silence. *AMM* music is supposed to admit all sounds but the members of *AMM* have marked preferences. An open-ness to the totality of sounds implies a tendency away from traditional musical structures towards informality. Governing this tendency – reining it in – are various thoroughly traditional musical structures such as saxophone, piano, violin, guitar, etc., in each of which reposes a portion of the history of music. Further echoes of the history of music enter through the medium of the transistor radio (the use of which as a musical instrument was pioneered by John Cage). However, it is not the exclusive privilege of music to have a history – sound has history too. Industry and modern technology have added machine sounds and electronic sounds to the primeval sounds of thunderstorm, volcanic eruption, avalanche and tidal wave.

Informal 'sound' has a power over our emotional responses that formal 'music' does not, in that it acts subliminally rather than on a cultural level. This is a possible definition of the area in which *AMM* is experimental. We are *searching* for sounds and for the responses that attach to them, rather than thinking them up, preparing them and producing them. The search is conducted in the medium of sound and the musician himself is at the heart of the experiment.

In 1966, I and another member of the group invested the proceeds of a recording in a second amplifier system to balance the volume of sound produced by the electric guitar. At that period we were playing every week in the music room of the London School of Economics –a very small room barely able to accommodate our equipment. With the new equipment we began to explore the range of small sounds made available by using contact microphones on all kinds of materials – glass, metal, wood, etc. – and a variety of gadgets from drumsticks to battery operated cocktail mixers. At the same time the percussionist was expanding in the direction of pitched instruments such as xylophone and concertina, and the saxophonist began to double on violin and flute as well as a stringed instrument of his own design. In addition, two cellos were wired to the new equipment and the guitarist was developing a predilection for coffee tins and cans of all kinds. This proliferation of sound sources in such a confined space produced a situation where it was often impossible to tell who was producing which sounds – or rather which portions of the single room filling deluge of sound. In this phase the playing changed: as individuals we were absorbed into a composite activity in which solo playing and any kind of virtuosity were relatively insignificant. It also struck me at that time that it is impossible to record with any fidelity a kind of music that is actually derived in some sense from the room in which it is taking place – its shape, acoustical properties, even the view from the windows. What a recording produces is a separate phenomenon, something really much stranger than the playing itself, since what you hear on tape or disc is indeed the same playing, but divorced from its natural context. What is the importance of this natural context? The natural context provides a score which the players are unconsciously interpreting in their playing. Not a score that is explicitly articulated in the music and hence of no further interest to the listener as is generally the case in traditional music, but one that co-exists inseparably with the music, standing side by side with it and sustaining it.

Once in conversation I mentioned that scores like those of LaMonte Young (for example *Draw a straight line and follow it*) could in their inflexibility take you outside yourself, stretch you to an extent that could not occur spontaneously. To this the guitarist replied that 'you get legs dangling down there and arms floating around, so many fingers and one head' and that that was a very strict composition. And that is true: not only can the natural environment carry you beyond your own limitations, but the realization of your own body as part of that environment is an even stronger dissociative factor. Thus is it that the natural environment is itself giving birth to something, which you then carry as a burden; you are the medium of the music. At this point your moral responsibility becomes hard to define.

"You choose the sound you hear. But listening for effects is only first steps in *AMM* listening. After a while you stop skimming, start tracking, and go where it takes you."
"Trusting that it's all worth while."
"Funnily enough I don't worry about that aspect".
"That means you do trust it?"
"Yes, I suppose I do." *

*Except from a dialogue on *AMM* by David Sladen.

Music is Erotic

Postulate that the true appreciation of music consists in emotional surrender, and the expression music lover becomes graphically clear and literally true. Anyone familiar with the basis of much near eastern music will require no further justification for the assertion that music is erotic. Nevertheless, decorum demands that the erotic aspect of music be approached with circumspection and indirectly. That technical mastery is of no intrinsic value in music (or love) should be clear to anyone with a knowledge of musical history: Brahms was a greater composer than Mendelssohn, though it can be truly asserted that Mendelssohn displayed more brilliance in technical matters. Elaborate forms and a brilliant technique conceal a basic inhibition, a reluctance to directly express love, a fear of self exposure.

Esoteric books of love (the *Kama Sutra* for example) and esoteric musical theories such as Stockhausen's and Goeyvaerts' early serial manipulations lose a lot of their attraction when they are readily available to all.

Love is a dimension like time, not some small thing that has to be made more interesting by elaborate preamble. The basic dream – of both love and music – is of a continuity, something that will live forever. The simplest practical attempt at realising this dream is the family. In music we try to eliminate time psychologically to work *in* time in such a way that it loses its hold on us, relaxes its pressure. Quoting Wittgenstein again: "If by eternity is understood not endless temporal duration but timelessness, then he lives eternally who lives in the present."

On the repertoire of musical memories and the disadvantages of a musical education

The great merit of a traditional musical notation, like the traditional speech notation i.e. writing, is that it enables people to say things that are beyond their own understanding. A 12-year-old can read Kant aloud; a gifted child can play late Beethoven. Obviously one can understand a notation without understanding everything that the notation is able to notate. To abandon notation is therefore a sacrifice; it deprives one of any system of formal guide-lines leading you on into uncharted regions. On the other hand, the disadvantage of a traditional notation lies in its formality. Current experiments in mixed media notations are an attempt to evade this empty formality. Over the past 15 years many special-purpose notation-systems have been devised with blurred areas in them that demand an improvised interpretation.

An extreme example of this tendency is my own *Treatise* which consists of 193 pages of graphic score with no systematic instructions as to the interpretation and only the barest hints (such as an empty pair of 5 line systems below every page) to indicate that the interpretation is to be musical.

The danger in this kind of work is that many readers of the score will simply relate the musical memories they have already acquired to the notation in front of them, and the result will be merely a goulash made up of the various musical backgrounds of the people involved. For such players there will be no intelligible incentive to invent music or extend themselves beyond the limitations of their education and experience.

Ideally such music should be played by a collection of musical innocents; but in a culture where musical education is so widespread (at least among musicians) and getting more and more so, such innocents are extremely hard to find. *Treatise* attempts to locate such musical innocents wherever they survive, by posing a notation that does not specifically demand an ability to read music. On the other hand, the score suffers from the fact that it does demand a certain facility in reading graphics, i.e. a visual education. Now 90% of musicians are visual innocents and ignoramuses, and ironically this exacerbates the situation, since their expression or interpretation of the score is to be audible rather than visible. Mathematicians and graphic artists find the score easier to read than musicians; they get more from it. But of course mathematicians and graphic artists do not generally have sufficient control of sound media to produce "sublime" musical performances. My most rewarding experiences with *Treatise* have come through people who by some fluke have (a) acquired a visual education, (b) escaped a musical education and (c) have nevertheless become musicians, i.e. play music to the full capacity of their beings. Occasionally in jazz one finds a musician who meets all these stringent requirements; but even there it is extremely rare.

Depressing considerations of this kind led me to my next experiment in the direction of guided improvisation. This was *The Tiger's Mind*, composed in 1967 while working in Buffalo. I wrote the piece with *AMM* musicians in mind. It consists solely of words. The ability to talk is almost universal, and the faculties of reading and writing are much more widespread than draughtsmanship or musicianship. The merit of *The Tiger's Mind* is that it demands no musical education and no visual education; all it requires is a willingness to understand English and a desire to play (in the widest sense of the word, including the most childish).

Despite this merit, I am sorry to say that *The Tiger's Mind* still leaves the musically educated at a tremendous disadvantage. I see no possibility of turning to account the tremendous musical potential that musically educated people evidently represent, except by providing them with what they want: traditionally notated scores of maximum complexity. The most hopeful fields are those of choral and orchestral writing, since there the individual personality (which a musical education seems so often to thwart) is absorbed into a larger organism, which speaks through its individual members as if from some higher sphere.

The problems of recording

I have touched on this problem twice already. I said that documents such as tape recordings of improvisation are essentially empty, as they preserve chiefly the form that something took and give at best an indistinct hint as to the feeling and cannot of course convey any sense of time and place. And later, that it is impossible to record with any fidelity a kind of music that is actually derived from the room in which it is taking place – its size, shape, acoustical properties, even the view from the window, and that what a recording produces is a separate phenomenon, something really much stranger than the playing itself, since what we hear on tape or disc is indeed the same playing but divorced from its natural context.

A remark of Wittgenstein's gives us a clue as to the real root of the problem. In the *Tractatus* he writes; "The gramophone record, the musical thought, the score, the waves of sound, all stand to one another in that pictorial internal relation, which holds between language and the world. To all of them the logical structure is common." (4.014) This logical structure is just what an improvisation lacks, hence it cannot be scored nor can it be recorded.

All the general technical problems of recording are exacerbated in the recording of improvisation, but they remain technical, and with customary optimism we may suppose that one day they will be solved. However, even when these problems are solved, together with all those that may arise in the meantime, it will still be impossible to record this music, for several reasons.

Simply that very often the strongest things are not commercially viable on the domestic market. Pure alcohol is too strong for most people's palates. Atomic energy is acceptable in peacetime for supplying the electricity grid, but housewives would rebel against the idea of atomic converters in their own kitchens. Similarly, this music is not ideal for home listening. It is not a suitable background for social intercourse. Besides, this music does not occur in a home environment, it occurs in a public environment, and its force depends to some extent on public response. For this reason too it cannot happen fully in a recording studio; if there is hope for a recording it must be a recording of a public performance.

Who can be interested purely in sound, however high its 'fidelity'? Improvisation is a language spontaneously developed amongst the players and between players and listeners. Who can say in what consists the mode of operation of this language? Is it *likely* that it is reducible to electrical impulses on tape and the oscillation of a loudspeaker membrane? On this reactionary note, I abandon the topic.

News has to travel somehow and tape is probably in the last analysis just as adequate a vehicle as hearsay, and certainly just as inaccurate.

Virtues that a musician can develop

1. *Simplicity* Where everything becomes simple is the most desirable place to be. But, like Wittgenstein and his 'harmless contradiction', you have to remember how

you got there. The simplicity must contain the memory of how hard it was to achieve. (The relevant Wittgenstein quotation is from the posthumously published *Remarks on the Foundations of Mathematics*: "The pernicious thing is not, to produce a contradiction in the region where neither the consistent nor the contradictory proposition has any kind of work to do; no, what *is* pernicious is: not to know how one reached the place where contradiction no longer does any harm".)

In 1957 when I left The Royal Academy of Music in London complex compositional techniques were considered indispensable. I acquired some – and still carry them around like an infection that I am perpetually desirous of curing. Sometimes the temptation occurs to me that if I were to infect my students with it I would at last be free of it myself.

2. *Integrity* What we *do* in the actual event is important – not only what we have in mind. Often what we do is what tells us what we have in mind. The difference between making the sound and being the sound. The professional musician makes the sounds (in full knowledge of them as they are external to him); *AMM* is their sounds (as ignorant of them as one is about one's own nature).

3. *Selflessness* To do something constructive you have to look beyond yourself. The entire world is your sphere if your vision can encompass it. Self-expression lapses too easily into mere documentation – 'I record that this is how I feel'. You should not be concerned with yourself beyond arranging a mode of life that makes it possible to remain on the line, balanced. Then you can work, look out beyond yourself. Firm foundations make it possible to leave the ground.

4. *Forbearance* Improvising in a group you have to accept not only the frailties of your fellow musicians, but also your own. Overcoming your instinctual revulsion against whatever is out of tune (in the broadest sense).

5. *Preparedness* for no matter what eventuality (Cage's phrase) or simply *Awakeness*. I can best illustrate this with a special case of clairvoyant prediction. The trouble with clairvoyant prediction is that you can be absolutely convinced that one of two alternatives is going to happen, and then suddenly you are equally convinced of the other. In time this oscillation accelerates until the two states merge in a blur. Then all you can say is: I am convinced that either p or not-p, that either she will come or she won't, or whatever the case is about. Of course there is an immense difference between simply being aware that something might or might not occur, and a *clairvoyant conviction* that it will or won't occur. No practical difference but a great difference in feeling. A great intensity in your anticipation of this or that outcome. So it is with improvisation. "He who is ever looking for the breaking of a light he knows not whence about him, notes with a strange heedfulness the faintest paleness of the sky" (Walter Pater). This constitutes awakeness.

6. *Identification with nature* Drifting through life: being driven through life; neither constitutes a true identification with nature. The best is to lead your life, and the same applies in improvising: like a yachtsman to utilise the interplay of natural forces and currents to steer a *course*.

My attitude is that the musical and the real worlds are one. Musicality is a dimension of perfectly ordinary reality. The musician's pursuit is to recognize the musical composition of the world (rather as Shelley does in *Prometheus Unbound*). All playing can be seen as an extension of singing; the voice and its extensions represent the musical dimension of men, women, children and animals. According to some authorities smoking is an extension of thumb sucking; perhaps the fear of cancer will eventually drive us back to thumb sucking. Possibly in an ideal future us animals will revert to singing, and leave wood, glass, metal, stone etc. to find their own voices, free of our torturings. (I have heard tell of devices that amplify to the point of audibility the sounds spontaneously occurring in natural materials).

7. *Acceptance of Death* From a certain point of view improvisation is the highest mode of musical activity, for it is based on the acceptance of music's fatal weakness and essential and most beautiful characteristic – its transience.

The desire always to be right is an ignoble taskmaster, as is the desire for immortality. The performance of any vital action brings us closer to death; if it didn't it would lack vitality. Life is a force to be used and if necessary used up. "Death is the virtue in us going to its destination" (Lieh Tzu).

Responses to Virtues, for Theorizing
(This critique of the foregoing was written by Michael Chant on 29th April 1968)

"Simple", if it is to be used to denote any aspect of what is true, must be taken to mean 'without parts'. However, we also want to use the word to convey a state of mind, or, further, an attitude of mind to what is the case. We want to be happy. 'Simplicity' cannot be a virtue, except in reference to a state of pure happiness. The world is then essentially without parts in that firstly, we discern no problems, and secondly, we sense no dichotomy between the internal and external worlds. We may say that we feel no discontinuities. In no sense can "simple" be used to signify "the opposite of complex", where by "complex" I mean 'multiform'. We cannot speak of a 'contradictory fact'. And I think we cannot tolerate a 'felt contradiction'. Logic – meaning 'system of reasoning' – must not be taken as standing for something absolute. A contradiction has reality only when it can be felt. If we discern a contradiction, we must resolve it by rejecting the mode of reasoning which generates it. Can we be happy while yet being aware of contradictions?

Integers are the abstractions of temporal discontinuities. Ordinal nos. are existentially prior to cardinal nos. To be happy implies the rejection of integrity. A person who respects integrity will perceive sounds as external disturbances, a musician will think of music as he thinks of words – a statement of a feeling (or expression of an external fact). Communication is an entirely internal phenomenon. Sounds which stand for themselves demand an effecting of communication by a rejection of the dichotomy between internal and external worlds. What subsists between man and his environment is the expression of a form.

To imagine oneself as exclusively concentrating on a one self is to ignore the relationship that exists between self and other. To imagine that one can alter one factor in this relationship without altering the other is to delude oneself. The relationship is a formal one – a continuity between altering the environment and altering oneself. Art is a statement of the further continuity of this relationship, it is an education. The ground lines are not static.

To imagine one can improve the external world by attempting to bring about its conformance to one's present ideal is thus seen to be an illusion. If something environmental is found grating, one must seek to adjust the relationship, not the external or internal world.

All that is needed is recognition that a relationship exists.

It is a distinctive feature of life that this sort of relationship exists, is called forth whenever we can speak of life. It calls forth time as a form. What is distinctive of consciousness is the control of this form. Art is the way of controlling this form internally. Music, as conventionally understood, is a record of the composer's experiences in this direction. We can go beyond this conception of music (and perhaps it may be as well therefore to drop the term) by letting a composition be a statement of how to control the form.

In pure happiness the relationship is null.

The Rite: Advice

Pages – No.2, Ed. David Briers – Winter 1970

[Cardew wrote this piece for Michael Chant's 25th birthday in January 1970. It is an analysis of Michael's 'rite' shown below]:

Play or Listen. If uncertain of anything at any time, go to where someone (if you are performing) is listening, or where someone (if you are listening) is performing, and ask him.
MCTR: A134 in Nature Study Notes (1969)

There is something hypnotic about entering into the analysis of this rite. Play or listen. The phrase implies that while playing you should play, not listen, and while listening you should listen, not play. It does not necessarily restrict your ability to switch from one to the other. In logical terms: Play or listen excludes Play and listen, but not Play then listen then ... etc. Or, to use more human phrasing: Play or listen, don't try to do both at once.

Now we come to a loophole (with a positive outlook): Suppose you are uncertain as to whether to play or listen. In terms of the rite, you cannot be uncertain until you are either a player playing or a listener listening, or rather the rite cannot deal with your uncertainty until you are one of those. Hence an implication that any prior uncertainty is your own problem. The positive outlook here is that this factor – about prior uncertainty being your own problem – removes the rite from the sphere of music therapy. (Looking through the loophole you establish that the department of music therapy is next door, near enough, maybe a little too close for comfort, but at least not right here). A prior uncertainty is not resolved by asking, only your uncertainties while playing or listening. My own suggestion would be (that is, if anyone were to ask me): if uncertain as to whether to play or listen, toss a coin. Tossing coins is excellent therapy. But here I speak as a therapist, not as a musician.

Anyway, having entered the rite, playing or listening, the rite then suggests that instead of getting into any other bad state, for example panicky, desperate, vicious, suicidal, etc.; you should become uncertain and then specifies the solution to that problem, namely, asking. Note that asking is a verbal matter, which adds a further dimension to the suggestion, as follows: If uncertain, verbalise your uncertainty, rather than a number of other possibilities, such as becoming paralysed by your uncertainty, or: silent pleading in one form or another, or: if you can locate it, elimination of what has made you uncertain.

'Sex: Uncertainty' is given as the pedigree of this rite. The idea of a pedigree is central to quite a number of the rites in *Nature Study Notes*, and so requires cursory elucidation. The prototype pedigree consists of three parts: firstly the Mother, who collected the rite or wrote it down as a rite (in our case it was Michael Chant); secondly the Father, the source of the idea (in our case it could have been a London policeman of whom Michael Chant asked directions, but that's just a guess); and thirdly an Ancestor or Archetype, identifying the basic human or non-human state, activity or event that the rite bears on. The Mother may choose to recall other relatives, and all kinds of deviant pedigrees are possible. For example, the pedigree of PDIR29 is given simply as 'Pedigree: Father', whereas the conventional notation would have been something like: Mother:- Philip Dadson Father:- his father Ancestor: – paternity. So in the case under discussion uncertainty is named not as the Father or Ancestor but as the Sex of the rite, and this, as intended, throws an interesting sidelight on the rite itself. What it suggests is that the mating situation does not necessarily arise from instincts of aggression, fitness to survive or what have you, as is sometimes supposed, but equally possibly from uncertainty, insecurity, unhappiness. I mean, that's really a very old dodge: going up to a perfect stranger and asking something (say, 'Excuse me, have you got a light?'). People talking together are very close, especially asking and answering questions; their minds touch (or should do) and an analogous reaction takes place as when bodies touch. I once read a children's book purporting to be narrated by a cat. In it the furry narrator formulates the following behavioural rule for herself: "When in doubt, wash". This rite proposes a rule of the same general form: "When uncertain, ask", and, substituting on the basis of what has just been said, this becomes – and let's assume this is outside the rite – "When uncertain, mate – copulate". So much for "Sex: Uncertainty". (For a rite that deals more explicitly with copulation, see CCDCRI32).

Now let's examine the rite with a view to improving it. Among other things we can eliminate the unreal distinction between playing and performing and correct the rather awkward formulation "... go to where ...and ask him." and rewrite the whole as follows:

Play or listen. If uncertain of anything at any time go up to a listener (if you are playing) or a player (if you are listening) and ask.

The first error that jumps to the eye in this cleaned-up version is this: it mentions 'a player' and 'a listener' as though these were different people, different types of people, whereas the original version refers in both cases simply to 'someone', a person, who may be either playing or listening. And in doing this we have eliminated a basic virtue of the piece, namely that it addresses itself not to a specified, limited group of people, but to all and sundry, with no distinction between musicians, non-musicians, performers, audience, etc.

That part of the clean-up that eliminates performing is valid, in my opinion. 'Performing' seems to indicate that people are performing for the benefit of the listeners, and that the listening people are listening to a performance. Better to have them simply playing (after all there may be no-one listening) or listening (there may be no-one performing). I think I am right in assuming that 'performing' implies the presence of a spectator. What I have just said brings up a new difficulty, however, a difficulty that arises only in extreme cases. All present playing, with no-one uncertain; no problem.

All present listening, with no-one uncertain, no problem. All except one playing, and all those playing uncertain; still alright, they can queue up to ask the one listening or even all ask at once. But all listening and all uncertain, for example, what then? Or worse still, all listening and one of them uncertain! Poor bloke!

One solution would be to set up a hierarchy, appoint officials: one steady player (again that regrettable anachronism 'the Player', the man who can't listen) and one steady listener, so that these sets are prevented from ever becoming completely empty.

Another solution would be to introduce a kind of homosexuality as a last resort: an uncertain player could ask another player if no listeners were available. In the rite as stated the 'normal', 'natural' relationships are upheld; those between members of opposite sexes, and this is something that might have featured in the ancestry of the rite: each class mating with its opposite.

Neither of these solutions is satisfactory; the situation will have to be dealt with as it arises. Possibly the unsophisticated footnote to PDIR29 will come in useful: "Be free at any time to calm whomever you feel is in struggle of some sort; but do so unobtrusively without making your presence felt". Yes, that sounds like just what I need. To return from far-out eventualities that are unlikely ever to occur to central issues that affect us every minute of the day.

The Crowning Glory of this rite lies in its remaining silent at the point where a normal composition would become garrulous. Having introduced the solution of 'asking', the rite does not go on to tell about answering. I see this as a graceful acknowledgment of the creative faculty resident in everyone to answer, to respond freely without instruction. And if such is not actually the case at present, the rite at least proposes that it should become so. To continue what threatens to become an uncontrollable string of sexual analogies: dogs, gorillas and other animals brought up in captivity without the opportunity of observing the procedure of their parents or others of their kind, have to be shown how to copulate. Humans – if we are to place faith in the fictional account by H de Vere Stackpool in *The Blue Lagoon* – don't. They can find out for themselves. Personally I don't place any faith in that account – on the sexual level I think we'd be just as helpless as any animal. But on the level of this rite I do believe it, and in this way: the rite does show you how to ask, and then the question will show how it is to be answered. This is the particle of genius in the rite. It points out the way, it doesn't take you by the arm and frog-march you down it. It inspires you with the consciousness of your own freedom and flexibility. It would have been very easy to go on and deal with answering procedures and I'm sure Michael Chant could have had a lot of fun doing it. My own composition *Schooltime Special* enjoys itself in just that way, for example. But he knew where to stop. He knew where to stop.

Now we're there. Now I can relate this rite to the ethic of the *Great Digest*, one of the four classic book of Confucianism. The second paragraph of the *Digest* begins: "only by knowing where to stop will you be able to go on to acquire certainty." Literally: "Know stop and only then have certainty. In Ezra Pound's inspiring but inaccurate version: Know the point of rest and then have an orderly mode of procedure." (The Chinese character for certain, or fixed shows a roof over rolls of cloth, a warehouse, as opposed to the character for peace, satisfaction, happiness, which occurs three lines further on in the sequence, which shows a roof over a woman, a home.) So one who knows where to stop is qualified to tackle the problem of uncertainty. This rite shows it.

Then again, the word 'ask', verbalise. In paragraph 4 of the *Great Digest* the phrase "seek precise verbal definition of the heart's inarticulate thoughts (the tones given off by the heart)" occurs as the last prerequisite for the acquisition of knowledge, or – depending on your choice between rival interpretations – enlightenment. When you can precisely verbalize – which in Pound's version of the Chinese etymology is pictured as "the sun's lance falling on the precise spot verbally" – When you can precisely verbalize your uncertainty, the rest will fall into place.

Of course this parallelism with the *Great Digest* is purely a coincidence – which in other contexts is called a miracle. Did Michael Chant go through all these reflections before or while or after writing the piece? Some maybe, but certainly not all. And this leads conveniently to the next proposition: When contemplating a rite (or any other artifact) you are not confronting a mind, even though there was a mind behind it. You are confronting an object, like a piece of nature, a mindless object, a stimulus limited only by the amount of attention you care to devote to it. Now the error of trying to correct or 'clean up' an object like this is quite apparent. Why should we expect a piece of nature, a mindless object, to conform to our individual mental processes? And if it doesn't why try and force it to do so? Such an attempt is among other things extremely unscientific – in the sense of pure rather than applied science, the observation of the way things are, not what they ought to be according to some arbitrary system.

Having applied this merciless critique to my own analysis, I now feel justified in carrying it back to the rite itself in order to set up the crucial point in the analysis by asking if the basic division 'play or listen' is a natural one or an arbitrary imposition. This means a switch from Confucian to Taoist terminology, the question now being: does this rite conform to the principle of Wu Wei – no action, or no action contrary to nature – or not?

The clearest illustration of Wu Wei is in Kwang-zi, the story of the butcher who cut up several thousand oxen over a period of 19 years without ever needing to sharpen his knife. He claimed that in the flesh there were infinitely small interstices and that by fitting his dimensionless knife-edge into these infinitely small interstices the carcass just fell apart – thunk!

I wish Kwang-zi were alive today to give us a similar analysis of how to use a cello bow, for example, for 19 years without the hairs wearing out. Obviously this business of observing the way things are is not such a simple pastime. Knowledge and insight such that at a touch things simply fall apart at their natural divisions, fully and accurately revealing their internal structure, i.e. the basis of an ideal natural science. Chopping things up by force – wei, action – according to an arbitrary grid will not fully and accurately reveal the internal structure, although this method is the one the computer or any other machine would obviously prefer.

Now: does the instruction 'Play or listen' conform to the principle of Wu Wei? Is there a natural division in music between playing and listening? Or is the separation of these two arbitrary and willful? The fact that music is something exclusively and uniquely human does not remove it from the domain of nature. Music, unless we believe that we were taught it in early times by visitors from outer space, is a natural function of man, and so we are quite justified in studying its nature. Composition today may be seen as attempting to dissolve itself; it is using the tools of notation to rediscover the nature of music in its pre-notated (natural) state. If this state is successfully re-established, notation and with it individual compositions will disappear. The reason this point (play or listen) is apparently bothering me so much is this: Anyone can play, anyone can listen, but not everyone can do both at once. (We can cursorily define listening as hearing plus comprehension, it includes a mental component as well as the physical one. As for playing; it is immaterial if we restrict this to sound producing activities or not). Anyone can play or listen, but not everyone can do both at once; Everyone is human, but not everyone is a musician (in a sort of professional sense, that their social function is to make music). Hence the easy step (and the word 'easy' is a powerful argument): Musicians are those who can play and listen at the same time, who can fuse playing and listening.

I'm not recommending this definition, I'm just trying to get it in perspective. In logical terms we have made the two classes 1) those who play or listen, and 2) those who play and listen, coincide with the two classes 1) those whose social function is other than making music, and 2) those whose social function is making music. In my experience these two pairs of classes are not congruent. Our confusion is caused by the two differing definitions of a musician, the one in terms of endowment or talent (being able to play and listen simultaneously) and the other in terms of social function.

Go back to the rite: some time earlier I said this rite eliminated the distinction between musicians and non-musicians, that all enter the rite on the same terms. On the basis of the endowment definition of a musician this now appears to be untrue. For non-musicians to play or listen means simply continuing in the state they naturally inhabit; for musicians to play or listen means doing something different from what they naturally do (i.e. playing and listening at the same time, fusing the two). In the light of this does the rite address itself to non-musicians, to musicians, or to both? Only in addressing itself to non-musicians (on the endowment definition) does it conform to the principle of Wu Wei – no action.

Now, although I certainly wish to see the principle of Wu Wei upheld, I don't see this argument as obliging the rite to address itself only to non-musicians. The rite addresses itself to all and sundry, anyone who's interested. Not everyone enters it on the same terms, but within it, by virtue of its varied suggestions, particularly about asking, the participants are encouraged to work towards mutual understanding of their different 'terms' – here, keep clear of the literal meaning of 'terms' and remember the context of 'people being on good terms' – with a view to eliminating odious comparisons involving personal value or musical potency, etc.

And let's consider this in particular and the analysis as a whole as a statement about the value of ritual, rather than the value of music. This seems appropriate as the piece forms part of a book of rites, not a book of music, the 'book of music' – music in its written form – being an object which, as you have quite correctly understood, we hope will disappear.

Scratch Music – 1972
Ed. Cardew
New Dimensions, Latimer – 1972

Introduction
What is Scratch Music? Scratch Music is one sector of the repertoire of the Scratch Orchestra.

What is the Scratch Orchestra? The Scratch Orchestra was formed on the basis of a Draft Constitution that I wrote in May 1969. It was founded by Michael Parsons, Howard Skempton and myself. The first meeting on July 1st 1969, was a gathering of about 50 people – musicians, artists, scholars, clerks, students, etc. – willing and eager to engage in experimental performance activities.

Scratch Music was one of several categories outlined in the Draft Constitution. Other categories were, improvising, playing compositions written by ourselves or other present-day composers, playing the Popular Classics in ways vastly different from the way their composers composed them and their audiences loved them.

Scratch Music was halfway between composing and improvising. I saw it as a necessary curb on the combined free expression of fifty players, and as a training ground. At the meeting of July 1st some of us already had examples of Scratch Music to show to newcomers. I wanted members to spend the next two months or so (there was to be no second meeting until Sept 30th) composing Scratch Music and preparing for our first sound-making experiences as an orchestra. Scratch Music never really caught on amongst the broad masses of the Scratch Orchestra, partly because I wasn't confident enough to put it over strongly (many people simply didn't understand what they were supposed to do) and partly because of inherent weaknesses in the whole idea of Scratch Music – its individualistic bias, 'doing your own thing' in a public entertainment context, and the resulting alienation.

From the first playing meeting of the Scratch, Scratch Music had a function. 'Scratch Members' punctuality was always lax, so to fill the time between the arrival of the first person and the (presumed) last, those who had Scratch Music played Scratch Music. Very beautiful it was on many occasions, with latecomers simply tuning in to the sound environment of the room and adding improvised music to the general texture of interacting Scratch Musics.

This mixed breed Scratch Music continued in use as long as meetings of that type continued in use. The form was: When I considered everyone was present I would clear my throat, the Scratch Music would gradually die away and the meeting would begin. I generally had several points to bring up: gig offers, rehearsal times, appeals for programme suggestions, appeals for volunteer work addressing letters, distributing posters, etc., etc. These meetings were always in batches, say 8 weekly meetings leading up to 4 concerts – and generally a few more arranged at short notice – in the last fortnight, so there was a strong short-term dynamism about the meetings. After half an hour or so of business – it seems now as if nothing I said was ever challenged, and our general ethic was 'no criticism before performance'; in fact challenge and criticisms used to rear their heads sometimes only after a delay of months, – after half an hour of business we would get down to work, distributing copies of pieces, rehearsing, trying out the ideas that people wanted to put in their concerts.

Did this all have to change? It changed. The internal contradictions in the Scratch got sharper and sharper until, possibly triggered by the civic and press response (we had a concert banned on grounds of obscenity and the press went to town on the scandal) to our Newcastle Civic Centre concert on June 21st 1971, I opened the doors to criticism and self-criticism. A collection of the resulting documents was circularised under the title 'Discontent'. The most radical critique came from Catherine Williams, who suggested the liquidation of the Scratch. (It is interesting that Williams' contribution to the present book, though much of it falls outside most definitions of Scratch Music, is the most progressive in that it deals with mass movements, with unanimity, something that the Scratch has definitely not yet arrived at.)

The Scratch was saved from liquidation by two communist members. At the August 23/24 discussions of the Discontent documents John Tilbury exposed the contradictions within the orchestra, and proposed the setting up of a Scratch Ideological Group. I and several others were glad to join this group, whose tasks were not only to investigate possibilities for political music-making but also to study revolutionary theory: Marx, Lenin, Mao Tsetung. Another aim was to build up an organisational structure in the Scratch that would make it a genuinely democratic orchestra and release it from the domination of my subtly autocratic, supposedly anti-authoritarian leadership.

It was in the context of this Ideological Group that I tried to reconstitute Scratch Music under the heading 'Scratch Music; first steps in composition' (see below). In the light of that text I had hoped to end this introduction on the note "Scratch Music is dead; Long live Scratch Music". However, the text has not been circularised amongst the Scratch; other ideas are in the fore-front, and may these develop fruitfully. Meanwhile I am forced to the following conclusion about Scratch Music: Scratch Music fulfilled a particular need at a particular time, at a particular stage in the development of the Scratch Orchestra. Such a need may be felt by other groups passing through a similar stage either now or in the future, and some or all of the basic notions of Scratch Music may again be useful, but for now, as far as the Scratch Orchestra is concerned, Scratch Music is dead.

(Extract from the Draft Constitution of the Scratch Orchestra, June 1969)

Scratch Music

Each member of the orchestra provides himself with a notebook (or Scratchbook) in which he notates a number of accompaniments, performable continuously for indefinite periods. The number of accompaniments in each book should be equal to or greater than the current number of members of the orchestra. An accompaniment is defined as music that allows a solo (in the event of one occurring) to be appreciated as such. The notation may be accomplished using any means – verbal, graphic, musical, collage, etc. – and should be regarded as a period of training: never notate more than one accompaniment in a day. If many ideas arise on one day they may all be incorporated in one accompaniment. The last accompaniment in the list has the status of a solo and if used should only be used as such. On the addition of further items, what was previously a solo is relegated to the status of an accompaniment so that at any time each player has only one solo and that his most recent. The sole differentiation between a solo and an accompaniment is in the mode of playing.

The performance of this music can be entitled Scratch Overture, Scratch Interlude or Scratch Finale depending on its position in the concert.

(Extract from the New Draft Constitution of the Scratch Orchestra, 1970)
Scratch Books

Your Scratchbook is your own personal, private document, and as such anything at all can go into it. However, the original idea of a Scratchbook was that it should contain Scratch Music at one end and Research at the other.

The aim of the Scratchbooks was to establish concern and continuity.

Scratch Music was proposed as a kind of basic training for participation in the Scratch Orchestra, the idea being that each person should write a number of pieces of Scratch Music equal to or greater than the number of people in the orchestra.

Scratch Music, recommended rate of composition, not more than one per day, is basically accompaniments. An accompaniment is defined as something that allows a solo, in the event of one occurring, to be appreciated as such. Each piece of Scratch Music should in theory be performable continuously (whether agonizingly or enjoyably depends on the type of person doing it and on the mood he is in) for indefinite periods of time.

For the notation of Scratch Music any medium may be used, visual, musical, verbal; the notations to be made in a Scratchbook which may be a plain notebook or any similar collection of blank units (e.g. peeled sticks, card index, …).

Ideally every piece of Scratch Music should be flexible enough to become a solo, if the player feels that way inclined (for instance, it may be played either sitting or standing, either muted or un-muted). When a number of people are playing together it is up to the judgement of the participants as to whether more than one can be soloing at the same time.

Scratch music – its composition – is thoughtful, reflective, regular, treasuring the transitory idea; it is also about privacy and self-sustenance.

Scratch Music – its performance – is about 'live and let live', peaceful cohabitation, contributing to society, meaningless and meaningful work, play, meditation, relaxation.

(10.6.1969)
Ask members to make up songs. Words and melody – without accompaniment. These will then be taught to the whole orchestra and sung in unison, either with or without scratch music.

(late 1970)
Think about: Rites and Scratch Music are vessels that catch ideas that would in the normal course of events be thrown away and forgotten, sometimes definitely rejected. So should they be discontinued? Does this depend only on their usefulness?

(23.5.1971)
For reasons of linguistic felicity the name Scratch Music has sometimes been used to describe quite other types of music than are dealt with in this book. E.g. music produced by the Scratch Orchestra that does not happen to fall under any other heading; or: performance to kill time by one or more individuals without verbal intercommunication relating to the performance. Such music might be thought of as 'unnotated Scratch Music', where it is known that notation is intrinsic to

Scratch Music in its original definition.

In the event of a record being produced one side might be entitled 'Scratch Music' and the other 'Unnotated Scratch Music' (Or perhaps 'False Scratch Music').

(Summer 1971)

BOOK OF SCRATCH MUSIC (much of the outline that follows has been rejected in the present book.)

Contents of the book would scatter over a wide range of categories, for example, Counting / Cyclical processes in general / Cosmic / Scrutinising Nature / Translation processes / Doodling / Programming / Games / Exercises / Traffic / Social / Privacy / Poetic visions / Variable versus invariable / Building – destroying / Exhaustiveness – Kombinatorik / Display / Bells.

The items – probably about 500 – would be plaited into a continuous rope wending its way amongst these categories. Frequently jostling together except for those that have specific visual presence. These should have preferential treatment (? use of colour and special papers). Individual contributors would be identified by some aspect, e.g. Jackman's items by their John Bull type and the fact that they always appear (say) in the NW corner of the page.

The ceaselessness of Scratch Music would be emphasised. Scratch Music is the basic music of the world, going on everywhere, all the time. Nothing that is not Scratch Music except regular Western musical compositions since CPE Bach.

(10.9.1971)

Particular and General in Scratch Music. Somewhere between the two, the notion of everybody active continuously on a reasonably quiet scale. This watered down version became accepted and was played often at Scratch meetings and probably for the last time at Alexandra Palace on August 31st 1971.

'Watered down' because in a group of say thirty people, not all have written Scratch Music (this book only records 16 authors of Scratch Music). So is it to end there? What about the ideals of conscientiousness, regularity and collective respect that are implied in the conception of Scratch Music? (Bringing ideas from the country into the 'civilised' environment, etc.)

Scratch Music is a method of uniting a group of people. Anybody can write and play it, it can be used in education, at all levels.

The superficially private and individualistic quality of Scratch Music must be seen in perspective. It fosters communal activity, it breaks down the barrier between private and group activity, between professional and amateur, – it is a means to sharing experience.

(6.10.1971)

Method.

The illustration spreads of Scratch Music were made up as follows, using random numbers to answer three questions: 1, How many pieces of Scratch Music on a spread? 2, Which people are these pieces written by? 3, Which items of Scratch Music from these people's Scratchbooks? Each composer of Scratch Music is allotted a particular position on the spread, and the items selected by random means are positioned on the spread in accordance with this allotment (e.g., Howard Skempton's Scratch Music always appears on the left page in the top left corner).

The way in which neighbouring items jostle one another and interact is improvised. Each spread can be seen as a possible performance configuration with the various items all taking place simultaneously. It should be borne in mind that although in graphic terms a particular item may be dominant in relation to others, in musical terms it may not do so. An item expressed simply as one or two words could be quite dominant in a musical situation, although graphically it appears insignificant.

Every effort has been made to be true to the appearance of the original pieces of Scratch Music. However, colour and size have had to be sacrificed. The illustration spreads have been reduced in size by a factor of 50%. This is linear measurement; the area of the original spreads is four times that of the printed spreads. Information about the colours (if any) of the originals can be obtained by looking up the individual items in the catalogue.

The random method of selection of items for each spread was chosen for its resemblance to the actual (or potential) situation in the Scratch Orchestra where each person comes to a playing session prepared to play a certain piece of Scratch Music without knowing what items the others will be playing. However, other grouping methods are also possible. For instance, collections could be made of all the items of Scratch Music written on a certain day (a lot of Scratch music is dated). Or, collections could be made of a number of items of Scratch Music relating to a certain theme. Or, any other method.

Needless to say, no Scratch Music is copyright.

Although in the original terms of Scratch Music it would naturally occur that a composer would play only his own Scratch Music, that in all likelihood he would consider himself the only one capable of playing his own Scratch Music, the presentation of a book such as this represents a default from these terms. But I reckon that Scratch Music can only survive and develop through having its current rules continually broken and modified, and submitting to constant redefinition.

(7.10.1971)
At different times I asked several people if they would like to write something linking Scratch Music and Activities. Michael Chant sent the following note:

I know no one who claims to understand what Cornelius Cardew means by "scratch music".

it may be – and that this book has reached an existence is a slight confirmation of this surmise – that he means it to be connected with experiments in notation.

but these examples of scratch music are mere phenomena, the noumenon of Scratch Music remains beyond the intellectual intuition of uncountably many individuals.

as for activities – as for activities I can only say that for me the transformation to music takes place when a certain philosophical cast is present in their direction.

this hesitant passage to the musical is manifested in a quickening, insensible, of the sense.

the common mystery that in action all the problems vanish may be why a scratch music and an activity are similar.

Michael Chant 1971

Extract from 'Composing for the Scratch' 13.1.1972
3) Scratch Music – First steps in Composition.
A piece of Scratch Music is a composition in the first instance to be played by the composer, alongside others similarly engaged. This lays the foundation of practicality: there is no point in writing something that you are not capable of performing. In the second instance (we are working along these lines at Morley College now) Scratch Music can be exchanged, so that A's piece is given to B to play while A plays B's piece. This lays the foundation for comprehensibility, your idea must be written down in a way that can be understood and performed by someone else. Through playing Scratch Music with others you gain experience of different ideas interacting with each other. This lays the foundation for composing pieces for several people.

Regular turnover is an important aspect of Scratch Music. The pieces should be played soon after they are written, so that the practical experience feeds back into the composing activity. (This differs from the original concept, in which a large number of pieces would be written before any were performed).

The dynamic range of Scratch Music. Because before the formation of the Scratch our fear was that everyone would be drowned out unless precautions were taken, much early Scratch Music consisted of 'minimal' activities. In practice, the Scratch Orchestra does not make a lot of noise except in certain conditions, e.g. when there are a lot of drums, or saxophones (or arguments) around. The new idea of Scratch Music is based on the idea that music should rise above the general (acoustic and other) level of the environment. So that dynamics is seen now as a question of balance. If the level is so low as to merge with the environment, the interaction with the other musicians is reduced. If it is so high as to dominate the environment then it has moved out of the sphere where it can be influenced by interaction from the other players.

The condition that it should be performable for indefinite periods of time is an important aspect of Scratch Music. This combats prodigal expenditure of energy (which would bring things to an early close). More important, it means that the composer has to visualise the development of his idea in time. A truism: over a long period of time, nothing remains the same. The dynamic control of changes in time is a big part of composition.

The development of imagination through the composition of Scratch Music. Not so much 'practical imagination', i.e. the lively development of the possibilities of a situation, but more 'theoretical imagination', i.e. the ability to imagine how an idea is going to work in practice, or simply the ability to imagine what it's going to sound like (cultivation of the famous 'inner ear').

Stockhausen Serves Imperialism
New Dimensions, Latimer, London – 1974

Contents

Introduction

Chapter 1
[Editor's note: The first chapter in the original publication of
Stockhausen Serves Imperialism was 'A History of the Scratch Orchestra',
written at Cardew's request by Rod Eley. This was based upon reports
submitted by different members of the orchestra. It offered a Marxist
interpretation of the orchestra's history and development and of
the crisis which arose in 1971-72 (the writer was a member of the
Ideological Study Group, and like Cardew he later became a member
of the Communist Party of England (Marxist/Leninist). This chapter
unfortunately had to be omitted from the present volume; it had been
intended to include it, but the author withdrew permission for it to be
reprinted. Interested readers may refer to the original publication. At the
time of publication the complete book (including this chapter) can
also be seen on the ubu website: www.ubu.com]

Chapter 2
Criticising Cage and Stockhausen
John Cage: Ghost or Monster?
Introduction to Cage's *Music of Changes* by John Tilbury
Stockhausen Serves Imperialism
On Criticism

Chapter 3
A Critical Concert

Chapter 4
Self Criticism: Repudiation of Earlier Works
Problems of Notation
Additional Material Presented at the Notation Symposium
Criticism of *The Great Learning*

Notes

Introduction

This book raises more questions than it answers. Two questions in particular have repeatedly posed themselves:

1) What are the relations of production in the field of music in bourgeois society? This is a theoretical question and can be clarified by sifting through the mass of data and experience available. However, the urgency of this problem is debatable.

2) What is the relative importance and significance of polemics such as those documented in this book in the context of the class struggles surging around us in the imperialist heartlands today?

I will just comment briefly on these two questions in this introduction.

1) Because of the law of copyright (which is supposed to give authors and composers control over the exploitation of their works) on the one hand and the idealist image many an artist has of himself as a 'creator' on the other, there is a tendency to imagine that the composer or writer is a 'free producer', that his product belongs to him to do with as he sees fit. In fact, a book or a composition is not an end product, not in itself a useful commodity. The end product of an artist's work, the 'useful commodity' in the production of which he plays a role, is ideological influence. He is as incapable of producing this on his own as a blacksmith is of producing Concorde. The production of ideological influence is highly socialised, involving (in the case of music) performers, critics, impresarios, agents, managers, etc., and above all (and this is the artist's real 'means of production') an audience.

In bourgeois society, the artist is in the employ of capitalists (publishers, record companies), who demand from him work that is, at least, potentially, profitable. And ultimately he is in the employ of the bourgeois state, which demands that the artist's work be ideologically acceptable. Since the state controls our main organ of mass communication, the BBC, it can determine whether or not a work will be profitable by exercising its censorship. An example is Paul McCartney's 'Give Ireland Back to the Irish', which was all set to bring massive profits to the capitalists, had its exploitation not been drastically curtailed by a BBC ban. The capitalists took their cue and the song became hard to find.

If this is the fate of a sentimental pop song under the bourgeois dictatorship, it is clearly impossible to bring work with a decidedly socialist or revolutionary content to bear on a mass audience. Access to this audience (the artist's real means of production) is controlled by the state. This is why Marx and Engels say that the bourgeoisie have reduced artists to the level of wage slaves (see note 6). The artist has a job, and the conditions of employment are laid down by the bourgeoisie.

2) In the age of large scale industrial production, the largest, strongest and most revolutionary class is the industrial working class. Marxists hold (and this book has been put together from a Marxist standpoint) that the overthrow of the bourgeois dictatorship will be led (as it has been, historically, in various countries) by the working class. Hence it is the ideological trends current in the working class that merit attention rather than those current in the intelligentsia or other minority sections of the population. Obviously Cage, Stockhausen and the rest have no currency in the working class, so criticism of their work is relatively unimportant. In fact this whole polemical attack, including this book, takes place outside the working class movement and is therefore politically relatively insignificant.

However, though Cage and Stockhausen have no hold on the working class, they did have a strong hold on me, Tilbury and others whose views feature in this book, and doubtless they still have a strong hold on many of the potential readers of this book. The violence of the attack on them is indicative of the strength of their hold on us; a powerful wrench was required to liberate us from this particular entanglement.

Political consciousness does not come like a flash of lightning. It's a process that passes through a number of stages. The stage documented in this book may be deemed unnecessary as far as the working class is concerned, but it was necessary for us. The Scratch Orchestra (whose history I found myself unable to bring up to date without becoming speculative and hence decided to leave as it was) did in fact go on to new stages, for instance, a movement to criticise music and films that do have wide currency in the working class. People in the Scratch Orchestra also took the line of integrating with the workers and fighting alongside them, as opposed to standing on the sidelines and cheering them on, or taking a stand above them and lecturing them on what they should be doing. The struggle to put this line into practice is still going on.

For the musician, the process of integrating with the working class brings unavoidable involvement with the ideological trends current in that class, both at the receiving end, among the 'consumers' of pop music, etc. and at the production end, through leaving the avant garde clique and integrating more with musicians working in the music 'industry' proper.

Integrating with the working class has two aspects: (a) integrating with the working class movement as a whole, and (b) integrating with the particular section of workers of which you are a member (in my case, working musicians). It is in the context of the second aspect that the clarification of the relations of production (point 1 above) has a certain importance. The first aspect brings another matter to the fore: the question of the political party of the proletariat, the vanguard Marxist-Leninist Party which stands for the interests of the working class as a whole, and without which the workers will not be able to topple the dictatorship of the bourgeoisie, seize political power and establish the Dictatorship of the Proletariat. (Today, because of the efforts of the new Tsars of the Soviet Union – phoney 'communists' like Khrushchev and Brezhnev – to subvert the whole terminology of Communism and 'revise' Marxism for bourgeois ends it is necessary to specify the political line of a Communist Party and draw a sharp distinction between Marxist-Leninist and revisionist parties.)

The 'study of Marxism and of society', which Mao Tsetung places alongside the question of integrating with the masses as an essential part of the work of class-consciousness artists and intellectuals, leads swiftly to the realisation of the necessity of building this proletarian Party. It also makes it clear that a genuine proletarian and revolutionary art will only develop under leadership of such a Party. Without such a Party, every effort on the part of progressive artists to produce revolutionary art is bound to be relatively isolated and relatively ineffective. This is not to say it is wrong to make these efforts, any more than it is wrong to go on strike because the gains therefrom will be limited and not 'revolutionary'. To discourage such efforts is to negate struggle and weaken the impetus of workers (whether intellectual or industrial) to change society. It is precisely through such struggles that political consciousness is aroused. Both ideological and economic struggles prepare the ground for building the revolutionary Party of the Proletariat.

As for this book: as a thing in itself, it can be seen as irrelevant to the working class movement. But no book is a 'thing-in-itself'; if this book gives background and perspectives to a particular form of class struggle in a particular situation, and shows this as something which is not static and final but developing from a particular point of departure through various phases to a new stage with wider perspectives; if this book can be read and understood in this way then its purpose will have been achieved.

I have provided continuity material (in italics) linking the various documents, and a number of notes (at the end of the book) to clarify references in the text. These notes are not subordinate to the texts, in fact they are often corrective to the texts and represent a later, firmer standpoint. Consequently, I would like them to be read with equal attention and as an integral part of the book.

As regards the arrangement of the chapters the Scratch Orchestra History is like a spring-board from which the critical articles jump off. The Criticism of Cage and Stockhausen began about the time the History ends (May 1972). The subsequent history of the Scratch Orchestra has provided even more food for thought than the early history and I would like to have given an account of it (it would also have provided more context for the last two chapters), but, as I've said, this has proved impossible.

C.C. 14th June 1974

CHAPTER 2

Criticising Cage and Stockhausen

The American composer and writer John Cage, born 1912, and the German composer Karlheinz Stockhausen, born 1928, have emerged as the leading figures of the bourgeois musical avant garde. They are ripe for criticism. The grounds for launching an attack against them are twofold: first to isolate them from their respective schools and thus release a number of younger composers from their domination and encourage these to turn their attention to the problems of serving the working people and second to puncture the illusion that the bourgeoisie is still capable of producing 'geniuses'. The bourgeois ideologist today can only earn the title 'genius' by going to extreme lengths of intellectual corruption and dishonestly and this is just what Cage and Stockhausen have done. Inevitably they try and lead their 'schools' along the same path. These are ample grounds for attacking them; it is quite wrong to think that such artists with their elite audiences are 'not doing anyone any harm'. When the attack was launched it had the advantage of surprise. In my early career as a bourgeois composer I had been part of the 'school of Stockhausen' from about 1956-60 working as Stockhausen's assistant and collaborating with him on a giant choral and orchestral work. From 1958-1968 I was also part of the 'school of Cage' and throughout the sixties I had energetically propagated through broadcasts concerts and articles in the press the work of both composers. This was a bad thing and I will not offer excuses for it, but it certainly contributed to our 'advantage of surprise'. In 1972 Hans Keller of the BBC Music Section, knowing the history of my association with Cage, asked me to write an article in *The Listener* to prepare the public for some Cage performances planned for the summer. The result must have surprised him, but it seems also to have pleased him, for shortly afterwards he asked me for an introductory talk to a broadcast of Stockhausen's *Refrain*. Bourgeois intellectualism is characterised by constant rivalry. The exponents of different schools are uninterruptedly cutting each other's throats and striving for advantage in all kinds of underhand ways, including the formation of temporary alliances. Thus the academic composers feel threatened by the avant-gardists, for example, fearing for their entrenched positions – but later you'll find them fraternising on some international panel, uniting to hold down some particularly promising upstart. Progressive intellectuals have to learn how to take advantage of such contradictions and use them. The Cage and Stockhausen articles were my first lesson and I made mistakes with the result that I temporarily lost my voice at the

BBC – my next talk On Criticism was neither broadcast nor printed. Punishments were also meted out inside the BBC on account of the Stockhausen broadcast which by mischance was heard by a high official of the Corporation. There are probably errors in the articles on Cage and Stockhausen, but I have left them as they were, adding footnotes where necessary. The version of the Cage article printed here is the first draft, which was considerably shortened for publication in *The Listener*.

John Cage: Ghost or Monster?

'My mind seems in some respect lacking so that I make obviously stupid moves. I do not for a moment doubt that this lack of intelligence affects my music and thinking generally. However, I have a redeeming quality: I was gifted with a sunny disposition.' (Cage 1968)

(An article on which the following is based appeared in The Listener *4th May 1972)*

Some years ago I received through the letterbox, as a free supplement with my regular copy of *China Pictorial*, Mao Tsetung's *Talks at the Yenan Forum on Literature and Art*. The *Talks* were written in 1942 [16]. In a recent edition I notice the Chinese commentator says "The *Talks* are a magic mirror for detecting the ghosts and monsters in our theatres (with reference to the bloodcurdling apparitions that were apparently a feature of traditional Chinese theatre)" [17]. It is a healthy exercise to hold up such a mirror to one's own work and the works of those one greatly respects or has greatly respected. Genuine criticism is motivated solely by the desire to strengthen what is good. Of course through strengthening what is good it will also contribute to the decline of what is not good, or no longer good. 'Good' is here understood to refer to everything that contributes towards social change in the desired direction, i.e. towards socialism.

"The first problem is, literature and art for whom?" (*Talks*). Whom does Cage's music serve? We can answer this quite simply by looking at the audience, by seeing who supports this music and who attacks it. Ten years ago Cage concerts were often disrupted by angry music lovers and argumentative critics. It was the most bourgeois elements in the audience that protested against it. But they soon learned to take their medicine. Nowadays a Cage concert can be quite a society event. The audience has grown and its class character has become clearer in proportion. What happens nowadays is that revolutionary students boycott Cage's concerts at American universities, informing those entering the concert hall of the complete irrelevance of the music to the various liberation struggles raging in the world [18]. And if it does not support those struggles, then it is opposing by them and serving the cause of exploitation and oppression. There is no middle course. "There is no such thing as Art for Art's Sake, art that stands above classes, art that is detached from or independent of politics" (*Talks*).

"Works of art as ideological forms are products of the reflection in the human brain of the life of a given society." (*Talks*). What aspects of present-day society are reflected in the work of John Cage? Randomness is glorified as a multi-coloured kaleidoscope of perceptions to which we are 'omniattentive'. Like the 'action' paintings of Jackson Pollock, Cage's music presents the surface dynamism of modern society; he ignores the underlying tensions and contradictions that produce that surface (he follows McLuhan in seeing it as a manifestation of our newly acquired 'electronic consciousness'). He does not represent it as an oppressive chaos resulting from the lack of planning that is characteristic of the capitalist system in decay (a riot of greed and exploitation). However, if progressive people begin to appreciate the music as reflecting this situation in fact, then it will become identified with everything we are fighting against. Many younger composers and artists have been deeply affected by Cage's work at one stage or another (and I include myself in this category) and he has become a father figure to a number of superficially rebellious movements in the arts. In the '30s and '40s his work was hard-hitting and realistic, but what is he writing now?

Cheap Imitation (1970) is based on a work by Satie. The rhythm of the original is retained, the notes are changed. Cage here contradicts the interdependence of all the aspects of a structure. Any content, as well as the dynamism that is characteristic of 'saying something', is automatically lost if one aspect of the language is systematically altered. But the resulting emptiness does not antagonise the bourgeois audience which is confident of its ability to cultivate a taste for virtually anything. The appreciation of emptiness in art fits well with imperialist dreams of a depopulated world. "The most, the best we can do, we believe (wanting to give evidence of love), is to get out of the way, leave space around whomever or whatever it is. But there is no space!" (Cage 1966)

Musicircus (1967) is a totally 'empty' composition – it contains no notations at all, except the demand that participants should regulate their activity according to a timetable which is not provided. By way of analogy I heard a lecturer recently describe the history of the Sarabande as follows: the Sarabande was originally a lively Spanish dance used by prostitutes to attract customers. It ended up in the French court as a slow, stately piece of music allowing for the most intricate and refined elaboration of the melodic line. Is the circus to go the same way? It used to be a many-sided spectacle and entertainment for the people, produced by itinerant bands of gypsies and 'other foreigners'. Much of this character is retained even in the modern commercial circuses, and they are still very much 'for the people'. But with Cage the circus becomes an 'environment' for the bewilderment and titillation of a cultured audience. Instead of a trained band of white horses with plumes on their heads, you may find a little string orchestra inaudibly playing Spohr in evening dress, while numerous other groups get on with their own things. Instead of the elaborate and highly decorated machinery of the fairground, you will find banks of TV tubes, amplifiers, modulators and 'spaghetti' of all kinds, ensuring that in the event of anyone wishing to say something coherent they will be totally inaudible to the public.

"The life of the people is always a mine of the raw materials for literature and art, materials in their natural form, materials that may be crude, but are most vital, rich and fundamental." (*Talks*). The Sarabande sacrificed its vitality on the altar of courtly culture and refinement. It looks as though Cage wants to dissipate the vitality of the circus into undifferentiated chaos and boredom.

Let's go back to *Variations I* (1958), which I regard as a key work in Cage's output. Unlike *Cheap Imitation*, the score of *Variations 1* emphasises the total interdependence of all the attributes of a sound. Transparent sheets of lines and dots make up the score. The dots (sound events) are read in relation to a number of lines representing the various aspects of that sound: time of occurrence, loudness, duration, pitch, timbre. A change of position of a dot means a change in all the aspects of that sound event. Once Kurt Schwertsik [19] and I, overcome with Cage's 'beautiful idea' of letting sounds be sounds, (and people be people, etc., etc., in other words seeing the world as a multiplicity of fragments without cohesion), decided to do a pure performance (no gimmicks) on horn and guitar, just reading the lines and dots and notating the results and letting the sounds be themselves. The result was a desert.

Contrary to his own 'beautiful idea', Cage himself, in his performance of this piece with David Tudor never let the sounds be just sounds [20]. Their performances were full of crashes, bangs, radio music and speech, etc. No opportunity for including emotive material was lost. And musically they were right. Without the emotive sounds the long silences that are a feature of the piece in its later stages would have been deprived of their drama and the piece disintegrated into the driest dust (as Schwertsik and I found out by painful experience).

The one merit of such a purely formal score is that it releases the initiative of the performer – it gives him participation in the act of composition and hence a genuinely educative experience. In the balance on the other side is the total indifference (implicitly represented by such a formalistic score) to the seriousness of the world situation in which it occurs. Can that one merit tip the scales? No, it can't, not even with the sunniest disposition in the world.

'Contrary to his beautiful ideas…' With the publication of *Silence* (1961) the rot set in. Beautiful ideas are welcome in every stately and semi-detached home and Cage became a name in the ears of the reading public, the intelligentsia.

There is a contradiction between the toughness of Cage's music and the softness of his ideas. The toughest of Cage's pieces that I have heard is *Construction in Metal*, one of three 'constructions' written about 1940. 'Collective violence' could describe this music; it might possibly awaken a listener to the idea that liberation requires violence.

His next book *A Year from Monday* (1968) includes a "Diary: How to improve the world (you'll only make matters worse)". In the Preface he states that he is now less interested in music, more interested in 'revolution', and recommends anarchism. In other words: the toughness (the music) is losing, the softness (the corrupt ideology) is winning.

For instance (just two out of literally thousands of such examples): "Difference between pennilessness now and pennilessness then: now we've got unquestioned credit" (Diary 1966). Who's we? John Cage and the Queen of England? It sounds as though Cage would say: Anyone can survive today provided they play the system, never mind how corrupt.

An earlier one: "We are as free as birds. Only the birds aren't free. We are as committed as birds, and identically." (*Lecture on Commitment*, 1961). One is tempted to joke back, 'How does he know?' and forget it. But this is dangerous and lazy. Cage is putting forward a poisonous line here: artists are on the same level as partridges on a game preserve (to take one of the more relevant of the available interpretations).

In the early 1960s, Cage's *Atlas Eclipticalis* was included in a concert at Lincoln Centre, New York, played by a conventional symphony orchestra. The parts for the musicians are again arrangements of dots and lines (this time traced from a star atlas) and every player has contact microphones attached to his instrument and an amplification system. The performance was a shambles and many of the musicians took advantage of the confusion to abuse the electronic equipment to such a degree that Christian Wolff (usually an even-tempered man) felt compelled to rush in amongst them and protest against the extensive 'damage to property'. Cage lamented afterwards to the effect that his music provided freedom – freedom to be noble, not to run amok.

I find it impossible to deplore the action of those orchestral musicians. Not that they took a 'principled stand' (I hope such stands may be taken in the future), but they gave spontaneous expression to the sharply antagonistic relationship between the avant garde composer with all his electronic gadgetry and the working musician. There are many aspects to this contradiction, but beneath it all is class struggle.

Life offers many lessons. Mistakes may be turned to advantage. The important thing for us artists and intellectuals is to "move our feet over to the side of the workers." (*Talks*). In so doing we may lose that part of our artistry and our intellectuality that is orientated towards bourgeois society and this loss should be celebrated, not bemoaned. The New York musicians gave Cage a lesson when they disrupted *Atlas*. Cage could have studied the reasons for this action – instead he coldly condemned it. The revolutionary students boycotting Cage's college concerts say quite clearly 'Your music is not saying anything to the world's people, it speaks only to a tiny band, a social intellectual elite'. But Cage waffles on about the 'haves and the have nots' as though it was all a question of pocket money, and ignores the lesson.

How can a composer truly reflect society if he ignores the lessons of that society? If a composer cannot or refuses to come to terms with such problems then the matter should be thrown open to public criticism. The artist serves the community, not *vice versa*.

Through broadcasts and public concerts a number of Cage's recent works will be heard in England this summer. *HPSCHD* (for 7 harpsichords, 52 tracks of tape, and a whole lot of audible and visible extras) is due for performance on 13 August. I have been engaged to play one of the harpsichords. I've heard that the part is complex and difficult, but I wasn't asked whether I could play the instrument – and I know why, because it makes not the slightest difference what I play, or how I play it or how I feel about it. On the same degrading terms many talented and intelligent people will participate in that concert. Basically judging from comments on an earlier performance "It was ensured that no order can be perceived" (Ben Johnston); "One of the great artistic environments of the decade" (Kostelanetz) – it will be a king-size electronic multi-media freak-out, and I don't recommend anyone to go to it.

People often speak of the 'dilemma of the bourgeois artist', as though he was trapped, paralysed, unable to act. This is not the case. Ghosts have some sort of dilemma; they can never be alive. Monsters have one; they can never be human. But I see no dilemma for Cage. It may not be all plain sailing, but there's no reason why he can't shuffle his feet over to the side of the people and learn to write music which will serve their struggles.

The performance of *HPSCHD* mentioned in the preceding article also included the pianist John Tilbury, who had earned a reputation as a performer of bourgeois avant garde music. Some time later his recording of Cage's *Music of Changes* was broadcast by the BBC and he was asked to contribute an introductory talk. My article had touched on a number of Cage's works without going into any one in detail; in his talk, Tilbury remedied this omission and on the basis of his thorough knowledge of the *Music of Changes* he criticised it in detail though not exhaustively. His talk is reprinted here in full.

Introduction to Cage's *Music of Changes*
by John Tilbury

The preface to Deryck Cooke's book *The Language of Music* contains the following passage: "At the present time, attempts to elucidate the 'content' of music are felt to be misguided, to say the least; the writer on musical matters is expected to ignore or only hint at what the composer had to say, and to concentrate entirely on how he said it. Or to put it in the contemporary way, he is expected to concentrate entirely on the 'form', which is not regarded as 'saying' anything at all. Thus the two inseparable aspects of an expressive art are separated and one is utterly neglected – much to the detriment of our understanding of the other. Instead of responding to music as what it is – the expression of man's deepest self – we tend to regard it more and more as a purely decorative art; and by analysing the great works of musical expression purely as pieces of decoration, we misapprehend their true nature, purpose and value. By regarding form as an end in itself, instead of as a means of expression, we make evaluations of composers' achievements which are irrelevant and worthless[21]."

Now it is just this question of content in music that I want to raise in relation to Cage's work. How, in fact, can we apprehend the true nature, purpose and value of the *Music of Changes*?

Let us begin with the facts of the piece. *The Music of Changes* was written in 1951 and is the embodiment, wholly or partially, in musical expression of Cage's view of the world. By that I mean that before Cage can function as a musician he has to live as a man, and not as abstract man, but historically as a real man in a particular society. In the *Music of Changes* Cage is saying something about the real world, secreted through the sounds and silences which constitute the piece. You will have the opportunity later, of hearing these sounds, experiencing these silences (and thankfully there is no substitute for that), but what of their origin, what is the nature of the compositional process that orders them?

Well, in fact this process is somewhat complicated though it is certainly not mysterious, and Cage has described it in detail in his book *Silence*.

Essentially, the arrangement of the material was determined by chance operations, by the tossing of coins. Charts of sounds, silences, amplitudes, durations were arranged so that they could interpret as musical material the coin oracle of the Chinese *Book of Changes*, so that they could accommodate a chance method of procedure. However readings of the charts always encompassed, for example, all twelve notes of the chromatic scale so that the effect of the chance operations (the tossing of coins) was balanced to a certain extent by the composer's initial choice of materials [22]. Technically, the result of Cage's application of this method is brilliant – the way in which the piano is used as a sound source to be explored rather than an instrument to be played, the extensive use of the third sustaining pedal to achieve a wide range of colours and textures, the subtly changing resonances obtained, the overall pianistic clarity and artistically, the effect is of stylistic coherence and originality.

But this is not all – in fact it is only half the story. For there is no such thing as an artistic conscience which is not governed by world outlook. In a class society such as our own an artist observes, selects, refines, in short, creates not simply according to his own needs but, more importantly, to the needs of a particular class – the musical ideas which created the *Music of Changes* are necessarily ideologically rooted and it is only within the context of ideology that the question of the true nature of a work of art can be meaningfully answered.

Ironically, in spite of Cage's professed desire to strip his work of subjectivity, to free it of emotional content, individual taste, tradition etc., ideas and concepts, Cage's ideas and concepts are expressed quite explicitly in the *Music of Changes* and you don't have to read Cage's writings (illuminating as they are) to grasp its ideological content. In particular there are three aspects of Cage's thought which the *Music of Changes* draws the listeners' attention to.

First there is his concept that sounds should be themselves, that they enter the time space centred within themselves, that they should be free from other sounds, free from human desire, free of associations, so that any relationship between sounds is quite fortuitous, i.e. unconscious [23].

This aesthetic inevitably requires a sympathetic attitude on the part of the performer. The American pianist, David Tudor, described it in a recent interview in *Music and Musicians*, "I had to learn," he says, "how to cancel my consciousness of any previous moment in order to produce the next one, bringing about the freedom to do anything." In other words, true consciousness is attained not by understanding one's historical crib, but by simply 'cancelling' it; not in order to understand the dialectical relationship between freedom and necessity, but in order to be free to do anything, presumably to anybody and for any reasons [24].

The *Music of Changes* in fact bears a strong resemblance to capitalist society, as Cage envisaged it in 1951; that is, as simply the sum total of its individual members who merely proceed on their own way, according to their own dictates. Each particle of this universe appears to be free and spontaneously self moving, corresponding to the free bourgeois producer as he imagines himself to be; events consist of their collisions and are the product of internal chance. However, a mysterious cosmic force holds all those particles together in one system; this mysterious force is simply the capitalist law of supply and demand [25].

The second aspect of Cage's thought that I want to mention is this question of chance. The majority of Cage's works use random procedures of one kind or another. Just as in capitalist society, and for bourgeois ideology, it is the free market, the iron law of supply and demand, which holds all the bourgeois producers together, inexplicably and arbitrarily determines and adjusts their relations to each other, and acts as the grand unifying principle – so in the *Music of Changes* (and many other of Cage's works) randomness, chance is exalted to become the controlling factor, and just as capitalist social relations engender wars, mass hunger, pollution, neuroses, so Cage himself has described the *Music of Changes* as an object more inhuman than human, having the alarming aspect of Frankenstein's Monster. And try as he may, Cage can no more resolve the contradictions of contemporary composition than he can the contradictions of contemporary capitalism. For to resolve a contradiction it is necessary to grasp the laws of motion and change, and act in accordance with them. This is something Cage is patently unable or unwilling to do. Cage's attitude to change is the third aspect of his theory that we find clearly expressed in the *Music of Changes*. Cage has often said that he is interested in quantity, not quality, and change in the *Music of Changes* is precisely quantitative, accumulative change. Thus the sound material does not develop and change according to its own inner contradictions but according to phenomena and conditions outside itself. In the *Music of Changes* a randomised compositional procedure is imposed mechanically on the sound material; tones and aggregates may be liquidated, or displaced to reappear at different points along the continuity in varying degrees of recognisability. This mechanistic thinking also explains Cage's obsession with technology. Thus, for him, the introduction of a new technique from without can resolve contradictions (i.e. effect radical change) within, so that, for example, the contradiction of capitalism can be resolved by our newly acquired T.V. –

inspired electronic consciousness. Cage postulates unconscious individual participation as opposed to conscious class struggle. What is crucial is that Cage totally ignores the revolutionary aspect of change, change in quality based on the development of internal contradictions. The revolutionary aspirations which Cage professes flake away under scrutiny to reveal a deep-rooted, pie-in-the-sky liberalism.

What I have tried to show, briefly and incompletely, is that the true nature of a piece of music, like any work of art, is inextricably bound up with the ideological stand or world outlook of its creator, and that the content of a piece of music is not something mysterious, unattainable or elusive. On the contrary, creative listening, that is, listening to music that involves the mind as well as the ears and heart, can attain a measure of understanding of what a composer is saying about the world.

In the passage I quoted at the beginning of the talk Deryck Cooke also brought up the question of the purpose and value of works of art. The purpose of a work derives from its nature and is inseparable from it; furthermore, the purpose of a work, objectively, can be at variance with the subjective intentions of the composer [26].

The purpose of the *Music of Changes* is to propagate a world view, more specifically to universalise a bourgeois class view (i.e. the dilemma of this particular ruling class is presented as the dilemma of the human race as a whole, as the human condition in general), its purpose is to obscure the laws of motion and change and thereby to attempt to help stave off revolutionary change.

In the *Talks at the Yenan Forum on Literature and Art* Mao Tsetung wrote, "A common characteristic of the literature and art of all exploiting classes in their period of decline is the contradiction between their reactionary political content and their artistic form." *The Music of Changes* exemplifies this thesis perfectly; a pianistic masterpiece rooted in bourgeois individualism, anarchism and reformism. And what is its value? To the working and oppressed people it has no value, it bears no relation to their life. Its value is to the ruling class, it serves the stability of that class and is a weapon in their fight against revolution. Its value, therefore, is its counter-revolutionary value to the status quo, to imperialism; this, in the last analysis, is its true nature.

[Cardew continues]
Cage serves imperialism and will go under with imperialism. But is it true to say that his music bears no relation to the lives of the working and oppressed people? In a way such music does reflect the conditions under which people

work, with the productive forces catastrophically out of step with the relations of production, and in doing so it intensifies our oppression. It is certainly true that it can have no positive value to the working class; workers would have no difficulty in identifying the *Music of Changes* as yet another horrible aspect of their oppressive environment – and they would not spend time going into just which characteristics of capitalism are peeking out at them through these calculated sounds and silences. But progressive artists have to settle accounts with their opposite numbers in the bourgeois camp, and there are some points outstanding.

Tilbury talks about three particular aspects of Cage's thought that this piece draws attention to. Rather does it reflect (draw attention to) three aspects of capitalist society, and three aspects of bourgeois ideology designed to mystify these aspects. The 'just sounds' idea reflects the conception of things as being isolated from one another, hence there is no point in investigating their interrelations, and if nobody investigates the relationships between things then the bourgeoisie will be able to maintain its rule. The 'randomness' idea is a familiar weapon of the bourgeois ideologists to divert the consciousness of the masses from the real laws (laws and randomness are counterposed) underlying the development of the world and human society. On the idea of 'quantitative change', Tilbury rightly points out that it denies the revolutionary aspect of change, even though Cage is constantly talking about 'revolution'. Thus we see that these are not just aspects of Cage's thought, but that Cage is propagating the main lines of the bourgeois ideological establishment. On the perceptual level his music may sound stranger but essentially he is singing the same old song.

So the *Music of Changes* does not 'resemble' capitalist society 'as Cage envisaged it' (Tilbury). Cage, claiming mental incapacity, has never given serious thought to capitalist society. What he does is to reflect capitalist society and the mess it's in, and he reflects this mess in the very way the bourgeoisie would like it to be seen, as something that is not their responsibility. Cage's music is in fact a much more genuine reflection of the straits of the present-day bourgeoisie than are the blue movies or Wagner operas that the bourgeoisie undoubtedly prefers for its cultural recreation. Cage at least tries to reproduce the world (the bourgeois world) and not the kingdom of heaven, as does Stockhausen. The aspect of Cage that engages our fury is his denial of the conscious role of the individual, of responsibility; in denying this, he is guilty of a vicious deception. No art drops from the sky; all art bears the imprint of the real world, even if its only reality is that it reproduces a lie being put about by the bourgeoisie. The area of criticism of the individual artist is the area of his conscious participation as an individual: what does he choose to reflect, for whom, from which class standpoint, and what intellectual and emotional penetration does he bring to it?

This raises problems that are not easy to deal with (and I don't propose to deal with them here), such as the degree of freedom of choice available to the bourgeois composer especially the nameless one who does not aspire to the influential position of a Cage or a Stockhausen. One thing is sure, discussion of these problems can in no way undercut the rightness of criticising Cage and Stockhausen, who have voluntarily come forward to take up the role of leading ideologists for the bourgeoisie on the artistic front. The articles above and the talk on Stockhausen that follows depict this servile role quite starkly and show it as an objective fact, whatever protestations the composers themselves may make to the contrary.

Stockhausen Serves Imperialism

[Editor's note: the following section was written as a broadcast talk for the BBC and later incorporated into an article for *The Listener* – 15 June 1972]

This talk has taken a different shape from the one I originally planned. I had meant to go into the development of the avant garde in Germany through the Nazi regime and after the war through the Darmstadt School [27]. However I soon experienced a real dislike for contributing to the already proliferous documentation of the avant garde. I decided to tackle the subject from a wider viewpoint.

Stockhausen's *Refrain*, the piece I have been asked to talk about, is a part of the cultural superstructure of the largest scale system of human oppression and exploitation the world has ever known, imperialism. The way to attacking the heart of that system is through attacking the manifestations of that system, not only the emanations from the American war machine in Vietnam, not only the emanations from Stockhausen's mind, but also the manifestations of this system in our own minds, as deep-rooted wrong ideas. And we must attack them not only on the superficial level, as physical cruelty or artistic nonsense or muddled thinking, but also on the fundamental level for what they are: manifestations of imperialism.

My saying something doesn't necessarily make it true. The task of this article is to make clear that Stockhausen's *Refrain* is in fact – not just in my opinion – a part of the cultural superstructure of imperialism. The task falls into three parts. To expose the essential character of the musical avant garde in general; to outline the particular development of the avant garde in which Stockhausen plays a role; and to indicate the position and content of *Refrain* within that development.

166

The avant garde period (consisting of successive avant gardes) is not the latest, but the last chapter in the history of bourgeois music. The bourgeois class audience turns away from the contemporary musical expression of its death agony, and contemporary bourgeois music becomes the concern of a tiny clique taking a morbid interest in the process of decay. I must avoid giving the impression that this tiny clique of the avant garde has its own kind of purity and honesty in representing the collapse of imperialism and bourgeois values in general. No, imperialism is rotten to the core and so is its culture. However the ruling classes – the big business men, the politicians, the field marshals, the media controllers etc. – don't just 'turn away' to groan and expire gracefully. They fight to stave off their collapse and in this fight they use all the means at their disposal – economic, military, political, cultural, ideological. The aim of the establishment is to use ideas not as a liberating force for clarification and enlightenment and the releasing of people's initiative, but as an enslaving force, for confusion and deception and the perversion of talent. In this way they hope to stave off collapse.

There has always been a mass of talent in the avant garde and some of this talent is keen to leave the restricted world of the avant garde and its preoccupations behind and take up a more definite role in the service of imperialism, a role with a larger following and bigger rewards. In 1959, the year he wrote *Refrain*, Stockhausen was ripe for this role. At that time he was a leading figure in the Darmstadt School which had been set up after the Second World War to propagate the music and ideas that the Nazis had banished. The Nazis branded the avant garde 'degenerate' and publicly disgraced it and suppressed it. In postwar Germany a subtler technique was used; instead of suppression, repressive tolerance. The European avant garde found a nucleus in Darmstadt where its abstruse, pseudo-scientific tendencies were encouraged in ivory tower conditions. By 1959 it was ready to crack from its own internal contradictions and the leading figures were experiencing keenly the need for a broader audience. For this the music had to change. *Refrain* was probably the first manifestation of this change in Stockhausen's work. Since then his work has become quite clearly mystical in character. In a recent interview he says that a musician when he walks on stage "should give that fabulous impression of a man who is doing a sacred service" (note the showmanship underlying that remark). He sees his social function as bringing an "atmosphere of peaceful spiritual work to a society that is under so much strain from technical and commercial forces".

In *Refrain* we can see the beginnings of the tendencies that his present music exhibits alongside the remains of his Darmstadt work.

The score itself is a gimmick typical of Darmstadt thinking. The music is obliged quite mechanically to accommodate itself to a crude piece of mobile two-dimensional design. It is written on a large card with music staves that bow into partial circles centred on the middle of the card. Anchored to this middle point is a strip of transparent plastic with some notations on it. These notations are the recurring refrain that gives the piece its title.

The instrumentation is piano, vibraphone, celeste, each of the three players also using auxiliary instruments as well as vocal exclamations and tongue clicks. Visualising the kind of musicians required for this, we see the beginnings of the specially trained band of players that are necessary for the presentation of his recent work.

The performance itself creates a situation of intense concentration and listening for the musicians. This listening activity of the musicians communicates itself to the audience and it is this intense concentration and concentration of sounds for their own sake that reveals the beginnings of the mystical atmosphere that Stockhausen has cultivated more and more theatrically since then.

Some may criticise Stockhausen on the grounds that he presents mystical ideas in a debased and vulgar form. This is true, but it is not enough. To attack debasement and vulgarity in themselves is meaningless. We have to penetrate the nature of the ideas that are being debased and vulgarised and if they are reactionary, attack them. What is this mysticism that is being peddled in a thousand guises, lofty and debased, throughout the imperialist world? Throughout its long history in India and the Far East, mysticism has been used as a tool for the suppression of the masses. Salesmen like Stockhausen would have you believe that slipping off into cosmic consciousness removes you from the reach of the painful contradictions that surround you in the real world. At bottom, the mystical idea is that the world is illusion, just an idea inside our heads. Then are the millions of oppressed and exploited people throughout the world just another aspect of that illusion in our minds? No, they aren't. The world is real, and so are the people, and they are struggling towards a momentous revolutionary change. Mysticism says 'everything that lives is holy', so don't walk on the grass and above all don't harm a hair on the head of an imperialist. It omits to mention that the cells on our bodies are dying daily, that life cannot flourish without death, that holiness disintegrates and vanishes with no trace when it is profaned, and that imperialism has to die so that the people can live.

Well, that's about all I wish to say about *Refrain*. To go into it in greater detail would simply invest the work with an importance that it doesn't have. No, my job is not to 'sell' you *Refrain*. I see my job as raising the level of consciousness in regard to cultural affairs.

At the outset I said *Refrain* is part of the cultural super-structure of imperialism. These terms: 'superstructure', 'imperialism', require some explanation if the level of consciousness with regard to cultural affairs, is to be raised, if we want to grasp the deeper roots of such surface phenomena as avant garde music. These terms are essential to Marxism, and yet a lot of people seem to regard them as some sort of jargon or mumbo jumbo. The truth is that in an imperialist country like Britain it would be a miracle indeed to find Marxism being taught in schools, since Marxism is directed towards the overthrow of imperialism, whereas the education system of an imperialist country must be directed towards maintaining imperialism. It is as well to bear this hard fact in mind.

In Marx's analysis, society consists of an economic base, and rising above this foundation, and determined by it, a superstructure of laws, politics, ideas and customs. The following quotation is to be found in Lenin's pamphlet entitled *Karl Marx*, which I have found the most concise and useful introduction to Marxism. Marx writes:

"In the social production of their life, men enter into definite relations that are indispensable and independent of their will, relations of production which correspond to a definite stage of development of their material productive forces. The sum total of these relations of production constitutes the economic structure of society, the real foundation, on which rises a legal and political superstructure and to which correspond definite forms of social consciousness. The mode of production of material life conditions the social, political and intellectual life process in general. It is not the consciousness of men that determines their being, but, on the contrary, their social being that determines their consciousness. At a certain stage of their development, the material productive forces of society come in conflict with the existing relations of production, or – what is but a legal expression for the same thing – with the property relations within which they have been at work hitherto. From being forms of development of the productive forces these relations turn into their fetters. Then begins an epoch of social revolution. With the change of the economic foundation the entire immense superstructure is more or less rapidly transformed. In considering such transformations a distinction should always be made between the material transformation of the economic conditions of production, which can be determined with the precision of natural science, and the legal, political, religious, aesthetic or philosophic – in short, ideological forms in which men become conscious of this conflict and fight it out" [28].

Marx lived in the age of the development of capitalism. He describes the development towards monopoly capitalism, which he calls "the immanent law of capitalistic production itself, the centralisation of capital". He says:

"One capitalist always kills many. Hand in hand with this centralisation, or this expropriation of many capitalists by few, develop, on an ever extending scale, the co-operative form of the labour process, the conscious technical application of science, the methodical cultivation of the soil, the transformation of the instruments of labour into instruments of labour only usable in common, the economising of all means of production by their use as the means of production of combined, socialised labour, the entanglement of all peoples in the net of the world market, and with this, the international character of the capitalistic regime. Along with the constantly diminishing number of the magnates of capital, who usurp and monopolise all advantages of this process of transformation, grows the mass of misery, oppression, slavery, degradation, exploitation; but with this too grows the revolt of the working class, a class always increasing in numbers, and disciplined, united, organised by the very mechanism of the process of capitalist production itself. The monopoly of capital becomes a fetter upon the mode of production, which has sprung up and flourished along with, and under it. Centralisation of the means of production and socialisation of labour, at last reach a point where they become incompatible with their capitalist integument. This integument is burst asunder" [29].

Marx, who died in 1883, did not live to see the imperialist wars of this century. It fell to Lenin to describe the development of imperialism in his pamphlet *Imperialism, the highest stage of capitalism* which he wrote in 1917. Here is what he says, with some omissions for the sake of brevity:

"Imperialism emerged as the development and direct continuation of the fundamental characteristics of capitalism in general. But capitalism only became capitalist imperialism at a definite and very high stage of its development, when certain of its fundamental characteristics began to change into their opposites... Free competition is the fundamental characteristic of capitalism, and of commodity production generally; monopoly is the exact opposite of free competition, but we have seen the latter being transformed into monopoly before our eyes... At the same time, the monopolies, which have grown out of free competition, do not eliminate the latter, but exist over it and alongside it, and thereby give rise to a number of very acute, intense antagonisms, frictions and conflicts. Monopoly is the transition from capitalism to a higher system... Imperialism is capitalism in that stage of development in which the dominance of monopolies and finance capital has established itself; in which the export of capital has acquired pronounced importance; in which the division of the world among the international trusts has begun; in which the division of all territories of the globe among the biggest capitalist powers has been completed."

Lenin brings out the aggressive, militaristic, brutal character of imperialism in his 1920 preface to the pamphlet. He says:

"Capitalism has grown into a world system of colonial oppression and of the financial strangulation of the overwhelming majority of the population of the world by a handful of 'advanced' countries. And this 'booty' is shared between two or three powerful world marauders armed to the teeth (America, Great Britain, Japan), who involve the whole world in *their* war over the sharing of *their* booty."

"One capitalist always kills many." Marx here graphically indicates the ruthlessness of economic development. In the economic base this produces the contradiction between free competition (i.e. private enterprise) and monopoly capitalism. How does this contradiction manifest itself in the superstructure? It manifests itself in multitudinous ways, but I will talk only about its manifestation in the field of art.

Here I must pause briefly to explain the word 'bourgeois'. The bourgeois class is that which becomes dominant with the development of capitalism. It is the class that lives by employing the labour of others and deriving profit from it. Bourgeois culture is the culture of this class. Concurrent with the development of capitalistic private enterprise we see the corresponding development in bourgeois culture of the individual artistic genius. The genius is the characteristic product of bourgeois culture. And just as private enterprise declines in the face of monopolies, so the whole individualistic bourgeois world outlook declines and becomes degenerate, and the concept of genius with it. Today, in the period of the collapse of imperialism any pretensions to artistic genius are a sham.

Earlier I drew attention to the fact that the ruling classes fight tooth and nail to stave off collapse. What are their tactics on the cultural front, the musical front in particular? The attention of the general public must not be drawn to the cultural expression of the collapse of imperialism, namely the degenerate avant garde. To actively suppress it would draw attention. We know that the Nazis' suppression of the avant garde in fact gave the impetus for considerable developmen 's of the avant garde. So it is fostered as the concern of a tiny clique and thus prevented from doing any real damage to the ruling class. In this tiny clique genius is still cultivated, especially when some composer (like Stockhausen or Cage) appear eager to propagate an ideological line – such as mysticism or anarchism or reformism – that is in so far friendly to imperialism in that it opposes socialism and the ideas that would contribute to the organisation of the working class for the overthrow of imperialism. So we see Stockhausen adopting all the hallmarks of the genius of popular legend: arrogance, intractability, irrationality, unconventional appearance, egomania.

But all this is a small scale operation compared with the tactics of the ruling class against the direct class enemy, the working class. In this area we find tactics comparable to the 'saturation bombing' technique of the Americans in Vietnam. There are two main lines of attack. First wide scale promotion of the image of bourgeois culture in its prime, the music of the classical and romantic composers (the whole education system is geared to this). Second, the promotion of mass-produced music for mass consumption. Besides bringing in enormous profits, their hope is that this derivative music (film music, pop music, musical comedy, etc.) will serve for the ideological subjugation of the working class [30]. Both these lines attempt to encourage working class opportunism. The first through a kind of advertising campaign: 'bourgeois is best', and the second through encouraging degenerate tendencies, drugs, mass hypnosis, sentimentality.

Lenin remarked that the English working class could never be kept under by force, only by deception. In other words the ruling class maintains its domination over the working people by telling lies and distorting the truth. The purpose of ideological struggle is to express these lies and distortions. You now have the opportunity to hear Stockhausen's *Refrain*. I've exposed the true character of the piece as part of the superstructure of imperialism, I've shown that it promotes a mystical world outlook which is an ally of imperialism and an enemy of the working and oppressed people of the world. If in the light of all this it still retains any shred of attractiveness, compare it with other manifestations of imperialism today: the British Army in Ireland, the mass of unemployed, for example. Here the brutal character of imperialism is evident, Any beauty that may be detected in *Refrain* is merely cosmetic, not even skin deep.

You might ask, Should I now switch off and protect myself from such ideas by not listening? Well, yes, by all means, that wouldn't be a bad thing in itself. But in the general context these ideas are too widely promoted to be ignored. They must be confronted and their essence grasped. They must be subjected to fierce criticism and a resolute stand taken against them.

What was the effect of the campaign against Cage and Stockhausen? I received a number of letters in response to the broadcast of 'Stockhausen Serves Imperialism', and the publication of the first half of this talk in *The Listener* provoked a storm in its correspondence columns. Seven letters were printed, most of them heatedly defending Stockhausen and attacking my music – but not my criticism. A review by Keith Rowe criticising a concert and TV appearance by Cage from the same standpoint appeared in *Microphone* magazine in June 1972 and created an equivalent flurry of correspondence. This led the editor, while contemptuously dismissing Rowe's review, to propose an entire issue of the magazine devoted to the questions that had been raised. These flurries demonstrated that there was a great eagerness to discuss artistic questions from a political point of view. The contradictoriness of the response showed that there was widespread lack of clarity on the basic questions of aesthetics and politics and their interrelations. Objectively there existed and still exists a need and a demand amongst musicians and their audiences for clarity on the question of the criteria to be used in evaluating music.

It was a symptom of this need that Hans Keller organised two series of talks on the BBC entitled 'Composers on Criticism and Critics on Criticism'. Naturally, in putting out these series, the BBC had no intention of achieving clarity on the question: rather the opposite. Their technique was to set up a large number of individuals to give their opinions in separate broadcasts and not allow any discussions which might have led to the issues being sorted out. My proposal for such a discussion was rejected on the grounds that it would require too much work! My own contribution to the series which was commissioned about the time of the Stockhausen talk, was rejected on the grounds that it was irrelevant!

The real reason for its rejection was, of course, that it was in fact relevant: relevant to the need and demand for the sober critical atmosphere that I mentioned above. I used the rejected talk as a lecture on a number of occasions and the discussions that it provoked proved its relevance. Despite numerous imperfections, some of which are taken up in the notes, the talk is printed here in full in its original form. This brings the chapter on the criticism of Cage and Stockhausen to an end.

On Criticism

To begin I'd like to read a quotation from John Cage.

"A most salient feature of contemporary art is the fact that each artist works as he sees fit, and not in accordance with widely-agreed-upon procedures. Whether this state of affairs pleases or displeases us is not exactly clear from a consideration of modern clichés of thought.

On the one hand we lament what we call the gulf between artist and society, between artist and artist, and we praise (very much like children who can only window shop for candy they cannot buy) the unanimity of opinion out of which arose a Gothic cathedral, an opera by Mozart, a Balinese combination of music and dance. We lament the absence among us of such generally convincing works, and we say it must be because we have no traditional ways of making things. We admire from lonely distance that art which is not private in character but is characteristic of a group of people and the fact that they were in agreement. On the other hand, we admire an artist for his originality and independence of thought, and we are displeased when he is too obviously imitative of another artist's work. In admiring originality, we feel quite at home. It is the one quality of art we feel fairly capable of obtaining. Therefore we say such things as: everyone not only has but should have his own way of doing things. Art is an individual matter. We go so far as to give credence to the opinion that a special kind of art arises from a special neurosis pattern of a particular artist. At this point we grow slightly pale and stagger out of our studios to knock at the door of some neighbourhood psychoanalyst. Or – we stay at home – cherish our differences, and increase our sense of loneliness and dissatisfaction with contemporary art. In the field of music, we express this dissatisfaction variously, we say; the music is interesting, but I don't understand it. Somehow it is not fulfilled. It doesn't have 'the long line'. We then go our separate paths, some of us back to work to write music that few find any use for, and others to spend their lives with the music of another time which, putting it bluntly and chronologically does not belong to them" [31].

This is what John Cage wrote in 1948 at the age of 36. Substantially the same analysis could be made today, and substantially I agree with it. It is an expression of disillusion and frustration. The composer's bright dreams wither up and die for lack of audience – discontent with the state of music today as compared with the music of the past, which he says, revelling in his isolation, does not belong to us. Actually it does belong to us, to do with as we see fit. We must make the past serve the present. But I'll come back to this.

I believe I speak for the vast majority of music lovers when I say, let's face it, modern music (modern classical music as it is called) is not half as good as classical music (which includes baroque classical, classical classical and romantic classical music etc.). What does 'good' mean in that sentence? It means effective, wholesome, moving, satisfying, delightful, inspiring, stimulating and a whole lot of other adjectives that are just as widely understood and acknowledged and just as hard to pin down with any precision. These are the judgements of the music loving public. By comparison with the effectiveness, wholesomeness, emotion, satisfaction, delight, inspiration and stimulus that we (that is, classical music lovers, and we are a class audience) [32] derive from Beethoven, Brahms and the rest, modern music (with very few exceptions) is footling, unwholesome, sensational, frustrating, offensive and depressing. Why is this? It is because the bourgeois/capitalist society that brought music out of church into the realm of bourgeois art, and reached undreamed-of power and imperial glory through the upheavals of the industrial revolution, and also undreamed-of power of artistic expression, is now in the last stages of decay, and modern music reflects that decay.

Because modern music is bad in this sense, decadent, it cannot submit itself to principled, objective criticism, it does not set up the criteria by which it would expose itself as nonsense.

I experienced this personally as a student at the Royal Academy of Music. The nearest we ever got to establishing a criterion was some remark like 'it has a good shape'. In fact, the handwriting, or the neatness of the layout of the score seemed to be a matter of more importance. There were some good sound practical considerations such as 'Can it be heard?' 'It looks interesting on paper but what does it sound like?'

In retrospect I appreciate the technical criteria dealing with the transformation of formal ideas into sound, even those to do with neat presentation, but the rest were so vague as to be useless. In fact I really can't remember what they were. I don't believe any criteria were applied.

The result was that when I came to occupy a teaching position myself at the Royal Academy of Music I instinctively took the line of 'no criticism'. Occasionally I might take issue with a technical point that seemed particularly crass, but generally as regards technical criticism I regarded it as secondary, and to apply secondary criteria while not applying the primary criteria would obviously result in misplaced emphasis.

Also in retrospect I realise that I am not at all qualified to apply technical criteria because in my own period of training I had never mastered anything more than the rudiments. The rest had seemed irrelevant in view of my desire to break with the traditions of tonal music completely. The fact that I was able to pass exams and get diplomas despite my extremely limited compositional technique is due entirely to the fatally liberalistic attitude that permeates our education system.

Liberalism is just as oppressive as the religious dogma of the nineteenth century that it replaces. Liberalism is a tactic whereby the sting is taken out of the huge contradictions that run right through our cultural environment, so that we are tempted to pass them over and ignore them.

If a rebellious composer has to confront the situation that he cannot graduate from the Royal Academy of Music then his rebellion may be broken if it is insubstantial in the first place, but if it is not then it will be immeasurably strengthened and his rebellion will be directed consciously against the establishment. This is a confrontation that the establishment is anxious to avoid, hence its tactic of liberalism.

'No criticism' in a teaching situation leads to psychologically insupportable emphasis on 'self criticism', resulting in introversion and lack of confidence. In 1969 Michael Parsons, Howard Skempton and I founded the Scratch Orchestra, a group of about fifty people devoted to experimental performance arts. Some were students, some office workers, some amateur musicians, some professional, and there were several composers. From the beginning our line was 'no criticism'.

The products of 'no criticism at all' are weak and watery; the products of 'no criticism except self criticism' are intensely introverted. The tension built up until, after two years, the floodgates were opened and the members of the Scratch Orchestra poured out their discontent. This stage represents 'collective self criticism' and from it emerged criteria that we could apply.

This collective self-criticism was fruitful not in terms of output – this decreased sharply – but in terms of the seriousness and commitment of the members. The collective self-criticism was also painful, and so the criteria that came out of it are the product of struggle in a human situation, not an abstract scaffolding erected for aspiring composers to hang their beautiful ideas on. Perhaps they are not even criteria, just questions whereby a composer can externalise his self-criticism and actually do something about it.

Firstly: what does a composer think he's doing? Why and in what spirit does he sit down to compose? Is it to express his inmost soul? Or to communicate his thoughts? Or to entertain an audience? Or educate them? Or to get rich and famous? Or to serve the interests of the community and if so what community, what class?

Secondly: does the music fulfil the needs of the audience? This immediately opens up two areas of study. First the different audiences that exist, where they overlap and what their class character is. And second, what the needs of the different audiences are, what are their aspirations, what are their standards (which means what are their criteria for appreciating music) and are we content to accept these or must we progressively change them?

Thirdly: do the compositions adequately meet the demands of the musicians playing them? A composition should give the musicians involved a creative role in a collective context. If a composition doesn't create a stimulating situation for the musicians involved it is very unlikely that it will stimulate an audience except in a negative way.

Fourthly, what is the material of a composition? It's not just notes and rests, and it's not just a beautiful idea that originates in the unique mind of a genius. It's ideas derived from experience, from social relations, and what the composer does is to transform these ideas into configurations of sound that evoke a corresponding response in the listener.

Fifthly, what is the basis of a composer's economic survival in society? He can take employment in education, in the service of the state, teaching what he has learnt to other composers, or investigating the 'nature of music' (whatever that may be). Or he can take employment in industry, writing film or background music, or commercial music of other kinds. Or he can attempt to win the support of an audience. Or a combination of these.

I must say, as a student at the Royal Academy of Music it would have been extremely useful if these matters had been brought up for consideration, never mind how reluctant I might have appeared at the time to take any notice.

Now I should like to talk about music criticism as a profession. Much propaganda is being done for the view that people are motivated by self-interest, the desire for money or fame or both. This is not true. The majority of people have a definite need to feel that they are serving the community in some way. We need the feeling that we are performing a useful function in society and not just living off society or other individuals in a parasitic way. Most music critics feel the same need.

Critics are an important link in the complex network that constitutes the relations of production of the musical profession. What can they do to serve the community?

A couple of months ago I noticed Andrew Porter saying something just at the end of a review of Wagner's *Ring* in Glasgow about Wagner's dream of the eventual end of capitalism as represented in Gotterdammerung. (This was in the *Financial Times*.) I must say, this inspired my curiosity. I have never seen a Wagner opera, although I have seen Hollywood's *Magic Fire* based on his life. *Magic Fire* bears about as much relation to reality as a Tarzan story [33]. I also know a piano duet version of the Prelude to Act III of *Tristan und Isolde* and once played in the fifth desk of cellos in a nonprofessional performance of the same piece. As regards Wagner's life I know that he was exiled from Germany for his part in a people's uprising in 1849 [34], the same year Karl Marx was exiled [35]. This is the sum total of my knowledge about the most controversial composer of the nineteenth century. I can hear someone saying, 'My lad, if you've reached the ripe age of 36 without having learnt anything about Wagner, you have only yourself to blame.' Well, I think the reason is different. The reason is that virtually everything written and said about Wagner and his music is extremely boring and irrelevant to the present time and reasonable musicians with a certain amount of work to do could not be expected to plough through it.

What does Wagner's music mean in relation to present-day society? If he had theories of Utopian socialism then it would be good to hear about them and criticise them. What is the historical basis of the myths that provide the material for the *Ring*? It would be wonderful to open a daily newspaper and find material of this kind, instead of yet another series of opinions and comments on performances, interpretations, readings of the score etc. The music critic should indicate the cultural and political context of a work, and point out how the work relates to it and what relevance these matters have to society today.

With regard to the work of living composers the critic's task is exceptionally important. On the one hand he is the spokesman of the people. He must demand works that relate directly to the issues and struggles and preoccupations of the present, and lead the way forward to a better society, a truly socialist society. And on the other hand he must stringently criticise such works from the point of view of both form and content, with the aim of building up their strength. He should do this conscientiously and thoroughly, so that strong links will be forged between composer, and critics, so that composer, and critics can feel united in the performance of a common task in the service of the community, namely the production of good music for the benefit of the people.

'Good music'? According to what criteria is it 'good'? And a basic criterion has already been implied, the criterion of the 'people's benefit'.

On the simplest level we can say any music is good that benefits the people, any music is bad that harms them, that tends in the long run to make their conditions of existence worse than they are now or the same as they are now. To make things stay the same is possibly the most grievous harm imaginable. This is the criterion of the people's benefit.

Then: by what criterion do people judge their conditions of existence to be better or worse? (Basically this is the same criterion that composers and critics apply to their work, because composers and critics are people too, with a productive social role like other workers.) Good conditions of existence are: when your needs, physical and spiritual, are fulfilled, when you are conscious of the way your work, your productive activity, contributes to the society you live in, and when – through this consciousness and because your needs are not frustrated – you are able to expand and develop your work so as to maximise its usefulness to society.

So the 'people's good' is this: their basic needs are satisfied, and they are conscious of their position in society; when these two conditions are met, the people's creative energy is released, they can contribute to changing the world. Everything benefits the people that (a) satisfies their needs, (b) raises their level of consciousness, and (c) following from the others encourages them to develop the energy and ability and initiative to change the world according to their collective needs. This is socialist construction.

Is capitalist society as we know it today orientated towards benefiting the people? Let's apply the criteria. Does capitalism satisfy the people's need? No, it regards the people as consumers, [36] and floods them with plastic bottles and white bread which bring vast profits to the manufacturers but no benefit to the consumers so that the majority of people remain in conditions of hardship while the ruling class and its hangers-on live more and more luxuriously and more and more wastefully. Does capitalism raise the people's level of consciousness? No, the mass media feed lies to the people (as, for instance saying that the miners in their strike were holding the nation up for ransom, whereas in fact they were not striking at the 'nation' but at the government and the ruling class), it feeds them platitudes under the guise of education, and crime and violence and sentimentality under the guise of entertainment. No, the mass media not only don't raise the level of consciousness of the people, they try to lower it, they aim to deceive the people.

Obviously these two negatives – not satisfying the people's needs and not raising their level of consciousness – do not produce a positive. In fact under capitalism today people are not encouraged to develop the energy, ability and initiative to change the world according to their collective needs. There is no such thing as socialist construction under capitalism, though Labour politicians will go on asserting that there is until they are blue in the face. There can only be socialist construction in opposition to capitalism [37].

I have been talking about politics. It's evident that the criterion of 'the people's good' is a political criterion. In music, the criterion 'good music is that which benefits the people' is a political criterion. 'Raising the level of consciousness of the people' is a political task. Everything that music can do towards raising the level of consciousness of the people is part of this political task, it subserves this political task. The artist cannot ignore politics. As Mao Tsetung says, "There is no such thing as art that is detached from or independent of politics." And I think I have also made clear what he means in the sentence: 'Each class in every class society has its own political and artistic criteria, but all classes in all class societies put the political criterion first and the artistic criterion second.' This is profoundly true, this point about the precedence of political criteria over artistic criteria. It can be seen to be true, objectively, in capitalist society and it will still be true in a socialist society [38]. To deny this is to cast yourself adrift in the realm of fantasy and, if you are an artist, your work will still be judged according to the political criterion first and the artistic criterion second and it will be seen – notwithstanding any artistic merit it may have – to be misleading the people; not raising their level of consciousness, and hence supporting capitalism and serving to prolong its domination of the working and oppressed people.

CHAPTER 3

A Critical Concert

I spent the year 1973 in West Berlin as a guest of the DAAD (German Academic Exchange Service) 'Berlin Artists Programme'. Every year this programme invites thirty or so artists from all over the world to live in Berlin and 'contribute to the cultural life of the city'. The people of Berlin and in particular the working people show a marked lack of enthusiasm for the contributions of these artists, and the German artists living in Berlin are also justifiably irritated by this importation of a highly paid elite from abroad to divide their ranks and cream off the juiciest commissions. Karl Ruhrberg, who was running the programme while I was there, claims to have been 'helping artists' for twenty-five years. Speaking to some of the artists he is supposed to have helped one receives a very different impression. Guests of the Berlin Artists Programme face a number of unacceptable alternatives when they arrive in Berlin, a frustrating battle to impose their work on an unwelcoming community; loneliness and isolation if they are unwilling or unable to do this; opting out by calling in at Berlin only to receive their cheques, and spending the rest of the time globe-trotting or in their native countries; or servilely collaborating with the Programme and accepting the degenerate social round of cocktail parties and receptions. Some of the artists use their well paid year as a kind of initial capital investment to build themselves an art career in Berlin, and continue to base themselves there afterwards. Others, who may accept the engagement because they are in financial straits, return home afterwards to find their economic outlook as bleak or bleaker than when they left.

One of the channels through which the musician 'guests' ('prisoners' would be more appropriate) of the Programme can present their work to the public is 'Musikprojekte', a concert series organised by the Berlin composer Erhard Grosskopf. Grosskopf, despite the economic discrepancy between him and the well paid guest composers, realises the necessity of uniting where possible with the visitors on the basis of opposition to the cultural oppression of capitalist society. Grosskopf engaged me to present a concert at the Academy of Arts on 7 April 1973. I decided to present Christian Wolff's *Accompaniments* and Frederic Rzewski's compositions *Coming Together* and *Attica*. These two American composers had both been aware of the development of the Scratch Orchestra (in fact, works of theirs had featured prominently in the early repertoire of the orchestra), and had also followed the process of its struggle and transformation with interest. The new work *Accompaniments* had been rejected for performance by the Scratch Orchestra in December 1972. *Coming Together* and *Attica* had already been heard in Berlin the previous summer, and had even generated a certain amount of enthusiasm. However, both these composers were presenting political themes and it was timely to submit their works to a critical appraisal in a public concert. The form of the concert was as follows; first the compositions were played (Wolff's first then Rzewski's), then I gave a short talk and led a discussion with the audience. To create conditions for the discussion, a programme book was printed which included, besides elementary programme material about the compositions (texts and composers' notes), a draft of my introductory talk and reprints of 'Stockhausen Serves Imperialism' and Tilbury's 'Introduction to Cage's *Music of Changes*'. The line that we intended to pursue in the discussion was thus clearly stated. For the present purpose I have rearranged the material slightly and added a 'report' written shortly after the concert. The programme material on the compositions is sandwiched between the Introductory Talk and the Report.

Introductory talk for discussion at Wolff/Rzewski concert

Nobody imagines we live in the 'best of all possible worlds'. In our personal relationships, our work, in our cultural activity, in everything we do we feel the oppression of a social system that is inimical to the vast majority of mankind. Capitalism is antihuman, it puts things first and people second. Logically, this system dictates that people too should become things, so that they may better be integrated into a society based on the production and consumption of things. In other words, for the evils that we experience in society today, the capitalist system prescribes anti-consciousness, a suppression of those human characteristics that enable a man to reflect on his environment and judge what is good and bad about it.

To regard this oppressive process as an inevitably determined one is to fall victim to anti-consciousness. The system wants to preserve itself, it is conscious.

The system is people, the people that control our environment in all its complex interactions – its legal system, political and cultural institutions, its armed forces, its police, its education, etc. In fact it is those people who we refer to as the ruling class who consciously disseminate anti-consciousness, in an effort to prolong indefinitely their rule, their control.

Unlike these people (who are resisting change), the vast majority of the rest of us feel the 'necessity for change' [39]. But if I now go on to say that the change that is necessary is the overthrow of the ruling, controlling class I am probably jumping ahead of a number of people. And in fact I am giving a false impression, an incorrect picture, even though the substance of it is quite right. It is utopian, the 'overthrow of the ruling class' is an abstraction, an ideal if I don't regard it from the point of view of the present situation[40]. (In fact in making such a jump I am opening the door to all kinds of ridiculous notions, for example that beings from outer space might overthrow the ruling class, or the working class might suddenly and miraculously wake up to its 'historic mission' to overthrow the ruling class. Such ideas are pure fantasy and cause harm.)

In saying that the change that is necessary is the overthrow of the ruling class I am denying or ignoring the fundamental truth that the basis of change is internal, and that external circumstances can only provide favourable or unfavourable conditions for change. The basis for the overthrow of the ruling class lies in the internal weakness of that class. The basis for the victory of the working class lies in the internal strength of the working class. The favourable conditions for the collapse of the ruling class are not only the growing strength and consciousness of the working class, but also the liberation struggles of the colonial and neocolonial peoples and many other factors. The favourable conditions for the victory of the working class – well, they are so plentiful it is hard to know where to begin. They range from the bankruptcy of imperialist culture and economic problems of imperialism to the shining examples of socialist China and Albania and the worldwide upsurge of revolutionary theory and practice.

It is seen that the victory of one class and the defeat of another form a dialectical unity. It is not their external, superficial strength or weakness that determines the outcome, but their internal, essential structure. The forces of imperialism are outwardly strong, but in the present and forthcoming struggles they will inevitably come to occupy their rightful position in the 'dustbin of history'.

A similarly dialectical process is at work in the development of the revolutionary movement. Here it is the dialectical unity of being and consciousness that is essential. It is fantasy to imagine that the working class and its allies will first became politically conscious and then rise to overthrow the ruling class.

The working class and other progressive sections of the population will become politically conscious, fully, only through the actual practice of overthrowing the ruling class in the real world, and then themselves becoming the ruling class.

When, through the social activity and circumstances of our lives we, as individuals, became conscious of the 'necessity for change', we experience the dialectical unity of being and consciousness. At that moment when we genuinely confront the 'necessity for change' in society, a process of change begins *in us*, we begin to grow and develop. We begin to participate in changing society and our consciousness grows alongside this. So, in terms of the individual human being just as in terms of society at large, the basis of change is internal. Outwardly, he tries to create the favourable conditions for this change to go forward. The revolutionary does not do this by retiring to a cave for cultivation of his immortal soul but by ploughing into the struggle against the old and the obsolete, against the decadent and the degenerate, against the human agents of oppression and exploitation (also in the field of culture and art), knowing that practical activity in this struggle provides the best possible external conditions favouring the development not only of his own personal consciousness, but also the consciousness of the vast mass of people who are materially and culturally oppressed under the present social system. In the struggle against the old and decrepit the new is born. In the fight against the political and cultural institutions of imperialism the proletarian revolutionary Party develops the capability to lead the working class in the overthrow of the ruling class.

In the field of music, an ever increasing number of people are taking the conscious road, in opposition to the anti conscious (or 'cosmic conscious') positions adopted by the various 'geniuses' of modern music who tamely – and some say unwittingly – allow their talents to be enlisted on the side of the ruling class. Those composers who take the conscious road necessarily submit to the test of practice. They can no longer take refuge in beautiful ideas, elegance of manner, logical completeness, formal perfection or the 'history of music' (which has no existence separate from social history), and nor do they wish to. In evaluating the work of artists who wish to be conscious, we must place content above form, effect above motive, the essential above the superficial. Rzewski and Wolff are two such artists, who have chosen explicitly political subject matter for their recent works. So the points we should discuss in connection with their works are, what are they saying in their pieces, to whom are they saying it, and whom does it benefit? What effect did they intend to achieve with such works and what effect are they actually achieving? Does the literal, superficial content of their work conceal a deeper, essential content, and if so, what aspects of the real world are reflected in this deeper content?

Accompaniments, text and programme note

The text for *Accompaniments I* is taken from an English translation of *China: the Revolution Continued* by Jan Myrdal and Gun Kessle. The speakers are a veterinarian and a midwife in the village of Liu Ling in the area of Yenan in Northwest China.

Veterinarian (male voice singing)

"My mother is very old now. I asked for leave of absence to go and see her. In such cases we're always granted leave. Obviously.

There are those who call looking after sick animals dirty work. But Chairman Mao has taught us not to be afraid of filth and excrement. And that's right. Chairman Mao has pointed out how necessary it is to develop stock breeding. And that's why we are getting ourselves more and more animals and why I'm studying all the time."

Midwife (female voice singing)

"We've been successful in our work. Now the new-born babies don't die any more. Formerly 60 per cent of all new-born infants died. The old way of giving birth to children was unhygienic. Dangerous both for mother and child. To begin with it was necessary to spread a great deal of information. But now there are no more problems over childbirth. Now the women understand why hygiene is important. Today, I deliver all the women in the village.

I'm also responsible for infant care. I teach the women. It's cleanliness that's so important. Their clothes must be clean, their hands must be clean. Their food must be clean. Cleanliness is the answer to disease. It is thanks to cleanliness our babies are surviving. Now the women too understand that three or four years should go by between pregnancies. Pregnancies that are too close together are damaging to health. Formerly many women were always pregnant. Most now understand that this is bad.

But we must go on spreading information. There used to be some men who spoke against contraception. It was easier to convince the women. But now even none of the men are against them. Now everyone says they agree. But some families are thoughtless. And of course there are accidents too. Today condoms are much cheaper than they were seven years ago. Now they cost only one yuan per hundred. And no one is so poor he can't afford that.

Other things are more problematic. There are so many bad old customs which must be combatted. There are those who aren't careful enough about their food.

Not everyone looks after their latrines properly. Dry earth must be used for covering them. There must be no flies. We have got quite a long way with our hygienic work but not the whole way. That is why unremitting propaganda is needed against the old bad habits. Not to look after latrines properly, that's one such bad habit. Hygiene is a political question. The old bad habits are deep-rooted, but we're fighting them all the time, and things are getting better every year that goes by.

This work we do during study meetings. To study and apply Mao Tsetung Thought; a good method. Good things can be praised. During these studies many people have come to realise that latrines too are a political question."

Wolff wrote to me that the piece had been written in response to a request from Rzewski for a piano piece[41]. He had the feeling that texts should be associated with whatever he wrote, if possible. The accompaniment chords had been worked out previously but he had not known what to do with them. For a number of reasons he had been reading about Marxism and about China, where (as he says) it really seems to be happening. The text struck him because it was direct and plain, practical about important matters (sanitation, contraception) which are ordinary, almost beneath the notice of 'serious', intellectual people; and because these matters are treated in a coherent and positive way, in relation to life as a whole, i.e. politically. He says the text expresses a sense of change in ordinary, specific problems necessarily related to change in the structure of society as a whole. He also chose the text because it was not 'propaganda' in the usual sense, but just statement of fact by the people experiencing it. His motive was to publicise the spirit of the text in a way he thought he could manage and that was congenial, i.e. with that music. He also had the notion that that music had an appropriate feeling (the formal ideas involve movement in cycles that also move forward and, incidentally, gradually upward, by transposition).

This performance is interspersed with instrumental interludes from *Accompaniments IV*. About this music Wolff says it came as a response to the spirit of the text and was written very rapidly, i.e. freely, within a few simple and, he hoped, clarifying restrictions, mostly harmonic, meant to give coherence and, again, a sense of moving forward. He says it is an attempt to write music with elements, melodic and harmonic, that are more directly and generally accessible than his earlier music.

The piece was originally conceived to be played by one person, Rzewski, whose performance as a pianist would be professional and as a singer, amateur. Wolff says that this mixture was deliberate, since the division between professional and amateur is something we've long been trying to break down.

Wolff's score divides the text into groups of 1, 2, 4, 8 or 16 syllables, each group associated with a set of 16 four note chords. One of these chords, a different one each time, is used to accompany each syllable of the text. Much is left to the performer to decide; the choice and order and timbre of the accompaniment chords, the rhythm and melody of the text (the score says simply that it is to be delivered 'simply'), etc. One could say that Wolff had provided the material but not the composition.

For this performance four composers worked on the material: Howard Skempton composed the rhythm, Chris May composed and instrumented the accompaniment as well as some of the instrumental interludes from *Accompaniments IV*, Janet Danielson wrote the voice parts, and I initiated and coordinated the work of these composers [42].

Coming Together and *Attica*: text and programme note

Text (spoken without accompaniment): 'In September 1971 inmates of the state prison at Attica in the state of New York, unable to endure further the intolerable conditions existing there, revolted and succeeded in capturing a part of the institution, as well as a number of guards, whom they held as hostages. Foremost among their demands during the ensuing negotiations was the recognition of their right 'to be treated as human beings'. After several days of inconclusive bargaining, Governor Rockefeller ordered state troopers in to retake the prison by force, justifying his action on the grounds that the lives of the hostages were in danger. In the slaughter that followed, forty-three persons lost their lives, including several of the hostages. One of these was Sam Melville, a political prisoner already known for his leadership in the Columbia riots and one of the leaders in the rebellion at Attica. According to some accounts, Sam was only slightly wounded in the assault. The exact cause of his death remains a mystery. The text for the following piece is taken from a letter that Sam wrote from Attica in the spring of 1971.

(Declaimed with musical backing): "I think the combination of age and a greater coming together is responsible for the speed of the passing time. It's six months now, and I can tell you truthfully, few periods in my life have passed so quickly. I am in excellent physical and emotional health. There are doubtless subtle surprises ahead, but I feel secure and ready. As lovers will contrast their emotions in times of crisis so am I dealing with my environment. In the indifferent brutality, the incessant noise, the experimental chemistry of food, the ravings of lost hysterical men, I can act with clarity and meaning. I am deliberate, sometimes even calculating, seldom employing histrionics except as a test of the reactions of others. I read much, exercise, talk to guards and inmates, feeling for the inevitable direction of my life."

(Spoken without accompaniment): "One of the leaders of the rising in Attica prison was Richard X. Clark. On February 8th 1972, Clark was set free from Attica. As the car that was taking him to Buffalo passed the Attica village limits, he was asked how it felt to put Attica behind him." He said:

(Declaimed with musical backing): "Attica is in front of me."

Programme notes (supplied by Rzewski): *Coming Together*, for a speaker and variable instrumental ensemble, was composed in January 1972. The text on which the composition is based, a letter written by Sam Melville in the spring of 1971, describes in eight terse sentences the writer's experience of passing time in prison. In the musical setting, each sentence is broken into seven parts, which are spoken at regular intervals; each sentence is heard seven times. The written music, a single continuous melodic line built of seven pitches, is a precisely defined structure within which a certain amount of improvisation is possible. The title refers both to a passage in the text and to the specific improvisational technique used. *Attica* is a shorter piece based on a quotation of Richard X. Clark with a similar but simpler structure.

Both compositions deal with a historical event: the uprising and massacre at Attica Correctional Facility in September 1971. They do not make a reasoned political statement about the event. They reproduce personal documents relating to it, and attempt to heighten the feelings expressed in them by underscoring them with music. There is therefore a certain ambiguity between the personal, emotional, and meditative aspect of the texts, which is enhanced by cumulative repetition, and their wider political implications. I believe this ambiguity can be either a strength or a weakness in performance, depending on the degree to which the performer identifies personally with the revolutionary struggle taking place in America's prisons and the world at large [43].

A report on the concert

The concert can be reviewed from several points of view. First, from my own point of view, the concert was very useful: I made many mistakes and we can learn from these by negative example. I'll go into the mistakes at the end.

The concert was also useful to me in that it provided a shared experience, a basis for future discussion and activity amongst the circle of my acquaintance in Berlin, thus breaking out of a situation of isolation and hearsay; my isolation from practising musicians in Berlin, their hearsay about my activities.

This all seems very personal. Nevertheless, in view of the frequent reproaches received about using music as a pretext for politics, etc., it is important to see that all these things are interwoven: people's personal lives, their individual consciousness, their class consciousness, their cultural habits, their political leanings or allegiance.

The second point of view is that of Rzewski and Wolff. A friendly contact exists with these composers and on this basis constructive criticism can be developed.

Coming Together is a piece which deals with a local event, the Attica prison uprising, occurring in a worldwide context of liberation struggles. It is very important material and highly suitable for musical treatment. The error of the piece is that it treats of its subject in a subjective way. The text is fragmented and repeated according to a mechanical plan, with the result that it becomes obsessive. The instrumental accompaniment, which refers to popular music and does actually engage the pop conscious audience and is a good initiative to that extent, nevertheless develops a negative aspect of pop music – its hypnotic or hysterical aspect – and none of its positive aspects.

The basic ideology of the piece is anarchism. I say this not because Sam Melville was an anarchist (I don't know if he was or not), but on account of the choice and treatment of this text for this purpose. The political activities springing from anarchism are reformism and terrorism, which is something we did not bring out clearly enough in the discussion. We came up against an important political theme and did not discuss it properly. The dialectical unity of reformism and terrorism was not brought out for example. For instance, in Northern Ireland the Civil Rights Movement ('a fair deal for Catholics') and the IRA are two sides of the same coin: they are both pleading for the most flagrant injustices to be removed, so that class relations can continue as before [44].

Anarchism is an ideology that springs from the decaying bourgeoisie. From the wreckage of broken bourgeois promises (e.g., individual freedom, etc.), the anarchist wants to leap into absolutes, 'total freedom', 'no government at all', etc. Its bourgeois origin is evident from the fact that it plays down the class struggle and the role of the masses in making history.

Hence, although this piece could potentially find some acceptance amongst the youth, as far as its language is concerned, it would not find acceptance amongst the class-conscious proletariat, since its ideology is not proletarian and in fact is not far removed from Mick Jagger's 'I can't get no satisfaction', and contributes just as little to revolutionary change. Marxists should therefore militate against the introduction of such works amongst the masses – they get too much of this already.

Accompaniments in the version we prepared, met with a totally blank reception from the audience, and I gather that things were not much warmer when the piece was first played by Rzewski in the USA. Why don't people respond to the piece? I think Wolff's mistake is in thinking that if something is simple it can be easily understood. This leads to the corrupt equation: simple = popular, implying that the masses are simple-minded. In fact in a complex world simplicity is achieved only by a process of abstraction, and abstractions are not easily grasped. Especially not by the masses whose daily activity tends to be more practical and hence has to deal constantly with the complexity of the real world. At some points in our version there were hints of that kind of simplicity that characterises a fairy story or a lullaby, but they were only hints and the context was lacking in which they could have been effective [45].

The main criticism of Wolff's piece centred on why this text was selected. The intuitive scepticism that had greeted this piece when I tried to introduce it to the Scratch Orchestra last year was illuminated by a flash of lightning when I received Christian's notes on the piece, in which he mentions the themes of the text as 'sanitation and birth control'. Of course, pollution and the population explosion, two of the great red herrings (secondary contradictions) that the bourgeoisie has brought out in the last few years in an attempt to distract people's attention from the principal contradiction, capital and labour. I don't imagine that Christian scoured the annals of the Chinese Revolution with specific intention of finding material that would be of use for a bourgeois propaganda campaign. But it's important to remember that there are whole armies of academics and journalists doing just that, and the fact that Christian was innocently drawn into something similar (though on a small scale) says something about how intensively and unremittingly we've got to fight against bourgeois ideology if we're ever going to manage more than 'one step forward, two steps back'.

From the point of view of the audience the concert was confusing. In the old Scratch Orchestra we used to work hard to create confusion, such confusion that the mind could no longer grapple with the overall situation and would thus submit voluntarily to the enslavement of 'mere phenomena'. In this concert there were extenuating circumstances and positive aspects to the confusion, but avant-gardists have to be on their guard against such notions that confusion is a good thing 'in itself' because it dialectically gives rise to clarity, and similar intellectual artifices.

Some false preconceptions were attacked. For instance, the idea that the musician or conductor (or even the composer) identifies with the music he presents. It became apparent that we had presented this music in order to criticise it. This seemed to create a slight sense of shock. But obviously it's essential that an intellectual audience takes a critical attitude to art, and this means, in the present wave of superficially political art works (such as Warhol's Mao prints, to take a crass example), developing the political criteria to deal with them. Often artists do not consciously support the political line that their art reflects, so when an artist reflects a bourgeois political line in his work (as do Rzewski and Wolff) this does not mean that we should necessarily regard him as a scheming enemy; there is a good chance that he is actually an erring brother. The path that should be pointed out to such artists is the path of investigation and study. Along this path it quickly becomes clear that there is no such thing as investigation and study above class and then the most crucial matter comes into the foreground: integrating with the masses. This is summed up in the slogan: 'Seek truth from facts to serve the people.'

One interesting fact about the composition of the audience for avant garde music came out. Besides the regular fans and cliques there are quite a few people who come on spec hoping to hear something new and above all something that means something. They are invariably disappointed and never reappear, but there are always more where they came from. Hence the fact that though the avant garde audience does not grow, it does not disappear entirely.

Now for the mistakes. In planning and organising the concert I gave the music a secondary role and the discussion the primary role. So far, so good. What I failed to take into account was that the primary role cannot be played properly if the secondary role is not played properly. The choice of instrumentalists, the preparation of parts, the amount of rehearsal time necessary – all these things I treated in a summary way, leaving it in the hands of others, while concentrating myself on the discussion material. The result was that we almost didn't have anything to discuss. Also, although there was some discussion and struggle amongst the musicians during rehearsal, it failed to develop strongly simply because of the pressure of work.

We learn from this that if you present something for criticism you must present it legibly. It was not a question of criticising Rzewski and Wolff personally (as if to say, you've gone wrong and deserve everything you get in the way of bad performances, etc.), but criticising their ideological and political lines, which also exist in the audience's mind and in our own. Our aim should have been, with the aid of this music, to bring these ideological and political lines out into the open and take a conscious stand against them and criticise them. By not presenting the music strongly enough we failed to generate that sense of community (basis of all music making) in which a meaningful discussion could have taken place – i.e. a discussion leading to a degree of unity at least among a section of those present.

20th May 1973

CHAPTER 4

Self Criticism: Repudiation of Earlier Works

Someone taking a stand, digging his heels in, making judgements on the basis of political criteria not only provokes a response (positive, in that the ideas put forward are taken up in discussion) but also in reaction (negative, in that people are knocked off balance and retaliate in a wild and flailing manner). The reaction to the criticism of Cage and Stockhausen often took the form 'What about your music? Your music is just as bourgeois and backward as theirs'. Maybe such critics hoped I would feel obliged to defend my own music and thus inevitably return to the straight and narrow path of servile ideologist of the bourgeoisie. Treacherous solicitude! The fact is that everything is involved in the process of change, including my ideas, and I make no bones about having produced music just as backward as anything a Cage or a Stockhausen is capable of. The main thing is not the mistakes one makes, but one's ability to learn from them and change direction.

The bourgeoisie has now given me two opportunities publicly to repudiate my own earlier compositions.

The first opportunity presented itself as an invitation to contribute to an 'International Symposium on the Problematic of Today's Musical Notation' held in Rome from 23-26 October 1972. About 100 scientists, musicologists, educationalists and composers were invited (no fee, but all expenses paid, even from the remotest corners of the globe) to contribute to this 'symposium' on a non-existent problem [46]. I participated in the symposium quite militantly, taking sides on a number of issues and refusing to vanish into thin air at the crack of any absurdly abstruse scientific or philosophical whip. The venue was the monumental neo-fascist edifice of the Institute Latino-Americano. The furnishings were plush in the extreme, individual arm-chairs fitted with head-phones providing simultaneous translation into four languages. My own contribution took the form of a talk on my composition *Treatise*, a 200 page so-called 'graphic score' composed 1963–67 as an attempt to escape from the performance rigidities of serial music and encourage improvisation amongst avant garde musicians.

Talk for Rome Symposium on problems on notation

What are the problems of musical notation today? There is no problem in dealing with new sounds on instruments, since the number of new symbols that can be devised is unlimited. On the other hand there are musical problems created by the systematic exploitation of the complexities available in the notation, for example in the avant garde music of the 1950s – but that would be the subject of a different symposium. In that music it's often not the music that's serial but the scores [47].

One might imagine problems of notation arising where the inspiration of the music is divorced from the fundamental assumptions of western musical notation, for instance if you want to write music that doesn't progress through rhythmic units, or that doesn't restrict itself to the division of the octave into twelve equal parts, or if your method of composing is by manipulating tape and you need a score not for production purposes but as a means to study formal relationships already existing in sound (on tape). However, it is probable that the inspiration of modern composers cannot escape the influence of the conventions of our music notation, and problems of this sort are likely to be soluble by extensions of the existing framework of notation conventions.

What I want to talk about is not such problems as these but what I feel to be diseases of notation, cases where the notation seems to have become a malignant growth usurping an absolutely unjustifiable pre-eminence over the music. I feel obliged to study these diseases on my own body, in my own work, rather than as they are evident elsewhere in the avant garde. One reason for this is that I can diagnose them with far greater certainty in the context of my own development than in someone else's and also I can speak with greater authority and full consciousness about the harmful effect of these diseases and how they hamper rather than enhance any development in one's musical thinking.

So far I have identified two main diseases, first, the idea that each composition requires or deserves its own unique system of notation. Let's be more accurate: the composer doesn't conceive of a piece of music so much as a notation system, which musicians may then use as a basis for making music, or more likely (as I would evaluate it today), aimless manipulations of the system in terms of sound [48].

Second, the idea that a musical score can have some kind of aesthetic identity of its own, quite apart from its realisation in sound, in other words that the score is a visual art work, the appreciation of which may depend on a consciousness of music and sound and the ways they have been notated, but with no certainty that the ideas of the composition can be transferred into and expressed through the world of sound. In my output I was preoccupied for several years with a large-scale manifestation of this second disease, the graphic score *Treatise*, and it is to this work that I wish to apply some more detailed criticism.

Of course diseases of this kind do not arise spontaneously. We must get to their roots and understand how they grow and what plants them and nourishes them. Then, as in medicine, the correct method is to devise a strategy for eliminating the root causes of a disease and tactics for dealing with its symptoms until such time as they disappear.

An adequately planned criticism of a work of avant garde art might proceed as follows:

First, to look at the score itself, to go into the superficial formal contradictions manifested, in the case of *Treatise*, in the graphic work.

Second, to try and uncover the ideas that it embodies, expose its content, and see whether these ideas are right or wrong, whether they truly reflect what we know about the real world.

Third, to examine the cultural environment of the avant garde, the place of the avant garde within the general production of music today.

Fourth, to see the social and economic factors that produce and mould that cultural environment.

These social and economic factors are not standing still, they are changing and developing. A result of this is the conflict between progressive forces, which recognise the inevitability or the necessity for change and actively promote it, and reactionary forces, which oppose change. This conflict is fought out in the realms of politics. The decisive thing is, who holds political power? And here I don't mean which political party but which class holds political power? At this point we should move on with our critical programme.

Fifth, to see how political power – and in capitalist society this means virtually 'money' – controls the manifestations of the fundamental conflict in the cultural environment, including the avant garde.

Sixth, to recognise the ideas, the world outlook, represented by a particular piece of avant garde music as being the ideas characteristic of the ruling class, ideas that do not challenge that class and its power, and hence support its continued existence.

Seventh, because these ideas are reactionary and do not accurately reflect the present stage of our knowledge of the world we see that their forms of expression (say, the graphic work of *Treatise*) are contradictory and incoherent, like the words of a liar who has lost all hope of deceiving his audience.

So it becomes clear that the roots of those diseases lie in society, not in the minds of misguided composers. Society develops through class antagonisms; bourgeois society is produced by the domination of the capitalist class and the subjugation of the working class. Bourgeois society was once immensely progressive in many fields, especially in the field of industrial production and also in the field of culture and artistic production. But bourgeois society is now in the last stages of decay and is the victim of countless diseases, including inflation, the pollution of the atmosphere, and cultural degeneracy. Does the fact that the roots of all our cultural ills lie in society absolve the individual artist from all responsibility for these ills? Certainly not. As Marx said of philosophy, 'It is not enough to understand the world, the point is to change it', so we should say to artists, 'It is not enough to decorate the world, the point is to influence it.'

The strategy for eliminating the root causes of our present artistic disease is the same strategy as is needed for eliminating the root causes of most of the evils of society today, namely the overthrow of monopoly capitalism and the bourgeois state and its replacement by socialism.

The great thing for artists to realize is that this step involves all sections of society including themselves. Having seen that the cultural environment is moulded by who hold political power, the artist must then quite consciously take a political stand in his art and life, and it certainly does not contradict the instincts of the bourgeois artist of the 'good old days' to take a progressive stand and not a reactionary one; the one thing that has to change is his class allegiance[49]. The bourgeois artist was never essentially a capitalist, he worked in the service of capitalism in its progressive stage. Now he should work in the service of the progressive, revolutionary class of the present, the working class. In doing so he is no longer a bourgeois artist coping with incurable cultural disease but a proletarian artist participating in the fight to change the world.

Such a change is not the work of a moment. For the composer it is not only a question of making a decision but of changing one's ideas. It is in this area that some tactics for coping with the symptoms of our cultural disease are useful. The main tactic that I have in mind is criticism, and that's why I outlined that 7 point critical method.

Such a critical method should be used on works that have a large effect on a large audience, in order to expose their true character and minimise their harmful effect. Happily for my peace of mind *Treatise* has not been so successful, and I am treating it merely as a test case. Rather than waste time on a systematic study of something which, though large, is of small importance, I want just to talk about some of the salient features.

In criticising art we should proceed from the basic standpoint that art contains ideas; it is an expression of consciousness, not just a phenomenon of the natural world, or a documentation of such a phenomenon. We live in the world, and our ideas are about the world. The sum total of our ideas constitutes our world outlook. Ideas are right or wrong in proportion as they reflect truly or distort the world[50]. They are relevant or irrelevant in proportion as they reflect the forces that are most active in the world today. The most active forces in the world today are not cosmic forces, or atomic forces, or spiritual forces (whatever they may be), but the social forces, the forces generated by large groupings of human beings.

Let's start with the idea – very widespread in the avant garde and implicit in the score of *Treatise* – that anything can be transformed into anything else. Now everybody knows (not only Marxists and farmers) that a stone, no matter how much heat you apply to it, will never hatch into a chicken. And that even an egg won't hatch into a chicken without the right external conditions. And yet in Cage's work *Atlas Eclipticalis* patterns of stars in a star atlas are transformed into a jumble of electronic squeals and groans. This transformation is carried out through a system of notation (a logic) that has no connection with astronomy and only a very sketchy connection with music.

In *Gruppen* Stockhausen transforms formant analyses of vocal sound into flurries of notes on orchestral instruments. In *Structures* Boulez transforms numerical systems into random successions of sound on two pianos. In graphic music a string of visual symbols is transformed into sound. True, there is a distinction between the Cage example and the other examples. Cage consciously refrains from imposing an image on the material generated by his transformations, whereas Stockhausen and Boulez do just that – they convert their fragmented material into a semblance of musical form, just as a mass of string can be shaped into the semblance of a human being; these semblances should of course be studied and criticised, from the point of view that the images of art should intensify, not falsify, our consciousness of the world.

Nevertheless, this distinction between Cage and the others is more apparent than real. Though Cage may refrain from forming his material into images, society does it for him – his works are played in concerts and hence are listened to as pieces of music, and the audience does its best to relate them to the world of their experience. And actually that's not too hard, for in its effect Cage's music does give an approximate reflection of some aspects of present-day life under capitalism. *Concert for Piano* sounds like a chaotic welter of individualistic conflicts, without harmony, without purpose. *HPSCHD* creates an image of society as a jumble of sense stimuli, flashing lights and tinkling sounds, in which the individual is reduced to the position of a mere spectator. These negative, pessimistic effects created by Cage's music reflect the surface character of the capitalist world, they do not reflect its essence. They don't indicate the direction of its change and development and worst of all they deny the positive contribution that individuals are capable of making towards this change.

Change is absolute, there is nothing that does not change. But it is just a stupid pun to say, on this basis, that everything is interchangeable, or by your actions to imply any such belief. Summer changes to winter, iron ore is changed into steel, a sequence of notes can be changed into a melody, but a tree can never be changed into a saucer of milk. Not in the real world. But in avant garde art it can (the mist might saw down the tree, scoop out a hollow and fill it with milk), and this is not only irrelevant to the social struggles going on in the world, but on a very fundamental level it is distorting reality, propagating lies, wrong ideas, about the real world. George Brecht's work on paradoxes is on this level – it operates on the pretence that a paradox can have a concrete existence and is more than just an error of formulation[51]. Such artists of course defend themselves with humour. But society needs art, it needs artists, quite seriously, that's why it has always produced them and it is not going to be satisfied with a bunch of intellectuals cracking jokes amongst themselves.

There are right ideas and wrong ones about the history of music. It is correct to say that music is produced to fulfill the needs of a society and that vast amounts, in particular, are produced to fulfill the need of the ruling class in that society to hold the subject classes down ideologically. It is quite incorrect to say that music is a world of its own, developing according to its own internal laws. It is, if possible, even more incorrect to say that musical *notation* is a world of its own, developing according to its own internal laws And yet this seems to be the premise on which *Treatise* is composed. As it says in the *Treatise Handbook* (a collection including the notes I made while working on *Treatise*), "The way the elements act on each other – it is like chemical processes: acid bites, circles roll and drag, and bend the stave lines of 'musical space'." *Treatise* arbitrarily combines images of transformations that occur in the real world: images of mathematical or logical transformations (multiplication of elements, relations between pairs of dissimilar elements, presence and absence of elements), and of physical transformations (by fragmentation, exploding, squashing, bending, melting, interpenetrating, etc.). And in amongst all these visual abstractions from reality a host of devices are used to keep the reader amused: 3 dimensional effects, pictorial effects, hints at concrete objects (trees, clouds, etc.) and enigmatic musical symbols.

This fits very well with what I said about the incoherence of the liar who has lost all hope of deceiving his listeners. He is quite likely to turn then to diversionary tactics just as a child does in a situation of embarrassment: standing on his head, singing a silly song, knocking over a jug of milk or simply pretending to be mad. Anyway, in *Treatise* the effect of these devices is as minimal as that of the *Notenbild*, the visual aspect of a traditional score – an undefined, subjective stimulus for the interpreter.

In performance, the score of *Treatise* is in fact an obstacle between the musicians and the audience.

Behind that obstacle the musicians improvise, but instead of improvising on the basis of objective reality and communicating something of this to the audience, they preoccupy themselves with that contradictory artefact: the score of *Treatise*. So not only is *Treatise* an embodiment of (not only irrelevant but also) incorrect ideas, it also effectively prevents the establishment or communication between the musicians and the audience.

Musical graphics are a substitute for composition. It is a truly laughable situation when you can compose a piece of 'music' without ever having heard or played a note of music. In fact nowadays you don't even have to use pen and ink, you can get a computer to draw it for you.

It is interesting to see from my own experience how the avant garde fights tooth and nail in support of its incorrect ideas. In the early days of writing *Treatise* (1963) I was studying the work of Frege [52]. In the *Handbook* I quote two phrases of his: 'The mysterious power of words devoid of thought', and 'No one will expect any sense to emerge from empty symbols'. Quite right. Words devoid of thought have the power only to mystify and confuse, and no sense will ever emerge from empty symbols. And yet, despite Rzewski's very reasonable suggestion that I should abandon the piece, I persevered with it for four more years.

What more graphic illustration of the astounding tenacity of bourgeois ideology, and what more telling indication of how ruthlessly that ideology must now be fought against in the avant garde!

How to account for this 'astounding tenacity' of bourgeois ideology in the avant garde? To quote the *Handbook* again: 'Psychologically, the existence of *Treatise* is fully explained by the situation of the composer who is not in a position to make music' [53]. The avant garde is isolated. By the process of alienation which has been going forward in giant strides since the beginning of the century, the modern composer has become isolated both from the working musicians and from any audience except a tiny intellectual elite. So, although the state will continue to support it and even promote some kind of audience for it, such support and such audience cannot cover up the fact that the avant garde is in desperate straits. It represents bourgeois ideology with its back to the wall.

The ideology of a ruling class is present in its art implicitly; the ideology of a revolutionary class must be expressed in its art explicitly. Progressive ideas must shine like a bright light into the dusty cobwebs of bourgeois ideology in the avant garde, so that any genuinely progressive spirits working in the avant garde find their way out, take a stand on the side of the people and set about making a positive contribution to the revolutionary movement.

During the symposium I made a number of shorter contributions and I publish these notes here for the sake of local colour, to give an impression of what the symposium was actually like.

Additional material presented in the course of discussion

There is a great difference between the remarks in my talk about notation problems and the statements of the scientists. I say that all problems of notation will be solved by the masses, i.e. through the efforts of working musicians and composers and also teachers and musicologists, engaged in the practical activities of music. What makes the scientists' position so difficult is that they want to study and analyse a language (or create a meta-language) in the laboratory, without contact with the people who speak it, and without interest in what is being said (they are only interested in *how* it says things). In this they reflect an attitude that is rife amongst composers – the tendency to become preoccupied with form to the exclusion of content.

The case of the Hukwe song in Carpitezza's lecture was revealing[54]. Of course the early transcribers of ethnic music were quite naive in their 'eurocentrism'. But what the talk brought out was that no progress has been made, only more sophistication. Music cannot be understood except in its social context. In any case let's think what the motive force is in ethnomusicology and related studies. Civilisation is destroying primitive man. The idea is to take possession of his resources. (Brazil, where they go out hunting Indians.) In order to convert the resources of primitive man – primarily his land – into bourgeois property, imperialism exterminates the people and, as a preliminary to this, it has his culture transcribed and makes this into bourgeois property too.

It is interesting that the same property relations can be seen in the field of pop music today. Many records are made without benefit of anything written. However, all pop records are transcribed, something is written down, because this is the only way the musicians can establish copyright, can assert their private ownership of the music. In tackling the question of musical *content*, Stefani takes up a number of avenues and subdivides many of them [55]. So we find under section 4 the two subdivisions, denotative and connotative meaning, and in the last of eight subdivisions of the field of connotative meaning, we find what he calls 'global axiological connotations'. He says, 'as any other reality, the musical work can form the object of moral and political evaluations.'

Most composers would agree that a composition is not an 'object to be evaluated' (property again), but a force to influence the consciousness of living people and *as such* it functions morally and politically. So this point should not be at the end of some remote cul-de-sac of the musicologists' categorisation, but in the direct forefront, occupying most of the screen. To what is the rest of his paper devoted? I don't pretend to understand it all, but it is obvious that if the most relevant aspect is dealt with in two lines and the paper is 24 pages long, there is a great deal that is irrelevant.

Of course there is a reply to this. I came up against it in connection with Ashley's talk – someone said, 'that's all very fine but this is a conference about notation, and Ashley just changed the subject and referred to politics'[56]. There are two points to be made here. Firstly, it is good to change the subject from something unimportant to something important. And in dealing with unimportant things (as we all have to do in daily life) it is *vital* to see them *in relation* to the important things. And in this sense, Ashley's talk was a positive contribution.

Secondly, it is the conscious tactics of a ruling class in a weak position to bring up unimportant points and treat them as important. This conference is an example – problems of notation are secondary to musical problems, musical problems are secondary to social and political problems. As one of the organisers pointed out, it has been quite easy to organise this very expensive conference devoted to a very minor issue, but if you want to get money from the state to improve music education in schools you come up against complete refusal.

So in the question of what is relevant we have to use our own minds, and not assume that something is relevant just because a lot of fuss is being made about it, conferences convened, etc.

It isn't possible to see the Brown/Evangelisti controversy as an isolated instance [57]. This is rampant in the avant garde. People like Kurt Stone would like to do something to improve it[58]. But with little chance of success, because these are symptoms of a very deep decay in avant garde music. Bad performances are so commonplace it is impossible for the composer any longer to imagine that this situation somehow has nothing to do with him, that he is innocent. In fact it wasn't just Earle's piece, the whole concert was bad and boring, the notations have failed to engage the energies of the performers. Even conventionally notated pieces fail to do this; performances are lifeless. So this problem is not specific to graphic music.

What a storm in a teacup. Individuals attack each other and there is great disunity. What is needed is for each person to take a sober look at his own activity in the context of the world political situation, and also in the context of his local involvement in a musical community, and come to a point of readiness to work together to produce a positive atmosphere and real development.

Our main subject should be, what progressive role can avant garde composers and musicologists play in society? Widmer and Stone are two examples whose work is socially directed, for the use of teachers, children, students, musicians[59]. They put collective needs above their individual inclinations (up to a point). Nattiez is the opposite – he is fascinated by the possibility that music and language (and possibly also micro-biological sequences) have formal features in common[60]. He experiences a kind of scientific ecstasy in thinking about this and wants everyone to share his enthusiasm. Many composers also seem to feel this way about their work.

I have characterised these two lines – following one's own inclination and fulfiling the needs of society – in different people, who we might say are mainly one or the other. However each single person has these two lines in himself sometimes they may even completely coincide (for example if a man is following his own inclination in serving the needs of society) and sometimes be completely divorced (follow your inclination at the weekend, and serve society during the week) [61].

Now if everyone in the avant garde could bring these two forces into equilibrium – their self-centred delight in their own activity and the consciousness of being active on behalf of the community – such enormous energy would be released that the problems of the avant garde would disappear overnight.

The forces fighting against this are: the philosophy of individualism (which is being promoted in all education) and the bourgeois state, the protector of the capitalists whose interests are in direct conflict with the interests of the masses of the people.

Of course I am not interested in solving the problems of the bourgeoisie (if I could provide a contented avant garde to replace the discontented one, I'd probably be in clover for the rest of my life). This is why we have to study politics and ideology. We must learn that if we become good children and serve our governments faithfully, we are definitely acting against the interest of the vast majority of the people. In balancing the individual and the collective we must become conscious of which collective, which class, it is whose interests we should put above our own. We must take our stand on the side of the working and oppressed people, the class that is in direct opposition to the ruling class and the state machinery under its control.

So it is definitely possible for composers and musicologists of the avant garde to take a progressive role. It is possible through resolving the contradiction between the individual and the collective approach and by developing class consciousness. The next question is: what role? It is too soon to answer this, but for a start we should take a general look at the vast field of musical production and realise that the avant garde is just a tiny pocket in that. An objective view of music consumption shows this. So it must be seminal – this is the only way we can illuminate things [62]. We must put our ideas and our music in such a way that they spread and grow elsewhere in the vast arena of musical production. And with this in mind we should take a very solemn and searching look at our music and our ideas and test them by every means available as to whether they are in fact healthy or poisonous, progressive or reactionary.

At this conference there has been a struggle:
– on one side, the musicians, who wish to throw out the original subject of the symposium because notation is unimportant relative to music, which again is less important than the social situation in which it occurs – on the other side the musicologists, who constantly wish to return to the problem of notation because it is the lifeline of their work.

This struggle is divergent – it cannot be resolved in the symposium. The scientists with whom the musicians might have liked to work are the scientists occupied with studying perception, the brain and the nervous system, or the physical properties of sound, acoustics. Obviously such scientists could not be called to a symposium on notation. So we see that the decisive factor was the original selection of the subject for the symposium – this determined the selection of speakers, which made it impossible for the conference to lead to progress in the field of musical production.

Treatise was a large-scale opus on which I wasted more hours of craftsmanship and intellectual effort than I care to recall. It would gratify me to sell the manuscript to a sleepy bourgeois at an inflated price and thus receive at least some compensation for that waste.

The Great Learning (1968-71) was an even larger scale opus and, because it definitely promotes a reactionary ideological content(Confucianism) and because some of its techniques of performance are effective and could potentially carry it beyond the confines of the avant garde, it merits criticism from a wider viewpoint than that of the avant garde. The opportunity to criticise it came up on the occasion of a performance of the first two paragraphs at the Berlin Philharmonic Hall in March 1974. I decided to accept the engagement with the proviso that I would write a relatively comprehensive article describing the nature of the piece and what I thought about it, and distribute this article to the concert audience and attempt to have the article used on all subsequent occasions when the piece might be brought before the public, e.g. in broadcasts, etc. In this way the reactionary composition can be used not only as an arena for ideological struggle but also as a carrier pigeon for revolutionary ideas. At that time there was a fierce struggle going on in China against Lin Piao's line and the ideas of Confucius and I tried to include my article in that frame of reference.

Criticism of *The Great Learning*

This article deals with paragraphs 1 and 2 of *The Great Learning*, my musical rendering of part of one of the Confucian scriptures, equivalent possibly to the Christian credo. As is the case with all works of art, ideas are being communicated in this music, ideas are being promoted in a particular present-day context, with a particular class character.

Confucian doctrine does not consist of absolute truths any more than does the Christian doctrine. Since class struggle began, well before Confucius's time, ideas have been born in class struggle, are used in class struggle and are constantly reinterpreted and changed in the course of class struggle. This year (1974) Confucius's ideas are at the centre of a veritable storm of struggle in their country of origin, the People's Republic of China. It is in the context of this struggle that I want to evaluate this aspect, the Confucian aspect, of my work *The Great Learning* and form a judgement on it.

The backbone of the ideological content of the work is the Confucian text. This will be dealt with first. But a body does not consist only of backbone; the flesh and blood of *The Great Learning* is sounding musical forms. Though these forms communicate non-verbally, they also communicate ideas. These forms are the product of historical development and are created for performers to play and for audiences to listen to. They are couched in contemporary musical language and embody ideas reflecting present-day reality, reflecting aspects of the class struggle as it is being waged in our own time. This flesh and blood aspect of the work's ideological content will be dealt with later in the article [63].

Finally I will attempt to evaluate the work from the class standpoint of the working class. From this standpoint the work stands out clearly as a piece of 'inflated rubbish' whose only value is its counter-revolutionary value to the ruling class. This being the case, the question arises: if I am genuinely adopting this standpoint, why do I allow the work to continue in use?

The aim is to use the work (such parts of it as are artistically more or less successful, that have a certain communicative power) as a carrier for its criticism. In this way, wherever the work is played its class character and its ideological content will be brought to light and criticised, and the consciousness of the progressive section of audience will be raised by repudiating the content of the work itself.

The Place of Confucius in the History of China

The transition from the slave owning societies of the Yin Dynasty (1520-1030 BC) and the early Chou Dynasty (1030-770 BC) to the feudal society of the Chin Dynasty (221-207 BC) and the Han Dynasty (202 BC-AD 220) was extremely turbulent. There were slave uprisings in the Spring and Autumn Period (770-476 BC), and the Warring States Period (476-221 BC) was characterised by intense political and military struggles. Reflecting these struggles, there was also warfare in the realm of ideas [64]. Confucius lived 551-479 BC, at the end of the Spring and Autumn Period, and the Confucian doctrine was developed in the succeeding centuries by generations of disciples, chief among them being Mencius (390-305 BC). *The Great Learning* is thought to have been written by a pupil of Mencius about 260 BC, the first chapter (on which my work is based) being attributed to Confucius himself.

In the ideological struggles of the Warring States Period the Confucians were on the side of reaction. By advocating revival of the old ritual culture they were advocating a return to the old social system of slavery – all under the slogan of 'benevolence and righteousness.' On the other side were the Legalists, a school of political thought that was looking forward to the feudal system which was to unite China under the Chin and Han Dynasties. Shang Yang (d. 338 BC) and Han Fei (280-233 BC) were the chief exponents of Legalism. They advocated a well defined code of law with a system of rewards and punishments to which all classes without exception were to be subject. Their legal system was devised to promote agricultural production and military strength. Many western historians of Chinese thought look askance at the Legalists, accusing them of bureaucracy, ruthlessness and other 'crimes'. The fact remains that, after centuries of internal strife, when the Prince of Chin put Legalist proposals into practice he was able to unify China in less than ten years, for these proposals conformed to the actual stage of development of Chinese society. The Chin Dynasty was short lived, but it finally established the feudal system. Later, during the Han Dynasty, the doctrines of Confucius were re-introduced to consolidate the autocratic rule of the feudal lords and lend it a more humanitarian and 'benevolent' appearance. Confucianism became the dominant, official religion in China, and remained so until the overthrow of the Ching (Manchu) Dynasty in 1911.

Backward people defend Confucius against the criticism of the masses in the period of the democratic and socialist revolutions in China

From 1911 to the present the struggle against Confucian ideas has been an integral part of the struggle for national liberation and the socialist construction of New China. The May 4th Movement of 1919 propagated the slogan, 'Down with the old (Confucian) morality; up with the new (democratic) morality'[65]. The present movement to criticise Confucius and Lin Piao homes in on 'restraining oneself and restoring the rites', the Confucian quote with which Lin Piao wanted actually to restrain the forces of socialism and restore capitalism.

Just as in his own day Confucius tried to prop up a decadent and dying social system, so it is the decadent and dying in our own time who try to prop up Confucius. According to Chiang Kai-shek – the stooge of US imperialism who still bleats about his Chinese 'nationalist revolution' from his island exile of Taiwan – Confucius was the 'eternal paragon of correct human relations' and, seeing that the 'traditional doctrine handed down by the sages,' is in danger of extinction, he moans that 'this is the biggest misfortune of our country and the biggest sorrow of the nation, and no peril can be greater or more imminent than this'[66]. With the downfall of Confucius he sees his own final defeat approaching.

According to Liu Shao-chi, the capitalist-roader who was removed from office during the Great Proletarian Cultural Revolution, the doctrines of Confucius and Mencius were a 'bequest useful to us'. Yes, if it were the desire of the Chinese people to restore capitalism. But this isn't the case and so they have no desire to inherit Confucius.

Lin Piao claimed to have detected historical materialism in the doctrine of

Confucius and this attempt to dress up Confucius in Marxist clothes is also being undertaken in the Soviet Union. They too claim that 'progressive aspects may be found in the early Confucianists', but one is hardly surprised to find that these progressive aspects are things like 'humanitarianism' and 'love of mankind', familiar enough concepts in the Soviet Union today, where every attempt is made to gloss over the class struggle and propagate an ideal 'State of the Whole People'. (Just as in the West, it is not the exploited and oppressed people in the Soviet Union who gloss over the class struggle, but the ruling class, the new bourgeoisie.) Indeed all these reactionaries seem to have one thing in common, they want to recreate Confucius in their own sugared pill image.

Who promotes Confucius in the West and what for?

In the West he has provided similar opportunities. The early missionary scholars sought Christian ethics in Confucius and found them. Ezra Pound sought the 'philosopher of fascism' and found that in Confucius. Since Pound has been the most active promoter of Confucius outside academic circles in the English speaking West, and since it was his version of the *Great Learning* that inspired my composition, I will go into his views more thoroughly.

Ezra Pound was an American poet who was active in the literary avant garde in the '20s, helping to build the reputations of such figures as T. S. Eliot and James Joyce. In the '30s he was an active supporter of fascism. He supported Oswald Mosley in England and publicly supported Mussolini before and during the Second World War, broadcasting his fascist views in English from Rome Radio. He was rabidly anti-semitic and anti-communist and, in a period when monopoly capitalism and imperialism were on the rampage, he chose to attribute all the evils of the world to 'usury'. Shattered by the outcome of the war he drifted more and more into visions of 'eternal light'.

In 1937, in a magazine *The Aryan Path*, Pound published an article called *The Immediate Need for Confucius* [67]. In it he takes up a posture of abject humility before the ancient scripture: "In considering a value already age-old and never to end while men are, I prefer not to write 'to the Modern World'. The *Ta Hio* (*Great Learning*) stands, and the commentator were better advised to sweep a few leaves from the temple steps." All this reverence is sham; he knows very well what forces in the modern world need Confucius and what for. "There is a visible and raging need of the *Ta Hio* in barbarous countries like Spain and Russia", obviously for quelling the proletariat!

"...There is also a question of milder and more continuous hygiene", i.e. to prevent risings of the 'stupid mob' in countries where the proletarian revolution was not currently on the move. Pound would dearly have liked to see the *Great Learning* put into direct political practice in the service of fascism – a wild dream, since the social system for which the *Great Learning* was conceived was already obsolete when the text was written. The political principles of the *Great Learning* never were put into practice and never will be; they function better in the ideological sphere as a means of deception. Pound's plans for it in this direction look like this, "The whole of Western Idealism is a jungle. Christian theology is a jungle. To think it through, to reduce it to some semblance of order, there is no better axe than the *Ta Hio*." Again: "The life of occidental mind fell apart [with the decline of religion] into progressively stupider and still more stupid segregations. Hence the need for Confucius, and specifically of the *Ta Hio*, and more specifically of the first chapter of the *Ta Hio*, which you may treat as a mantra, or as a mantra reinforced, a mantra elaborated so that the meditation may gradually be concentrated into contemplation."

Pound's aim has been summed up by J. S. Thompson, "To abstract, from the histories of tyranny and oppression, those things that worked to ensure order, 'a world order', the 'social coordinate of Confucius and Mussolini'.[68]"

How the musical *Great Learning* came into existence

Like many other mis-educated products of a bourgeois upbringing, it was to the very wildness and contradictoriness of Pound's work that I fell victim when in 1968, stimulated by a commission from Macnaghten Concerts for the Cheltenham Festival, I decided to make a musical version of the first chapter of his *Great Learning* translation. As a politically backward composer wrapped up in the attractions of the avant garde, I was not concerned about Pound's politics and it mattered little to me that his mystical interpretation contradicted the findings of most scholars. I had not read and would not have heeded Shang Yang's warning about ancient texts: "Anyone who studies ancient texts without a teacher, trying to discover what they mean merely by the use of his own intelligence, will not to his dying day make out either the words or their general meaning." Pound of course set great store by his own intelligence and I followed him in this. Indeed with a career in the avant garde to think about it was expedient to consider things in an isolated, fragmentary way, otherwise one's ideas would tend to coincide with other people's ideas which would lead to the charge of banality and of being an 'epigone'. So in setting the first paragraph I followed Pound's instruction 'to keep on re-reading the whole digest until he understands', and thus hit on a rendering which reflects Pound's 'mantric' interpretation of the text although this interpretation was unknown to me at the time.

An attempt to reform the first two paragraphs of *The Great Learning*

"If a textbook is too summary, pupils will be able to twist its meaning; if a law is too concise, the people dispute its intentions" – (Han Fei). Shelves full of Chinese scholars' tracts and a fair number of European translations prove the applicability of this Legalist thesis to *The Great Learning*. A literal translation of the first two paragraphs yields:

"*The Great Learning's* way consists in: polishing bright virtue; caring for the people; resting in the highest good. Knowing where to rest one has certainty. Being certain one can be calm. Being calm one can have peace. Having peace one can lay plans. Laying plans one can succeed." In class society there is no literature or philosophy above classes, and we have seen Confucius's class standpoint above – he stood on the side of the slave owning class which was basically finished but still fighting for survival. From the politics of the present-day ruling class – the bourgeoisie, which is also basically finished but still fighting for survival – we know that 'caring for the people' means dividing them and playing them off against each other so that they don't rise against their oppressors. The imperialists stockpile armaments and murder millions in the name of 'peace' – all they want is to continue their exploitation of working people and underdeveloped countries in 'peace'. The only 'plans' the bourgeoisie make are plans for the further exploitation and oppression of working people, and as for 'success', in bourgeois society your success is measured by your parasitism and profitability.

Let's see how pupil Pound twists the meaning to suit his own ends:

"*The Great Learning* takes root in clarifying the way wherein the intelligence increases through the process of looking straight into one's own heart and acting on the result; it is rooted in watching with affection the way people grow; it is rooted in coming to rest, being at ease in perfect equity.

Know the point of rest and then have an orderly mode of procedure; having this orderly procedure one can 'grasp the azure', that is, take hold of a clear concept; holding a clear concept one can be at peace internally; being thus calm one can keep one's head in moments of danger; he who can keep his head in the presence of a tiger is qualified to come to his deed in due hour."

Pound's version is tailored to fit his idea of a 'conspiracy of intelligence' to protect Order and Civilisation against the onslaught of the 'mob'. He makes intelligence a matter of introspection. He advocates detachment: an inner sanctum of 'perfect equity' where he reclines at ease 'watching with affection' (as if through a window) the struggles of the people. His 'calm' is the calmness of intellectual superiority; his 'peace' is internal. Only along this road can one 'qualify' to take action.

In 1972 I and the Scratch Orchestra were offered the opportunity to present these two paragraphs in a Promenade Concert at the Albert Hall, London. For this occasion I came up with yet another 'translation' of *The Great Learning*. By this time our political consciousness had been at least awakened and we were taking the first steps along the road of developing political discussion and music making in the service of the proletarian revolution. Taking as our guideline Chairman Mao's thesis 'Works of art that do not serve the struggle of the broad masses can be transformed into works of art that do', we devised a performance which was formally much more disciplined than the original and which included banners bearing four slogans which expressed our feelings about revolution and the *Great Learning*. These banners were banned from the performance by the BBC, who also censored the programme note to remove all political statements except such as were smuggled into the translation. Here is the new 'translation' together with the slogans:

"*The Great Learning* means raising your level of consciousness by getting right to the heart of a matter and acting on your conclusions. *The Great Learning* is rooted in love for the broad masses of the people. The target of *The Great Learning* is justice and equality, the highest good for all."

First slogan: "Make the past serve the present."

Second slogan: "Revolution is *The Great Learning* of the present."

Third slogan: "A revolution is not a dinner party, it is an insurrection, an act of violence by which one class overthrows another."

Fourth slogan: "Apply Marxism-Leninism-Mao Tsetung Thought in a living way to the problems of the present."

"We know our stand (on the side of the working and oppressed people) and so our aim is set (the overthrow of monopoly capitalism). Our aim being set we can appraise the situation. We appraise the situation and so we are relaxed and ready. We are relaxed and ready and so we can plan ahead despite all danger. Planning ahead despite all danger we shall accomplish our aim."

I now consider that this effort to 'reform' *The Great Learning* needs to be just as severely criticised as does the work in its original form. In order to harmonise the reactionary ideology of *The Great Learning* with the revolutionary ideology of Marxism-Leninism we were obliged to stand on our heads, and from such a contorted position one can perform no useful service to the revolution. Capitalism cannot be reformed, it must be overthrown. Bourgeois ideology cannot be reformed, it must be smashed. The attempt to reform *The Great Learning* was a logical consequence of a fundamentally 'reformist' attitude which reaches far back into my work as an avant-gardist in the '60s and permeates the activities of the Scratch Orchestra (for whom most of *The Great Learning* was written), from its inception up until the time when it began to liberate itself from bourgeois ideology.

What were these 'reforms' that we struggled for in the Scratch Orchestra, and that find their expression in the paragraphs of *The Great Learning*? They are reforms in the interest of certain oppressed individuals. We wanted to break the monopoly of a highly trained elite over the avant garde, so we made a music in which 'anyone' could participate regardless of their musical education. We wanted to abolish the useless intellectual complexity of the earlier avant garde, and make music which was quite concretely 'simple' in its assault on the senses. We wanted to devise a kind of music that would release the initiative of the participants.

In breaking out of the elite we succeeded only in forming a kind of commune and were just as isolated as before. In rejecting intellectual complexity we landed ourselves in situations of brutal chaos in which mystical introspection supervened as a method of self-preservation. And in releasing the initiative of the performers we slipped into the cult of individualism. Hippy communes, mysticism, individualism – our various 'reforms' led us straight into a number of cul-de-sacs of bourgeois ideology that are being widely promoted today.

The ideology of Reformism has a class character; a bourgeois class character

People who set out to reform some of the blatant evils of bourgeois society often do so with the 'best of intentions' and think like we did that they are acting at least in the interests of some oppressed individuals in society. (In the case of social workers, etc., many believe that they are working on behalf of the drastically oppressed sections of the working class with which they come in contact.) Actually such people are carrying out the wishes of the ruling class, of the bourgeoisie. They are the more often than not deluded servants of the bourgeoisie. Reformism is an ideological trend emanating from the bourgeoisie. The bourgeoisie would like nothing better than that the evil symptoms of oppression and exploitation would disappear while the facts of oppression and exploitation remain. The very life of the oppressing and exploiting classes depends on their ability to conceal and mystify their true character. This ability is now wearing very thin. The oppressed and exploited classes are learning in great numbers that they cannot place any faith in promises of reform, whether these promises come from Social Democrats, Divine Light Missionaries, Revisionists or Fascists. They are learning that only through building their own organisations, the organisations of the working class, the genuine communist parties, can the reasonable course be put into practice, the course of proletarian socialist revolution. In the context of this learning, the mystical delights of *The Great Learning* are just butterflies in a blast furnace.

Criticise *The Great Learning* from the standpoint of the working class

A reformed *Great Learning* can never be more than an armour plated butterfly, and for this reason I decided to present the work in future in its unreformed state. No longer do I want to conceal the facts about bourgeois society, I want to expose them. My standpoint in criticising *The Great Learning* is the standpoint of the working class. For the working class *The Great Learning* is – or would be if they ever got to hear it – a piece of inflated rubbish which obviously has no role to play in their struggles; its role is to promote and consolidate bourgeois ideas in one guise or another amongst the intelligentsia.

Through my position as a bourgeois composer I have the right (which is denied to the vast majority of musicians employed by capitalist and state-supported enterprises under the dictatorship of the bourgeoisie) to express my ideas about my own work and those of other bourgeois composers in this form. I hope that in doing so I can promote amongst progressive people a conscious and critical attitude – and finally an attitude of rejection – towards bourgeois music and encourage them to turn their attention to, and integrate themselves with, the progressive forces in present-day society, namely the politics and culture of the working class in its upsurge to wrest political power from the hands of the monopoly capitalist class.

27th March 1974

Participating in the Berlin performance of *The Great Learning* was a painful and – as it seemed – debilitating experience for me. Holding the view that music's main function is to bring people together, to unite them, it was a contradictory situation to have to direct a performance – which had to be a 'good' performance so that people could get to grips with its content – for the sole purpose of leading the audience, through the accompanying article, to repudiate that content. A 'good' performance is one in which the musicians and audience are totally engaged. In contravening this principle – by disengaging the audience – I had set myself the job of launching a sizable lead balloon. I accomplished this quite successfully and it was a worried little audience that wended their way out of the hall at the end. This disturbed me; I wished I had had something better to offer, something which we could have united around. Then I reflected (on the basis of some quite concrete experience) that if I had had such a work ready it would doubtless not have been performed in those circumstances, and this depressed me still further. Later I realised the cause of these depressions, I was clinging very tenaciously to the role of the bourgeois composer. Shortly after the concert, *Peking Review* brought out a further article on the subject of criticising Confucius, this one by an old professor who had previously espoused the Confucian cause, just as I had. What he wrote inspired me greatly. I realised that the business of changing one's class stand, remoulding one's world outlook, is no easy thing, no 'lover's bed', but a long and complicated process of struggle, no 'benevolence and righteousness' about it. This struggle may be invigorating or painful or both by turns. On the personal level it brings about important changes, it gradually breaks down all complacency, all loneliness in the process of integrating with the working people, joining the fight to change the world and shatter the present oppressive conditions finally. In this fight there is, besides hardship and sacrifice, great companionship and great happiness.

Professor Feng Yu-lan of Peking University Department of Philosophy is an old man, but not too old to be warmed by a new world and new ideas as these emerge through the difficult struggle against the old world and its rotten ideas. After his lecture denouncing Confucius he said:

"When the mass movement to criticise Lin Piao and Confucius started last autumn, I was at first rather uneasy. I said to myself: now I'm for it. Before the Great Cultural Revolution started I had always revered Confucius. Now, there is going to be criticism of Lin Piao and criticism of Confucius and the worshipping of Confucius, this means I will also be criticised.

On second thoughts, however, I found this frame of mind wrong... I should join with the revolutionary masses in criticising Lin Piao, criticising Confucius and criticising the worship of Confucius.

When the university leadership knew how I felt, it encouraged me to speak at a meeting of faculty members and students of the philosophy department on my present understanding of Confucius... As I worked on the speech, my misgivings gradually disappeared... In the concluding portion of the speech I said:

'...I'm nearly eighty and have worked for half a century on the history of Chinese philosophy. It makes me very happy to be able to live to see this revolution, and to take part in it makes me feel all the happier.' After I delivered my speech at the meeting, the response I got was a great encouragement to me [69]."

Notes

6. This use of the term 'petty bourgeoisie' refers to these people's world outlook and cultural aspirations, not to their actual relations of employment. As Marx and Engels say in the *Communist Manifesto*: "The bourgeoisie has stripped of its halo every occupation hitherto honoured and looked up to with reverent awe. It has converted the physician, the lawyer, the priest, the poet, the man of science, into its paid wage-labourers." The same is of course true of the students of these professions.

16. In May 1942 the Chinese Communist Party organised a three week forum on literature and art. Chairman Mao gave the opening and closing speeches, pointing out the general line that the forum should take and summing up the results. The forum took place in Yenan, a town in China's northwest. Yenan was the centre of operations for the Communist leadership in the Anti- Japanese war of 1937-45 and the capital of the Shensi-Kansu-Ninghsia Border Region, one of the liberated areas under the provisional government of the Communists. It should cause no surprise that the Chinese Communist Party could find the time in the thick of war to run a three-week forum on literature and art. Culture is as vital to human survival as food and drink; man's so-called spiritual needs are just as real as his material ones, and there is no sharp dividing line between the two. Mao put this point across very incisively when he wrote (in 1944), "An army without culture is a dull-witted army, and a dull-witted army cannot defeat the enemy."

17. It was in 1967, during the Great Proletarian Cultural Revolution in China, that *China Pictorial* reprinted the *Talks* as special supplement to celebrate their 25th anniversary. The *Talks* were an effective weapon in the Cultural Revolution not because of any magical properties but because of their firm proletarian line and their sharp dialectical materialist analysis. These qualities are vital in the struggle of the working class to exercise leadership in all fields and prevent the bourgeoisie from staging a comeback by usurping positions of authority in fields of culture and ideology. By the time the 30th anniversary of the *Talks* came round

(1972), artists the world over were tackling the problems of applying the *Talks* to the concrete conditions of their own countries and their own work. To name two examples: in West Berlin a conference was called by the Communist student organisation KSV to study and apply the *Talks*; in London the Scratch Orchestra's Ideological Group were studying the *Talks* collectively over a relatively long period. One thing that the Cultural Revolution had brought home to us very forcefully was the need to develop criticism of bourgeois culture: we too need to attack the 'ghosts and monsters' in our cultural environment. We should tie the label GHOST to the tails of those artistic and intellectual trends that promote the ideology of anarchism and reformism, and brand the word MONSTER on the faces of those artistic and intellectual trends that promote the ideology of fascism.

18. This was hearsay from a source I had and have no reason to doubt. Cage denies that such boycotting took place, maintaining that the incident in question occurred in connection with a Stockhausen concert.

19. Kurt Schwertsik is an Austrian composer and hornist who saw clearly the growing alienation of the avant garde from working musicians and the music loving audience. In the sixties he became interested in light music and dropped out of the avant garde, earning his livelihood as an orchestral horn player in Vienna.

20. The high standard and unique quality of this American pianist's playing and personality had a large influence on the piano compositions of Cage and Stockhausen and a number of other composers. He has been a close collaborator of Cage's since around 1950. In recent years he has virtually abandoned piano playing to devote himself to live electronic performance.

21. Tilbury quotes Deryck Cooke's remarks appreciatively because they 'swim against the tide' of current bourgeois musicological theory. Cooke's lament is justified, but when it comes to a statement of his own musicological theories, there is little there that a materialist could support. His definition of music as "the expression of man's deepest self" betrays an idealist world outlook which sees the highest reality deep in 'man's' soul and not in the outside world. For a materialist, intellectual and artistic activity is a partial and partisan reflection on expression of objective reality, in particular the objective reflection of social life. These realities, at least since the emergence of class societies on page one of recorded history, make it quite impossible to speak of 'man' in the abstract, above class. Cooke's use of this term is an example of the partisan character of his own

intellectual activity: it is in the interests of the bourgeois class that he glosses over the question of class.

22. Cage's intention seems to be to reflect mechanically, unconsciously (that is with no purposeful composition intervention) the present stage of the historical development of the musical material, and thus cover up the decisive factor in the historical development of the musical material, namely social development and conscious participation. In this he mirrors the 'objectivity' of those *bourgeois* scientists who mechanically assemble and process tons of data: their 'objectivity' is a veil to conceal the class standpoint from which their researches are carried out.

23. Cage's mumbo jumbo about self-centered sounds should stimulate us to clarify the actual mode of existence of sounds. Our concept of sound derives from our faculty of hearing, which in turn probably evolved as a mechanism for detecting and evaluating a particular range of matter-in-motion phenomena. Sound is audible vibrations in a medium produced by some forms of activity. We have developed activities specifically to produce sounds which convey through their character and combination our experience of the world as we know it from our particular standpoint. These activities constitute music making, a specifically human affair, to which we may obviously compare a whole range of non-human and non-audible activities (bird 'song', 'music of the spheres', the 'music of your smile', etc.) but which is firmly rooted in and cannot be detached from the social life of human beings. Cage calling his music 'sounds' (rather than music) therefore represents an attempt to remove it from the human sphere (categorically impossible, since the activities of human beings can never be non-human), from which he promises himself a double advantage: (a) it would absolve him from his human responsibility for his actions as a human being, and (b) it would give his music the superhuman 'objective' authority of a phenomenon of (blind, unconscious) nature. In fact, man and his thinking are themselves a part of 'nature', whose products are by no means all wise, harmonious and graceful, as can be seen from such blatant examples as the dinosaur and Cage's metaphysics.

24. Engels expressed the dialectical relationship between freedom and necessity as follows: "Freedom is the appreciation of necessity." For instance: freedom for the working class can only consist in recognising the historical necessity of overthrowing capitalism and actually doing so.

25. Actually the capitalists' first commandment is 'maximise profits' which means

essentially 'maximum exploitation of labour'. The so-called 'law of supply and demand' is a complex affair of creating, conquering, dividing up and destroying markets, involving cut-throat rivalry amongst the bourgeoisie and a nearly total disregard of the 'demand', the actual needs of the human consumers who make up these markets. The capitalist (say, the grain hoarder in India) will not supply goods where there is a demand for them (grain to the starving) unless the rate of profit is adequate (to his greed).

26. Cage generally disclaims any subjective intention in his work ('just let the sound be sounds', and so on). At his boldest he might say that he wanted his music to make people free. Its effect is the opposite: entangling people.

27. The Nazi campaign against 'degenerate' art is viewed differently by different classes. For the bourgeoisie, the main victims in this campaign were the bourgeois avant-gardists: Klee, Kandinsky, Schoenberg and others whose work did in fact reflect the ideological degeneration of the bourgeoisie into metaphysics. From the proletarian point of view, the main victims were the Communist artists of the Weimar Republic: Georg Grosz, Kathe Kollwitz, Hanns Eisler, Bertolt Brecht. The German capitalists brought the fascists to power as a last resort, a desperate gamble to stave off collapse. On the cultural front their attack was two pronged: on the one hand they suppressed the culture (the bourgeois avant garde) that reflected the bankruptcy and weakness of their own class, and on the other they suppressed the culture that reflected the growing consciousness and militancy of their enemy, the working class. The anti-semitic line of the campaign was just a red herring. There was no need for the Nazis to ban Mahler's works, for instance, but they did because he was a Jew. Possibly the main advantage the Nazis derived from their racist anti-semitic line on the ideological front was that it enabled them to outlaw Marxism (Communism) not because it was proletarian, but because Marx was a Jew!

When the Darmstadt Summer School for New Music was founded after the war its claimed intention was to reinstate and develop that music which had suffered persecution at the hands of the Nazis. Because the West German state was again a bourgeois state, the Darmstadt Summer School of course reinstated the bourgeois composers who had been victimised by the Nazis, not the socialist composers. Darmstadt propagated the so-called Second Viennese School – Schoenberg, Berg and Webern – and offered encouragement to young composers – Boulez, Stockhausen and Nono became the leading names – to proceed further along the road of serial music. What they turned out was a kind of atomised 'music for its own sake', appreciated only by a tiny circle of composers, musicologists and their admirers, plus a certain number of even younger musicians who, because they felt alienated by the sterility and banality of the musical establishment, were attracted by certain progressive catchwords current in Darmstadt circles. These catchwords were, as far as I remember, 'science', 'democracy', 'consciousness', 'progress', and we were to see them all turn into their opposites in subsequent years: mysticism, dictatorship, anti-consciousness and reaction. In the climate of political reaction of the 1950s', with the Cold War, the death of Stalin and the growth of a new bourgeoisie in the Soviet Union, the Darmstadt school flourished. By 1970, when the world political climate had changed dramatically for the better, with national liberation struggles on the increase throughout the world, great successes of the Great Proletarian Cultural Revolution in China and growing working class militancy in the imperialist heartlands, Darmstadt had become a stagnant backwater.

28. Karl Marx, *Contribution to the Critique of Political Economy*, Preface.

29. Karl Marx, *Capital*, Vol I.

30. In a sense this music is indeed 'derivative', but it was wrong to use this word, which has a pejorative character in bourgeois criticism. In fact there is no art production that is not derived in some way from things that went before, and above all there is no art that is not 'derived' from social practice. It was wrong to 'knock' popular music in a general way because the vast mass of working musicians, employed in popular music under very oppressive conditions, represent the basic musical resources of the working class. Despite the restrictive relations of production, which hamper cultural development just as they hamper economic development, this mass of working musicians has achievements to its credit, especially technical achievements. Genuine artistic achievements on a grand scale are of course not possible under the dictatorship of a degenerate bourgeois ideology.

31. John Cage, *Defence of Satie*. (A lecture delivered at Black Mountain College in 1948.)

32. I was not clear on the class character of this audience when I wrote the talk. The audience for classical music consists largely of educated and professional workers – wage slaves all, despite their non-participation in manual labour. When

people speak of the 'bourgeois audience' this refers to the fact that this audience is to a great extent under the influence of bourgeois ideas and claims the cultural privilege that are held out to them to distinguish them and divide them from the manual workers. The 'snobbish' character of a certain part of the audience derives from its acceptance of these and other privileges in return for non-participation in the class struggle on the side of the workers. However, at the present time large numbers – including some of those that enjoy bourgeois music – of these non-manual workers (civil servants, teachers etc.) are becoming class conscious and are adopting the methods of class struggle that were previously thought to be peculiar to the industrial proletariat and other manual workers. For instance, they go on strike. In proportion as this becomes the general trend the fascination of bourgeois concerts – all that wholesomeness, delight, inspiration, etc. – is likely to grow continually paler.

33. Since writing this talk such fantasies have lost all their charm for me. More often than not they are not only distorting the truth, they are deliberately spreading metaphysical or even fascist ideas.

34. 1848-49 is often referred to as the 'Year of Revolutions'. 1848 saw the first ever armed rising of the proletariat as a class acting on its own behalf, in Paris June 23-26. This rising was brutally suppressed by the bourgeoisie.

In 1849 there were risings of a different type: popular, uncoordinated risings in several German states in support of the new (bourgeois) Constitution adopted by the parliament in Frankfurt in March 1849, which various monarchs had refused to recognise. The rising in Dresden was put down by Prussian troops on 9 May 1849.

Wagner was director of the Dresden Opera at the time and was filled with enthusiasm for the revolution, which he hoped would open the way to the realisation of his artistic dreams. He participated in the rising and as a result spent the next 13 years in exile bitterly regretting it all and servilely begging forgiveness. His political views were a hotch-potch and his fidelity to them completely unstable. (The ideological and political content of his music is another subject, and can't be dealt with here.)

Much stauncher in his support of the bourgeois revolution was Wagner's assistant in Dresden, Rockel. He spent 3 years in prison for his part in the rising and resolutely refused to sue for pardon or renege on his views.

35. Marx was persistently hounded by the authorities in 1848 and 1849. Banished

from Belgium early in 1848, he made his way to Cologne via Paris. In Cologne he edited the *Neue Rheindische Zeitung* for about a year. During this time he was put on trial, but was acquitted in February 1849. In May he was banished from Germany and went to Paris, was banished from Paris and went to London, where he lived for the rest of his life. (For a short account of Marx's life, see Lenin's essay *Karl Marx*.) The reason he was thus hounded was that the theses set out in the Communist Manifesto, drawn up by Marx and Engels early in 1848, were consistently borne out by the historic events of that year, and Marx was contributing continuously to the growing consciousness of the rising workers.

36. This is one-sided. Primarily, capitalists regard the people as labour power capable of producing 'surplus value', from which they derive profit. Part of this surplus value goes to expand production, and expanding production sends the capitalists in search of markets to consume their multiplying products, and where no legitimate market exists they use advertising techniques and other means to create an artificial one. Cigarettes are a better example than plastic bottles and white bread, because while bringing in vast profits, cigarettes not only don't benefit the people, they actually harm them.

37. This sentence is incorrect. In fact there can only be socialist construction when the capitalist system is overthrown.

An economic system such as capitalism or socialism protects itself with a political dictatorship, in which one or more classes (within which there may well be democratic institutions) holds sway over the rest (for whom these democratic institutions are little more than scraps of paper).

The capitalist system is protected by the political dictatorship of the monopoly capitalist class, exercised through its organ the bourgeois state, with its 'democratically elected' government and its obviously anti-democratic armed forces and police. By no stretch of the imagination can your right to vote once every five years or so be considered a meaningful participation in the political affairs of a country, whereas the 'right' of the police to arrest and intern people for doing nothing whatever (creating an obstruction, etc.) is well known to all. These are features of the dictatorship of the bourgeoisie. Its aim is to hamper the development of socialism.

A socialist economy must equally be protected by a dictatorship, whose aim is to prevent the re-emergence of capitalism. This dictatorship is the dictatorship of the proletariat, which deprives the bourgeoisie and other exploiting classes of all political rights. Only under such a dictatorship can socialism be built. This goes for both economic affairs and cultural affairs. Hence the need for any socialist composer worth his salt to do propaganda for socialist revolution and the dictatorship of the proletariat.

38. When the capitalist class holds political power it takes all available measures to censor and stifle proletarian revolutionary art. This is its first law in the field of art and it is a political law. The same applies in a socialist country like China. True, after liberation the business of rescuing the economy from the ravages of war took precedence over cultural matters, and despite a healthy growth of proletarian culture the art of the exploiting classes continued to dominate the stage. The Great Proletarian Cultural Revolution set the course for rectifying this contradictory state of affairs, and now if works by Chinese artists show traces of bourgeois ideas or smack of capitalist restoration they are criticised and if necessary suppressed. If such works are allowed to see the light of day, then only for the sake of denouncing them and preventing the further growth of such trends. The reasons for this are political: if bourgeois art were allowed to flourish it would undermine the dictatorship of the proletariat.

39. 'Necessity for Change' is the title of a document prepared by the Internationalists for the 'Necessity for Change' Conference, held in London in August 1967. In this Marxist-Leninist document the aspiration of the youth and student movement of the '60s to actively participate in and change things is summed up. Its first sentence is: "Understanding requires an act of conscious participation, an act of finding out." The first part of the document deals with the phenomenon of 'anti-consciousness' referred to in the talk.

40. Utopia, literally, 'nowhere'; a never-never land purified of all social injustice. In the Communist Manifesto of 1848 Marx and Engels roundly criticised the 'Utopian Socialism' of such bourgeois thinkers as Owen and Fourier, whose tendency was to 'invent' ideal social systems without taking into account the actual laws governing the development of society. By these means they lulled the workers with sweet dreams instead of arming them with correct theory to guide them in their battles in the real world. To 'utopian socialism' Marx and Engels opposed 'scientific socialism', and made it their business to investigate the laws of social development and place their discoveries in the service of the working class and indicate the immediate line of advance. (See Engels, *Socialism: Utopian and Scientific*.)

41. The formulation in the following three paragraphs are taken directly from a letter from Wolff received in response to a request for programme notes for the piece.

42. Most of this work had actually been done when I proposed the work for inclusion in a Scratch Orchestra concert in Birmingham in December 1972. On that occasion, despite my impassioned resistance, the Scratch Orchestra finally barred the work from the concert on the general grounds that it ridiculed the Chinese revolution (making it out to be a question of cows and condoms) and did not mention the role of the Communist Party and the fighting spirit of the masses. Whether or not Wolff had the intention of ridiculing the revolution is a secondary matter, the main thing being the effect that the piece had. Everyone knows that the most ridiculous statements are usually made with a serious mien; in fact this seriousness is no small ingredient in the ridiculousness of the effect. The fluency of Wolff's statements reported in the programme note must be regarded with suspicion. Either it conceals a real naivety (which needs to be overcome, as there is no room for naivety in the struggle against bourgeois ideology) or he is pretending to be naive in order to ridicule the Chinese revolution.

43. Rzewski here off-loads his responsibility for the contradiction (he calls it 'ambiguity') between the subjective character of the piece and the political events to which it draws attention on to the shoulders of the interpreter.

Further material from Rzewski on *Coming Together* (from a letter accompanying the score) was published in the third issue of the magazine *Soundings*. The technical procedures employed in the piece are described in more detail, and in the final paragraph more light is shed on Rzewski's attitude. Here is the extract:

"The text for *Coming Together* is taken from a letter written by Sam Melville from Attica Correctional Facility in the spring of 1971. Sam Melville was murdered by the state in the assault on Attica last autumn.

The score for *Coming Together* consists of a single melody written in the bass clef. There are several ways of interpreting this piece, depending on the number of persons available. The simplest possible version can be done by one person who both plays the melody as it is written and recites the text at the same time. I have performed it this way at the piano. Ideally, however, there should be one person reciting the text and a number of musicians accompanying him in the following way:

One musician at least plays the melody straight through in very strict time on a bass instrument, preferably electric bass or bass guitar. The others do not play at all at first but enter gradually, playing long notes in the beginning with silences between them, then gradually shortening the duration of the long notes and the silences so that they become notes of medium duration, groups of notes, short melodies and fragments of melodies and so on. Most of these notes are octave doublings of notes in the bass line which are then sustained for as long as the player wishes before going on to the next doubling. What happens is this, that a number of melodies arises, as many as there are players, the sum of which however is as it were a freely articulated orchestration of the principal melody. In addition, however, the musicians should try to interpolate freely improvised passages that depart from this rule, with the condition that they do not get lost. It is very hard not to get lost, so that to be free in this situation really requires a struggle. As the music approaches the end (the piece lasts about half an hour) the durations become shorter and shorter so that for the last section everyone is playing in unison or octaves. Dynamics are free, although basically loud, and a percussion part may be improvised, as long as it helps to keep people together.

Regarding your comment (presumably referring to the editor of *Soundings* No 3) on the pessimism presently affecting American composers, I would only like to point out that, where this phenomenon is manifested, it is usually a trivial and naive pessimism which does not really reflect their long term attitudes and it can be corrected by further discussion of the question, 'Whom are we serving?' In particular, and by further politicisation in general. A new stage of revolutionary optimism is now beginning among American artists, I think, although this has to be expressed in concrete actions and although a certain component of intellectual pessimism should perhaps, at the same time, be retained. Pessimism is the basic philosophy of the ruling class for whom change can only be for the worse, whereas for us the prospects for change are good, although this may require long duration and effort."

Rzewski's assessment of pessimism as a characteristic of the ruling class in its period of decline is correct, so why does he plead for the retention of 'a certain component of intellectual pessimism'? This shows an ambivalence in Rzewski's attitude.

44. In implying that the provisional IRA is a 'terrorist' organisation I fell victim to bourgeois propaganda. The real terrorists are the British Government and their army in Ulster. There may be disagreement as to their aims and tactics, but the provisional IRA are organising armed struggle against British imperialism, against the forces of reaction, and to this extent they are playing a progressive role.

45. Thank heaven for that! But the fairy story element should have been criticised anyway, for its utopian (see note 40) tendencies. To sing, to a middle class American audience, obsessed as they are by hygiene, about the revolutionary necessity to wash your hands before meals – this crassly divorces the Chinese revolution from the concrete conditions of the west.

46. Goffredo Petrassi, 'grand old man' among Italian composers, opened the symposium with the remark that it was about a 'false problem', that notation was not in any way a real 'problem' facing composers today.

47. A clear example is Stockhausen's *First Piano Piece*. It sounds like a fairly haphazard juxtaposition of notes and chords, but involves the pianist in very abstruse technical problems, such as playing a ten note chord where each note must have a different degree of loudness, or passages where changes of tempo are expressed as complicated ratios (e.g. eleven quavers in the time of twelve, within which there may well be other complicated ratios to cope with) in relation to a basic tempo which is 'as fast as possible for the shortest rhythmic values used in the piece'. Another example is Cage's *Music of Changes*. In both these cases the development of notational complexities in line with serial (mathematical) compositional techniques led to complexities of performance that would not otherwise have arisen and that had no appreciable effect on the sounding result.

48. *Autumn '60 for Orchestra* and *Solo with Accompaniment* are two compositions of mine that fall into this category. Other examples include Pousseur's game-like pieces and much of Christian Wolff's music. In these cases it is not so much that each composition is a unique system, but that the composer develops over a number of pieces, his own unique system of notation – a kind of hopeful guarantee for the uniqueness of the resulting music, on which the avant garde composer's reputation depends.

49. 'The Good Old Days' of bourgeois art is what is being referred to here, i.e. the period when artists were voicing the aspirations of the ascendant (progressive in that context) bourgeoisie. An example of such progressive aspirations is the slogan 'liberty, fraternity, equality' under which the French bourgeoisie mobilised the masses to overthrow the reactionary monarchy in the French Revolution. The bourgeoisie are still touting this when they talk of the 'free world' and the 'western democracies.' Working people and other progressive people are pretty clear as to

the fraudulence of these claims today. They ask, 'Free for whom? Democratic for whom?' and face the fact that we live and work under the dictatorship of the bourgeoisie. They are now demanding freedom and democracy for the working people, which means smashing up the freedom and democracy of the bourgeoisie.

50. This mechanical notion has cropped up twice in this talk. It omits to mention that our ideas about the world, our world outlook, are determined by the social position from which we view it, by our class standpoint. There is no abstract knowledge, no abstract right and wrong, only partisan knowledge, class ideas.

51. George Brecht, American artist, was active in the 'Happenings' period of avant garde art in the early sixties. His work has had an influence on such movements as Concept Art and Minimal Art.

52. While working on *Treatise* I was preoccupied with the philosophical writings of Ludwig Wittgenstein in the fields of logic and language. One of Wittgenstein's sources was the German philosopher Gottlob Frege (1848-1925), particularly his book on the *Foundations of Arithmetic*.

53. This remark does not account for the 'tenacity of bourgeois ideas in the avant garde.' It's not the ideas that are tenacious, it's the avant-gardists: they cling to the ideas to maintain their feeling of self-importance. The remark quoted was prompted by the fact that from 1962–70 (with a few longish breaks) I worked in an office as a graphic designer, pursuing music as a spare time activity. Hence the escapist character of the music; it was a 'fantasy' to which I attached vast importance. It helped me to overlook the fact that I was just a wage slave of the capitalists like millions of others.

54. Carpitezza (he must have been a professor of ethnomusicology) had played a tape of a man of the Hukwe tribe (in Africa, I think) singing to the accompaniment of a log drum. The lecture brought in four independent transcriptions of this song by students in an American university, and pointed out the vast differences of interpretation displayed in these. 'Interpretations' here referred not to any understanding of the meaning or function of the song but simply to the physical data on the tape, which the students 'interpreted' in the light of their existing 'Eurocentric' framework of formal criteria for evaluating musical sounds.

55. Professor Stefani (Italian musicologist) gave the leading speech on musicology, the longest and most systematic.

56. Robert Ashley is an American avant garde composer teaching in a Californian university. I don't remember the subject of his speech, and as for his political statements I only retain an impression of his desperation at the bankruptcy of bourgeois culture in the U.S.

57. During the symposium there were concerts in the evenings. At one of these concerts Earle Brown's composition *Synergy* had been badly performed, and Brown took it upon himself publicly to denounce the Italian composer Franco Evangelisti – in so far as he was responsible for the concert – as dishonest and irresponsible in his attitude, and as having wilfully travestied Brown's intentions with regard to the notation.

58. Kurt Stone, American professor, had pleaded for codification and standardisation of all new notation symbols introduced in new music, on a continuous long-term basis with the aid of government grants, computer time, office staff etc. If one turned a blind eye to the scandalous waste of money and resources involved, his proposal seemed quite reasonable. It hoped to draw composers and players together to co-operate in solving their problems, etc., etc. However, Stone's proposal drew a lot of censure from the individualistic composers of the avant garde (people like Ashley). They felt threatened in their 'freedom' to develop personal and unique notation ideas, hating the thought that these might become common property. In the intervening period, I have heard no further news of Stone's project.

59. Widmer was a music teacher or educationalist from a South American country. His talk was about the use of new notation systems for school music.

60. Nattiez was a French-Canadian scientist, who could have carried away any prize offered for abstruse terminology.

61. Because it does not take up the issue of classes in society, this paragraph degenerates into woolliness. (The subsequent paragraph takes a turn for the better.) 'Serving the needs of society' in a bourgeois academic context (like Widmer and Stone) means serving the needs of the ruling class in society, and the more co-operative and 'social' their way of doing this the more effectively their work can be used against the oppressed classes. The most that can be said for such

people is that they are serious and workmanlike, and these qualities could become useful to the oppressed classes if these people were to change their class stand. The out and out individualists, on the other hand (whether avant garde composers or scientists like Nattiez) are not so much serious as fanatical and obsessive, building their careers on 'drunken speculation.'

62. Despite my moralistic exhortations to composers to take 'solemn and searching looks' at their work, etc., this passage still betrays the arrogance of the avant-gardist. In offering avant-gardists a 'seminal role' I appealed to their vanity, and real progress is out of the question when one's sole basis for unity is bourgeois vanity. I now realise that I capitulated at this point to the ideological climate of the symposium, i.e. I lapsed into a tacit assumption that the bourgeois avant garde is in some sense a 'vanguard', is 'advanced'. It's not; it's backward. That's its dominant aspect. On the question of what role avant garde composers can play in the class struggle, it would have been more correct to speak not about 'our ideas' and 'our music', but about the ideas and the music of the militant working class and encourage the composers and others to place their work potential in the service of that class.

63. This promise is not kept in the article, so I will deal with it here.
Paragraph one of *The Great Learning* opens with a chorus of clicking stones. Then comes an extended organ solo characterised by long, changing conglomerations of notes. Then the chorus divided into two sections re-enters. One section speaks the text and the other plays long held notes on all kinds of whistle instruments. The text over, one of the whistlers breaks into a bird like interpretation of a string of graphic 'phrases' derived from Chinese calligraphy, while the other whistlers continue holding their notes. The text is then spoken again and another whistler plays the solo and so on until all the whistlers have played a solo and the text has been repeated a final time, during which the whistlers all drop out. Thereupon only a three note organ chord remains and on the striking of a small bell the organ is switched off. The air pressure dies out slowly in the pipes, creating strange sliding sounds which gradually fade to nothing. The effect is extremely solemn and ritualistic, provided, that is, that it is not disrupted by justifiably irreverent laughter. The fragile yet raw naturalistic 'nature' sounds of the stones and whistles set off the succulent religiosity of the organ solo. The result, if successful: a mystic awe at the grandeur of the universe. Against this backcloth the human element, the speaking chorus humbly voices its submission. The bell at the end is like a benediction on this quiet submissiveness, and the divine presence fades away

about its business. There is no hint of struggle or excitement, and the human element in the piece is of a tameness that would have warmed old Confucius's reactionary heart.

Paragraph two is scored for a number of groups of singers, each accompanied by a drummer and an instrumentalist. The groups (usually four or five groups) are positioned around the hall so as more or less to enclose the audience. The drummers all start together choosing one out of twenty-six available rhythms. Each drummer acts independently of the others: choosing his own tempo, he repeats his chosen rhythm over and over while the choral group behind him sings through a phrase of long notes, led by the instrumentalist. At the end of each phrase the drummer chooses a new rhythm until he has used up twenty-five of the rhythms. The first drummer to arrive at the last rhythm establishes a tempo to which the other drummers conform as they too arrive at their last rhythms. The drummers thus end the piece with a semblance of unity: they are playing different rhythms but in the same tempo. Throughout the piece the drums dominate; the rising and falling phrases of the voices only just manage to penetrate. Only very occasionally does a chance constellation produce a strong harmonious sonority.

Superficially this stormy piece is the antithesis of the first paragraph, but the essential schema is the same: nature, the stormy racket of the competing drums, again holds sway over the human element, the voices, this time subjugating them by sheer brute violence. Here indeed there is struggle and excitement, the vocal part is taxing in the extreme; but the outcome of the struggle is defeat.

64. See *Peking Review* Nos. 8 and 9, 1974, 'Struggle between Two Lines in the Ideological Sphere during the Spring and Autumn Period and the Warring States Period', by Yang Jung-kuo.

65. The following extract on the May 4th Movement is taken from *Peking Review* No 9, 1974, page 5. "In early 1919, not long after the end of World War 1, an imperialist conference was convened in Paris to share the spoils – the colonies. This was the so-called Paris Peace Conference. The imperialist countries at the conference arrogantly turned down China's just demands for abrogation of imperialist special rights in Shantung Province. When this news reached China, it aroused the great indignation of the Chinese people. On May 4th that year, patriotic students in Peking held mass meetings and demonstrations in front of Tien An Men. They demanded: 'Uphold our sovereignty! Punish the traitors!' and 'Down with imperialism and the traitorous government!' "

The movement spread swiftly throughout China and, from June 3rd onwards, workers in Shanghai and other places went on strike and held demonstrations. The working class stood like a giant in the forefront of the struggle against imperialism and feudalism, playing a most powerful part. Stirred by the workers' and students' actions, shopkeepers in all major cities put up their shutters and joined in the struggle. The May 4th Movement thus became a nation-wide revolutionary movement with the proletariat, the petty bourgeoisie and bourgeoisie taking part.

"On the eve of the 55th anniversary of the May 4th Movement this year the Peking University Committee of the Chinese Communist Youth League and the Students' Union jointly held a commemoration meeting and organised a lecture.

Basing themselves on what is happening in the current struggle, the students conscientiously studied Chairman Mao's brilliant works *The May 4th Movement* and *The Orientation of the Youth Movement* and reviewed the historical experience of the May 4th Movement. The students came to a profound understanding that the May 4th Movement came into being at the call of the October Revolution and of Lenin. It was at once an anti-imperialist, anti-feudal political movement and a great cultural revolution. With its spearhead directed at the doctrines of Confucius and Mencius, the movement raised the clarion call 'Down with the Confucian shop', lit the torch of struggle against Confucius and won magnificent achievements."

See also Lu Hsun's contribution to the criticism of *Confucius, Confucius in Modern China*, reprinted in *Chinese Literature* No. 4, 1974. The article was written in 1935.

66. *Peking Review* No. 8, 1974, page 8.

67. Anthologised in *Ezra Pound: Selected Prose* 1909-1965, Cookson (ed), Faber 1973.

68. *Literature and Ideology* No. 8, 1971, *The political theme of Ezra Pound's Cantos.*

69. Peking Review No.12, 1974, page 14.

The Situation and Prospects of Art Students Today

[A talk given at Falmouth College of Art on 13th June 1974 and again at the School of the Art Institute of Chicago on 8th January 1975. These are notes from which Cardew presumably extemporised.]

Art school is an educational establishment financed by the state (by the taxpayer). Why does the state give people education? Why doesn't the bourgeoisie just pocket the money they filch from the taxpayer? Why do they spend it on these expensive schools?

Clipping from Daily Telegraph to support the following. [Lost] They take the taxpayers' money and invest it in a project, education, in which they have a vested interest, from which they expect to derive profit.

Schools are funded, organized and run in the interests of the bourgeoisie, not in the interests of the students.

However, the students want education – in their own interest to serve their own development. The vast majority of people, students included, have the aspiration to go forward, to learn, to be more productive in their lives, etc. etc.

Since the state serves its own interest by educating people, while the students want to serve their own interests through education, a conflict exists objectively, in all educational establishments in bourgeois society, Eton and Oxford not excepted.

1. Illustrate with my own experience at the Royal Academy of Music.
– My experience as a student was as a passive recipient, superficially rebellious on an individual level.
– Unawareness of the process of creaming off of top talent for elite establishments, orchestras, film composers (like Richard Rodney Bennett), while the rest are flung unprepared into the commercial profession.
– Later, as a teacher there, (still without political commitment) I wanted to develop the students' ability to solve their own problems (not push for exams etc.). As a result I found myself without students.
– One student of mine several times attempted suicide, not because of any wish to die, but because (partly) the RAM refused to provide the teaching that she felt she needed. They of course tried to make out that it was her problem, that there was something wrong with her which was not the case. (Contradictions for teachers in such establishments is another subject, which I won't go into here. This talk is for students.)

The conflict exists. The interests of the state and those of the students are opposed.

What are the interests of the students in a school like this? With a bit of imagination we can paint quite a pretty picture. The all-round development of art skills and talent, both for functional application and fine art production, so that the artists can participate in an urban community, reflecting its material and spiritual life in their work, communicating their superior (acquired) skills to children and amateurs in their spare time, participating in productive work and in the design and decoration of the environment, etc. That's practical work.

On the theoretical side, to learn how the skills you are learning have developed historically, how they were stimulated and called into existence by social movements and upheavals, the role played by art in past and foreign societies, the characteristics of present day society and new developments in the constantly fluctuating interaction of art and society.

Then there would be technical scientific work on the actual materials in current use, the physical properties of colour and light, as well as the subjective factors in the perception of art and the environment, the eye and the brain not only as receptive machinery, but as evolved organs producing ideas and consciousness, grappling with the realities of the outside world as this too has evolved in constant interaction with human societies.

All this work would be done collectively, so that the individual's responsibility is not to be the best student of the year or get one of the rare scholarships offered, but to have acted responsibly in relation to the collective, not wasting the resources that were made available, etc. etc. That's a very rough sketch that could be varied in every detail.

Now what are the interests of the state in a school like this? We have to deal with two aspects: the economic interest and the ideological interest i.e. a) capitalist industry has its interests in developing specialised productive labour power, and b) the bourgeois class as a whole is interested in developing an ideological climate in which its basic position as the ruling class is not seriously questioned – basically a climate in which the question or social classes is obscured and distorted. (It's quite convenient for the state to develop these two interests side by side despite the basic difference between them, because it's highly desirable that the skilled art workers who will go into industry should be infected with ideological confusion so as to inhibit their later natural development into class-conscious workers, aware of their exploitation and oppression and eager to do something about it.)

However, the development of industrial artists is a definite financial investment, profits are at stake, so we find that art schools are relatively departmentalized from quite an early stage. If you invest capital in training a highly skilled professional fashion artist, or ceramic designer, etc., that artist or designer is providing the maximum return on capital only when engaged in that specific job. He must therefore be taught from early on to keep his nose to that particular grindstone and not mess about with artistic ambitions.

On the ideological side there are again two departments: artists and art teachers. I don't know how sharply defined these are in today's art schools. Perhaps there's no specific educational, teacher training course, in which bourgeois educational theory (? the art of coping) is instilled into students with artistic talent who reject a bourgeois art career (or at least don't aspire to it) in favour of a job where they feel (however illusory) that they have a chance to be socially useful, as a teacher. It doesn't matter;

many fine art students in fact end up in education at one level or another – as lecturer, technical assistant, school teacher or even in private practice (just as musicians take private pupils) – even if they don't go on to teacher training college after art school.

Also for the fine art students, the principle thing is to develop fanatical egocentricity, self-absorption, extreme individualism, alongside a desperate search for material novelty, the more farfetched the better. Competition, on which capitalism rests, and which is a social thing still in the industrial art fields (people can at least compare their work, for instance, with a view to improving it), in the fine art field this competition reaches its apex (and destroys itself) in total isolation. Ideologically, this 'training' (to be totally self-centred and unique) is backed up with a wide range of theories. Freud, Harekrishna, Wittgenstein, Confucius, Dr Goebbels, half-boiled mysticism, glorification of sex, witchcraft, the Death Wish, you name it, they push it – a veritable rogues gallery of ghosts and monsters. This Ancient and Modern Hymnal of ideological claptrap is supposed to set up such a din that the students are not capable of facing with sober senses their actual conditions of existence, their real situation. This is no joke – there is a real possibility of permanent (or at least long lasting) damage to the world outlook of such students after they leave college.

And what awaits these students after they leave college? Years of isolation and tribulations of all sorts are often the price of a successful career. Only in this process is the ego tempered, does the ego reach the dimensions required by the bourgeois art market. (This is a fiercely competitive process of elimination. Show how the successful artist too is an oppressed wage slave – certainly not 'free').

Or you can drop out, degenerate and pretend to make 'living' your art. Or exhibit on the railings of Hyde Park, or paint skies or trees or hands on the 'original oil paintings' sold in Woolworths (sweated labour). Maybe after the talk we can discuss some case histories.

Anyway, the main thing is: none of these courses can be viewed as desirable for the student, as representing his interests in anyway.

The conflict exists. The interests of the state education system and the interests of the students are opposed.

When students become conscious of this a struggle breaks out inevitably. Some individuals may resist passively – become withdrawn and disinterested. Others may capitulate and throw themselves with fervour into the course mapped out for them by the bourgeoisie. Some, the most conscious, begin to question the real situation, to investigate what's going on, study society, see who has what to say about it, and what can be done about it. They will also wage ideological struggle against the ideas being promoted, they will fight for progressive content in their courses.

What are the specific difficulties of struggle in art schools? The main one is individualism. The fact that the interests of the state, specially in art schools, is to develop the ego, the bourgeois individuality, of the student, creates the impression that the interests of the state and the student are identical: i.e. development of the student. It is hard for the student to realise that this particular exaggerated development of his ego is actually harmful to his development as a person. It is hard for the student to resist a development which is presented to him as being his own development.

Another difficulty is the particular character assumed by the Students' Union branches in art schools. I don't know the history of this particular Union within the Trade Union movement. Obviously the Students' Union, whose members will later join other unions, has a special place in the Trade Union movement, but is nevertheless an integral part of it. Like most unions, it must have been formed as a defence organisation, to defend the interests of the students against the interests of their 'employer' the state. Because although the students are not yet employed in productive labour, they are being trained for such employment, so in a sense their exploitation as productive labour, though not yet begun, already exists in embryo.

The Students' Union fights for reasonable social amenities in colleges, edible food and decent common rooms, for adequate accommodation facilities and for a living grant.

Perhaps because of the romantic notion, of the artist as someone who dies of consumption in a garret, these union struggles tend not to be actively supported in art schools (or am I wrong here?). At the RAM we used to regard the union as something which existed for our individual benefit, to supply our individual needs, for practice rooms, cheap travel, what have you. Very few students recognised the character of the SU as representing our interests as a whole, as a collective. I imagine it's much the same in art schools.

However, a new situation has developed. The student movement as a whole, since the risings of 1968 and after, has taken on a new dimension, over and above its essential struggles on the economic front for grants, etc., a specifically political dimension in fact. So for instance the NUS has adopted a resolution calling on its branches to use whatever means necessary to prevent known fascist and racist ideologists from speaking in colleges. With this resolution the union has reached a stage where it can potentially become very active indeed in art schools. For in art schools fascist and racist ideological lines – and a whole lot of other anti-people lines – are rampant, even if not in the crude clarity displayed by such characters as Eysenck.

The stage is developing when the conscious art student will be able through the SU to demand progressive content in lectures and classes, and through uniting the majority of students around this demand to actually bring pressure to bear (through boycotts, pickets, etc.) to get rid of reactionary lecturers and engage progressive teachers of their choice. When the student body demands majority student representation (for instance) on the committees where educational decisions are made, the bourgeois state will be forced to resist, and the consciousness of larger and larger numbers of students will be aroused. In ways like this it is definitely possible for the struggle in art colleges, despite specific difficulties in this area, to develop to a relatively high level. Cultural revolution is not something that can only happen in China.

But I'll end with an instance from China which I hope will encourage you to take up the struggle here, and not passively wait e.g. for the working class movement to mature. I think it was during the Chinese War of Resistance against Japan (1937-45) a revolutionary art movement was launched. The revolutionary writer Lu Hsun was active in this movement. In the course of just a few years over 10,000 separate collections of woodblock prints with revolutionary and educational content, in editions ranging from 50 to several thousand, were produced by Chinese artists. This great movement, which played an important part in educating the masses and freeing them from the fetters of feudal society – and unleashing their militancy against it – was encouraged and led by the Communist Party of China.

Now I don't think such a movement could be launched right here, right now*. But such a stage will inevitably develop, when the class struggle of the workers rises to even higher levels, and when the leadership of a Marxist-Leninist Party has emerged. Then such movements will be launched, and play their part in developing the revolutionary ideology of the working class. And that's not in the dim and distant future, so we'd better start preparing.

* hand written note "Why not?"

Cornelius Cardew – interviewed by Adrian Jack
Music and Musicians – May 1975

Born in 1936, Cornelius Cardew became known in the 1960's as the most innovatory composer in England. His works were published by Peters Edition (including the substantial graphic score, *Treatise*, begun in 1963, which took several years to evolve) and Universal Edition. The Experimental Music Catalogue published *The Great Learning*, which began as *The Great Digest* in 1968. Getting people together to perform one of this collection of seven pieces led to the formation in 1969 of the Scratch Orchestra, which encouraged non-musicians to join. By the summer of 1971 discontent within the Scratch Orchestra caused it to split into two groups: those who, with the pianist John Tilbury, were committed to the politicisation of music intended from a Marxist viewpoint, and those not.

The influence on the Scratch Orchestra's political development came from the Communist Party of England Marxist-Leninist. This party is critical of the Communist Party of Great Britain and was first formed as a group called the Internationalists in 1963. It is the strand in the left-wing movement which Cardew is still interested in and which he thinks 'will win through'. The history and the break-up of the Scratch Orchestra are outlined in a book published at the end of last year and reviewed in *M & M* in March: this is a collection of articles by Cardew and others with the title *Stockhausen serves Imperialism*.

Cardew has now turned his back on what he regards as elitist avant garde or experimental music. In 1973 and 1974 he wrote several pieces for voice, piano, violin and piano, or pop group, which are mainly based on Chinese revolutionary songs or settings of texts expressing proletarian protest. They use a squarely phrased tonal idiom. The performers of these pieces have so far most often been Cardew himself, John Tilbury and a pop group called *People's Liberation Music*. Cardew still associates himself with performances of his earlier music, but has accompanied them with a talk or discussion in which he repudiates the music.

*   *   *

Adrian Jack   The implications of what you say in some of the articles collected in *Stockhausen serves Imperialism* as well as the implications of the music you have written since 1972 are, I think, Stalinist. You had, come to think of it, a picture of Stalin on the platform at your concert with *People's Liberation Music* at the

Purcell Room on March 5th, 1974. But what really brought this home to me was the reference in the book to the People's Republic of China: you said that bourgeois works should be suppressed if necessary, as they are in China, or – if they are performed – only performed in order to be repudiated and held up as examples of what not to do.

Cornelius Cardew In China this has actually been done, not with music but with films.

AJ Do you think it should be done with music, then?

CC Well, I've learnt to keep my mouth shut rather about China. We could get into a long discussion about where the word Stalinist comes from, and it just prevents us from discussing the issues that are actually facing us. It's the same with China, although I'm still just as interested in what is going on in China. The same objections keep cropping up: 'Have you ever been to China? No? Well I have and I know this, that and the other…' The whole argument goes over to China and you get lost there.

AJ Well, the question of China is very important to people because you seem to admire it. Therefore they take everything they know about China as a blueprint of your ideal, although you would reject the word 'ideal'. I am worried about whether you really are interested in suppressing Stockhausen, Cage and so forth, whether you believe in the imposition of a standard musical aesthetic if you like: that is what I mean by a Stalinist idea.

CC To go back to China, often you get the conception that there is a unified cultural programme. There certainly is a very integrated cultural programme, but it's got so many different aspects and they are developing many different kinds of music. In the national minority areas they are developing all the folk music. The way that the Russians influenced style, like the *Yellow River Concerto*, and how that is transformed in the provinces is all very complicated. There are many different directions. So I don't think there is a unified standard aesthetic. I don't think there can be, and I would never think of imposing it. But I'm not too worried about it because I think that such decisions should never land in the lap of one person. To decide that Stockhausen or Cage should be banned is something I am never likely to be in the position to do. If it was to do with me, I wouldn't ban them, because I think really they are banned in London, for example, by lack of support. And although you can say that this is manipulated by the media, that they discriminate against certain types of modern music, you can actually see that when people aren't interested in it, then it dries up, and I think that has happened. If music is about the things people are interested in, they will welcome it. If it's just about mathematics or the arrangement of notes, they won't be interested.

AJ But don't you think that one of the functions of the artist is to show things to be interesting that aren't obvious? Things that take a certain amount of working at; that people haven't thought of at all?

CC Even then you can say there's a situation that exists that very few people understand or that not everybody understands or that everybody understands only in a superficial way, and then some composer comes along and goes into a particular aspect of that, which he then understands very deeply; and then in the judgment of people that listen to the music it is only a very minor aspect...

AJ Do you really place so much value on the judgment of people who listen to music?

CC I'm not really talking about the individual judgment. I'm talking about collective judgment, although the whole of our conversation is in very ideal terms, because we are leaving out of account for the moment the ideological promotion of certain schools of music, which is something that exists objectively. It's quite possible that there are very good composers working today who, because of their ideology, are suppressed and prevented from reaching any kind of audience. If for a moment we leave that out of account, then I certainly place a lot of confidence in the judgment of the audience as a collective thing. Although the violin is very difficult to play, people persevere with learning to play it because they realise the potential. It's possible that there would be very difficult music which would be very good music, that people would be interested in persevering with and hearing several times.

AJ It's a question of familiarity. Your analogy with learning the violin is not really relevant because there people hear the results which are within their experience: they have lived with old music for many years, they've been exposed to it. They just haven't been exposed sufficiently to modern music.

CC There's a place in the book where it says that most modern music is footling and unsatisfying compared with the classics. Now are you suggesting that the achievements of modern composers are as satisfying as those of the classical composers?

AJ Yes I am, and I'm saying that lack of familiarity militates against their experiencing modern music in the same way as the classics. It's just a question of exposure, of something being shown to them enough.

CC I used to think that. I used to think that you could recognise the beauty in any old sound.

AJ I don't think that!

CC What you're saying relates to the idea that the human being is totally conditionable. I don't agree with that. I think you could expose people in unlimited doses to certain things and they still wouldn't welcome them.

AJ I am not saying at all that you only have to expose people to something to make them accept it. That is on a very low level. I think you have to expose them to many examples of new music to put them in the position where they can discriminate. For instance it's not until you have lived in a country for some time that you can discriminate between buildings with similar architecture.

CC What you say is quite right from the aesthetic point of view, but I maintain that the main thing will be whether the building is a palace or a wash house: if there is a fantastic building which was the palace of a particularly vicious Renaissance family, you will appreciate its aesthetic qualities but you won't like it, because of what it stands for.

AJ But you can divorce its aesthetic qualities from its function, can't you?

CC Well, I would never want to, you see.

AJ You must admit that the working classes don't like Beethoven or Mozart very much.

CC I'm not at all surprised that the working class doesn't like Beethoven or

Mozart, because they are the composers of the bourgeoisie.

AJ   Then what is suitable music for the working class? The music you have written recently sounds almost deliberately bad for instance – those pieces from the *Piano Album* that John Tilbury played at the Purcell Room on March 5th last year. Why are they not better composed? You could certainly manage better, couldn't you?

CC   Well, it's a matter of education. When I was at the Academy I was more interested in writing like Stockhausen, and the 19th-century pastiche I had to do I never took very seriously.

AJ   What are you trying to do? A year ago you said that you didn't claim they were ideal music for the workers, that you were experimenting.

CC   Well, I don't even think that's true now. I think we simply don't have access to a working-class audience. These pieces were written for a definite audience. It is a definite audience which comes to the Purcell Room – or the students in colleges round the country where you might get a gig. It's not an audience of workers in their work environment or even in their recreation time. It's music for a consciously culture-orientated youth. I never believe I claimed it was reaching the working classes. I acknowledge there are compositional shortcomings in these pieces, and I don't make any claims for them. The advantage of them is that they draw the attention of the listeners to social issues. If you have a concert of arrangements of Irish songs, it does draw attention to the culture of the Irish and also to their fight.

AJ   But the fact is that most of the audience laugh at this music, so that you bring the cause disrepute.

CC   I've found that not to be true actually. Maybe we play the pieces better now, but certainly on the American tour I went on early this year the audiences didn't laugh. There were some people that thought it was trivialising the causes it was setting out to champion.

AJ   What pieces did you play on the American tour?

CC   Some of the *Piano Album* pieces and the *Thälmann Variations*. Some music students were delighted that they could use their traditional performing skills in the *Thälmann Variations*.

AJ   The 19th-century style you have adopted in such pieces evolved out of composers' interest in their private feelings. Yet you are not concerned with exploring your own sensibility.

CC   Every artist has to use his individual sensibility, otherwise how could he communicate? We want to change the emphasis from the subjective to the real world. But you have an obligation to bring your individual sensibility, your passions, to bear upon your music. To deny the subjective quality of art would be to deny life.

AJ   Do you want to make your future pieces innovatory in a technical way, or do you want to use an idiom that is very familiar?

CC   I would like it to be more simple. I'm not terribly interested in breaking new ground, as I feel we were trying to do in AMM. [Cardew was a member of this experimental improvisation group from 1966 to 1972.] New ground is being broken all the time, and I have certainly participated in that, but to make that your aim is pretty irrelevant. I'm much more interested in the national liberation struggles in Africa than I am in the latest technique of Stockhausen. Your work reflects whichever interest occupies you more. Because I don't think those inventions are terribly important. I probably won't contribute to them much. I would be much happier if music were much simpler, more straightforward and communicated about something in the real world.

AJ   Whom do you want to communicate with?

CC   The same old audience. Gradually changing. Certainly the audience will shift. More left-wing people will be interested in coming to the concerts as this trend becomes more general and as more avant garde composers become more left-wing in their political views.

AJ   But you don't think much of some of the composers who have shown this trend, do you?'

CC   No, I think a lot of it is mystifying.

AJ   What about Erhardt Grosskopf's latest music? [See review of the German Month at the ICA in *M & M* January, 1975.]

CC I think he is making efforts in the right direction, just as I think Christian Wolff is making efforts in the right direction; [See review of the Berlin Festival in *M & M*, December 1974.]

AJ Do you think that avant garde means soften the blow and obscure the message?

CC I feel, like the Chinese musicologists, that modern music is in a very deep sense pessimistic and that not much can be done with it. But there may be composers who will prove me wrong. I mean a Stockhausen piece like *Momente* or *Gruppen* – there's no reason why such a piece of music should not have progressive content. But it's very unlikely in the present circumstances that such music would receive State support.

AJ How will it have progressive content? By means of texts?

CC Maybe. Or perhaps like the way that Nono used to do it. In retrospect I think that what Nono was doing was fairly valid. And what he is doing now is fairly valid.

AJ That strikes me as odd, because it seems that Nono's music dissolves the text away too easily for those who aren't interested in it.

CC Yes, but one is never interested in the people who don't want to pay attention to it. The core of the audience is those who are interested in what one has to say. One's efforts are directed to the most conscious section of the audience.

AJ Do you think it is a good idea to do, as John Tilbury did on two occasions: repudiate the ideological implications of the music he plays with either a programme note or a talk or discussion after the performance?

CC Well, all I can say is that we thought it right at the time. When I worked with Steve Reich, I had no authority over the presentation of the concerts – I was there simply because I was paid. It would have been extremely difficult, for me to organise any kind of discussion. Of course I could put on a concert of Steve Reich's music here and now and have a discussion about it, but don't think it's that important. I think I now see things in a more balanced way and that maybe having discussions about other composers in those days was not so good. There are some audiences it is good to upset, but it is not good to upset the majority of audiences, and it certainly isn't what I want to do now. It's good to make them think about things they haven't thought about before, but not to cause dismay.

AJ Some people feel that it is hypocrisy for you to perform avant garde music which you disapprove of.

CC I know those people. They are the ones who want you to go out in the desert and die of starvation and rub yourself off the face of the earth because you're bringing up these troubling questions. I've got a perfect right to earn a living – in the easiest way I can actually. I feel that we were in danger of taking the line of isolating ourselves from what we'd been involved in. If John Tilbury and I got out of the avant garde musical scene, there would be plenty to take our place. No possible dent would have been made. There would have been no promotion of our ideas. It would just be a ridiculous dream.

AJ How do you feel about the revision you made in 1972 of Paragraphs 1 and 2 of *The Great Learning*? Would you rather have the revised version or the original performed now?

CC The original, because it engages the participation particularly of the players in the situation that existed then – which was the formation of the Scratch Orchestra. That was a genuine real life situation and in no way artificially constructed; through that experience it already shatters their notion of the conventional establishment. And because it's a very loose organic kind of experience and not a tight frightening one, it gives you a more flexible basis to do future work on. If people have participated in that kind of activity they can feel the satisfactions there are in it and also the dissatisfactions there are in it – which are many. They can express what they feel about these reactions and on the basis of that move on to something else. I don't really believe that a bourgeois piece of muslc can be reformed. You can only adapt it, and the adaptation certainly wouldn't be better than the original.

AJ So what are you doing at the moment apart from your employment as a freelance musician?

CC We are trying to develop *People's Liberation Music*, and Laurie Baker in the *PLM* is starting to organise things like benefit concerts for working-class causes.

I'm wondering it there isn't some similar possibility in classical music, the problem being that with modern music, even if you had quite well-known people doing it, the money you would raise would be absolutely minuscule. But it might be good for the musicians who took part. And then all the people in the *PLM* have started becoming not necessarily active but at least consciously participating in the Musicians' Union. And I very much want to get back into teaching now.

AJ   Are you still a professor at the Academy?

CC   I'm available in theory, but they don't give me students.

AJ   Why?

CC   I think it's just a hangover from the old avant garde days. They didn't like the Scratch Orchestra and the fact that I didn't care if students went in for exams. They feel that any person who thinks it isn't necessary to have that kind of training is a threat to the Academy.

AJ   Yet in your book you said that the training isn't thorough enough, and you criticised what you considered the low level of demands in diploma exams.

CC   Exactly. There's that little paragraph which explains why *Piano Album* is not very well composed. The whole education is lacking. Certainly those institutions have a role. In the Scratch Orchestra we were thinking of a Utopian society: not having been to the Academy would not prevent anyone from making music: *everyone* should be able to make music. Kodaly's ideas were tending towards a situation where everybody participates in music – very desirable, very important for the future. So I'm still very interested in amateur music making – not amateur as opposed to professional but in the sense of amateurs making genuinely new music, not just aping the professionals. Now at the Academy all the students have been through a process of selection that is quite stringent. Everyone coming straight from school there is already pretty special in their instrument. So I am trying to get a teaching job in an establishment outside London where competitive pressure isn't so high. I think what you realise is that the actual craft of making music is not all that important. The product of music is ideological influence, and I want to direct this influence in a particular direction. The question is how: by writing a piece of music – which I've tried – or do you do it by teaching other people to write music or being in a situation where they are developing skills in writing music and where you can participate in directing the development of those skills? That is a situation I'm very interested in.

AJ   I don't agree with your point about influence. You can wield it in teaching, but the influence of music is far more indirect. After all, all your recent pieces use a text or are based on a song with a political text. It is the text which is drawing attention to ideological matters.

CC   But I'm not sorry that I did that, because it acknowledges that music does come from somewhere, it's not just abstract. By using Irish music you open up the channel from where that music came. If I decide not to carry on writing music in that tonal idiom, it will be because I don't think it is terribly effective, not because I think there is anything wrong with it. Another thing that could be done and ought to be done is to present the social background to a composer's music, for instance, when John Tilbury plays Debussy. We could put on concerts of classical music, with the proper background. That's something they're beginning to do in Germany. That's another thing one can do in the teaching situation. One could do research which would draw attention to the social aspects. There are still many thousands of young people who still don't think of culture in terms of class. It's rather amazing that we were able to operate in the Scratch Orchestra without a definite consciousness of that kind. There were people with working-class backgrounds but no ordinary manual workers. I was quite pleased to hear recently at the Royal College of Music some students talking about Tippett and Britten in terms of their world outlook, though.

AJ   The image of the sort of music you've been engaged in recently is a kind of cultural slumming.

CC   Yes, which is very bad.

AJ   Why shouldn't the workers have the best?

CC   There's the whole question of how you apply bourgeois culture. There is a working-class culture, you see.

AJ   In England?

CC   Folk music.

AJ   Surely that's middle-class dabbling.

CC   There is that too, of course.

AJ   You get very little spontaneous singing in pubs or places of work now.

CC   No, but there is a consciousness, like in the mines. There are mining songs. It's a dying tradition, I know that, because as industrialisation has taken place the kind of work to which you sing has been reduced. Also with the growth of mechanical reproduction and pop music it's become less necessary, but it's there. If you think of pop music as being a kind of working-class culture – not necessarily progressive pop.

AJ   I don't think of pop music as being a working-class culture at all. It's entirely manipulated by middle-class exploiters.

CC   Yes, well then you've got to distinguish between the part which is manipulated and the part which has actually grown up. Naturally, once we have produced a music which can be manipulated, it will become middle-class, as happened to negro culture. But pop music has its roots in oppressed people's music. That is to say the influence of Beethoven and Stockhausen is minute. The people who are involved in it are more likely to be working-class than people who are involved in symphony orchestras. It's directed at the masses and consumed by the masses, though it is also consumed by the middle classes as a kind of accompaniment to a party. If it's possible through *PLM*, all the members of which are experienced professionals in the pop field apart from John Tilbury and myself, to influence the people that produce pop music and encourage that trend which already exists – that music should become more class-conscious, that we should have songs about working-class heroes – then that would be a very good thing, because this is a channel through which working class ideology is really influenced.

AJ   But the main re-inforcement for pop music surely is its commercial advantages. As soon as your ideas are expressed in pop music to an effective point, promoters won't want to touch it.

CC   That's perfectly true. I have no illusions about the bourgeoisie allowing us on the air. But if people (like Paul McCartney) occasionally write progressive songs and these are suppressed, then people see that they are suppressed and

243

they have an incredible influence then. If it is known that they take a stand, this has an influence. And there can arise a situation where pop artists are not dependent on the media. Particularly in Black America there are progressive, class-conscious groups who are not readily available on record, though they might be available on labels which are distributed through their own channels. They simply play for their audience and make a living from that.

A note on Frederic Rzewski
The Musical Times – January 1976

Frederic Rzewski (born 1936) is one of a number of unpublished American composers who are beating a path out of the cliquishness and formal aridity of the established avant garde towards a politically conscious mass audience. 'Musicians and artists', he has said, 'must listen to the sounds of struggle if they are to contribute anything in the way of harmony.'

Rzewski's musical career began early: at the age of nine he was giving recitals of Beethoven sonatas. Later, at Princeton, he made the acquaintance of another avant garde prodigy, Christian Wolff, and their friendship has remained fruitful. Rzewski stepped outside the confines of an avant garde career and made overtures to the mass audience of discontented youth. A Ford Foundation fellowship in Berlin 1964-5 led to a prolonged stay in Europe (he was based in Rome until recently) during which he did pioneer work on live electronic improvisation and music making with untrained players.

English audiences have had only fragmentary glimpses of Rzewski's work. In the 1960s he attracted astonishment and admiration with a talc enshrouded rendering of Stockhausen's *Klavierstuck X* at a BBC Invitation Concert. Later, Musica Elettronica Viva (of which he is a founder member) visited England at the invitation of Music Now; on one occasion they participated in a pop concert on Parliament Hill, only to be greeted with hurled hot dogs and Coke tins. After 1970 some of his compositions and improvisatory pieces appeared in the repertory of the Scratch Orchestra, and the interest generated thereby was one factor leading to the Prom performance in 1974 of his *Les Moutons de Panurge*, rendered by an expanded Intermodulation.

Les Moutons (1969) is a good example of Rzewski's compositional method: a lively modal melody is developed by progressively adding notes and then compressed by subtracting notes from the beginning. His favourite instrumentation is aggressive percussion and penetrating wind, and intensity is sustained by a continual teetering on the verge of anarchy.

In his concert at St Pancras Assembly Rooms (January 22) Rzewski will be presenting two more recent works (again at the invitation of Music Now). *Coming Together/Attica* (1972) develops the systemic techniques of *Les Moutons* but uses them to present two texts of extraordinary emotional striking power. Part I is a letter written by Sam Melville from Attica prison before the rebellion by the prisoners in which they took possession of part of the prison; the state governor ordered troops to recapture the prison, which they did, and 40 people were killed in the process. Melville was among the dead. Part 2 is a brief reply by Richard X. Clarke, another Attica inmate, to a question put to him as he was leaving the prison. Assisted in this performance by rock and jazz artists, Rzewski uses dynamic, driving elements from popular music to embody the urgency and total commitment of those killed.

Since 1972, *Coming Together/Attica* has generated heated discussion among musicians and audiences in Europe and America, and that has undoubtedly given impetus to the development of Rzewski's thinking. Of far greater impact – and this is true of large sections of American youth and intellectuals – has been the coup in Chile in 1973 in which the USA government was implicated. Rzewski's contribution to the movement of solidarity with the people of Chile under the present right-wing regime is a 35 minute set of piano variations on *El Pueblo Unido Jamas Sera Vencido*. This beautiful song by Sergio Ortega is a product of the New Chilean Song Movement which flourished under the Allende regime. In his variations Rzewski poured out his abundant compositional and pianistic virtuosity: his political consciousness released a flood of creative energy that would otherwise have remained dormant.

Struggle Sounds
Time Out – 16th January 1976

Cornelius Cardew previews Music Now's outstanding concert of the season: 'Music of Resistance' at the St. Pancras Assembly Rooms, January 22nd 1976.

Musicians and artists must listen to the sounds of struggle if they are to contribute anything in the way of harmony. Frederic Rzewski's remark shows quite a change of outlook for a composer/pianist who has made a name playing Cage and Stockhausen.

English audiences have had only glimpses of Rzewski's work. He gave the first English performance of Stockhausen's *Piano Piece X* at a BBC invitation Concert and Music Now has invited his live electronic improvisation group Musica Elettronica Viva to London on a number of occasions. After 1970 some of Rzewski's compositions and improvisatory pieces began to appear in the repertoire of the Scratch Orchestra: *Les Moutons de Panurge* (1969) in particular became something of a favourite, and was later featured In a 1974 Prom by the live electronic group 'Intermodulation.'

In his January 22 concert, subtitled: 'Music of Resistance', Rzewski will be presenting more recent works. *Coming Together/Attica* (1972) develops the 'systemic' composition techniques of *Les Moutons* – techniques which combine and permutate note patterns. But it uses them to present two texts of extraordinary emotional power. Part One is a letter written by Sam Melville from Attica prison prior to a rebellion by the prisoners in which they occupied part or the prison. The then Governor of NY State, Nelson Rockefeller, ordered troops in to recapture the prison, which they did, killing 40 people in the process. Sam Melville was among the dead. Part Two is a brief reply by Richard X Clarke, another Attica inmate, to a question put to him as he was leaving the prison. He was asked how it felt to be leaving Attica.

Commenting on this work in *Stockhausen Serves Imperialism*, a collection of articles in book form reviewed in this magazine last year (TO 256), I criticised it for its underlying anarchism and for the intensely subjective effect of the 'systemic' fragmentation of the text, I also felt that Rzewski had emphasised neurotic and obsessive aspects of popular music in his piece. Certainly this is not music with any kind of 'socialist' perspective. In the sense of looking towards a new social order. But it is a powerful statement of spontaneous resistance to the class and racial oppression characteristic of US society.

Since 1972, *Coming Together/Attica* has generated heated discussion among musicians and audiences in Europe and America, and this has certainly given impetus to the development of Rzewski's thinking. A more powerful factor has been the fascist coup in Chile in 1973 in which US ruling circles were deeply implicated. Rzewski's contribution to the world-wide movement of solidarity with the people of Chile is a mammoth set of piano variations on *El Pueblo Unido Jamas Sera Vencido* (*The People United Will Never Be Defeated*), the song by Sergio Ortega and Quilapayun that has become almost the anthem of the Chilean Resistance abroad.

Both politically and musically this represents a new stage in Rzewski's work. Politically, such a piece raises definite issues of socialism. In particular the issue of the so-called 'peaceful road to socialism.'

Musically, the piece represents an attempts to shake off the formalism, the 'systemic' character of most of his compositions up to and including the Attica pieces.

So Rzewski's *Music of Resistance* concert on January 22 is not 'just music', it is about something. And it is not just 'about' the subject matter of the different compositions, it is about a very big issue of how to resist and challenge the prevalent culture, which represents for me such a powerful weapon of repression against the working people of this country. Those who identify with this objective

Wiggly Lines and Wobbly Music

Studio International – No. 984, Vol. 192 November/December 1976

Without wishing to turn this article into a personal statement, I have to say at the outset that I was engaged throughout the 1960's in writing – I should say drawing – and performing so-called 'graphic music'. I also wrote articles which contributed to the speculation that grew up around the genre (on which academics and students are still feeding) and attempted to provide it with theoretical justification or at least interest. Then in 1971 the ripples of a new revolutionary political movement upset this fragile coracle (as far as I was concerned) and tipped me out into the maelstrom of the class struggle. A period of 'settling accounts' with my avant garde activities followed, and I detected (as have previous generations of artists who wanted to serve the people) a clear antagonism between the bourgeois (artistic) avant garde and the proletarian (political) vanguard, i.e. the revolutionary party of the working class. In 1972 I was asked to speak at a conference on problems of notation in Rome, and spoke of my own composition *Treatise* as a particularly striking outbreak of what I diagnosed as a disease of notation, namely the tendency for musical notations to become aesthetic objects in their own right. Today, four years later, such problems have been largely displaced (as far as I am concerned) by more pressing ones, such as how to produce and distribute music that serves the needs of the growing revolutionary (political) movement.

I may as well confess that this article springs from no 'inner necessity'. I was asked to write it, and accepted because of a certain 'external necessity' with which I am sure most readers are familiar. My opinions on graphic music are no longer those of an active participant, in fact they are quite detached, in that I attempt to view it as a phenomenon (among other phenomena, all interrelated) of a particular historical juncture. I want to go beyond opinions and arrive at an objective assessment of the role played by graphic music as one strand among many in the post-war musical avant-gardist. And because the artistic avant garde is a component – and an ideologically active (should I say virulent?) component – of the superstructure of western imperialist society (it's no accident that many of the composers I'll be talking about are American), and hence helps to protect that society against radical social change, the assessment is bound to be negative in the overall political sense. What it boils down to is that graphic music 'proper' (we'll go into that in a moment) was a constellation of misconceptions and mystifications that contributed to confusing the basic issues facing musicians in bourgeois society, namely: the question of content in music, how music expresses and embodies ideas, and whose interests does it serve.

* * *

Casting about for a point of entry to the subject: What do people mean by the term 'graphic music'? Can one draw a picture of a sound? Are there aural equivalents of visual effects? What led people to think of 'drawing' music instead of writing it? What is the importance of the graphic aspect of ordinary musical notation? What does it mean when visual artists and critics talk about drawings and paintings in musical terms (loud colours, etc.)?

* * *

All our sense organs transmit information to the brain. The very fact that the brain can distinguish visual from aural from tactile from olfactory stimuli implies that it can also relate them to one another. Any new stimulus is also related to the stored experience of a lifetime of social practice. So there can be no purely aural, or purely visual let alone purely musical (as Stravinsky would have us believe) or purely aesthetic experience. Even though there are areas of the brain that specifically deal with certain stimuli (visual, aural, etc.) these areas are not closed off from one another. They often interfere with one another. 'Synaesthesia' is the name for a condition where the brain jumbles up stimuli of different sorts. If a man watching a solar eclipse finds it so loud that he blocks his ears instead of closing his eyes, then his eyes may be damaged, and we would consider this a result of a malfunction of his brain. But some degree of 'synaesthesia' is present in everyone, and can be developed from a less conscious to a more conscious level. It's this faculty that allows us to experience 'rhythm' in paintings, 'light and shade' in orchestral 'colour', the 'smell' of decay in a photograph, or 'personality' in an abstract painting. (Closely observed, each of these examples would present special features and problems, unique contributory factors, etc., but the general gist of what I'm saying is clear, I hope). All these parallelisms, whether intuited ('felt'), inducted, deducted, constructed, cannot amount to equivalence. In my view, any correlation of the different varieties of, for example, 'blue' notes with the various shades of the colour blue would be arbitrary.

Many such parallelisms boil down to problems of social etymology: what social conditions, cultural milieu, linguistic confluence gave rise to the expression 'feeling blue', for instance? But there are some cases where the idea of the equivalence of qualitatively different phenomena forces itself upon us. One such case is the similarity between acoustic 'beats' and visual 'moire'.

Acoustic beats are produced when two notes of nearly the same frequency are sounded together. A string producing 440 cycles (vibrations) per second and another producing 441 cps cannot be distinguished by the ear as producing different notes. What the two strings *do* produce sounds like a single note waxing and waning in intensity in cycles of one second (441 minus 440 equals one). Sound is transmitted through a medium (generally air), with the result that all sounds occurring simultaneously in the same location combine into a single waveform, a single complex shape of disturbance in the air (although this shape will be different in different parts of the room depending on the proximity of different sound sources, for example). The ear analyses this waveform back into its components, thus distinguishing the different instruments playing, etc. (Hence the practicability of reproducing music from the single groove of a record). In our case the nodal points of the two sound waves coincide once every second, so that the resulting waveform repeats itself once a second (rather than 440 times per second as would be the case if both strings were tuned to 440 cps). If the difference between the two frequencies was two (440 and 442) the nodes would coincide twice every second. This is a physical phenomenon occurring in the air, independent of any listener.

With moire effects the situation is different. A simple moire effect (kinetic art enthusiasts be patient) can be achieved by drawing the same pattern of concentric circles on two transparent plastic sheets and superimposing them. If the centres of the circles are made to coincide the image appears still; if the centres are slightly displaced the combined image appears to rotate (note 1).

This is an 'optical' effect, in the sense that it is not the image that moves, but the eye of the beholder that creates the effect of motion. The structure of the combined image obliges the eye to rotate. So these apparently similar aural/visual effects are not equivalent in fact, and if one were to make a graphic score composed of such moire patterns the process of converting them into accurately corresponding patterns of acoustic beats would have to be governed by a complex series of arbitrary rules and conventions.

But such a score can quite easily be converted into sound (or even music) 'intuitively' or semi-intuitively. Such intuitive reading of the score is a fundamental aspect of graphic music. Rather than serving as notations, many graphic scores were intended rather as an 'inspiration' to the musicians, or as an aid to improvisation. In this sense graphic music (or musical graphics) represents a reaction against musical notation – though often preserving relics of musical notation – as opposed to graphic notation which represents a development of musical notation.

At this point it is worth looking at the history of musical notation. That will give an idea of what is implied in the term notation, and then we can see to what extent graphic music either functions as or departs from musical notation.

* * *

Musical notation as schoolchildren learn it today has been in existence broadly unchanged since about 1600, but the fundamental inventions that brought it into existence go back much further. Guido d' Arezzo, a monk born in AD 990, is credited with the general introduction of the 'staff', a bundle of equally spaced horizontal lines on which notes could be placed so as to indicate their relations to one another in pitch (high/low) and in time (left/right as in our script). It would be interesting to research the whys and wherefores of how the need for notation arose – the social/political/ideological matrix that gave rise to Guido's revolutionary contribution – but it lies outside the scope of this article. Assuming that notation was designed to preserve musical forms by putting them on accurate written record, the actual effect of its introduction was to pave the way for a great diversification of musical forms. It was also the chute down which a new type professional, the composer, the person who designs and manages the musical activity of executant musicians, was catapulted into the arena.

This type of notation – staff notation – shows the shape of the music as it is to be heard. It coexisted and frequently had to compete with systems of notation called tablatures, which depicted what the musician was supposed to *do*, rather than showing what was to be *heard*. Such tablatures were prevalent, particularly for keyboard instruments and lutes, from about 1450 to 1800. They consisted usually of a kind of picture of the fingerboard or keyboard of the instrument; with numbers or letters placed on it to show the position of the fingers. New ones are still being invented today: for example, a tablature is often used for teaching recorders in schools. Their disadvantage is that if the instrument which is being 'tabulated' becomes obsolete, so does the tablature. Guitarists who today unearth old lute music cannot try it out directly because the guitar is built, strung and tuned differently from the lute. So they have to convert the particular tablature into the general staff notation.

The history of staff notation is a history of increasing differentiation, increasing precision. In the service of this increasing precision a wealth of data accumulated around the basic notational parameters of pitch and rhythm. Tempo indications, at first rough and ready (andante, vivace, etc.) were later supplemented by a notation of the precise number of beats per minute, made possible by Maelzel's invention of the metronome in the early 19th century. Dynamics, or nuances of loud and soft, were indicated with more and more precision and supplemented by expression marks (dolce, energico, etc.). The more differentiated and precise the notation became, the stronger the hegemony of the composer over the art of music. Elements of improvisation and ornamentation, i.e. independent contributions from the interpreter, were gradually eliminated.

The main use of this refined and flexible compositional instrument, musical notation, was of course to enable the composer to communicate to the executant musicians what they were to play. With the development of electronic music in the 1950s an area opened up in which notation could not play this main traditional role of providing performance material for the sounding composition. Electronic music was composed once and for all in the studio; thereafter it could be reproduced from tape. Therefore no score and parts for musicians were required; hence no notation was necessary as far as performance was concerned.

But many electronic composers still felt the need to score their works – either before or after composing them – and in the early 1950s many different types of notation on graph paper began to appear. The score of Stockhausen's *Study 2* serves mainly to elucidate, or at least present in readily surveyable form, the formal characteristics and layout of the piece.

Cage scored his *Imaginary Landscape No 5* on graph paper for purely practical reasons, and the notation functions in the traditional way as an intermediary between composer and performer. The instruments in this piece are mechanical reproducers – record players – and to play them is a matter of starting them and stopping them and adjusting the volume controls (it's like an orchestra of DJs). There is no need to notate the sound, for that results automatically if the indicated starts and stops are carried out.

When the technique of combining pre-recorded electronic tapes with live performance began to develop, notation again became necessary for the parts of the live performers and also for the electronic parts, as a point of reference for the players. In cases where the players were expected to synchronise or accurately accommodate their parts to the electronic part, certain modifications of traditional notation were almost unavoidable (were in fact avidly desired (note: 2.)), since electronic music of that time tended to be measured decimally in seconds rather than in crotchets and quavers, bars and beats, etc. So for instance a proportional notation of time became a virtual necessity, with a regular time span allotted to each line of the score.

In notating the electronic parts, some composers contented themselves with indicating points where the tape should start or stop (as in the Cage example described above), but others developed a shorthand to give the players a rough and ready impression of the types of sound they would hear and their relative pitch, loudness and length. This sketching-in of a rough picture of the sound developed its own conventions, drawing where appropriate on the conventions of traditional notation. An example is Stockhausen's *Kontakte*, where the sketched-in notation of the electronic part is a perfectly adequate guide to the performing musicians.

An approximate notation of this type, which represents music already composed in every detail, is very different from an approximate notation that is intended as a score for musicians to play from. Logothetis' *Odyssey* is a piece of graphic music that differs visually very little from the *Kontakte* example, except that it is tangled up into a kind of labyrinth with a superimposed red line running through it to indicate the 'path' to be followed by the musicians.

Composers who adopt such approximate graphic indications of what their music is to sound like have lapsed ideologically into the fallacy that music can consist solely of a series of doodles, textures, outbursts, stops and starts. Never mind how artfully arranged, this amounts to adopting the attitude that your score can be used by anyone, to express any ideas, in any context.

These rough and ready graphic composers abandon all musical discipline, and if they are to cover their nakedness at all it is only by applying a certain amount of graphic discipline to their scores – which then become 'aesthetic objects in their own right, regardless of whether or not they are used for making music', i.e. they become fully fledged musical graphics.

Such activity is a safe refuge for the musically incompetent. And a fair number of young composers turn to it. About 25% of the scores I had to read in a recent contest were wholly or partially graphic, and about half of these were of this type, which may be described as the cheapest variety of graphic music. It is a far cry from the type of graphic music established by Earle Brown in his *December 1952*.

December 1952 is sharp and clear. Brown was fascinated by the constructivist movement in art, by Calder's mobiles and 'action' painters such as Jackson Pollock. This score is a single rectangular sheet with blank lines and rectangles floating on it. The white space predominates; the impression given is of precise little dashes (horizontal and vertical) of different weights on a white ground. The instrumentalists – any number and kind of instruments – all read from copies of the same sheet, but they may read it any way up. I think that originally interpreters were expected to measure the coordinates of any rectangle and locate a sound correspondingly in the overall range of his instrument. This measuring

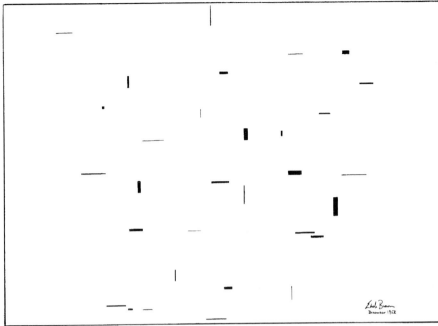

Earle Brown *December 1952* c Associated Music Publishing inc.

later became softened. Of a 1964 performance in Darmstadt, Erhard Karkoschka says that it was Brown's conducting rather than the score that stimulated the performers, for some of the effects produced were irreconcilable with the appearance of the score. So geometrical and precise in appearance, what the notation of *December 1952* amounts to is an exhortation to be geometrical and precise in your playing. It is a frequent characteristic of graphic music that it seeks to suggest an *attitude* or quality of playing to the performer. In Brown's case this exhortation is generally disregarded. When Brown himself conducts it, one has the impression that the score is merely the starting point of an improvisation which unfolds under Brown's control.

Assuming for the moment, however, that *December 1952* was intended to be a musical score rather than an inspiration to improvise, it raises one of the big problems of graphic music: its two-dimensionality. Whatever the limitations of staff notation, it is an instrument designed to describe and serve the needs of a musical continuum, with its host of interwoven dimensions. In *December 1952* you've got the opposite: the music has to be designed to imitate a two dimensional black and white drawing or diagram. However conscientious your measuring, a score like this uses only a tiny fraction of a trained musician's ability and initiative (which may account for the fact that it is sometimes more rewarding playing this music with untrained people); and the rest is likely to come out in horseplay, improvisation, etc., of a friendly or antagonistic kind depending on the particular social and human relations. When composers and musicians are engaged in harmonious collaboration and share common preoccupations all goes 'well'. But when the musicians feel they are being conned or exploited by the composer, you get the type of horseplay that led to the vandalization of electronic equipment by orchestral musicians in Cage's New York performance (1964) of *Atlas Eclipticalis*.

Cage wrote *Atlas* in 1961. It is a good example of that type of graphic music which comes under the proposition: Anything in the universe that has been or can be given a graphic representation is a possible notation for musical activity. Star maps provide the material for the notations of *Atlas*. Cage traced the constellations on tracing paper and then used chance methods to decide some aspects of how they are to be translated into sound. The orchestral parts retain the basic features of staff notation – the 5 line staff is used where applicable, and progress from left to right regulates the disposition of the events in time.

A practice which contributed considerably to preparing the way for graphic music was the proportional (as opposed to symbolic) notation of time. The factors leading up to this innovation are outside the scope of this article, but it can be appreciated how this innovation gave a 'graphic' appearance to the musical scores in which it occurred and changed the way the musicians had to 'read'.

Take a page of an ordinary book: 'graphically' it is what a typographer would call a 'grey page'. 'Literarily' it is the sense of the words in the context of the language and culture that produced it. In reading music one normally 'reads' the symbols for how long and short the individual notes or chords are supposed to be, but when time is notated proportionally (say 1 cm = 1 second, or some other arbitrary, or even arbitrarily changing unit) you are supposed to 'scan' the page with your eye. You let your eye travel from left to right, and when it picks out an obstacle you play the appropriate note. It is a slightly dehumanising method, because it aims to replace thought (reading) with an automatic physical reflex (scanning). Normally the speed with which we experience events in the world depends on how much food for thought they provide, or how much attention we decide to devote to them. Of course we do the same when reading graphic music, but not without some feelings of guilt at our failure to accurately reflect in the sound the proportions laid out in the graphic score.

It's true that in normal notation the graphic aspect has a role to play (I've heard that people who select educational music take care to select pieces that are largely in crotchets and quavers, rather than semiquavers and demi-semiquavers, in order to avoid the hysteria produced in young learners by a 'black 'page'). But it is not a dominant role. In graphic music, the graphic aspect of the notation has become dominant.

It's appropriate here to spend some time on graphic notation, as opposed to graphic music. Graphic notation is a perfectly justifiable expansion of normal notation in cases where the composer has an imprecise conception. And I don't mean merely a failure of musical sensibility, because his conception may be quite precise as to its overall characteristics but imprecise as to the minutiae. For example, if a composer wants a string orchestra to sound like a shower of sparks, he can interrupt his 5 line staves and scatter a host of dots in the relevant space, give a rough estimate of the proportion of plucked notes to harmonics, and let the players get on with it. This is graphic notation in the best sense of the word – vivid and clear. Such methods are used by many relatively established avant-gardists, from Ligeti to David Bedford to Penderecki, and have proved their viability (note 3).

Graphic music proper, on the other hand, tends to be conceptual rather than pragmatic. One graphic score I looked at recently consisted of that classic series of split second photographs which shows a bullet passing through a soap bubble. Such a score obliges the interpreter(s) to make strange decisions: what aspect of the score should one use to determine the type of sound to be used? Bubbling sounds and rim shots (naturalism?) is one possibility. Or you might decide that slow motion is the crucial aspect of the score.

To 'compose' such a piece no musical training or experience is necessary (which may account for the fact, that conservatories often take an over-resolute stand against it). This is a contradictory phenomenon and has its history. Cage's ideas had a considerable influence on the development of American avant garde painting of the 1950s and 1960s, particularly Rauschenberg and Jasper Johns. Other visual artists became so interested that they took up composing themselves. George Brecht was one, and he developed a neat kind of conceptual music often employing musical events in a visual context and vice versa (like piling bricks inside a grand piano). Brecht popularised the expression 'Intermedia' to denote twilight zones between the various traditionally defined arts. My contribution to Intermedia was the graphic score *Treatise* (1963-67): it's a cross between a novel, a drawing and a piece of music. In performance it was sometimes more of a 'happening' than a piece of music.

Another visual artist who took up composing was the English painter Tom Phillips. He participated in the Scratch Orchestra, so when I was asked to get a book of Scratch Music together I wrote to Tom for a contribution. He sent eight picture postcards as examples of his *Postcard Compositions Opus XI*. The idea was to assume that the postcard image depicts the performance of a piece of music. Then you have to deduce the rules of the piece and perform it yourself. There were a number of visual artists in the Scratch Orchestra: and between them they produced a host of compositions of this type, all of which come under the heading of graphic music.

In the last analysis graphic music is part of musical notation, in that it conveys a composer's conception to executant musicians, however loosely defined. But the examples given show how graphic music leaks out into various other areas that have nothing to do with music notation. The type of notation that we call graphic music (or musical graphics – I've come to the conclusion that these two terms are interchangeable) is characterised by an element of *juggling* with the concept of notation, and indeed with other concepts too, such as composing, performing, reading, playing, listening, etc. And in this it shares common ground with a lot of conceptual music, 'intuitive' music and verbal scores – all of which are going to have to fall outside the scope of this article.

*   *   *

A word on the economics of graphic music. Because the service that composers perform for the bourgeoisie is primarily ideological, we tend to overlook the economic aspect, which though secondary is not negligible. For instance, certain music publishers played a role in consolidating graphic music as a definite genre. Peters Edition brought out works of Cage, Feldman and Wolff in 1962 (a single part of Cage's *Atlas Eclipticalis* and there are 86 in all – now costs over £7). Associated Music Publishers (NY) printed Brown's graphic scores. In Europe Universal Edition has dominated the genre, though many smaller publishers have also got involved. One of these – Moeck Verlag of West Germany – brought out Erhard Karkoschka's book on *Notation in New Music* (which deals quite thoroughly with graphic music) in 1966. Universal published an English translation in 1972. Something Else Press (NY) published Cage's anthology *Notations* in 1969. Exhibitions of graphic music have been organised on a number of occasions as a means to publicise avant garde music in general. Publishers' showrooms are often decorated with enlargements of graphic scores. I don't think a graphic score has yet appeared in a Coca-Cola ad, but at the Venice Biannale this year all the posters and programmes for concerts were liberally sprinkled with graphic scores. Almost all of them date from the 1960s. Almost none of them was actually scheduled for performance in the festival.

While it's clear that publishers cannot create a genre, they can influence considerably the extent to which it becomes established. They determine whether or not a genre – and this applies particularly to graphic music, where the score, the printed object, has such pre-eminence – passes into musical history in the sense of becoming a subject for study in colleges and universities.

While researching this article I was sobered to find that graphic music and related phenomena occur these days in university curricula. Our carefree fancies of the 1960s are now doing a 'fine job' wasting the time and confusing the minds of the next generation of composers. While this is no place for remorse, it does bring home the necessity of revolutionizing music education and throwing out the formalist garbage that has accumulated over the last 70 years or more. It may well take another 70 years to do it, so we should start in right away!

One hears the view that Cage exerted a 'liberating' influence on the intellectually musclebound musical avant garde of the Darmstadt period (the 1950s), dominated by the theories and products of Boulez and Stockhausen. Cage's work certainly led to an explosion of irrationalism in the 1960s. But neither of these directions gave any serious thought to the question of the role of new music in western imperialist society. Certainly a number of people with relatively progressive ideas were swept into the avant garde and dallied for shorter or longer time with the manipulative techniques and pseudo-intellectual ideologies that were currently on show. But where could they go? Their subjective rebellion against the establishment left them in limbo. Today the establishment holds the field and the avant garde is in retreat. To be sure it's a slightly updated establishment, expanded to include many erstwhile rebels: people like Nono, Feldman, Bussotti, Ligeti, Xenakis. However, the body of the new music establishment is composed of people who played a minor role, if any, in the avant garde: Henze, Berio and in England Maxwell Davies and Birtwistle. All these and many others make a reputable living out of composing and are well stocked with commissions. Behind them stands the old establishment: Britten, Malcolm Arnold, Roger Sessions, Copland, Petrassi, Lutyens, Alan Bush, many of them veterans of the anti-fascist movement of the 1930s. Clustering around their skirts are the more traditionally minded of the younger generations: Maw, Bennett and others in this country (and a crowd of university composers). And seated over everything, the mythic heroes on the their thrones: Schoenberg, Stravinsky, Ives, Webern, Stockhausen and Cage, who have given their lives (and souls) in the struggle to find – for the bourgeoisie – a way out of the stifling moribundity of bourgeois music (note 4).

This is a rough sketch, but it suffices to show the tree and its branches (I haven't

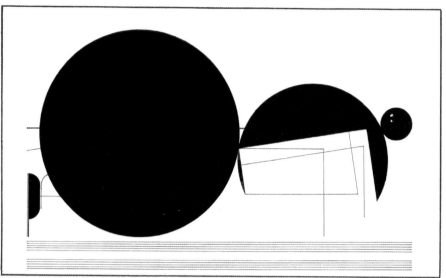

Cornelius Cardew. A page from *Treatise*

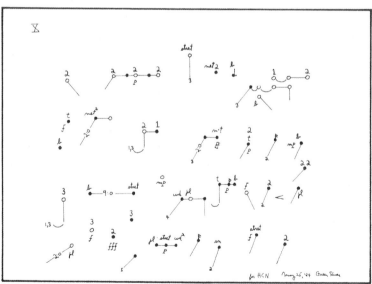

Christian Wolff. Last page from *For 1,2 or 3 People* 1964

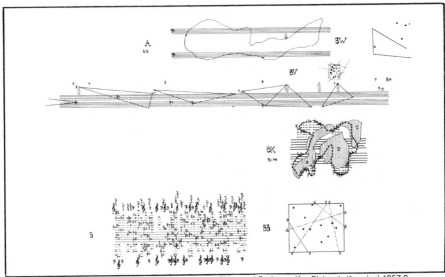

John Cage. A page from the solo piano part of *Concert for Piano and Orchestra* (for Elaine de Kooning) 1957-8

touched on the roots this time), and to ask the crucial question: where in this vast hierarchy is the struggle going on for a new music that genuinely serves the people? Is it where composers are using subject matter that is more 'socially relevant'? I suppose Barry Guy's *Songs for Tomorrow* (commissioned for the 1976 Proms) would qualify as socially relevant, with its theme of the pathos of poverty. So would Cage's *HPSCHD* which, with its 52 tracks of electronic tapes and 7 amplified harpsichords simultaneously playing music by Mozart and other composers, could be said to reflect the surface anarchy and turbulence of the current political situation. Or is it where composers are trying to write music to appeal to a mass audience? Bernstein is the only example that springs to mind.

Or does the whole tree serve the bourgeoisie, regardless of all the skirmishes going on along the branches and twigs? It's possible in fact that the struggle for a new music that serves the people is not actually fought in the field of music at all, but somewhere else (and I don't mean in heaven). It's possible that a new music that serves the people will be a completely new tree, springing from different ideological roots, developing leaves, branches and a trunk over a long period while the old tree rots away, overburdened with its 'cultural heritage' until the people one day come along and cut it down – or leave it standing as a skeletal reminder.

A last example – not strictly 'graphic music', but its lean and elegant notation justifies its inclusion, and provides a good example of a skirmish on the avant garde branch of the old tree. Christian Wolff's *Wobbly Music* (1975) is scored for voices and a 5 piece instrumental ensemble. Its four sections use texts from US labour history in the period 1908-13: the first is a setting of the Preamble to the Constitution of the Industrial Workers of the World (known as the 'Wobblies'); the second a setting of 'John Golden and the Lawrence Strike' (by Joe Hill); the third contains excerpts from Arturo Giovanitti's speech from the dock (an indictment of wage slavery); and the fourth is a setting of part of a speech by Bill Haywood beginning 'It was a wonderful strike'. Wolff's settings are sparse and quite monotonous, so that the content of the text determines any dynamism in the work. In the first and last sections words and syllables are passed between different groups of singers creating a sense of sensitive interdependence, like walking with linked arms over stepping stones, or passing something delicate from hand to hand. The Joe Hill movement takes the form of a bouncy but irregular monodic song. The Giovanitti speech is mostly declaimed against grumpy chords on electric guitar with altered tuning (a tablature notation is given). The whole is preceded by three labour movement songs of the period, presented quite directly in community sing style.

It's hard to tell what effect all this will have in performance and how it affects listeners is one of the main criteria for judging whether a piece of music is progressive or not – but certain things can be seen just from the score. First, that Wolff is thinking about political subject matter, and it must be considered positive that he has chosen to popularise (never mind to how small an audience) a passage of the working-class history of his own country. Secondly, that he has striven for complete intelligibility of the texts he has chosen – which wasn't the case in certain other of his recent compositions, e.g. *Changing the System*. And thirdly, he alludes – more or less discreetly – to sounds and characteristics of pop music. The question is: does all this amount to a struggle against what is reactionary in the avant garde, or does it merely constitute an 'alternative', which implies – because of the relations that prevail amongst the composers of the avant garde – that it is simply in competition with the rest of the avant garde on the basis of its 'novel' subject matter and certain idiosyncrasies of its style and presentation ('ordinary' singing at the outset, etc.)? Such questions will be discussed when the piece has its first performance in England on 28 November at the ICA.

One thing seems certain. When we're thinking of progressive/reactionary, new/old in modern music we have to struggle to separate the man from his music. If the new music that serves the people is a completely different tree, we need the people from the old tree to help it grow, but they have to leave their bourgeois music and outlook on the old tree. Only then can they start to make a new music out of the life and struggle of the people. And the more they participate in that life and struggle the more vivid will be their artistic contribution.

'And graphic music in this context?' I hear an editorial murmur. 'Graphic music' will doubtless curl up and get comfortable in the dustbin of history.

LEFTOVERS
Graphic music is a type of musical notation. But it differs from traditional notation in one very important respect. Whereas a traditional score can be designed to look like anything from Magna Carta to computer print-out (given the services of a cunning music typographer/designer), in other words it doesn't matter what it looks like except from a purely practical point of view (legibility), in graphic music the graphic form of the score is fixed by the composer – the way it looks is crucial, hence the term 'musical graphics' as opposed to musical notation. But we must keep to the broadest definition of musical notation, as anything used or intended to be used as a directive in the activity of music making.

One can say of a 'free improvising' musician that he uses the world as a directive, however. And of Indian musicians or jazz musicians that they use established, orally transmitted norms or forms such as specific modes or the 12 bar blues as directives in their music making. But although these things direct such a musician in his playing, he does not have to read them. The written directive is the characteristic development that led to the separation out of the composer as a distinct type of musician; as one who works with his head and hence dominant (in bourgeois society) over those who work with their hands (the players).

The composer of graphic music sets himself against this separation, but only succeeds in heightening it. How? By composing 'graphically' he tries to re-appropriate a manual role; he no longer just writes, he develops graphic skills. He also tries to remove the 'reading' aspect from playing a score (to a greater or lesser extent). But in liberating the player from the domination of the written score, he liberates (divorces) himself from the activity of music making.

It's the same with his newly acquired manual (graphic) skill: there is no conventional framework for linking his new skill with the skill of the players. To take two extremes (and such things do actually happen in the arcane world of avant garde music): enormous playing technique can be deployed in giving a musical rendering of a child's scribble; and conversely, someone who has never before played a violin can nevertheless use it to interpret a highly refined graphic score (assuming certain intellectual predispositions).

The role of idle fancies in the development of notation.
A Renaissance monk designs a composition in the shape of the Virgin Mary, or a Valentine card manufacturer bends a melody into the shape of a heart. The one is a devotional meditation and the other a commercial gimmick – neither has anything to do with music. For a composer to lapse into such conceits amounts to an apology, a failure to grasp or recognize music's expressive capacity, how it conveys ideas. What decides whether a notational form or system survives is its viability, its usefulness in the currently developing musical praxis.

It is a quite mistaken view – similar to that which holds that computers make reasoning redundant, or equivalent bullshit – that a highly developed notation (however mechanical in its conception) eliminates the interpretative function of the performers. It's true that the complexity of notation reached intimidating proportions in the avant garde music of the 1950s, but this did not essentially threaten the interpretative role of the performer. It reduces this; and a case can be made out for saying that such reduction in the area of interpretative flexibility makes the area remaining that much more crucial. The whole issue of reducing, interpretative 'freedom' hinges on whether you see the composer/performer relation as an antagonistic one, in which case each inch of interpretative freedom will be hotly contested. The composer won't rest until he has eliminated the performer completely (e.g. through electronic music, or mechanical or self activating instruments), and the performer won't rest until he has banished the composer (free improvisation). Performers can be found who hated electronic music (it devalued their skills), and others can be found who welcomed it (it relieved them of a burden). Composers can be found who despise improvisation (as a surrender to subjectivism) and others who welcome it (they can use it to put pep in their music). Much depends on what electronic music and what free improvisation is being talked about and who is talking about it. Nothing conclusive is going to emerge from anecdotes.

Since composed music has existed (i.e. since there have been composers as a separate type of musician), composers and performers have collaborated in the production of music. Within this collaboration there have been all kinds of head-on collisions, ideological and stylistic disagreements, walk-outs and sit-downs, but the collaboration is the primary thing.

Just as the production of a jet plane is inconceivable without design and management skills, so a complex orchestral form communicating a definite ideology is inconceivable without composition skills. Naturally it doesn't have to be a single, individual composer, or one who is not also a performer, but the act of 'composition' is a necessity.

To compose is to have an overall conception of what is to be communicated combined with the knowledge and experience: and on this base also the searching out and inventing – of the musical means necessary to convey that. This embodies the fundamental tenet that it is new content that calls new forms into existence, and that without new content all formal novelties reduce to trivia and decoration.

Since composers and interpreters primarily collaborate, the division of labour between them is not a hard and fast line. In the crisis of extreme formalism that occurred in the post-war avant garde (the titles are indicative: *Structures*, *Kontrapunkte*, etc.) a reaction was inevitable. Catchwords like 'Open Form' and 'Indeterminacy' that drifted over from the States in the mid-1950s were eagerly welcomed by young avant-gardists who felt stifled by the dominant determinism of the European scene. Under these catchwords the genre of graphic music flourished. It not only reinstated the interpreter as an active participant in a non-mechanical way in the musical process, but also enabled improvising musicians (who often have not learned traditional notation) and amateurs to participate in the production of avant garde music.

Notes:

1. In acoustics too there are effects created in the ear; the ear has its own acoustic properties like everything else. If the ear is over-stimulated it will distort the sound just as a microphone will.

Other phenomena common to both hearing and seeing are the ability to hear and see things 'inside your head', both as a result of just listening and looking (as it were at the back of your closed eyelids), and as a result of projecting them in your imagination (thinking through a familiar tune, for instance). Then there are those phenomena where the image you 'see' in your head is provoked by a non-visual stimulus, e.g. the stars you see when a policeman's truncheon lands on your head.

Again sounds can be transmitted to the brain through the bone structure of your skull. This accounts for the fact that you can never hear your own voice as others hear it. You hear it simultaneously as vibrations in the air picked up by the ear, and as vibrations transmitted through bone – whereas everyone else hears only the vibrations in the air.

2. Many composers in the 1950s felt that traditional notation imposed restrictions. It imposed certain rhythmic relationships and certain pitch relationships, and composers exercised their initiative to try and break out of these restrictions (see

remarks on proportional notation for time). Electronics was one way, graphics was another. We tried to simplify, for the sake of flexibility, and complicate, for the sake of control and precision. It was possible to break out of the established rhythmic and pitch relationships by relaxing the tension between performer and score (graphic music), by saying to the performer: 'This is not an obligatory exam paper that you have to fill in, but a flexible guide to action'. In electronic music the established relationships could be overthrown quite mechanically. Or could they? The 'restrictions' referred to did not actually spring from notation, but from the accumulated practice of centuries of music making. The notation merely embodied them in a handy conventional form.

3. I can't hold it against such cultural workers that they battle on in the 'struggle for production', even though it's our duty to inform them that every new technique and invention that they come up with will be used against them (against the people, I should say, because the inventors themselves may well come in for some greater or lesser material reward) until the obsolete, fettering social system under which we all labour has been thrown over.

4. What is the place of graphic music in this hierarchy? Graphic notation is an integral part of it, in the sense that new techniques and new procedures require new notations and these are bound to have a certain 'graphic' character as long as they are new. 'Graphic music' as a genre is already in its grave, however.

This article included a number of graphic score illustrations:

Earle Brown's *December 1952*
Cardew' *Treatise*
Wolff's *For 1,2 or 3 People*
Cage's *Concert for Piano and Orchestra*

Role of the composer in the class struggle

Transcribed from a handwritten text – delivered as a talk – probably 1978

I'll start by talking about two cultural movements that occurred in Britain in 1977. Firstly the 'Silver Jubilee', the celebrations of the 25th Anniversary of accession of Elizabeth II, in the course of which the most chauvinistic culture was thrust on the people in large quantities. Secondly – and this was an international phenomenon – the commemoration of the 150th anniversary of Beethoven's death.

The Queen, the royal family, the whole institution of the monarchy is regarded by the majority of people either with indifference, or as a joke, or with anger. The Silver Jubilee set out to convince people that a) the Queen is some sort of impartial being, above all class distinctions, non-party and benevolent. And b) beyond that that the monarchy itself is a great institution that stands for Britain's 'civilising' influence throughout the world, that it is a symbol of Britain's 'greatness'. To carry out this propaganda campaign every area of culture was drawn in – film, TV, posters, etc. and music. On the pop music side we had the Sex Pistols' 'God Save the Queen' with its Union Jack poster, and the so-called 'bubble gum' single 'Queen Elizabeth'. On the classical music side Malcolm Williamson – Master of the Queen's Music – got together with John Betjeman and wrote an atrociously sentimental Jubilee Hymn. Obviously this wasn't going to convince anyone to support the Monarchy, so the main emphasis was on the tradition of classical music in England in association with the Royal Family. Some Coronation Odes by Purcell were raked up; all kinds of anecdotes about the musical talent of Henry VIII, George III. All the record companies and publishing houses produced Jubilee stuff and the music press went to town on the promotion of national chauvinist British music.

The kingpin was the composer Edward Elgar. This composer was adored by the Royal family because of his chauvinistic marches, songs, oratorios, etc. In particular, his *Land of Hope and Glory* which glorifies the British Empire as one which brings freedom and progress to the colonial countries. When the words were proposed to him, even Elgar was dubious. But when it became clear that the King wanted them, he agreed. Elgar was a sycophantic lackey of the British imperialists.

Next point: Elgar was an instrument of a definite policy of the British Imperialists that they have pursued ever since they started to build the empire. This policy consists in trying to win the support of the ordinary people for the British Imperialists' aggression against the other countries in the world. Then the people are told that the people of other countries are savages who are incapable of governing themselves, who are not ready for democracy, etc. etc. – ideas that imply firstly the superiority of the British people, and secondly the superiority of the white race; by cultivating such ideas the British Imperialists have implemented their racist policies of white supremacy. By doing constant propaganda for Britain's greatness and 'white supremacy' they have tried to win the support of the ordinary people for their atrocities throughout the world. Elgar went along with this policy, consciously participated and has thus ensured the hatred of all progressive people. This is not spoken lightly: this chauvinism and phoney patriotism forms the basis of the fascist movement in Britain, and the whole Silver Jubilee exercise was manure to the fascist movement – it gave them every opportunity to grow.

For this reason it was absolutely necessary to oppose the Silver Jubilee and bring the real issues to the fore. The Communist Party of England (Marxist-Leninist) organized a campaign 'Down with the Monarchy' to promote the facts of the matter: that the Queen is a leading monopoly capitalist, a parasite, that the Monarchy is a racist, colonialist institution that historically has collaborated with fascism, and is used to promote fascism today. Within this campaign I and other musicians in Progressive Cultural Association put on a number of concerts in the major cities of England under the slogan 'Down with the Monarchy'. We played anti-fascist and anti-monarchist songs from all over the world, and wrote a new song to sum up the feelings of the working people of Britain: 'Rip down the Union Jack, British Workers/ It's a flag of aggression and war/ It belongs to the ruling classes/ and we wont stand for it any more' and sing it to the tune of an Irish song.

SONG

A brief digression: Why is Irish patriotism OK and British patriotism reactionary? Why do we sing an anti-nationalist song to an Irish nationalist tune? The basic difference is that Ireland is an oppressed nation (oppressed by British Imperialism and other forces) struggling for national independence, whereas Britain is a nation that oppresses other nations. For this reason, nationalism in Britain is an oppressive force, whereas nationalism in Ireland is a liberating force. Of course there is such a thing as Irish chauvinism – you find it in IRA circles, where the idea exists that all Brits are bad and should be shot – this is reactionary, it harms the struggle, because it interferes with the unity of the British and Irish people in their fight against their common enemy: the British ruling class.

The second cultural movement of last year was an international one: the celebration of the 150th anniversary of the death of Beethoven. In the PCA we took up the task early in the year of producing an article on Beethoven; this article has still not appeared. We have not yet taken a definite stand on Beethoven.

However, all I can do is give one account of our thinking on the question. The first thing to reject is the idea – promoted during the 100th anniversary by Ernest Newman – that Beethoven was the vehicle for the divine to manifest itself on earth. We don't accept these days that genius is an absolute mystery, transcending space and time, etc. Most people now agree that composers are a product of their age and their society, and that Beethoven was a child of the French Revolution and an eloquent spokesman for bourgeois ideas in a period when these ideals were struggling for supremacy in Germany, against the backward forces of moribund feudalism. Amongst serious musicologists it is accepted that Beethoven wrote political music, and its content reflected the bourgeois revolutionary movement. However, amongst Marxists another metaphysical view has asserted itself to replace the old metaphysical view that Beethoven's genius transcends time and space. This new view (not so new – it dates back the 1940s) holds that Beethoven's revolutionariness and progressiveness is something eternal that transcends time and space, by which they mean that Beethoven's music is revolutionary and progressive in terms of the proletarian revolution going on today. Thus you find delightful books promoting Beethoven – with a Marxist colouration – being produced in East Germany. You find the old DKP in W. Germany publishing a Beethoven record in 1970 to mark the 200th birthday of his birth; and most recently you find the new regime in China (after Mao's death and the coup against the so-called 'Gang of 4') broadcasting part of the fifth symphony on the date of the anniversary last year.

In the field of culture as in all other fields there is an irreconcilable antagonism between the proletariat and the bourgeoisie: what is good for us is bad for them and what is good for them is bad for us. So Beethoven, who is eminently good for the bourgeoisie as is obvious from the wide promotion he gets, is bad for the working class. The most striking instance is his choice of text for the 9th Symphony: "All men are brothers" is a bourgeois slogan that covers up the class contradictions in society and preaches class collaboration.

Someone has said to me "You Marxists are very black and white", so at this point we should go into one of the shades of grey. However, the discussion so far has been about dead composers and it is very important to come up to the present and speak of the living participation of composers today in the class struggle – and how this participation can become conscious and progressive. So let's draw a line under this preamble – and return to it for discussion if people want to.

We are part of the classical music field, our music speaks to a particular section of society: the educated stratum. We, of the educated stratum, are brought up to regard this musical heritage as our own. Through our schooling we appropriate this music and it becomes part of our culture. It becomes a privilege which distinguishes us from the working masses, and which separates us from them, and gives us the impression of being superior to the working class. From the working class point of view this culture is hostile and oppressive, it is something enjoyed by all the well-to-do and their petit-bourgeois hangers-on in well-heated concert halls and lecture theatres like this one, to which the working class has no access in capitalist society. Not only is this culture hostile by the mere fact of being a privilege that working people don't have access to, it is hostile by virtue of its content and ideology. Bourgeois plays and operas are not about the lives of working people, and they don't express their aspirations and hopes: they are about individuals – whether heroic or miserable – wrestling with their inner contradictions, agonizing over subjective states, or blandly deals in abstractions.

So this whole field of bourgeois culture (including classical music) is foreign to the working class, and is a burden on their backs. It is parasitic in the sense that without the productive labour of the workers there would be no surplus value out of which to make and distribute this high-flown culture. In short it is reactionary and oppressive.

There is only one road for the composer to play a progressive role in the class struggle, to break out of the bourgeois cultural establishment and go amongst the working people. And there is only one progressive way of going amongst the working people, and that is to participate in organizing for the overthrow of the oppressive system.

This is very black and white, and because this is an issue of principle it has to be black and white – on matters of principle there are no shades of grey. But let no-one distort this with evil intentions and say "Either you're a bourgeois composer or you're a revolutionary, there's nothing in between". This is not what I said. What I said is that there is only one road and the characteristics of roads is that they have length and lead from one place to another. The important thing is to set foot on this road and keep persevering along it; through a long and arduous process of struggle, of remoulding one's thinking through practice and participation, we can definitely serve the people and make a contribution to the revolutionary cause of the working class. Obviously not everyone will go all the way along this road but as long as they stick to this road they are progressive regardless of how far they get. But if we don't set foot on this road, but merely try to apply some Marxism, for example, to some problems of musical composition, or profile our careers in music by writing about the ruling class – then we will not make any contribution, but will continue to be a heavy weight on the backs of the people.

Having set foot on this road what becomes of the bourgeois composer? He still has a job and has to make a living, and there's nothing wrong with that. Here in this bourgeois festival there is plenty to be done: to raise the right issues for discussion, to encourage the struggle for more democracy, to fight against backward ideas, and inspire the musicians to engage in struggle and integrate with the masses and so on. Since the vast majority of musicians are ideologically oppressed and materially exploited, there is a great undercurrent of resistance to bourgeois rule. And the progressive composer has to tap this resource and unite the people and the ideals of the working class and transform them into into a fighting force. In the course of this the bourgeoisie will try and get rid of us and we have to fight back. But the main thing to remember is that only the working class can lead a successful struggle against the bourgeoisie.

Before throwing the debate open, just a word on the concept of 'Art that serves the people'. Is art what the people need? And can art be given to the people?

I am no liberal who'll leave these provocative questions unanswered! One of the great issues that Socialism has to resolve is the division between mental and manual labour. Art is a synthesis: in a physical and concrete way it expresses the spiritual ideals of a society. It is the revolutionary people who will create the art of the revolution. Out of their revolutionary activity will come revolutionary art. In our experience in PCA, trained artists too often impose their conceptions of art – of what art is, and by what standards to apply it – on the people. The point is to serve the people as a person – to apply ourselves to solving whatever problems may be facing them – rather than as an artist. By standing shoulder to shoulder with the working people in battle, by sharing weal and woe with them, we will then be in a position to make some art that is of the people and for the people.

The idea that artists can make a purely cultural contribution to the revolution is a bourgeois idea; it rests on the conception of the artist as a special individual with a special way of looking at the world. This is why the revisionists love Beethoven so much: his contribution to the bourgeois revolution was purely cultural: he didn't go out to fight for it, he just wrote music for it. And the revisionists try to make out that the same is true of the proletarian revolution – that you can make your contribution from an armchair or from a notebook. But as I have said: this revolution is different, and it is very often the artists who stand in the way of revolutionary art and oppose it; and the revolutionary fighters have to brush aside their cultural comrades in order to produce the revolutionary art.

I'll end with a song sung by an Irish comrade, an amateur singer.

Speech of Party Representative at
International Youth Concert, London – 9th August 1980

Comrades and friends, on behalf of the RCPB(ML) [*Revolutionary Communist Party of Britain (Marxist/Leninist)*] I should like to thank the Canadian comrade for his warm and militant words and say how pleased we are to participate in this Internationalist Youth Concert, organised by PCA [*Progressive Cultural Association*] and Stalin Youth Brigade, along with performers from the CCWC [*Canadian Cultural Workers' Committee*], from the West Indian communities in Britain and Canada, and the Indian community in Britain. It is for us a great honour to receive this visit of the Canadian cultural workers and representatives from the West Indian community in Canada, as well as a delegation of the CYUC(ML) [*Canadian Youth Union of Canada (Marxist/Leninist)*], who are in the audience. All have just come from Germany, where they participated with our youth and cultural comrades in a militant and highly successful Youth Camp Internationalist. This is the first visit of Youth and Cultural delegations from Canada to this country, and we hope the first of many. It reflects the close historical ties between the working peoples of our two countries, and also the close and long standing links between our two ML [*Marxist/Leninist*] parties, which go back to the mid1960s. We are sure that the visit of the delegations will further strengthen the unity and cooperation between our two parties and peoples.

I want to make three points about the significance of these concerts, which have been held in Manchester, Birmingham and now London this week. Firstly the songs and poems performed in the concerts are the beginning of a new culture, a culture fired by the struggles of the working people of all countries against imperialism, social imperialism and reaction; aimed at serving the interests of the working people; and following the line of our ML parties. But when we say new culture, we do not mean that this culture starts only at this point in history, like the so-called new culture of Mao Tsetung, who talked of drawing "beautiful characters" on a blank sheet, as if no culture existed before. This type of culture can only be a culture of slogans, of philistinism. When we say new culture/proletarian culture we mean, as Lenin said, a culture which must assimilate and rework the best of all previous cultures. Marx's theories, which have guided the struggles of the world's peoples since his time, including their struggles on the cultural front, were not some invention. Marx's great contribution to history was that he studied the entire more-than-2000 year wealth of knowledge, of human thought and culture, criticised it, tested it on the working class movement, and reached conclusions impossible to anyone bound by bourgeois limits and prejudices. So our new culture must be the most advanced development of all previous cultures. These concerts are a beginning, and as they develop so more and more our cultural work in this country will assimilate the great traditions of the British working class – not the traditions of 100 years of labour aristocrats compromising and selling out with the rich – but the traditions of the great struggles of the Chartists, the struggles to found the trade unions. the great class battles of the early years of the century, the great struggles immediately after the First World War, and many others since. And not only does the British working class have its great fighting traditions of struggle, but rich cultural traditions which go along with this, for instance the culture of the miners. Much of this culture has either been suppressed, sabotaged by the social democrats, or just submerged under the weight of imperialist culture. But as our cultural work develops, so these traditions will be increasingly assimilated. So when we say this is the beginning of a new culture, we mean in quality, in the directness and clearness of its aims, but at the same time a development of all the best traditions of the British working class, and the progressive art of the other classes in history.

Secondly, these concerts have been Youth Concerts. In them has been stressed the important role of the youth, of the young people, in the fight for freedom and emancipation of the working people. The youth, by nature, are for the new and against the old, ready to fight for everything progressive and revolutionary. They are full of energy, aspirations and dreams for a better life, genuine freedom and a better world. But what outlet do these energies and aspirations have in countries such as ours – the capitalist countries of the West and the formerly socialist countries of Eastern Europe? What prospects do the youth have in these countries? In this country increasingly large sections of the youth have only the prospect of the dole queue, the street corner, attack and harassment by the police, petty crime, drug detention centres. And of course recruitment into the armed forces to be used as cannon fodder by the imperialists in their squabbles with each other over raw materials, markets and labour. Not to mention the wholesale pessimism, mysticism, confusion promoted by the bourgeois culture offerings. As these songs and poems say, there is only one future for the youth: to unite with the working class and its Party to bring about socialist revolution. It is only in this way that the energies of the youth can find a satisfactory outlet, that their dreams of a better world can be realised.

Thirdly, these concerts are Internationalist Concerts. They express the unity of working people of all lands in the struggle for freedom, democracy and socialism. These particular concerts are a concrete illustration of the close links between the working people of Britain, Canada, India and the West Indies. These links are forged firstly by history, as a result of the forcible movement of millions in slavery or the equally forcible movement caused by the anarchy and cruelty of the capitalist system, which has forced other thousands and millions of toilers to leave their homelands and sell their labour, their only possession, in whatever market the capitalist system happens to provide. Then, wherever they have gone, they have united with their class brothers in struggle against the common enemy. Then, they have also united with the working masses in other lands, since the imperialists and social imperialists, despite their differences, plot together to step up the exploitation of the working people and stop revolution. So by history, by experience and by necessity, the working people of the world must and do unite. This is the spirit of the workers of all lands, the most conscious expression of which can be seen in the unity between the ML parties of the world.

These poems and songs performed today speak of and are part of the struggle for a new world. As the title of the concert states: We sing for the future. But when we talk of a new world we are not talking of some far-off dream. Old workers and communists from Britain saw this new world being built in the Soviet Union in the 30's and 40's, before the betrayal of the Kruschovites. The delegation of our Central Committee which recently visited Socialist Albania saw this new world being built now with their own eyes. Throughout the world the peoples are struggling with this new world as an immediate aim. In every corner of the globe the working people are rising up against the savage, aggressive and exploitative policies of the imperialists, social imperialists and all reaction. As Comrade Enver Hoxha says: "The world is at a state when the cause of revolution and national liberation of peoples is not just an aspiration and future prospect, but a problem taken up for solution."

These concerts are an inspiration to fight to achieve and build this new world, to strengthen our revolutionary work in the different countries and to solve the centuries old problem of winning a new world free from the exploitation of man by man.

GLORY TO MARXISM-LENINISM AND PROLETARIAN INTERNATIONALISM!
WORKERS OF ALL COUNTRIES UNITE!

Programme notes for Piano Album 1973

Cornelius Cardew Foundation – 1991

I have discontinued composing music in an avant garde idiom for a number of reasons: the exclusiveness of the avant garde, its fragmentation, its indifference to the real situation in the world today, its individualistic outlook and not least its class character (the other characteristics are virtually products of this). I have rejected the bourgeois idealistic conception which sees art as the production of unique, divinely inspired geniuses, and developed a dialectical materialist conception which sees art as the reflection of society and at the same time promoting the ideas of the ruling class in a class society. At a time when the ruling class has become blatantly vicious and corrupt, as it must in its final decay, it becomes urgent for conscious artists to develop ways of opposing the ideas of the ruling class and reflecting in their art the vital struggles of the oppressed classes and peoples in their upsurge to seize political power.

In taking this course a number of questions arise: what musical material is available, on what musical sources and traditions should we base our work? And in what style should that material be presented, bearing in mind that it must be accessible to the broad masses of so-called 'uncultured' people? The pieces I am presenting here are tentative experiments in a number of different directions, seeking provisional answers to these questions.

The first four pieces are based on material from China. *Charge* is an arrangement of a battle song with the theme 'Workers and peasants make revolution'. *Song and Dance* is a song about a soldier preparing to go into battle, his consciousness of the enemy and class hatred. Both are from a collection of Chinese 'Historical Revolutionary Songs' published in Peking in 1971.

Bring the Land a new Life is an aria from the Peking opera *Taking Tiger Mountain by Strategy*, describing the oppression suffered by the peasants and their aspiration to go forward and make a better world under the leadership of the Communist Party. *Sailing the Seas* is one of the best known and most popular songs from present-day China. It can be heard, played by Chinese instruments, at the beginning of the opera *On the Docks*.

The People's Republic of China is the most advanced socialist country in the world, and for this reason it is attracting the attention and the enthusiasm of more and more progressive artists and people throughout the world.

The working class movement in the West has frequently been sold out by its leaders and has not yet succeeded in seizing political power. However, the working class in the West is certainly not without culture, and it is the responsibility of communist artists to research this culture and strengthen it. *The Red Flag*, a poem by Jim Connell about the martyrs of the working class movement, is sung to an old German Christmas carol *0 Tannenbaum*. In England it is sung at Labour Party rallies and has come to stand for much that is backward in the English labour movement. In this arrangement I have changed the metre of the song. Probably I have avoided petty bourgeois sentimentality only to fall into bourgeois tragedy.

The Red Flag arrangement is in the style of a Romantic prelude. The next piece *Soon* uses a contemporary style that does not present barriers to an audience of ordinary people. I composed the song in September 1971, basing it on the final paragraph of Mao Tsetung's *A Single Spark can Start a Prairie Fire* written in 1930, 19 years before the communists came to power in China. Paraphrase: Soon there will be a high tide of revolution in our country. When I say 'soon' I don't mean 'perhaps' or 'probably' or 'possibly'. It's like the sun rising in the east whose rays can already be seen from the mountain top. It's a child waiting to be born, restlessly turning in its mother's womb.

The history of the Irish peoples' struggle for national liberation is of vital interest to all genuine communists in England. The rising of 1798 is one of the most glorious chapters in Irish history. Numerous songs and ballads celebrate the heroic deeds of the people in their efforts to achieve liberation from the British colonial yoke and a social revolution under the leadership of the bourgeoisie along the lines of the French revolution of 1789. The British used savage means to provoke a premature outbreak of the revolution, and once they had provoked it they suppressed it with equally savage cruelty. County Wexford in the south-eastern part of Ireland was one area where the British met with fierce resistance. The revolutionary forces, armed largely with pikes, scored several brilliant victories before they were defeated. The two folk songs that follow both describe the events in County Wexford. The *Croppy Boy* describes the capture, trial and execution of a young rebel. *Father Murphy* is the story of a Catholic priest who played a leading role in the Wexford rising and fought side by side with the people. In the song he says: 'Now priest and people must fight or die'. Probably still today there are progressive priests in the north of Ireland who on the basis of their daily association with the people also support their just struggles. The support given by Buddhists to the Communists in South Vietnam is a similar instance.

Four Principles on Ireland, based partly on an old Irish melody, is a new song written in support of a campaign by the Communist Party of England (Marxist-Leninist) The four principles are: (I) that Ireland belongs to the Irish people and that British Imperialism's criminal interference – not only its military interference but also its economic, political and cultural interference in Ireland's internal affairs – must cease, (2) that the Irish people are one people, and that the partition of Ireland in 1920 and the present attempt to divide the North on religious lines have been engineered by the British Imperialists as measures to enable them to continue their exploitation of Ireland, (3) that the Irish can solve their own national problems without outside interference, including the problem of their own treacherous comprador bourgeoisie whose aim is to sellout Ireland's resources to foreign capital, and (4) that a nation oppressing another nation cannot itself be free (Engels), i.e. that Britain's colonial and neo-colonial hold on Ireland acts as a powerful brake on the working class movement in England, and this brake must be released. The song ends with the prospect of close coordination between the Marxist-Leninist parties in England and Ireland so that British Imperialism can be attacked simultaneously from within and without.

Commentaries

Cardew's *The Great Learning*

Brian Dennis

The Musical Times – November 1971

The seven paragraphs of Ezra Pound's translation of the Confucian classic provide the text for the seven pieces of Cardew's *Great Learning*. Each is quite long, autonomous and rich not only in musical but often in visual, philosophical and ritualistic possibilities, Only a collage in the manner of Cage's 'Mosaic' in *A Year from Monday* (an essay on Schoenberg presented in fragmentary quotations and commentaries) could give even a fractional idea of the work's complexity or of the variety of Cardew's innovations. One need only stress the importance of the Scratch Orchestra's involvement and influence in the work (from Paragraph 2 onwards) to give an impression of its social manifestations. Because the Cagean idea of 'each reacting in his own way' is taken a stage further to 'each learning in his own way' (the work is educational in the broadest sense), no single commentary can do justice to the implications of a work where personal involvement is 'written into the score'. Perhaps one should simply point out that the score has 23 pages, that the cover is blue and that the excellent calligraphy of the composer is reproduced clearly throughout,

An alternative might lead to an experiment in creative criticism. We live in an age where fragmentation can only assist (paradoxically) in clarifying our view of our art, our society and our environment. Let each reader create his own imaginary 'collage' of ideas and quotations. The Pound Confucian text provides an inexhaustible supply of material. One might select randomly like Cage or intuitively (without blindfold):

> The Great Learning takes root in clarifying the way wherein
> the intelligence increases through the process of looking
> straight into one's own heart and acting on the results.
> Know the point of rest and then have an orderly mode of
> procedure.
> Given the extreme knowable points, the inarticulate thoughts
> were defined with precision.
> From the emperor down to the common man singly and
> altogether this self-discipline is the root.

Knowing some of those who have performed the work would be invaluable; impressions may range from the physical exhaustion of having sung Paragraph

2 against the insistent thunder of countless drums (Michael Parsons: 'Buddhist monks go to a waterfall to practise chanting; the waterfall can't be drowned but it inspires the voice to high levels of power and quality'; Cardew: 'Singers may justifiably feel proud of surviving the piece to the end'). The veterans of Cardew's class at Morley College remember the first stones and whistles collected for Paragraph 1 and being choked by the dust from the beaten cushions (the 'Sonorous Substances') of Paragraph 4. More recently the unifying calm of Paragraph 3 with its deep tones and stratified singing (on a staircase) in the German Institute after 16 simultaneous concerts[1] (the Wandelkonzert of May 13) will be still fresh in the memory – the religious atmosphere of the church performance of Paragraph 4 and the DGG recordings of 2 and 7 also.

Having heard the broadcasts of 1 and 2, one could draw considerably on the composer's own introductions: 'Failure exists in relation to goals. Nature has no goals and therefore it can't fail – often the wonderful configurations produced by failure reveal the pettiness of the goals'. 'Moral certainty springs from an unassailable moral authority and Confucius locates this authority "inside".' 'Parallel with the dawning of the age of individual responsibility, there is the increasing amount of information available to individuals forming their own judgment.' '… that bad kind of politeness which consists of sparing people's feelings as opposed to engaging their feelings.' 'If music was a purely aesthetic experience it would not occupy the central place it does in our affairs. It must make waves in our environment'.

There is the music itself, particularly those sections which speak only in the purity of sounds – the Stones Chorus and organ solo of Paragraph I – the relentless almost machine-like pounding in Paragraph 4 – the intricate rhythms of 2 (the drum figures) and the rich harmonies of 3. Cardew's fascination for calligraphy perhaps drew him to the ideogram as a source of material. The whistle solo of Paragraph 1 and the guero parts in 4 are derived very simply as this example shows:

TA   HSUEH   CHIH

It is not another randomisation technique like Cage's use of the imperfections in paper or John White's adoption of random permutations; for one, the calligraphy demands a certain type of instrument (whistle or guero) and secondly creates distinctive patterns which affect the character of both rhythm and pitch arrangements.

Pound's interest in the pictorial basis of Chinese writing, (firmly obscured over many millennia) acts as a romantic, almost sentimental influence in his poetry. For example: (*a*) = a tree (*b*) = the sun (*c*) = the sun tangled in the tree's branches, meaning now the east. With Cardew the appeal is more abstract; the

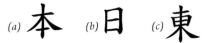

shapes and the sounds provide the inspiration. For instance the romanticization of the characters provides the material for the Stones Chorus as follows:

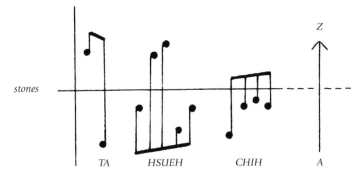

Something of a rarity in recent music, this technique resembles Schumann's use of letters and ciphers. The ideogram remains the essential source however, and this example from Paragraph 2 shows how the longs and shorts of the characters are translated into rhythms:

short, short, long, long,
short, short, broken, short:

short, long, long, short:

The simplicity of numbers provides the control for Paragraph 7 whose repetitions of words and phrases strangely resemble the *Drinking and Hooting Machine* of John White (another influence from Cardew?). Each word or phrase is sung softly for the length of a breath as often as indicated (the singers moving in their own time):

sing 8   IF
sing 5   THE ROOT
sing 13 (ƒ3)   BE IN CONFUSION

(ƒ3 = any 3 repetitions should be loud)

The numbers are derived as follows:

 8 strokes

 5 strokes

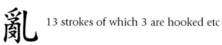 13 strokes of which 3 are hooked etc

None of these techniques is important in itself, but the fact that Cardew has chosen to provide *specific* performing material (especially in Paragraphs 1,2,4 and 7) is very significant in terms of his development.

Paragraph 5 is Cardew's 'view of the composition of the Scratch Orchestra as it now exists (1970) with its high level of differentiation of actions and functions'. A symposium, 'an amusement arcade' (Cardew: 'I simply included everything which cropped up at the time') – Paragraph 5, as yet unperformed, begins with a Dumb-Show, proceeds through eight verbal pieces '(The Compositions') becomes an Improvisation Rite ('A dense forest that presents no obstacle to mind or eye (or other sense)') with optional chanting, an Action Score, a Number Score, Ode Machines and a host of other activities. Examples:

MOUNTAIN TOP MUSIC: Mostly winds. Taking off. Flying high. 'Blow your problems and solutions to the four winds.' In the middle get quiet but no less blowy for that. Think of the mountain contours all around 'cutting the horizon fold over fold.'

SKIPPING ODE:

I'll tell your mother I saw you kissing ... (a boy's name)

Do you love him? Yes, no, yes, no

(Continue upward until no higher note can be sung. The last word is the answer)

NUMBER SCORE:

A		2					
B	3	5 ·					
C	2			6	11	8	10
D					2	9	etc

Add to these fragments and Improvisation Rite from the Scratch Orchestra's *Nature Study Notes*.

Mix in works from the Scratch *Anthology of Compositions*. Add pictures, slides and moving film; maps and journeys; the new Scratch Opera; but above all attend performances of *The Great Learning*. Participate if possible. If Paragraph 2 seems no more than a primitive accumulation of drumming and chanting, move amongst the players and sample the intricacies of their rhythms. Provide new 'branches' for tree-like productions of Paragraph 3 – spread upwards from the 'firm roots' of the work. 'Blow your problems and solutions to the four winds.' Musicians note the economy of the organ solo of Paragraph 1 – how each single note or action affects the sound – the power achieved with so few notes. Listen to the whistles in the final section and their delicate interaction within the sustained organ chord. There is something for everyone – for lovers of complexity and simplicity – of beauty or of danger – for those who wish to work alone or in company – to analyse or shake to pieces.

> He who can keep his head in the presence of a tiger is qualified
> to come to his deed in due hour.

The Great Learning, for any number of untrained singers and instrumentalists, contains a whole world and a wealth of potential activity. It is one of the finest and most significant works of recent times.

Note 1. The 16 groups of musicians (Intermodulation, Gentle Fire, AMM, the PTO etc.) performed mostly simultaneously in all the different rooms of the building and the audience was able to wander freely between each.

Cornelius Cardew's *The Great Learning*
Michael Nyman
The London Magazine – December 1971/January 1972

With simultaneous ceremony and jubilation, Paragraph 5 is to be finally lowered into place on 21 January 1972, and the second stage of Cornelius Cardew's *The Great Learning* achieves completion. The first stage, the writing, occupied Cardew from Spring 1968 to Summer 1970; one by one six of the seven paragraphs have been performed, mainly by the Scratch Orchestra, in a variety of locations in and out of London.

My own initial experience of the first two paragraphs was as a listener/critic. My reviews in 'The Spectator', separated by a period of seven months, were curiously similar. Of Paragraph 1 I wrote that it was 'as real as a drizzly afternoon, gradually eating away at our blinded and cluttered musical mentalities', and of Paragraph 2 as being 'one of those rare works of such power and freshness that seem to reinvent music from its very sources by somersaulting musical history'.

Now, over two years later, not only do I still hold to those opinions (if not precisely to the way of expressing them) but they have been reinforced through close contact with *The Great Learning* as a performer – though such is the incorruptible latitude of the score that each participant ideally fulfills the roles of performer, listener, critic and composer.

This incorruptibility, which is coupled with a meticulous generosity, derives from Cardew's personal acceptance of the principles laid down in the Confucius text on which *The Great Learning* is based and the way in which they are translated into direct, non-symbolic musical terms (on a more profound level than the accepted banality of 'expressing the text in music'). Not only does this subtly help one along the road of 'correct behaviour' during a performance, it beneficially affects one's mode of procedure in everyday life.

An apt analogy is tidal. As the sea progressively reaches the seashore, there is a period of maximum immersion when the sand is completely covered; equally gradually, and inevitably, the water recedes, drawn away by its own forces; the sand looks much as it did before. But who can say what effect the experience has on the sand?

The book of *The Great Learning* is one of the four classic books of the Confucian religion. The first chapter is said to have been written by Confucius himself in the sixth century BC; it lays down a basic ethical code. The first chapter is divided into seven paragraphs, and Cardew has taken each of these seven paragraphs 'as the basis of a sizable composition for an unlimited number of performers'.

The Confucius text as Cardew has pointed out, is concerned with the development of an unassailable moral authority, an authority that Confucius locates *inside*. In the first paragraph he speaks of 'looking straight into one's own heart and acting on the results' and in the second paragraph he advises to 'know the point of rest and then you will have certainty'.

So to Gene Youngblood's statement* that 'the act of creation for the new artist is not so much the creation of new objects as the revelation of previously unrecognized relationships between existing phenomena, both physical and metaphysical' we must add 'and ethical'; and note that whereas Youngblood sees these relationships as being revealed through an ever-spiralling complex of electro-technological hardware, *The Great Learning* comes to rest at a point of redefinition of the natural, concrete, basic physical properties of things. These properties make themselves felt as though totally independent of 'composition'.

(* in *Expanded Cinema*, Studio Vista, 1970)

In this respect it was not simply to make *The Great Learning* accessible to large bodies of untrained musicians that Cardew has avoided using traditional instruments; for in these, as Cardew noticed when improvising on his cello in AMM, there resides a permanent and inescapable portion of musical history. In *The Great Learning*, one is made intensely aware, as if for the first time, of the physical intention of sound: of wind as it issues from blown pipes (Paragraph 1), from organ pipes (Paragraphs 1 and 4), or from the human throat, in singing (2, 3, 5, 7) or speaking (1, 4, 5); of objects struck against each other – stone against stone (1), wood on skin (2), mainly metal on metal (Crash Bang Clank Music of Paragraph 5) or scraped (the gueros of Paragraph 4): of bow against string (5); or of raw physical gesture (as in the highly disciplined Introductory Dumb Show of 5).

This vast reservoir of existing natural sound phenomena is coupled with an equally important reservoir of methods for causing these sound resources to be activated. *The Great Learning* seems to me to have a status akin to that older experimental 'classic', Cage's *Concert for Piano and Orchestra* (1957-8): each accumulates a rich multiplicity of notations, but with one very significant difference (at least). Cage's notations, especially in the piano part, propose ways of organising the production of sounds, whereas Cardew's propose various ways of organizing people to produce sounds. Organizing is the wrong word; the extraordinary thing about reading Cardew's notations is the way in which one is immediately and directly stimulated to musical action, whatever type of notational symbols he has adopted or invented. It applies equally to the sign-event complexes of *Octet 61*, the matrices of *Solo and Accompaniment*, the brilliant, exhaustive graphic 'journey' of *Treatise*, the cryptic diagrams, hints and texts of *Schooltime Compositions* as to *The Great Learning*.

It is equally remarkable that Cardew's concern with liberating human resources (rather than 'sounds') has developed on a consistent line over the past ten years. In the instructions for *Octet 61* the attitude revealed in the following 'this piece is an opportunity for an interpreter. It demands no very sophisticated formal approach: the performer does not have to be a composer, he merely has to discover and use that modicum of creativity that is available to all' is continued in 'Towards an Ethic of Improvisation' in which, in reference to *Treatise*, Cardew says that 'Ideally such music should be played by a collection of musical innocents; but in a culture where musical education is so widespread (at least among musicians) and getting more and more so, such innocents are extremely hard to find. *Treatise* attempts to locate such musical innocents wherever they survive, by posing a notation that does not specifically *demand* an ability to read music': and finally comes home to roost in the foundation and constitution of the Scratch Orchestra, which was actually born out of the need to find a large pool of musicians to perform Paragraph 2 of *The Great Learning*.

The summation of social and musical experience that *The Great Learning* represents far transcends the situation towards which Cardew was groping when, in connection with *The Tiger's Mind* (1967), the notation of which required only 'a willingness to understand English and a desire to *play* (in the widest sense of the word, including the most childish)', Cardew remarks, somewhat sadly perhaps, that this 'still leaves the musically educated at a tremendous disadvantage. I see no possibility of turning to account the tremendous musical potential that musically educated people evidently represent; except by providing them with what they want: traditionally notated scores of maximum complexity.'

The reservoir of resources that is *The Great Learning* magnificently succeeds in encompassing the 'needs' of the musician whose 'individual personality (which a musical education seems so often to thwart) is absorbed into a larger organism, which speaks through its individual members as if from some higher sphere', as well as those who just wish to indulge in play, and musical innocents who have no ability or desire to read standard musical notation.

The methods of stimulating the growth of the larger organisms are perpetually fascinating and account (in part at least) for the internal vitality of *The Great Learning*. Quite often the 'social ritual' is static and draining, as in Paragraph 1, which grows through the straightforward democratic process of the addition of a series of solos for whistle instruments (supported by a multiple drone provided by non-soloists). Each whistler does his solo in turn according to his personal reading of the curling graphic notation. Each solo is separated from the next by the other large group of performers speaking the Confucius text.

Paragraph 2, though similarly concerned with group music, allows of less individuality; its ritual is tough, its discipline exuberant. Each group consists of a number of singers and a drummer. The drummer repeats rhythmic patterns over and over again, as the singers sing the text through to slow pentatonic phrases. For the singers: progressive exhaustion; for the drummers: progressive exhilaration; when all the singing has stopped all the drummers finally come together in a state of metric agreement. For the listener: each group, proceeding at its own pace, produces as 'out-of-syncness' in relation to all the others – a multi-spatial, multi-rhythmic, multi-tonal experience out of a common, unitary notation (unitary in that one single score is used by the groups, independently of each other).

At the other extreme, the unitary scores of Paragraphs 6 and 7 provide for a personal ritual threading through a communal network, in a climate of silence or near-silence. In Paragraph 6 personal responsibility for making music is at its most acute, as one has to wait and judge the correct context into which to place one's fragile sound. Working through the score at your own pace means that this context is different for each player; your context depends on theirs, and is simultaneously part of theirs.

Paragraph 7 also works on the 'network' principle. One of my most beautiful musical experiences came from taking part in a performance of this piece in a low-lit Portsmouth Cathedral. Sounds fanned out in space and time as singers, standing still or circulating in a slow procession, passed on their sounds to someone in close proximity, and with great reverence, picked up sounds in the same way.

Paragraph 5 is *The Great Learning* spectacular, and for Cardew 'in a way is my view of the composition of the Scratch Orchestra as it now exists, with its high level of differentiation of actions and functions'. The range of differentiation of the material, the scope it gives for every and any member of the Scratch Orchestra no matter what their level of development, interest or ability, is an astonishing achievement on Cardew's part.

The Introductory Dumb Show, for instance, is to be performed with the normal teacher/pupil relationship viewed through the wrong end of a telescope: 'A player who thinks he will be relatively slow in performing the dumb show gets up in front like a teacher. Another who thinks he will also be slow gets up and faces the "teacher" who now performs sentence 1 while the other watches. The watching one then becomes teacher in his turn, and another gets up and watches him perform sentence 1.' And so on, so that the fastest start last; a handicap game.

The Action Score and Number Score seem to harness the energy potential of mind and body, concept and action on an entirely new and fruitful level of participation, and as far as musical activities are concerned the Ode Machines, elaborate solo vocal melodies and The Compositions which outline, in very general terms, a process of activating various sound resources, represent two extremes of the musical spectrum.

Two of the Compositions' notations are so rich in suggestions as to require no further comment:

SILENT MUSIC No sound. Silent and still. Occasionally a movement watched by all, never more than one at a time... Comprehend the movements as deeply as possible – physically, referentially, plastically, symbolically – as they occur. Very heavy music.

BEAUTIFUL SOUND MUSIC Players make sounds they think are beautiful, making them beautifully, spacing them and arranging them in a manner they think beautiful in the general context. Three times try and make the neighbouring sounds sound stupid or ugly in the general context. Three times make sounds that you think are stupid or ugly... Try to go forward to ever more beautiful sounds. If no more beautiful sound occurs to you repeat the last one over and over ever more beautifully. If it gets less beautiful, stop.

And so begins the third stage of *The Great Learning* as it takes off into the world.

Improvisation
Eddie Prévost
Cornelius Cardew Memorial Concert programme – 16th May 1982

Cornelius joined AMM in 1966. By then Lou Gare, Keith Rowe, Lawrence Sheaff and myself had all but relinquished our 'jazz' heritage. We were developing an experimental and improvisational music into which we could inject our ideas and experiences, free from the constraints of any commodity ethos and free from any naive appreciation of the American jazz model. This development on our part obviously made Cornelius' entry to AMM easier; having had a conservatory training and already a known 'avant gardist' meant that many of the conventions of jazz were perhaps unobtainable by him. However, even though the last vestiges of jazz were perhaps receding from our music, Cornelius insisted that he was joining a jazz group. At the time this was the source of much affectionate amusement at Cornelius' expense. But probably his appreciation of the essence of jazz music was nearer the mark than ours.

Cornelius' influence helped to harden the purer form of improvisation that AMM was developing. For already there had evolved an openness of perspective to which Cornelius could respond and contribute. And – in those early days – it was becoming clear that the improvising ethic was needed to sustain the musical treatment of his magnum opus *Treatise* – the huge 193 page graphic score. Thus Cornelius' relationship with AMM was a strong factor in his determination to 'humanize' music. In *Treatise Handbook* he wrote: "What I hope is that in playing this piece each musician will give of his 'own' music – he will give it as a response to 'my' music, which is the score itself…" In addition Cornelius gained the unique kind of fellowship implicit in collective improvising. The association was a fruitful symbiosis of differing cultural origins. The result was an integrated form of collective music-making that arose from the meeting of creative minds mutually assured than any innovation would receive understanding and support. Cornelius wrote in 1969: "AMM in like a cradle: however violent or destructive you feel, it holds you, it won't let you hurt yourself."

In effect, Keith, Lou, Lawrence and myself found our way to a purified form of the aspiration we had intuitively recognised in jazz. It was a self defining activity for which any socially or culturally alienated group must search. The history of jazz is littered with such examples right from the early days in New Orleans, when against a backcloth of economic deprivation a beleaguered ex-slave black community (progressively hemmed in by the infamous 'Jim Crow' laws) sought their self defining culture – of which jazz was a part. With hindsight it is clear that in AMM Music we were asserting ourselves as creative beings – although not in any fashionable bid for notoriety as our rejection of the commodity ethos confirms. Cornelius also was not unmoved by the history of jazz and he too, despite the obvious educational and musical advantages he had enjoyed, felt repressed and alienated by the conventions of society in general and the musical establishment in particular. Later, of course, after he had left AMM, the former considerations dominated his life. However, it is characteristic of the AMM ethic to enable musicians of varying backgrounds to work collectively towards a more satisfactory basis for musical life. For during its existence AMM has also included Christopher Hobbs, Christian Wolff and John Tilbury – all conservatory trained musicians. Given these varying backgrounds and differing predilections it is interesting to note that the internal relations in music-making were commensurate with our mutual aspirations. Obviously, what we all had in common was a rejection of the predominating modes. However, I would repudiate the superficial assumption that we shared a camaraderie based upon a destructive dislike of an unsatisfactory form. No intense long-term creative relationship is likely to be sustained upon a negative basis. What AMM did – and still does – was to supersede the unsatisfactory ways of making music.

The classical and romantic tradition which still predominates, superseded the less formal ways of making music characteristic of pre-industrial society. There the composer and performer were interdependent and often the same person. Dowland's close friend Henry Peacham, author of *The Compleat Gentleman* (1622) said: "…it is a sign of good breeding to play extempore." Clearly the musicians of that time had a more integrated relationship to the music they performed than the later orchestral players of the classical and romantic periods. Size of music-making ensembles has much to do with the diminution of autonomy for the individual musician. Although whether the reduction of individual autonomy followed the creation of the modern orchestra, or whether the demotion of the musician to factotum preceded it, is something worthy of examination. I feel, given the general ethos of a burgeoning industrial/capitalist society, that market forces must inevitably have made an impact on the musicians' general relations towards their music and audiences. Whatever the case of musicians in those times, the commodity ethos prevails in our own times – even if it is camouflaged by an 'art for arts sake' mentality, which professes a neutral apolitical appreciation of culture attached to neo-Platonist notions of the perfect form.

Cornelius, even though he improvised with as much commitment as the other musicians, did retain a certain detached perspective. He also retained the composer's aspiration: to organise and develop the relations between musicians.

The AMM Music experience however was different in kind to all other aspects of contemporary musical life and the very notion of directed play within AMM Music an obvious contradiction. Nevertheless, Cornelius did write a piece especially for the AMM musicians, *The Tiger's Mind*, an imaginative drama text designed to stimulate a sense of the direct inter-active relations which characterize improvisation. And although it is an inessential format for the experienced improvising musician it is an intriguing intermediary stage for the aspirant. These concerns have not been without effect upon the subsequent working and thinking of AMM – even after Cornelius had departed. Of particular significance is our current concern to identify and promulgate the distinguishing moments of the improvisational form and to contrast it with the 'classical' mode. In this respect we offer the two key 'moments' in the form of the following analytical propositions:

a) Western 'classical' music demands a solution to most of the technical problems of making music *before* the music can be performed. Whereas – although most improvised musics demand a high level of technical competence – the elaboration of a theme on a chord sequence or the direct response of musical dialogue, demands the application of 'problem-solving' techniques *within* the actual performance.

b) In improvised music there is a creative and inter-active dialogical relationship between performers, whereas a composed work acts as a medium between the various instrumental components. The relationship between musicians loses its social significance; lessened by the agency of an external element e.g. the composition.

We would subsequently argue that an interpretation of the contemporary improvised music form, as simply a negative reaction to the predominating modes i.e. the classical and the commodity based popular musics, is incorrect. There are fundamental structural differences in the way these musics are produced and, consequently, the critical perspective has to reflect these changes in cultural emphasis.

Contemporary improvised music – as much of jazz history indicates – is a positive response to the deprivation, the absence or even the inadequacy of a fulfilling cultural expression. It does not simply negate the negating strictures of dehumanizing forms, characterized in our own times by the more extreme examples of 'serialism'. Contemporary improvised music humanizes and thence supersedes all the alienating forms which preceded it and, is distinguished from earlier forms, which also had strong personal and social aspects, by reflecting the technology, the problems and the ensuing aspirations for a modern democratic society.

Much of this Cornelius appreciated. He was our first articulate spokesman and instigated the desire for that analytical perspective. Later, in his tragically shortened life, he had a sense of urgency that could be assuaged only by entering a more overt political life. However, the AMM experience of which he is a part, reveals the complexity of human beings who whilst innocently making music together perceive that they had found a more cogent basis for both music and life.

Cornelius Cardew

John Tilbury

Contact No. 26 – Spring 1983

This article is a revised version of the text of 'Cornelius Cardew –a Memorial Lecture', delivered at the Goldsmiths' College School of Adult and Social Studies, in association with the Music Department of the college, on 26 April 1982.

I first met Cornelius Cardew at the Dartington Summer School in August 1959 when we were both 23 years of age. My recollections of that month are hazy and of no particular significance, but some kind of rapport must have been established because soon after my return to London I received a phone call from Cardew. He had a project in mind, a concert of experimental music for one and two pianos (music by the Americans Cage, Feldman, and Wolff, and by Cardew himself), and asked me if I would like to be the other pianist. In January of the following year the concert look place at the Conway Hall, London. Cardew's performances, in particular of the music of Morton Feldman, constitute to all intents and purposes my first lasting memory of the man as artist. Those floating, sourceless sounds, which he played with an unerring sense of timing and an artistry that was as convincing as it was unconventional, evoked an emotional response quite unlike any other I had experienced in listening to music, and which was intensified by Cardew's profound identification with Feldman's work.

How did Cardew's preoccupation with the American avant garde come about? This is an important question in the light of the subsequent influence of North American culture on Europe, especially in the sixties, Cage, Buckminster Fuller, and the abstract expressionist painters, in particular Robert Rauschenberg and Jasper Johns (to whom Cardew dedicated his Octet 61). Cardew received his formal musical education at the Royal Academy of Music between 1954 and 1957. At this time the Academy was an extremely conservative institution and it did not look kindly on the music of Schoenberg, let alone Boulez or Stockhausen. So it was inevitable that inquiring, restless young souls like Cardew and his friend Richard Rodney Bennett should have reacted in the way they did, rejecting what they regarded as the narrow-minded and bland conservatism of the English musical establishment. The European avant garde, on the other hand, centred in Darmstadt, paraded some progressive slogans; serialism was associated with the scientific method, progress and discovery, and some apologists, such as René Leibowitz, even claimed that serialism was the musical equivalent of the classless society. The music that Cardew wrote during his time at the Academy, notably the second and third piano sonatas, certainly owed more to Webern and Boulez than to his professors. And the performance that he and Bennett gave at the Academy of Boulez's *Structures*, besides being a considerable technical and musical feat, was probably tantamount to an act of rebellion in the climate that prevailed there.

Under the circumstances Cardew's decision to continue his studies and, as it turned out, to work with Stockhausen in Cologne was not surprising, though the consequences were not without a certain irony. The conditions he found in Germany in 1957 were as oppressive as anything he had left behind – though in a different way: total serialism had achieved the status of a religion whose followers defended and counter-attacked with all the fanaticism and intolerance of true believers. It needed the intrusion of John Cage into those closed European musical circles to alleviate a situation that had become intolerable. Even Boulez, hardly an innocent party in the proceedings, commented 'In Darmstadt between 1952 and 1958 the discipline of serialization was so severe it was ridiculous. Cage represented a liberation from this.'

In 1958 Cardew attended concerts of American avant garde music in Cologne by John Cage and David Tudor. The radical content of this music, its freshness and audacity, coupled with Tudor's phenomenal musicianship, made a deep impression on both Cardew and Stockhausen and was without doubt the source of inspiration for Cardew's indeterminate pieces of the early sixties, and probably for Stockhausen's first 'moment-form' works. Cardew's *Two Books of Study for Pianists*, completed in the year of Cage's visit to Cologne, reflects the disruption caused by the American invasion. The continuing influence of Stockhausen is discernible in the application of a scale of six dynamics and in particular in the mobile character of the material (within the given space of time the sounds may be distributed freely by the performer), but the ideological source of the music is to be sought elsewhere – the isolation of tones, the feeling of discontinuity (which later Cardew rather harshly criticised as 'laboured spontaneity') and the wayward harmonic language (though still constrained by European considerations of structure) reveal that the new American aesthetic had taken root in European music.

In an illuminating diary entry on 1st September 1964, in which he looks back on *Two Books of Study*, Cardew comments:

"What I composed in this piece – the image that hovered in front of my mind's eye – was a 'Musizierweise' (mode of music-making). I invented a way of making music and limited it to such an extent that musicians without constructive ideas of their own are in a position to adopt this musizierweise."

The indication here is already of his moving away from music as object towards music as process, and of a concern for the problems of the performers. Cardew was one of the first Europeans to grasp not just the musical but also the social implications of the new American aesthetic. And this was because his response to the music was not merely a cerebral rejection of the predominant Western European compositional method – total serialism – but a deep-seated reaction to content and meaning, to the new ways of thinking and feeling, to the idealism, both moral and philosophical, that seemed to inform the new American music. 'There is no room for the policeman in art' Cage said in one of his polemics against the Europeans. Cardew's originality was that he created out of the new aesthetic a kind of music utterly different from that of the Americans. *The String Quartet Movement* (1961), and in particular *February Pieces* (1959-61) for piano solo, perfectly exemplify this new departure, prefiguring the ideological content of most of Cardew's output in the early sixties. The influence of both Cage and Stockhausen is residual; the music possesses a strong improvisatory quality, but the dangers of excessive subjectivism (self-indulgence) are circumvented by the highly idiosyncratic and individual application of aleatoric principles. The result is a curious, compelling discontinuity; weird juxtapositions, irrational outbursts, fleeting references to other musics, past and present, create a kind of psychological disorientation, a hypersensitive music which haunts and disturbs the memory, reflecting a mysterious, impenetrable world in total disorder.

This expression of human agency at large, the spontaneous quality in the music – albeit in a chaotic, incomprehensible environment – constituted Cardew's bourgeois humanist world outlook at that time; the thrust of his creative work throughout the sixties served to sharpen the various facets of the contradiction, the subject/object dichotomy, and this continued until he espoused dialectical materialism in the seventies. The late Bill Hopkins, that most perceptive of critics, made the point in his review of *Three Winter Potatoes* in the *Musical Times* in 1967 'Cardew was compelled to weigh up the claims of artifice (selection and ordering) against those of the spontaneity which for him represents musical truth.' Cardew himself expresses the dichotomy with reference to improvisation in a diary entry of 1967:

"I compose systems. Sounds and potential sounds are around us all the time – they're all over. What you can do is to insert your logical construct into this seething mass – a system that enables some of it to become audible. That's why it's such an orgiastic experience to improvise – instead of composing a system to project into all this chaotic potential, you simply put yourself in there (you too are a system of sorts after all) and see what action that suicidal deed precipitates."[2]

For a short period serialism had been a source of intellectual fascination for Cardew and had acted as a 'logical construct' in his student works, but in the last analysis the mechanistic philosophy that underpinned it was anathema to him and he rebelled to free himself of it . This dualism – on the one hand asceticism, the desire and respect for dogma and purity (which also expressed itself in his preoccupation over a lengthy period from the age of 23 with Wittgenstein's writings and later with Marxism-Leninism), on the other hand the spontaneous and libertarian actions that characterised his life style – is the key to an understanding of Cardew's motivations and achievements, both musical and political.

The references to serialism in his diaries are mostly negative and occasionally humorous. In 1967, by which time, of course, serialism was for him very much a thing of the past, he wrote:

"Since the war folk music has become dissipated and internationalized (at least in Europe and America) to the point that one can hardly call it folk music. This fate can be compared to the heroic pseudo-scientific universalism of serial music in the early 50s; at that time you were quite likely to hear serial compositions by a Bulgarian, a Japanese, or a South African on the same programme and be virtually unable to tell the difference between them. At that time serial music was not available on disc, so we may attribute the effect to the pervasiveness of the idea. However, death in a vacuum is not a happy thought and around 1960 many of the reputable composers were beating a hasty retreat, taking with them just as much of the original idea as they were able to carry. Nono went into political music. Stockhausen into the grand operatic tradition. Boulez into impressionism and a glorious career as a conductor." [3]

In a related entry, on 12 September 1967, he wrote:

"From America Columbus brought us back syphilis, or Death through sex; there is no reason why the compliment should not be returned with myself as the humble vehicle, in the form of total serialism – of Death through music. In the case of serialism the damage has already been done, Schoenberg is the bearer of that intolerable guilt." [4]

Having rejected both tonality and serialism, it was not surprising that a radically minded young composer should have felt attracted to the American avant garde. But in fact Cardew's admiration for Cage had little to do with Cage's compositional techniques (though he once described the notation for Cage's *Variations* 1 as a 'giant step forward');' [5] what he admired was Cage's rejection of the commodity fetishism that had invaded musical composition, for which the super-objectivity of serialism and its corollary, the preoccupation with the perfection of the ideal object, was largely to blame. What also impressed him was Cage's liberation of the performer from the constraints of oppressive notational complexities, and perhaps most of all the 'democracy' inherent (at least in theory) in Cage's scores. And here is the crux, because this concern for freedom and democracy, displayed in a number of highly sophisticated indeterminate compositions from the early sixties, though in an abstract and intellectualised fashion, informs Cardew's entire musical career. With him 'indeterminacy' was not simply another compositional technique, displacing a previously discredited one, it was a logical musical expression of his humanism: humanism is the vital thread that runs through all his musical activities, making for a continuity that overrides even the most radical stylistic changes in his work. His rejection of total serialism freed him as a composer; with his espousal of indeterminacy, creative freedom was also extended to the performer.

In the magazine *Performance* the composer David Bedford described his experience with Cardew's indeterminate pieces:

"Speaking as a performer in many of Cardew's early works it must be said that the experience was totally rewarding. Our creativity was constantly being challenged, and the empathy of the performers, channelled into producing a coherent piece of music despite sometimes sketchy and sometimes paradoxical instructions, was often remarkable. It should be pointed out that none of Cardew's works ever gave total freedom to the performer. The instructions were a guide which focused each individual's creative instinct on a problem to be solved – how to interpret a particular system of notation using one's own musical background and attitudes. " [6]

These comments highlight the all-important difference between Cage's and Cardew's applications of aleatoric techniques. Cage's notational systems presuppose a denial of the influence of musical background (that is, history), whether Cage's own or the performers', and moreover generally allow for no spontaneous expression during performance. The thrust of Cardew's musical development, already evident in the indeterminate scores of the early sixties, was in precisely the opposite direction – towards an ethnic, spontaneous music making, which found its ideal expression between the years 1966 and 1971 when Cardew was a member of the improvisation group AMM.

What Cardew did share with Cage was the ability to take calculated risks: risk taking is part and parcel of both indeterminacy and improvisation. *Octet 61*, for example, is an indeterminate piece, that is the performer has an active hand in determining its form; it consists of 60 signs derived from conventional musical notation, each of which constitutes a single musical event. The task for the performer is not only to interpret each sign but to join the signs together to create musical phrases, musical continuity (Example 1). Of the *Octet* Cardew wrote:

"The greatest music is always explicit – like Webern, if you dig him. In *Octet 61* I realise that explicitness has been sacrificed. In this research it is always necessary to sacrifice trusted concepts. Afterthought. As long as there is no blur in the thinking … " [7]

Example 1 – Octet 61

During the next five years, from 1963 to 1966, Cardew made two such sacrifices: the first was of traditional notation in favour of graphic notation; the second was of notation in favour of improvisation. Two activities tower above all others during this period: his mammoth 193 page graphic composition *Treatise*; and the improvisation group AMM. A diary entry on New Year's Day 1963 anticipates this radical development:

"A good man watches, experiences, the complete devastation of his private world and survives. Then he moves back into the real world and grasps it with his mind. So he recreates it, and it is no longer private. It is everybody's world. To do something constructive you have to look beyond yourself. Humanity in general is your sphere (not people). Self-expression lapses too easily into mere documentation."

Later in the year, on 4th September, there is another philosophical entry, but now containing a direct reference to *Treatise*:

"My age of romanticism is over. Sensations, moments drop away. My desire is to experience long-term continuities as beautiful. – In *Treatise* to create the coherent code which expresses the truths we do not know and cannot live up to. To be aware of the psychological groundings of your musical strivings (being timid physically as a boy, I became bold in spirit) and still leave the ground."

In Buffalo in 1966 Cardew described the genesis of *Treatise*:

"I was 23 when I first come across Wittgenstein's *Tractatus* : right from the first sentence, handwritten by Slad [David Sladen, an old school friend] as a foretaste before he gave me the book. 'The world is everything that is the case.' It made a deep impression on me. The name *Treatise* (from Tractatus): a thorough

Example 2 – Treatise

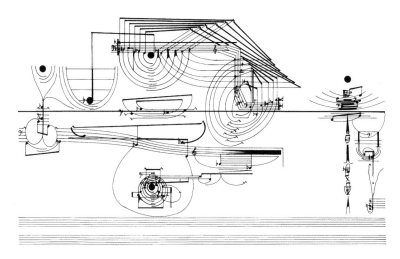

investigation of what? Of everything, of nothing. Like the whole world of philosophy. I started work on it in 1963 and have worked on it inconsistently ever since. In that time it has lost some of its abstract quality, autobiographical aspects have crept in. But then there are autobiographical wisps to be read into Wittgenstein's *Tractatus* – the whole takes on a slightly different autobiographical slant in view of his later rejection of part of it." [8]

Treatise finally appeared complete in 1967. It is a continuous weaving and combining of a host of graphic elements (of which only a few are recognisably related to musical symbols) into a long visual composition, the meaning of which in terms of sounds is not specified in any way. Any number of musicians, using any media, are free to participate in a reading of the score, and each is free to interpret it in his own way. The graphic subject matter appears in various guises: triangles, circles, circle derivations, squares, square derivations, irregular shapes, etc. (Example 2). One way of interpreting *Treatise* might be to match these graphic: symbols with musical categories – triads, trills, irregular tremolos, periodic rhythms, etc.; shapes and positions of symbols could be used to determine, for example, dynamics. This might be the method of interpretation that a conventionally trained musician would adopt – a non-reading musician might take a much freer, more spontaneous approach. What Cardew wanted was that in playing *Treatise* "each musician will give of his *own* music – he will give it as his response to *my* music, which is the score itself." [9]

The history of *Treatise* is documented in detail by Cardew in the *Treatise Handbook*, which appeared in print some years after the completion of the score.

The first part of the *Handbook* consists of working notes, which shed light on many aspects of Cardew's musical thought.

"Notation is a way of making people move. If you lack other ways like aggression or persuasion. The notation *should* do it. This is the most rewarding aspect of work on a notation. Trouble is: just as you find your sounds are too alien, intended 'for a different culture', you make the same discovery about your beautiful notation: no one is willing to understand it. No one moves."[10]

Visually *Treatise* is sensational, so beautiful as to be inhibiting for all but the boldest spirits – its visual impact disconcertingly puts most performances of it in the shade. *Treatise* releases music from the constraints of conventional notation; it demands new concepts of time, new sounds, and new attitudes to old sounds, which many classically trained musicians seem unable to bring to it.

In 1964-5 Cardew worked on a number of pieces concurrently with *Treatise*. But *Treatise* was the dominant activity to the extent that at least two of these pieces, *Bun No 2 for Orchestra* (1964) and *Volo Solo* (1965), are versions of *Treatise* in some form. Why 'Bun'? He gave me two off-the-cuff reasons when I asked him: a bun is what you give to an elephant at the zoo, and that was how he felt when he gave the work to an orchestra to play; and the piece is like a bun – filling but not substantial! Of the other works of this period *Material* (1964) is a transcription for any ensemble of harmony instruments of the *Third Orchestral Piece* (1960). *Three Winter Potatoes* was completed in 1965 and *Bun for Orchestra No 1* was written for Petrassi's composition course, which Cardew attended in Rome between February and June 1964.

David Bedford remarks that Cardew "brought a typically English elegance and wit to even some of his apparently more eccentric compositions." *Memories of You* and *Solo with Accompaniment* (both 1964) are two cases in point, but an ironic gloss conceals their true significance. Both these works seem to be nostalgic reflections on Cardew's musical past, referring respectively to the two composers whose influence shaped his early career. *Memories of You* is a homage to Cage. The score consists of 22 diagrams of a grand piano with instructions to make sounds at specific points in and around it; Cage's *Concert for piano and orchestra* (1957-8) contains virtually the same notation. The accompaniment part of *Solo with Accompaniment* consists of a number of 'matrices'; the parameters of the basic elements in a matrix wax and wane according to the composer's complex system of notation, which seems to allude to Stockhausen's *Plus-Minus*. The relatively simple solo part is thrown into sharp relief by an extremely busy and complex accompaniment so that an ironical comment is made on the traditional relationship between the two.

In AMM Cardew encountered, perhaps for the first time, musicians as uncompromising as himself, who had already entered the uncharted territory of improvisation and who would risk all in the making of each performance. A short entry in Cardew's diary for 1965 reads like a prophetic description of AMM music.

"Music is a vagrant; it has no fixed abode. It's a menace to society. It needs cleaning up. The impossibility of abolishing music. Its omnipresence. Its uncatchability. Perhaps after all we have to step down and let music pursue its own course." [11]

The importance of AMM for Cardew cannot be over-estimated, as he acknowledged himself. Mutual understanding within the group reached a depth that he had never experienced in concert hall music. The four original members of AMM were Keith Rowe, Eddie Prévost, Lou Gare and Lawrence Sheaff, all of whom came from a jazz background. They met regularly for sessions that generally lasted about two hours, with no formal breaks or interruptions, though there would sometimes occur extended periods of near silence. In an essay entitled 'Towards an Ethic of Improvisation' Cardew wrote:

"It is not the exclusive privilege of music to have a history – sound has history too. Industry and modern technology have added machine sounds and electronic sounds to the primeval sounds of thunderstorm, volcanic eruption, avalanche and tidal wave. It is to the 'history of sound' that AMM tries to contribute something. 'Informal' sound has a power over our emotional responses that 'formal' music does not, in that it acts subliminally rather than on a cultural level. This is a possible definition of the area in which AMM is experimental. We are *searching* for sounds and for responses that attach to them, rather than thinking them up, preparing them and producing them. The search is conducted in the medium of sound and the musician himself is at the heart of the experiment." [12]

It was the humanising component of spontaneity in improvised music, which finds expression in the creative dialogue between musicians at the point of music making, that Cardew valued so highly. In AMM he found the embodiment of his ideas and feelings about music and freedom taken a stage further. On the relationship between *Treatise* and AMM he wrote in 1970:

"I now regard *Treatise* as a transition between my earlier preoccupation with problems of musical notation and my present concerns – improvisation and a musical life. AMM was the turning point, both in the composition of *Treatise* and in everything I had thought about music up to then." [13]

The latter part of the sixties and the early seventies parallel the immediately preceding period: *Treatise* and AMM, the related dominant preoccupations of the earlier period, are matched in the later one by two mutually determining activities – *The Great Learning* and the Scratch Orchestra.

The monumental *Great Learning* (1968-70), Cardew's masterpiece, incorporates experimental techniques into tonal and even modal frameworks. Indeed, it is a significant feature of many of the pieces of this period, including *Volo Solo* and *Three Winter Potatoes* (both 1965) – brilliant virtuoso piano works and compendiums of avant garde pianistic techniques – that they contain paragraphs that lend themselves easily to tonal analysis; the tonal references here go a good deal further than the fleeting allusions in, for example, *February Pieces* of 1959-61 (Example 3).

Example 3 – Three Winter Potatoes, no 2

The reason for the adoption of a more traditional language in his compositions is clarified by a consideration of the direction Cardew was taking socially and even politically in the latter part of the decade. Throughout the period he was becoming less and less concerned with beautiful artefacts and more and more involved with people and their ability to make their own music. He began to assume a more educative role – to which he was perfectly suited through his strong democratic sentiments, his ability to teach by example, and not least his genius for improvising. Musical education is what *Schooltime Compositions* (1967) is about. The work is a notebook of observations, ideas, notations, hints, diagrams, concepts, scientific experiments, geometric analogies – some direct, some oblique, but mostly presented as 'facts' with no covering instructions. For Cardew each composition was a matrix to draw out the interpreters' feelings about certain topics or materials. Here the different matrices grew around such things as words, melody, vocal sounds, triangles, pleasure, noise, working to rule, will/desire, keyboard. Some of the matrices serve as a measure of virtuosity, others of courage, tenacity, alertness, and so on. They point to the heart of some real matter, mental or material. The score tells the interpreter the general area of his potential action – he may wish or have the talent to play, or sing, or construct, or illumine, or take exercise of one sort or another, and can draw out his interpretation in that direction.

For Cardew there were no two ways about it: people could be encouraged, inspired, or even cajoled, but ultimately they had to be trusted to make their own music on the basis of their own background, experience, and attitudes. In these new compositions he subtly defines the areas – emotional, physical, psychological, and historical – in which the performer operates, but there is no question of controlling the interpretation, either directly or by some back-door method involving 'chance operations'. At the same time, however, he was still grappling with the idea of involving musically educated people (people trained in musical establishments) in his compositions. In 1967 he wrote:

"I see no possibility of turning to account the tremendous musical potential that musically educated people evidently represent, except by providing them with what they want: traditionally notated scores of maximum complexity. The most hopeful fields are those of choral and orchestral writing since there the individual personality (which a musical education seems so often to thwart) is absorbed into a larger organism, which speaks through its individual members as if from some higher sphere." [14]

The Great Learning, a large-scale choral work in seven movements (the duration of the whole is around seven hours), based on one of the Confucian scriptures, is the magnificent realisation of this projection. As Michael Nyman points out: "The ethical purity is mirrored by Cardew's use of sound resources. *The Great Learning* appears to come to rest at a point of redefinition of the natural, concrete, real physical properties of (sounding) things." [15] The 'sounding things' are of every sort: stone struck against stone, metal against metal, wood on skin, bow on string, whistles, drums, voices, reciting, shouting, singing, chanting, howling, laughing, gueros, rattles, jingles, musical boxes, toy pianos, jews harps, water drops. *The Great Learning* includes games, improvisation rites, dumb shows; there are single line extended melodies (odes) written in conventional notation, and graphic notation as the basis for improvisations. But each of the seven paragraphs has a clear-cut image, such that it would be impossible to mistake one for another.

Despite his reputation as a controversial figure, as the *enfant terrible* of the English musical scene, Cardew never insulted or abused his audience, he never subscribed to the theory of épater le bourgeois; his music, even in the later political and militant works, is never in the least aggressive. But he was marvellously unpredictable and original: the music sharpens social and psychological contradictions so that, from confronting the music, the audience finally comes to confront itself. This unpredictable music naturally produces unpredictable responses. At a performance of the first paragraph of *The Great Learning* at the Cheltenham Festival in 1969 the audience split into two factions, one supporting and one opposing the music, which because of the uproar could hardly be heard. In the artists' room after the concert an elderly gentleman, who looked like a retired colonel, pushed through the crowd to confront the composer; he grabbed Cardew's hand and said: "Thank you Mr Cardew, what a relief to hear your music after all this horrible modern stuff."

The Scratch Orchestra, to whom *The Great Learning* is dedicated, was founded by Michael Parsons, Howard Skempton and Cardew himself, and emerged out of Cardew's composition class at Morley College in London in 1969 (in fact at least two paragraphs of *The Great Learning* had been completed before the Scratch Orchestra was formed). It was an enterprising body of around 40 performers of varied skills, who played all kinds of experimental music – by Cage, Cardew, Wolff, Riley, Young, Rzewski, and themselves – in all kinds of situations and for all classes of people: for Cornish farm workers in village squares, for the young industrial workers of the north-east, and for both urban and rural communities on the Continent, as well as for music lovers who frequented the Royal Festival Hall. The Scratch Orchestra consisted of an assortment of people from various walks of life, some of them with considerable artistic talent, who loved and needed music. There was no more enthusiastic, more committed collection of individuals working in the field of contemporary art at that time.

Despite the ultra-democratic procedures that the Scratch Orchestra evolved for every aspect of its activities, Cardew was very much the unproclaimed authority, a father figure to whom people looked for guidance and inspiration. The Scratch Orchestra bore his stamp, and in fact it was the embodiment and realisation of the ideas he had formulated about musical life over a long period. The first two years of the Scratch Orchestra's existence were idyllic, and the performances and compositional output were prolific. But the nature and intensity of its activities created problems, and complaints and disillusionment began to surface. Cardew opened a 'discontent file', which functioned therapeutically for a while but did not relieve the underlying tensions. The situation eventually reached crisis point. At one of the meetings two members of the Orchestra presented an analysis of the predicament, which pinpointed a fundamental disunity of theory and practice as the principal source of discontent and frustration: in theory the Scratch Orchestra believed in integration and gregariousness, in practice it was isolationist and parochial; in theory it rejected the musical establishment, in practice it asked for support (Arts Council grants, BBC television and Festival Hall appearances); in theory it wished to be an instrument of inspiration, in practice it appeared to many as a pessimistic symptom of a system in decay; and so on. The Scratch Orchestra was trapped in the classic anarchist's dilemma; it willed one thing and caused its opposite. The corner-stone of the analysis was a lengthy quotation from the English Marxist Christopher Caudwell, which generated considerable discussion. The passage concerned, which comes from Caudwell's essay on D. H. Lawrence, deals with the function of art and the role of the artist in bourgeois society:

"But art is not in any case a relation to a thing. It is a relation between men, between artist and audience, and the art work is only like a machine which they must both grasp as part of the process. The commercialisation of art may revolt the sincere artist, but the tragedy is that he revolts against it still within the limitations of bourgeois culture. He attempts to forget the market completely and concentrates on his relation to the art work, which now becomes still further hypostatised as an entity-in-itself. Because the art work is now completely an end-in-itself, and even the market is forgotten, the art process becomes an extremely individualistic relation. The social values inherent in the art form, such as syntax, tradition, rules, technique, form, accepted tonal scale, now seem to have little value, or the art work more and more exists for the individual alone." [16]

The Caudwell essay made (I believe) a profound impression on Cardew, not because it imparted new thoughts, but because it crystallised his own thoughts and feelings, and he began to identify with Marxism. The formation of the Scratch Orchestra was the culmination of Cardew's career within – or at least on the fringes of – the musical establishment. His profound commitment to the democratic ideals of the Orchestra led inevitably to his, and several other members', politicisation. His socialism was the logical consequence not just of his involvement with the Scratch Orchestra but of the experiences and direction of his life up to that point. His deeply rooted morality and tenacious humanism finally found a political purpose, which embraced and broadened previous preoccupations and achievements.

Inevitably Cardew's music changed, but not as violently as some critics have tried to make out. *The Turtledove* for voice and piano is an interesting product of a period of transition. Written in 1973, it is the third of *Three Bourgeois Songs*, settings of Chinese poems from an anthology selected by Confucius, and is an arrangement for voice and piano of a melody from Paragraph 5 of *The Great Learning*. In an introduction to a performance of the songs Cardew wrote:

"The reason for presenting these songs is to get to grips with bourgeois thought, bourgeois emotions. In short, what is bourgeois ideology?… The third song, *Turtledove*, purports to have been written by a woman, this time in praise of her ruler. He is depicted as the wise, benevolent, generous and modest ruler, above all he is the mirror of nature – his way is natural, therefore destined to survive

10,000 years. It is not hard to see who these sentiments serve. In the first poem they serve the man, and in this one they serve the ruler. Further they glorify the social relations that put the man or the ruler in the position he's in. For this reason, no matter whether written by the lowest serving maid, these poems are ruling class ideology. That's the intellectual side. What about the emotional side? Basically ecstatic submission, either to the power of the man, or to the eternal processes of nature whereby the master knows best just like the mother turtle over her children. "[17]

In the early seventies Cardew spent considerable time and energy criticising and repudiating his earlier works, including *The Great Learning*. In China the Communist party had initiated an anti-Confucius campaign in which, as a European supporter of Mao, Cardew participated vigorously. His subsequent repudiation of Maoism may invalidate part (but certainly not all) of his fierce polemic against the avant garde in his book, *Stockhausen Serves Imperialism* (1974), which was written during his Maoist period. He claimed that the aspirations of the avant garde, which had attracted young composers like himself, had turned into their opposites. Scientific investigation had become mystical pseudo-science – for example, in Stockhausen's *Gruppen* investigation of the structures of vocal sound had been applied in a totally unscientific way. Consciousness and sensitivity had become super consciousness in an ever narrowing sphere – for example, the human ability to cope with mathematical relationships and other complexities of performance had developed at the expense of social consciousness and the ability to communicate. And consciousness of the formal problems had increased so much as to exclude consciousness of the content. Progress and discovery at the frontiers of a new kind of music had become detached from the source of all progress and discovery, namely the life of the people; cut off from this source the new music had withered and died, and inevitably become a reactionary weight holding back further development. The avant garde had finally made the transition from illusion to disillusion.

At the time of his death I think it is true to say that Cardew's position on the avant garde and modernism had not changed. But he had shown a renewed interest in improvised music, and on Keith Rowe's invitation he had agreed to take part in an AMM performance of *Treatise*. The blanket repudiation of the past was associated with the discredited Mao, and in a speech on 'Culture', which Cardew delivered at an Internationalist Youth Concert in London on 9 August 1980, as representative of the Revolutionary Communist Party of Britain (Marxist-Leninist), he said "When we say 'new culture', 'proletarian culture', we mean, as Lenin said, a culture which must assimilate and rework the best of all previous cultures." Cardew's position may have begun to approximate to Brecht's who remarked that there was no need to worry about presenting bold and unusual material to a working-class audience as long as the members of that audience felt they could relate to the content of what was presented to them, as long as that content corresponded in some way to their reality.

Hanns Eisler, a composer whom Cardew greatly admired, once said "I have always striven to write music that serves Socialism. This was often a difficult and contradictory exercise, but the only worthy one for artists of our time." [18] Throughout the last ten years of his life Cardew grappled with this 'difficult and contradictory exercise' and it is part of the tragedy of his death that, in the opinion of many, he was on the brink of achieving a valid and meaningful result. Initially he made what he himself regarded as bad errors, such as his commitment to Maoism, but his active involvement in politics gave his artistic work a new focus and direction. In 1980 he organised and directed an international choir at the International Youth Camp in Germany.

"I'm convinced [he once wrote] that when a group of people get together and sing the Internationale this is a more complex, more subtle, a stronger and more musical experience than the whole of the avant garde put together. This is not a pseudo-scientific fantasy but represents real people in the real world engaged in the most important struggle of all – the class struggle."

Cardew took up the struggle in the field of music and culture, performing and singing at May Day and anti-fascist demonstrations, and in support of the Irish people's struggle for national liberation. He played in many parts of Ireland, including the Andersonstown Community Centre, a Republican stronghold in Belfast, where during his performance of *Lid of me Granny's Bin* four armed British soldiers entered the hall and began to harass the audience. Later Cardew and his musician colleagues were arrested by the RUC, held and questioned for several hours.

Cardew's commitment to socialism during the last decade of his life is awe-inspiring. His notebooks reveal the depth of his study of Marx and Lenin and, most important, the way in which he applied these principles to every situation. His activity reached heroic proportions; he was involved 24 hours a day, composing, performing, touring, organising, writing, lecturing, analysing, meeting, discussing, demonstrating on the streets (for which he was imprisoned), and militantly opposing a decadent exploitative system and its ugly, ever growing offspring, racism-fascism. An entry in his diary reads:

"The artist should think to himself do I really want the revolution to come? Or is it simply an 'inspiring' possibility to juggle with? Genuinely desiring the revolution, this implies the correct class stand and the proletarian world outlook. Only from this position can the 'benefit of the people' really be considered. The people will benefit (in the long-term) only through revolution. Making the revolution = serving the people. Two questions that occupy me at present. The necessity of building the Party. The necessity of building a revolutionary culture."

He recognised that these tasks were enormous. On the problem of presenting political music, revolutionary music, to an audience, he wrote:

"Music backs up, supports the social conscience of its audience (which is also its indirect producer). Thus when we try and write revolutionary music for the usual audience we're faced with the insurmountable problem of giving it a form that backs up the bourgeois class consciousness of the audience. If we succeed then the revolutionary content is turned around to serve the bourgeois audience in its ideas and prejudices. If we fail, then the revolutionary content remains but does not touch the audience – you get the negative reaction either on the grounds that it's bad music, or on the grounds that it is an attack on the audience (on their bourgeois consciousness)."

Elsewhere Cardew gives a concrete example of this complex composer-audience relationship. A diary entry in 1973 reads:

"*The East is Red*, for violin and piano, is a virtuoso piece, depicting the transformation of a simple folk tune into a solemn national anthem and then showing the lilt of the folk tune within that: it was played in a concert of modern music in the British Centre Berlin on February 10th. The audience responded enthusiastically and the piece was played again: the other pieces were received with sighs and groans. The critics could make nothing of it; one could not make out whether it was ironic, and another could not detect any critique of socialism in the piece. Was I backward to compose it? Were the people backward to enjoy it? This is nonsense. There is nothing to be gained by restricting the productive activity of artists." [19]

The majority of compositions during this period were political songs, written usually with a specific function in mind. He collaborated on songs with his American socialist composer friends Wolff and Rzewski; songs for Brecht's *The Measures Taken* (1976) were written in collaboration with the 'Songs for our Society' class at Goldsmiths' College; and *Resistance Blues* (1976) was composed for a concert at Brixton Prison. *Bethanien Song* (1974) exemplifies Cardew's internationalism; it was written for a campaign (in which Cardew himself was active) to save a children's hospital in one of the poorest quarters of West Berlin.

The authorities had planned to pull down the hospital and erect an 'artists' centre' in its place. In an introduction to the song Cardew explained:

"It (*Bethanien Song*) embodies our demand for a children's polyclinic in Bethanien, not an artists' centre. It sings of our children's future, threatened by the myriad abuses of capitalist society. It derides bourgeois art, exposes the politics of the urban planners, and indicates the perspectives of revolutionary change, with the the working people of all nationalities uniting to take their destiny into their own hands."

Bethanien Song was taken up by the people and became the rallying song for the huge campaign.

As well as some instrumental solo pieces – *Mountains* (1977) for bass clarinet, and *The Workers' Song* (1978) for violin – Cardew produced several large-scale 'concert' works for piano during the seventies: *Piano Album* (1973), *Thälmann Variations* (1974), *Vietnam Sonata* (1976), *Boolavogue* (1981) for two pianos, and *We Sing for the Future* (1981). The pieces in *Piano Album* are the first essays in a new piano style. In the accompanying notes Cardew wrote:

"I have discontinued composing music in an avant garde idiom for a number of reasons: the exclusiveness of the avant garde, its fragmentation, its indifference to the real situation in the world today, its individualistic outlook and not least its class character (the other characteristics are virtually products of this)."

Cardew's concern for the English national tradition became increasingly evident in the later years, not only in his speeches and conversations but also in his music. Arrangements of songs such as *Watkinson's 13* and *The Blackleg Miner* reflect his commitment to folk and popular music, while both *Boolavogue* and *We Sing for the Future* clearly reveal a debt to 16th- and 17th-century art music – the influence of the Fitzwilliam *Virginal Book*, for example, is apparent in sections of *Boolavogue* (Example 4). At the same time there are textures and rhythmic devices which, in an interesting way, betray the influence of Cardew's earlier, avant garde music. He was still an 'experimentalist', but now the music is imbued with a spirit of passion and drive which reflects the intense political life he was leading. Cardew did not really begin to write 'different' music in the seventies; it was always his music, which developed and changed inexorably on the basis of his activity as a committed revolutionary.

In his obituary in the *Süddeutsche Zeitung* on 29th December 1981 Dieter Schnebel wrote, 'Cardew's originality lies in his abandonment of originality'; he went on to remark that whatever influences Cardew quite openly embraced – whether Cage, Stockhausen, Petrassi, or even Tchaikovsky – all his music bears an unmistakable, individual stamp. What Cardew renounced over the last ten

Example 4 – Boolavogue for two pianos

years was the market mentality, a corollary of which in the West has been an obsession with 'originality', the often unconscious need to produce something 'new' at all costs. In this sense he abandoned originality, but never his individuality, which he consciously placed in the service of the socialist collective.

The composer John Paynter quoted a letter from The Guardian:

"Having sat through most of Act I of a ballet at the Royal Opera House while two ladies next to me talked incessantly l risked a polite remonstrance. One of them replied, 'But it's only music.' Is there any reply to this?" [20]

Cardew would have relished such an opportunity more than most. Over the last ten years of his life he came to see the development of music as inseparable from man's struggle against privilege, injustice, systematised greed, and exploitation. He believed that it was only through the combination of artistic and political action that contemporary music could be dragged out of its isolation.

Cornelius Cardew was a complex man. If we neglect or ignore aspects of his character because they are uncomfortable, we are in danger of doing both him and ourselves a disservice, and we shall neither understand nor appreciate his life. Cardew became a revolutionary; he was always a poet. Soon after his death an American composer friend Alvin Curran, wrote in a letter to me, "Cornelius was always a true revolutionary, but his poetry was far more interesting and natural." In the heat of the last ten years it has been easy to forget the poetry. (He had put it aside himself, though it always emerged.) His best music and music-making had a floating, poetic quality: the inscription at the beginning of one of his last pieces, *Boolavogue*, reads 'try and make it float'; the same quality characterised his performances of Feldman's music in the early days, and his bold but sensitive piano playing is turned to great advantage in his recordings of Ives's violin sonatas with Janos Négyesy.

In his essay 'Towards an Ethic of Improvisation' Cardew includes seven virtues that a musician can develop. The seventh virtue is the acceptance of death. The essay ends with these prophetic lines:

"From a certain point of view improvisation is the highest mode of musical activity, for it is based on the acceptance of music's fatal weakness and essential and most beautiful characteristic – its transience.

The desire always to be right is an ignoble taskmaster, as is the desire for immortality. The performance of any vital action brings us closer to death; if it didn't it would lack vitality. Life is a force to be used and if necessary used up. 'Death is the virtue in us going to its destination.'[Lieh Tzu]. "[21]

My last memory of Cornelius Cardew is of an anti-fascist concert, which he had organised himself, only a week before he was killed. He was playing the piano, accompanying, and singing to a packed audience in a community hall in Camden. Many members of London ethnic groups were in the audience and participating. It was a far cry from the international festivals of contemporary music where he had begun his career, but it was the destination he had consciously chosen, and which he had reached by forcing his music into life, by making the act of composition something more than the mere manipulation of sound.

Notes

1. *Musical Times*, vol 108 (1967) p.738.
2. Diary entry,18th February 1967, headed 'Lecture for Univ. of Illinois, 25.11.67.
3. Notes for a lecture delivered at the State University of New York at Buffalo, 1967.
4. Ibid.
5. Diary entry, 1st September 1964.
6. *Performance* (April-May 1982).
7. Diary entry, 17th February 1963, headed 'for lecture on Indeterminacy'.
8. Diary entry, headed 'Nov 18th '66 Buffalo'; Cardew was living in Buffalo at that time.
9. *Treatise Handbook* (London, Peters Edition, 1971), p. x . [113]
10. Ibid, p.iii. [99]
11. Diary entry, 25th February 1965.
12. *Treatise Handbook*, p.xviii. [127]
13. From the introduction to a BBC broadcast of *Treatise* on 8th February 1970. [113-114]
14. *Treatise Handbook*, p.xix. [130]
15. Michael Nyman, *Experimental Music: Cage and Beyond* (London Studio Vista, 1974), p.104.
16. Christopher Caudwell, *The Concept of Freedom* (London: Lawrence & Wishart,1965), pp.11-13.
17. Diary entry, headed 'Concert, March 5th 1973'.
18. Address delivered to a conference of delegates from the German Composers and Musicologists Union, Berlin, 23-4 February 1957.
19. From an article entitled 'Propaganda through the Medium of Art', handwritten in the diary: the entry is undated but was made between January and April 1973.
20. Letter from Derek Parker, February 1980; quoted in John F. Paynter, *Music in the Secondary School Curriculum* (Cambridge University Press, 1982), p.133.
21. *Treatise Handbook*, p.xx. [133]

Editor's note: numbers shown in [ ] refer to pages in this book.

The Great Learning

Programme notes by Michael Parsons, John Tilbury, Howard Skempton and Dave Smith for the first complete performance of *The Great Learning*. This event, spread over two days, was coordinated by 'Radical Themes in Contemporary Music'* at The Union Chapel, Upper Street, Islington, London on 7th and 8th of July 1984, as part of the Almeida Festival.

The Great Learning by Cornelius Cardew is a large-scale composition in 7 paragraphs, based on Ezra Pound's translation of the Chinese text of Confucius. The music was written between 1968 and 1970, and is dedicated to the Scratch Orchestra. The first chapter of the Confucian classic is used as a basis for a wide variety of musical and visual interpretations, and the complete work calls for a large number of trained and untrained musicians, singing, speaking, drumming, playing stones and whistles, performing actions and gestures, improvising, using conventional and unconventional instruments and other sound resources. This is believed to be the first complete performance of the entire work, lasting altogether about 9 hours.

Cornelius Cardew was born in 1936 and died in 1981. For over 20 years he had a unique influence on English music. After a brilliant studentship at the Royal Academy of Music (1953-57) and a close association with Stockhausen, Cage and other avant garde composers, he began to use graphic and verbal notations and to work with untrained performers, and in 1966 became a member of the radical free improvisation group AMM. The foundation of the Scratch Orchestra followed 3 years later arising out of an experimental music course which he started at Morley College in 1968.

The Great Learning and the work of the Scratch Orchestra between 1969 and 1972 represented an important stage in Cardew's progress away from the purely aesthetic concerns of the musical avant garde towards the more overtly political, Marxist-Leninist commitment of his later work. His great achievement lay in his ability to communicate his belief in the power of music not as an abstract and specialised pursuit but as a vital and essential social activity.

* 'Radical Themes in Contemporary Music' was a concert producing initiative set up by John Tilbury, Keith Rowe and Eddie Prévost.

The Great Learning

Paragraph 1, for chorus (speaking, playing stones and whistles) and organ.
"The Great Learning takes root in clarifying the way wherein the intelligence increases through the process of looking straight into one's own heart and acting on the results; it is rooted in watching with affection the way people grow; it is rooted in coming to rest, being at ease in perfect equity."

Paragraph 2, for singers and drummers.
"Know the point of rest and then have an orderly mode of procedure. Having this orderly procedure one can grasp the azure, that is, take hold of a clear concept. Holding a clear concept one can be at peace internally. Being thus calm one can keep one's head in moments of danger. He who can keep his head in the presence of a tiger is qualified to come to his deed in due hour."

Paragraph 3, for large instruments and voices.
"Things have root and branch; human affairs have range and origin. To know what comes first and what follows is to be close to the way."

Paragraph 4, for chorus (*shouting and playing ridged or notched instruments, sonorous substances, rattles or jingles*) and organ.
"The men of old, wanting to clarify and diffuse throughout the Empire that light which comes from looking straight into the heart and then acting, first set up good government in their own states. Wanting good government in their states, they first established order in their own families. Wanting order in the home, they first disciplined themselves. Desiring self-discipline they rectified their own hearts. And wanting to rectify their hearts they sought precise verbal definitions of their inarticulate thoughts, the tones given off by the heart. Wishing to attain precise verbal definitions they set to extend their knowledge to the utmost. This completion of knowledge is rooted in sorting into organic categories."

Paragraph 5, for a large number of untrained musicians making gestures, performing actions, speaking, chanting and playing a wide range of instruments, plus, optionally, 10 solo singers singing 'Ode Machines'.
"When things had been classified in organic categories, knowledge moved towards fulfilment. Given the extreme knowable points, the inarticulate thoughts were defined with precision, the sun's lance coming to rest on the precise spot verbally. Having attained this precise verbal definition, this sincerity, they then stabilized

their hearts. They disciplined themselves. Having attained this self-discipline, they set their own houses in order. Having order in their own homes, they brought good government to their own states. And when their states were well governed, the empire was brought into equilibrium."

Paragraph 6, for any number of musicians using any sound materials.
"From the Emperor Son of Heaven down to the common man, singly and all together, this self-discipline is the root."

Paragraph 7, for any number of trained and untrained singers.
"If the root be in confusion, nothing will be well governed. The solid cannot be swept away as trivial, and nor can trash be established as solid; it just does not happen. Mistake not cliff for morass and treacherous bramble."

Apart from paragraph 1, which was commissioned by Macnaghten Concerts and first performed at the Cheltenham Festival in 1968, the composition of *The Great Learning* was essentially bound up with the formation and growth of the Scratch Orchestra in 1969 and 1970. For many years Cardew, together with many other musicians who took part in the Scratch Orchestra's activities, had been deeply dissatisfied with the social and musical climate in which new music existed. Throughout the 1960's he had been searching for ways to draw upon the musical resources of untrained performers and improvisers, and of those who had developed skills other than the ability to read and interpret complex notation. Works such as *Treatise*, *Schooltime Compositions* and *The Tiger's Mind*, which used graphic and verbal notations, were stages in this development, as was his experience of extended free improvisation with the group AMM between 1966 and 1972.

Cardew's intention was not to replace trained with untrained performers, but to bring them together into a participatory situation in which different abilities and techniques could be fruitfully combined and contrasted, and in which performers from different backgrounds could learn from each other, and so extend the creative capacities of all participants, often in unexpected ways.

In paragraph 1, for example, the chorus is required not to sing, but to strike stones together, to speak in unison and to play whistles, interpreting a graphic notation derived from the characters of the original Chinese text. The organist is invited to explore the idiosyncrasies of the instrument, making use of isolated notes from widely separated pipes and false tunings obtained by gradual pulling out or pushing in of stops.

This unconventional approach to sound, characteristic of the whole of *The Great Learning*, immediately creates a fresh and vital awareness of its actual physical, spatial and acoustic properties; in contrast with the abstraction of much avant garde music, it deals directly with the real physical materials of sound as such: with speech and song, with wind issuing from blown pipes, with the striking of stone, wood, metal and skin, with scraped or plucked strings, and with the actions and gestures of the human body.

Paragraph 2, in particular, provided the initial incentive for the formation of the Scratch Orchestra in 1969. The work was originally conceived for a group of individual performers who would both sing and drum, and it was in this form that it was first rehearsed at Morley College in January 1969. Soon it became clear that a much larger body of singers would be needed to stand up to the incessant and overpowering drum rhythms; each of the regular participants in the Morley College group brought in friends, students and colleagues to swell the chorus, and the work was transformed into an exhilarating and exhausting struggle between singers and drummers. After trial performances with groups of students at Leeds and Hornsey Colleges of Art, in which it was discovered that the rough and unsophisticated sound of large groups of untrained voices was ideally suited to the nature of the work, the first public performance was given at the Round House, London, on 4th May 1969, in a 7 hour concert which also included works by LaMonte Young, Christian Wolff, John Cage, George Brecht, Terry Jennings, Howard Skempton and Christopher Hobbs.

As an illuminating reference for the paragraph 2 Cardew liked to quote the story of Tibetan Buddhist monks who go to a waterfall to practice chanting; the sound of the waterfall cannot be drowned, but it inspires the voices to new levels of strength, quality and perseverance.

The five or more chorus-groups, widely separated in space, each with its own lead singer and drummer, move independently through the vocal part, each at a rate determined by the collective breath-length of the singers in that group and the leader's timing of the entry of each new note; starting roughly together, they gradually diverge, and as one group forges ahead and another falls behind, a freely canonic structure emerges, generating harmony and counterpoint across the space, as if for the first time; as Michael Nyman wrote after the first performance, the work 'seems to recreate music from its very roots'.

Out of the large and heterogeneous body of trained and untrained performers which came together for this occasion, the Scratch Orchestra was formed later in the same year. The rest of *The Great Learning* was written in 1969 and 1970 in response to the orchestra's developing characteristics and abilities, and performances followed as opportunities arose, culminating with the first performance of paragraph 5, again under the auspices of Macnaghten Concerts, at the Cecil Sharp House, London, on 21st January 1972.

Each paragraph makes use of a different set of sound resources, and approaches the question of combining trained and untrained musicians and performers in new and original ways. In paragraph 3, large bass sustaining instruments play slow ascending scales, the players timing the notes in response to what they hear being played around them, always returning to the low A flat, which provides a continuous drone. Singers relate each word of phrase of the text to specified pitches, or to other notes which they hear in the scales being played by the instruments; here, as elsewhere in *The Great Learning*, it is not enough to be able to read music: players and singers have to develop the ability to listen and make choices; the time-scale is open.

In paragraph 4, a multilayered organ part (with optional groups of other instruments) is to be realised by the performer from the pitch materials provided, which contain a wealth of possibilities. This is juxtaposed with a chorus part in canon, in which an extended declamation of each sentence of the text alternates with interludes for ridged and notched instruments, following a graphic notation which is again derived from the Chinese characters. The basic instrument for this paragraph is the wand, which is used to scrape the ridged instruments and also to accompany the vocal declamations by rhythmically striking a 'sonorous substance' (usually a cushion).

Paragraph 5, the most diverse and complex part of *The Great Learning*, brings together a variety of visual and musical elements, including gestures, activities, songs, games, and free improvisation. It begins with a 'Dumb Show', a visual translation of the graphic elements which make up the Chinese characters into gestures derived from a hybrid of American Indian sign languages, which were developed for communicating with whites during the 19th century; this was among the range of subjects which Cardew was studying at the time. When all the performers have completed this dumb show, there follows a sequence of 7 verbally notated compositions, which are not rationally related to the text: Crash Bang Clank Music, Bowed Sound, Plink, Beautiful Sound Music, Loud and Soft Laughter Music, Silent Music, Mountain Top Music. These compositions may occur in any order, and are interspersed with recitations of the complete text, and vocal renderings of each sentence by individual singers. The compositions embrace extreme opposites, from sustained to pointillistic, beautiful to ugly sounds, noise to silence, poker-faced to hilarious activity, from the solemn to the grotesque. An optional alternative to participating in the compositions is to interpret the 'action and number scores', in which the material is predominantly visual; performers are called upon to make actions using a repertoire of gestures, objects, instruments, ideas and relationships, and to combine them in specified ways.

Concurrent with this whole structure are the Ode Machines, a set of 10 elaborate solo songs, any number of which may be performed simultaneously. These are settings of poems from the Confucian *Book of Odes*. They begin one by one, and end approximately together with the last of the compositions.

After the profusion and diversity of paragraph 5, paragraph 6 is predominantly quiet and sparse. Any sound materials may be used, but in contrast with the unrestricted improvisation with which paragraph 5 finishes, the number and type of sounds which can be made is here precisely defined: isolated individual sounds, constellations of up to 5 sounds, sounds to be synchronized with those of other players; sounds which must follow a general pause; optional sounds, which may be played, heard, or quasi-accidental; occasional long or loud sounds. What is specified here is the relationship between each sound and its immediate context, which can only be discovered by attentive listening; the context will be different for each player, as each moves through the instructions at an individual rate. A subtle network of interrelated points and groups of sound is created, the player-listeners spanning the intervening silences with concentrated awareness of each others' actions.

Paragraph 7, finally, the only paragraph for voices alone, is again essentially based on the process of listening and responding to other performers. It is accessible to anyone familiar with the procedure, regardless of previous musical experience; each singer, beginning with a freely chosen note, sings the first word for a specified number of full breaths, and then, moving around in the space, chooses for each successive word or phrase a new note from among those which can be heard from other singers. This provides a completely original solution to the problem of creating music for a large group of trained and untrained singers, in which all can participate on an equal basis, by giving them a framework within which individual responsibility and choice and the sense of community and interdependence with other participants is made meaningful.

The process is no way exclusive; if some of the singers should happen to introduce deviations in sustaining their notes, or in taking up and prolonging notes heard from other performers, these will in turn be passed on to other singers and so become incorporated into the texture of sound as the performance unfolds. The music as heard is not fixed in the score, but arises out of differences in individual breath-length, vocal quality and abilities. It does not exist in an ideal realm of aesthetic perfection, but in the here-and-now, in the physical, acoustic and human circumstances of each particular performance.

Michael Parsons

The Great Learning – Polemics and Controversy

In an introductory talk to a broadcast recording of the first performance of Paragraph 1 of *The Great Learning* at the Cheltenham Festival in 1968 Cardew remarked, "If music was a purely aesthetic experience I don't think it would occupy the central place it does in our affairs. It must make waves in the environment and have repercussions beyond the concert hall." In fact, this reference to his musical credo was prompted by the furore which the work has created amongst the audience on that occasion. The public had split into two factions, participating through vocal approval or disapproval, and Cardew's radical attitude towards music-making found expression in his reaction to the event. Moreover, he draws political parallels in a way that foreshadows his later commitment to revolutionary politics. Just as we should cultivate our own individual responsibility socially and politically, and only rely on our own judgement, so the audience at Cheltenham had every right, in Cardew's view, to act upon their judgement of a piece of music, and he applauds their lack of 'politeness'. His summing up of the affair is characteristically political in its formulation: "When you find a certain situation intolerable you can attempt to change it, or terminate it."

Of course, the basis for the hostilities at the Cheltenham performance was psychological and aesthetic – not political. At the time Cardew had adopted a radical aesthetic which involved an expanded time scale (in relation to conventional western musical practices) and a Cagean preoccupation with 'informal sound', which he contrasted with 'formal music'. "Blow a sound and make it glow," he wrote in a diary entry at the time. Elsewhere he wrote, "From Cage you learn that all sounds have life, from David Tudor you learn that this life can be nourished, from LaMonte Young you learn that you can *totally* identify yourself with this life of a sound. It is something so big and powerful you can surrender yourself to it, instead of feeling obliged to protect something that is intrinsically fragile and weak. At this point the term sound has to be abandoned, and the term music steps in to take its place."

The Great Learning hovers around this area between informal sound and formal music and it is this radical aesthetic which placed such a strain on the relationship between Cardew and some of his audience in performances of *The Great Learning*.

But what of the Confucian text? What attracted Cardew to a text which, after a relatively short period of time had elapsed, he was to condemn in a thorough-going critique in his book *Stockhausen Serves Imperialism*. As Bryn Harris, prominent member of the Scratch Orchestra, has remarked, Cardew attempted "to vitiate the Confucian world outlook with democracy, attempting an eclectic amalgam of a philosophy based upon a tribute-paying society (Confucianism) and that of a bourgeois-democratic socio-economic formation." And he goes further, drawing a parallel, provocatively, between the Confucian idea of the 'virtuous man' as an aristocrat wielding power over the populace and Cardew's own relationship with the Scratch Orchestra – a relationship of which, it must be said, Cardew himself became more conscious and more critical as his politicisation intensified.

Cardew's highly idiosyncratic approach to the text is evident in a interview with Hannah Boenisch (a German film-maker who filmed the Scratch Orchestra on tour) in 1972. Cardew rationalizes his pragmatic method, defining and elucidating themes from *The Great Learning* which he has regarded as important for the Scratch Orchestra and for himself. "people wouldn't wish to live by the principles outlined in *The Great Learning*. But they have an effect. Many of the principles are patently breaking down in the present state of society – like the absolute importance of the authoritarian structure of the family, for instance." (To pursue Bryn Harris's analogy mentioned above, at the time of the interview Cardew's own authority (as father figure) in the Scratch Orchestra was under siege and the Orchestra's disintegration had begun.) "But in *The Great Learning* it's a central theme. The theme I find most important is what is actually central in the text: self-discipline is the only discipline… There are other principles in *The Great Learning* like love the people, that I think are very important. *To watch with affection the way people grow…* The Scratch Orchestra doesn't dominate the audience – in the way that in conventional concerts the audience is dominated by the music. So, my feeling is that we should have an affectionate attitude towards the audience, not a lecturing attitude. And another principle, the one in the last Paragraph about the *solid cannot be swept away,* and *trash cannot be established as solid.*"

Cardew's extraction and emphasis of these particular principles, and his exclusion of underplaying of those which lay uncomfortably with his own and the Scratch Orchestra's liberal anarchism remains unconvincing for many of his political comrades, several of whom have refused to take part in the Almeida performance of *The Great Learning,* upholding Cardew's later repudiation of the work. In fact, already in 1972, by which time his politicisation was underway, Cardew produced a revised version of the first and second Paragraphs, attempting to rescue the music from the text, for a Promenade Concert performance. The new version involved altering the text so that it was relevant to contemporary politics, the use of revolutionary slogans and banners, and a watering down of the radical aesthetics which Cardew felt had become too closely associated with the original text. Thus, the altered text and banners supplanted the compositional element. In the Promenade Concert the BBC went so far as to ban the slogans, and banners were not allowed to be displayed during the performance. Cardew regarded the revised version a mistake; it was never revived, nor did he thereafter show any interest in *The Great Learning* except as a negative example. His later uncompromising hostility to the work as a whole may be partly explained by his acute embarrassment at what he regarded as a naive and irresponsible choice of a reactionary text. My own view, and that of my co-directors of the Almeida project, is that whatever qualms one may have about the historical origins of the text, the music of *The Great Learning* is a clear and profound expression of Cardew's humanism at a time when he was moving towards an understanding of the political and social roots of musical life. Michael Nyman aptly describes *The Great Learning* notations as 'people-processes': "They give each performer (or group of performers) the identical notation and set of rules which allows them to proceed through it, progressively, with few restraints on personal or group independence and spontaneity – a unique combination of freedom and restraint which largely accounts for the freshness and vitality of these works."

Cardew also draws attention to the way in which the text and music-making complemented each other; for example, the text in Paragraph 5, "they disciplined themselves," and the essentially improvisatory quality of much of the music in that Paragraph. "I see such self-discipline as the essential pre-requisite of improvisation. Discipline is not to be seen as the ability to conform to a rigid rule structure, but as the ability to work collectively with other people in a harmonious and fruitful way. Integrity, self-reliance, initiative, to be articulated say on an instrument in a natural, direct way; these are the qualities necessary for improvisation. Self-discipline is the necessary basis for the desired spontaneity where everything that occurs is heard and responded to without the 'aid' of arbitrarily controlled procedures and intellectual obscurity."

Cardew's attitude to music-making can be seen to contrast sharply with that of John Cage. Whereas with Cage generally little or no spontaneous expression is permitted during performance, Cardew never denied the performer's history and background. He never exerted backdoor control whether by a mathematical series or by chance methods, but preferred to focus a performer's creativity on problems to be solved. In an article in *Tempo* magazine Michael Nyman compares Cage with Cardew: "Through his evident isolation as a composer Cage is still taking steps towards the socialization of music. For Cardew these steps have already been taken; the Scratch Orchestra, a successful experiment in such social music-making, lived and died while Cage was still scratching his head." Cardew's commitment was to social music-making, and *The Great Learning* goes back to the roots of musical practices and experience. It is a means of renewal, a reaffirmation of moral, social and aesthetic principles as the basis for collective music development – principles which for many musicians 'modernism' has negated through the tyranny of baton control, the reduction of the performer to the role of skilful technician, and the commodity fetishism of the modern score-to-be-analysed.

It is this very radicalism that continues to evoke controversy. Critics have praised it as "one of the finest and most significant works of recent time" (Brian Dennis), or denounced it as "deliberate infantilism" (Gerald Larner). Its unpredictability produces unpredictable responses. After the furore of the first performance of the first Paragraph at Cheltenham an elderly gentleman, who looked like a retired colonel, pushed through the crowd in the artists' room to confront the composer. He grabbed Cardew's hand and said, "Thank you, Mr Cardew, what a relief to hear your music after all this horrible modern stuff."

In the Eighteenth Brumaire Marx wrote, "The social revolution of the 19th century cannot draw its poetry from the past, but only from the future." The idealism and utopianism of *The Great Learning* in these dark times need not embarrass us. On the contrary, in its anticipation and imaginative expression of music-making in a new society – a peaceful, creative and collaborative future where people manage and determine their own lives – it can inspire and sustain us.

John Tilbury

The Great Learning – a conversation between Howard Skempton and Dave Smith

DS Hearing a performance of Paragraphs 1 and 4 in 1971, it seemed as if there was something special for people taking part from the point of view of individual reward – something to do with the balance between freedom and restraint, I suppose.

HS The frustrating thing was that there was perhaps too much freedom. The piece introduced enough restraint to make performance satisfying. Looking at the score, I think Cornelius was trying to produce effective material for the Scratch Orchestra. For example, one thing that interests me is the medium … the Scratch Orchestra in its early days was too noisy – people were using electronics and saxophones. In *The Great Learning* he either calls for voices or simple percussion instruments, on the whole.

DS Do you think that he did this specifically with a mind to curbing the kind of excesses that could happen in, say, improvisations? Paragraph 7 seems tailor-made for curbing excesses: Bryn (Harris) told me with some glee about the competition between himself and Chris Hobbs to finish last: that's not breaking the rules.

HS Is the simplicity of the instructions an attempt to restrain the performers or a way of encouraging the non-musicians?

DS Both.

HS This restraint – Cornelius was always interested in restraining in order to reveal subtleties, as LaMonte Young was. If you set severe limitations then you appreciate more within those limitations. At the same time, composers weren't sure about electronics – Cornelius certainly wasn't. He felt that loudspeakers weren't yet good enough to justify their use.

DS How much of *The Great Learning* uses appreciable volume? Paragraph 2 of course and Crash Bang Clank Music.

HS No, they're exceptions, especially Crash Bang Clank Music. It's not a piece for listening to.

DS It's a contrast to the other compositions of Paragraph 5.

HS The simplicity of the material intrigues me. Why use pentatonic scales in Paragraph 2? I think that the problem for a composer was what to do if you didn't like electronics and wanted to avoid serialism. Petatonicism was one answer – very simple triadic material … Paragraph 3 as well … it's is not only a means of making life easier for the non-musicians.

DS Using pentatonic scales means that pitching for the singers shouldn't be too difficult. Also it means that the result will be pretty consonant.

HS Later on Paragraph 3 becomes dissonant when different sentences are combined. Also singers pick out notes of scales freely chosen by the instrumentalists.

HS The organ writing in Paragraphs 1 and 4 looks more dissonant that it actually sounds.

HS There seems to be three elements – triads, clusters and pentatonic material. It's difficult to know if the work is primarily characteristic of the composer or primarily dictated by the needs of the Scratch Orchestra.

DS The two are interrelated. It's a logical extension of Cornelius' earlier work. For that matter it was logical that the political stance followed. It's never seemed contradictory.

HS Do you think the listener can get much out of *The Great Learning*?

DS I think so. For instance, you mentioned LaMonte earlier. Paragraph 7 could be seen as presenting 'LaMonte Young for the people' – no need for just intonation! The effect is not dissimilar. I would have thought that this 'beautiful sound' element is present in other Paragraphs as well.

HS What about Paragraph 4?

DS Brings 'Death Chant' (LaMonte Young) to mind! It's very ritualistic and there's a lot repetitive and ethnic music with that quality. And watching people beating cushions increases the effect.

HS This is the third thing that strikes me. Firstly there's the medium; secondly the material (pitch and so on) and thirdly the inclusion of actions and ritualistic elements … which is also very much of its time.

DS How?

HS Probably because experimental composers at that time were uncertain about the nature of music. George Brecht's events, primarily theatrical, were regarded as music.

DS Which probably helped people to feel even more uncertain …

HS Yes, but I think there was a need to challenge received views about what music should be. The Action Score of Paragraph 5 is symptomatic of this.

DS Remembering that Paragraph 5 was written for the Scratch Orchestra at a certain point in time, I'm wondering whether these theatrical elements developed within the Scratch, or if Cornelius always had them in mind.

HS The Action Score could well have been a means of restraining exhibitionists within the orchestra.

DS But both the Action Score and the Number Score offer opportunities for the exhibitionists …

HS Yes, but they had to earn the right! … by reading the instructions. Cornelius insisted that they did.

DS Fair enough; if you want to draw attention to yourself, you have to work hard for the privilege.

HS In 1972, did you find performing in Paragraph 5 a satisfying experience?

DS Yes, except for the Improvisation Rite. In Scratch improvisations people tended not to listen or to take account of what others were doing. I feel that the improvisation in Paragraph 5 is essentially idealist … impracticable for the Scratch at the time. It falls outside of the material of the rest of *The Great Learning* because it doesn't have that restraint.

HS Cornelius' attitude to composition was inclusive. He once said that you should include everything you like in a piece. He also said that he regarded the Scratch Orchestra as an oracle. *The Great Learning* is a combination of the two ideas and contains everything he was interested in at that time. Each Paragraph is a homage to a particular field of new music. Paragraph 1 is an exception. It was written before the Scratch Orchestra was a twinkle in his eye. Paragraph 2 is probably a homage to Terry Riley.

DS In what way?

HS Simply the idea of a cell being repeated. 6 is possible a homage to Christian Wolff and 7 a homage to Feldman.

DS Rather than LaMonte Young?

HS Perhaps 3 is Feldman and 7 LaMonte Young. 5 is a Cagean mix for the Scratch Orchestra.

DS Yes, it's not a single-idea piece … also there are other homages – the Ode Machines for John White. What about 4?

HS I've never been sure about 4. It's an extraordinary piece in many ways … think of the medium – massed gueros! … cushions … I'm happier with listening rather than ritual, with pure sounds rather than atmosphere and magic. There seems something unnecessary about the performers sitting in a line.

DS There's a good practical reason for that. It's a canon in which you have to be aware of what the person ahead of you is doing.

HS Cornelius later criticised *The Great Learning* for its mystical aspects. He suggested that there was a danger that simplicity can become mysticism. I think he was far too practical, too good a composer … I would say that a good composer was essentially practical.

DS What aspects do you see as being mystical? The content – the Confucian philosophy? The Ezra Pound translation? The 'beautiful sound' angle? The idealism of the Improvisation Rite?

HS The Number Score could have a mystical aspect, but the way in which Cornelius describes the preparation of the Number Score is too humorous to run the risk of degenerating into a purely mystical experience. I think he was always essentially a humanist, a materialist. The sheer length is worrying – he described it later as inflated rubbish and it's difficult not to accept the view that it's inflated. But the standard length of a piece of experimental music was half a concert, just as the standard length of an SPNM work is 12 minutes or the standard length of an American masterpiece is, so Feldman tells us, 26 minutes. It was the most useful thing to do to write a piece lasting 45 minutes – the concert had to be filled. But as far as I am concerned, that's a basic criticism of the piece – it operates on far too grand a scale. The duration of each Paragraph is more to do with this standard length of time rather than any heroic vision on the composer's part. I don't think he was setting out to write a masterpiece.

DS Or even a significant statement? I've never felt that any Paragraph outstayed its welcome. The nature of the material seems to demand a reasonably substantial duration – it's certainly not boring to listen to. For the performer presented with 45 minutes of such material, there's some sort of convenient ratio of concentration to reward – it's not too long to be burdensome. Steve Reich's aim in composing *Drumming* was undoubtedly to create a chrome gloss masterpiece; Cornelius' aims, both musical and social, were very different of course.

HS Paragraph 1 was a commission. The rest was a response to the needs of the Scratch Orchestra and the Morley College group. The aim was to find something within the reach of everyone but which could curb the woefully anarchic side of the character of both groups.

Cornelius Cardew
Richard Barrett
New Music – 1987
(ed. Michael Finnissy and Roger Wright) OUP, 1987 (amended by the author 2005)

1 (Auto) biographical

Cornelius Cardew was born on 7th May 1936, in Winchcombe, Gloucestershire. He was a chorister at Canterbury Cathedral from 1943 to 1950, and from 1953 to 1957 studied at the Royal Academy of Music. It seems that his official studies there (composition with Howard Ferguson, piano with Percy Waller) turned out to be less important to him than the opportunity to study, support, play, and learn from the contemporary European avant garde, which became a strong influence on his early work (no doubt to the bemusement and/or annoyance of the predominant conservatism at the Academy). Having received a RAM scholarship to study electronic music in Cologne in 1957-8, Cardew met Karlheinz Stockhausen, with whom he worked as assistant from 1958 to 1960 and 'collaborated' on the score of *Carré*. According to Stockhausen, "I left the independent working-out of composition plans to him. Our common experiences have shown how such collaboration might be further developed."[1] Cardew later wrote "This score... would be the score of a piece for four orchestras by Karlheinz Stockhausen and no mistake about it."[2] Stockhausen pursued what he saw as a collaborative line of development (*Ensemble* (1967), *Musik für ein Haus*, and *Aus den sieben Tagen* (1968), etc.) without at any time denying the centrality of his own personality, finally coming out in favour of promoting a 'new serving mentality'[3] in his associates.

Having begun in the late 1950s to absorb the ideas emanating from the American experimental movement (primarily John Cage and David Tudor) and its genuine attempt to think about and work with such unquestioned (in Europe) musical areas as the composer/performer relationship, the role of notation, the composition of other than the 'sounding result', etc., Cardew began to react against the doctrinaire serialists on the European scene. As a profoundly humanist musician (this quality becomes a constant factor behind what may seem to constitute several radical changes of direction subsequently), he was attracted by the experiments of composers like Cage, Wolff, and Bussotti who in their different ways invited the performers of their music to take an active part in the process of musical realization. The presence of a performer like David Tudor was certainly a catalyst for this development, since composers needed to have the faith that such openness on their part would be constructive (i.e. the performer making real, musical decisions). Boulez and Stockhausen, together with most European composers, treated the idea of the performer's choice as no more than an interesting technical device; Cardew saw what it was really about – music as a collaborative phenomenon in the true sense.

On his return to Britain at the beginning of the 1960s, then, Cardew had placed himself at several removes from the musical establishment. His major work of this period, *Treatise* (1963-7), is to an extent a product of and a reaction to his enforced living conditions at the time – earning a living as a graphic artist. 'Psychologically the existence of the piece is fully explained by the situation of a composer who is not in a position to make music.'[4] It might thus be said that *Treatise*, consisting of 193 pages of undefined, sometimes quasi-notational graphics, is not music but a substitute for music (but what would that be?) and also obviously represents an interest in graphic invention as an end in itself. I shall return to the subject of this work, which must be the most introverted and personal in the whole of Cardew's output, but which paradoxically led to his involvement in the least introverted area of music making: free improvisation, with his joining the group AMM in 1966, consisting at that time of the ex-jazz musicians Lou Gare, Eddie Prévost, Keith Rowe, and Lawrence Sheaff.

Towards the end of the 60s, Cardew became important as a teacher of music, both at the RAM (at which his first pupil, Christopher Hobbs, was his only one for some time; the Academy had not changed that much in the 10 years since Cardew himself studied there) and at Morley College, where he had the opportunity to attract and work with numbers of like-minded people. His most important work, *The Great Learning* (1968-71) is the work of a composer who is in a position to make music. By the time it was complete, the Scratch Orchestra, a large collective of musicians, artists, performers of all kinds both trained and untrained, had been in existence for several years and was about to begin its traumatic process of politicization which was to lead Cardew's work into a new phase and his activities into a different arena; namely his concern for the class struggle.

By the time of Cardew's DAAD scholarship to work in Berlin for a year in 1973 he was trying to undo all the work he had put into producing and publicizing the avant garde music of the 50s and the experimentalism of the 60s, both his own work and that of others, because his critical approach to music now had as its prime criterion the relevance and appropriateness of a work to the revolutionary liberation of the working classes. When invited by the BBC the year before to write and present a talk introducing a performance of *Refrain* (1959) by his ex-colleague Stockhausen, Cardew produced the text 'Stockhausen Serves

Imperialism' – later collected with other musical/political writings in a book of the same title[5] – in which the work of the avant garde is subjected to examination on Marxist-Leninist-Maoist principles. The same process was applied to Cage and the experimentalists, and to Cardew's own previous work.

Not that Cardew was losing interest in composition during this time; he was actively involved until the end of his life in the process of evolving a music which would serve the interests of the working-class revolution, and this process, while remaining unresolved at his death, did indeed produce a great deal of music worthy of his unique musicality. One may speculate on his eventual contribution to music in this country had he lived. In the autumn of 1981 he began a course in analysis at King's College, London, in order to familiarize himself with historical techniques, the better to 'make the past serve the present'. In November of that year, a vaguely familiar looking figure distributing political leaflets at the refectory of King's College (where I was studying at the time) turned out to be Cardew. There was a brief conversation of little consequence; my own political awareness was nothing to speak of at the time. Several weeks later I heard that he had been killed by a hit-and-run driver on 13 December, near his home in Leyton, East London. Half-way through the next term I left the College, for reasons summed up by an attempt to organize an afternoon session of improvisation at the music department, which I was the only person to attend.

In 1984, taking part in the first complete performance of *The Great Learning*,[6] I began to realize the unique importance of this work and its implications and, as a result resumed an earlier commitment to improvisatory musics.

I began work on these notes in 1985, at first intending to request interviews and/or opinions from colleagues of Cardew. I eventually decided against this; knowing of the work in hand towards documentation and appraisal being carried out by John Tilbury, one of Cardew's most authoritative and faithful collaborators (as well as a major influence on Cardew's own politicization), any attempt by myself would be incomplete and redundant. What follows is a collection of reactions and reflections by a musician (painfully) aware of the responsibility of all creative musicians to attempt to come to terms with the issues raised by Cardew's work in all its manifestations.

2 Piano

If I begin with Cardew's piano music, which spans his entire career and might be said to be the least radical (i.e., experimental) area of his work, this is because the not inconsiderable literature on Cardew frequently gives a view of him (merely) as a 'man of ideas', rather than a composer of *music* whose qualities need no moral support from their conceptual infrastructure, and which may be judged on the same level as any music by composers less concerned than he was with the nature and status of themselves and their work.

The piano music is the work of an accomplished pianist; anyone who heard Cardew in his earlier days as an exponent of the newest music would testify to this, and he has left eloquent and powerful recordings, with Janos Négyesy, of the four Ives violin sonatas[7] which confirm such a view. As a composer for his own instrument, he shows ever renewed fascination with its sonorous possibilities, whatever changes his style underwent, inviting comparison with another English composer-pianist, Michael Finnissy. In the piano works of both, a strong and continuing source of ideas is experience of the instrument itself, and both eventually assimilated both the post-war avant garde pianism and that of the nineteenth century virtuosi into their scheme of things, albeit in entirely different ways. Whereas Stockhausen, for example, designed his piano pieces as compositional etudes, 'drawings' for more finished and expressive works, Cardew and Finnissy project through the medium something very basic about their musical personalities; the piano is somehow at the heart of their respective aesthetics, a prime contributory factor to my conviction that they are the two most important writers for the piano that this country has produced.

Cardew's *Piano Sonata No. 3* (1958) shows these pianistic qualities to a greater extent than his previous works; the *Second Sonata*, for example, bears the stamp of Boulez's *Structures* 1 for two pianos (of which Cardew and Richard Rodney Bennett had given the first British performance, at the RAM) in its astringent use of integral-serial methods. The third, however, despite displaying just as abstract a musical skeleton, breaks into streams of grace notes which glitter across the keyboard as subsequently completed works of Stockhausen (e.g. *Klavierstuck VI* and *X*) were to do: a rapprochement has been achieved between serial aridity and an irrepressible need to use the piano as more than an analytical projector of structure. This sonata is followed by the *Two Books of Study for Pianists* (also 1958) (Ex. 1) which is separated from the earlier work by the 'American experience'. The ideas which generated Stockhausen's *Klavierstuck XI* and Boulez's *Third Sonata* have already been more fully appreciated by Cardew, who, stemming as he did from a virtually negligible sense of indigenous musical tradition, was perhaps more susceptible to take a path contrary to the European mainstream. Not that Cardew was now slavishly following the Cagean line of abstraction from sound during composition – the *Two Books* define not a precise musical object but, in Cardew's own term, a 'musizierweise',[8] a mode of music-making, information which, imparted by means of the score to the interpreters, enables them to

Example 1

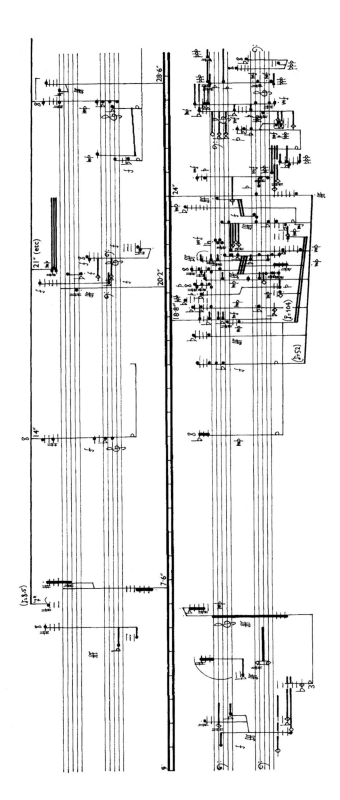

337

understand and operate within the limits which constitute the piece. The definition of such limits in exact accordance with the performer-and perception-related aspects of the proposed music becomes a more and more important compositional concern of Cardew's through the 60s, culminating in *The Great Learning* as a supreme example of just enough information to create a musical identity for a work, without compromising the responsibility placed on a performer to think out and contribute his or her own music. In the *Two Books*, however, and the piano music which follows, these ideas are seen in terms specifically of a pianist (or pianists) and, again in contradistinction to Cage, the 'taste and memory' of that pianist, the vast area of connotation around the fact of being a pianist. The next work for piano, *February Pieces* (1959-61), focuses further in on 'pianistic psychology', rushing headlong and irrationally through a wide scale of 'receivedness', figurational familiarity, expressive disjointedness. The process of working with the piano continues through the *Three Winter Potatoes* (1961-5), the first of which is actually a realization of the cryptic symbols constituting *Octet 61*, thus emphasizing Cardew's view of the piano as a theatre of, as it were, *concrete* music making. The symbols are transformed into a more fully notated music which is not only psychologically consistent (at least within the framework of aleatoric fragmentation) but also characteristically pianistic in its deployment of the gestural suggestions. A further 'concretization' which, at least as far as its performance history to date is concerned, relates to the piano, is *Volo Solo* (1965). This was written as a 'virtuoso piece' for John Tilbury, although it may be performed, omitting pitches outside the available range, on any instrument: it consists of 'the entire formal scheme of *Treatise* transliterated into well-tempered pitches'; [9] most aspects of interpretation are free except that each of the swarms of pitches, separated by gaps, which constitute the score are to be performed at a (subjectively) reckless pace. 'The instrument' Cardew wrote, 'should seem to be breaking apart.' [10] Ex. 2, from the preface to the score, shows an excerpt in which the pitch range of a bassoon (as an arbitrary example) is delineated by horizontal lines, and then the same excerpt in a hypothetical performing version for that instrument. Despite all this, the fact that the piano is the only readily available instrument which can play all the notated material, as well as being the instrument most able to account for the piece's manipulation of the 'as fast as possible' instruction by rapid variations, i.e. the extent to which the music lies under the hands (however fortuitous this may be), marks *Volo Solo* as a piano piece at heart. In a similar way *Memories of You* (1964), a homage to Cage and especially to his *Concert for Piano and Orchestra* (1957-8) could have been written with virtually any instrument in mind, but in fact consists of diagrammatical

338

instructions as to where in relation to a piano the (undefined) sounds should occur. The title of this piece may relate to Cage. It may also refer to the piano itself, to which Cardew, at least as a composer, bade a temporary farewell during the *Treatise*/AMM period. The attitude of the work to the instrument is ambiguous: the three sound sources A, B, and C may actually involve the participation of the piano, or equally, may be connected with it only by proximity, as if Cardew's journey into musical experiment had progressed beyond the point where piano music is possible.

Example 2

Once Cardew, in the early 70s, had decided to deny himself the bourgeois individualism of such eccentricity, the piano once again becomes the centre of his musical activity, not least through being virtually omnipresent in potential performing spaces. In the *Piano Album* 1973, brief and uncomplicated melodies (mostly Irish and revolutionary Chinese in origin) are adapted in an equally simple, almost naive, but profoundly pianistic manner. *Father Murphy* (Ex. 3) has this characteristic lack of sophistication but is one of the most hauntingly emotional pieces one could wish to hear: its sparse gestures spring out of the piano with great freshness and poignancy. The *Thälmann Variations* of 1974, named for the chairman of the German Communist Party who was interned in 1933 and executed in 1944 by the Nazis, is equally inventive with piano sonority, from the harp-like broken chords at the beginning onwards, but suffers, together with other examples of avant garde or experimental composers adopting a melodic/tonal style (Stockhausen, Takahashi, etc.) from being harmonically and

Example 3

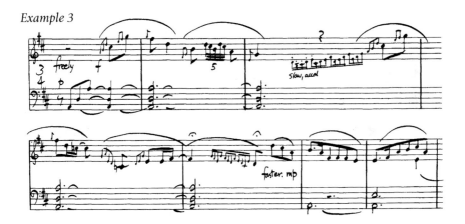

formally rather clumsy, seemingly disjointed when it should be mellifluous and *vice versa*. Perhaps this clumsiness was deliberate. In any case, Cardew's last compositions for piano, *Boolavogue* (for two pianos) and *We Sing for the Future*, both 1981, show a greater integration of the procedures of tonal music especially of the baroque and earlier. The latter piece involves strict contrapuntal working, and both use folk music or folk like material (much as did their models in earlier music) for its innate characteristics and for the (partly submerged) emotional effect of its subject matter. (Both types of impact were certainly in evidence when John Tilbury, announcing *Boolavogue* at a London concert during the miners' strike of 1984-5, mentioned its performance in mining country shortly before – one of the tunes used in the piece is *The Blackleg Miner*.) The road towards a reconsideration of sophistication in Cardew's music had begun by 1981; with these two pieces we shall have to content ourselves with only the beginning.

3 Improvising

Treatise may on one level be a reaction to Cardew's prevailing circumstances, but there is a great deal more to it than that: any examination of the score reveals it as a valuable contribution to the discussion of notation, its purposes and priorities, as well as a highly accomplished and beautiful piece of design, and an enigmatic but powerful stimulus to music production.

The score itself is a complex, quasi developmental treatment of 67 elements[11] which generates, upon silent reading, the impression of a large-scale, almost symphonic, musical span, with areas of relaxation and areas of climax (notably the build-up to the enormous burst of black circles on page 133, (Ex. 4) which never fails to evoke a reaction hardly different from that of a particularly cataclysmic passage in 'real' music). Several of Cardew's more explicitly notated works (they

Example 4

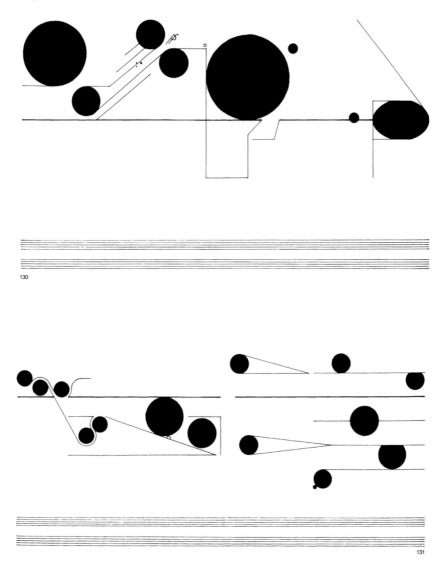

could hardly be less) of the 60s are 'realizations' of parts of this massive score: *Volo Solo* has already been mentioned; *Bun No. 2* for orchestra (1964) is another example, and there may be others which Cardew did not advertise as such. Nevertheless, *Treatise* has become a work to be realized as it is, usually in the form of more or less premeditated improvisation. Rather than representing an alternative mode of realization to the ones mentioned above, this exemplifies Cardew's hope that

Example 4 continued

'in playing *Treatise* the performer will give of his own music in response to my music, which is the score itself'.[12] But as Tilbury says, 'its visual impact disconcertingly puts most performances of it in the shade'.[13] I have experienced myself the exquisite frustration which results from attempting to create sounds as an interpretation of the score: any consistent treatment of the elements on a given page is inevitably contradicted by the presence of one or more contradictory features. The resultant impression is that there is a sonic analogue to what is on the page, that it will remain forever just out of reach, but that something about *Treatise* consistently makes musical sense.

It was of course impossible for Cardew to pursue this line; like Wittgenstein in the *Tractatus Logico-Philosophicus*, from which Cardew's title is derived, he had said everything possible given a certain view of the field of enquiry. The only logical step after the experience of 'performing' *Treatise* was for Cardew to enter more fully the world of free improvisation, which he did upon joining AMM. I do not propose to dwell upon the work of AMM as such, since Cardew, it should be remembered, was in no sense its leader or even a *primus inter pares*, but it is important in the light of his work as a whole to attempt to appreciate what he meant by improvisation, which was not exactly what a jazz player or non-Western musician would make of the word. In *Towards an Ethic of Improvisation*, published in the *Treatise Handbook*, Cardew significantly adopts the method of the later Wittgenstein, who in *Philosophical Investigations*, for example, 'has abandoned theory, and all the glory that theory can bring on a philosopher (or musician), in favour of an illustrative technique'.[14] Although AMM music was generally quite individual and recognizable, Cardew in no way gives a 'recipe' for it, confining himself to a list of 'virtues a musician can develop': simplicity, integrity, selflessness, forbearance, preparedness, identification with nature, and acceptance of death. What then takes place musically is nothing more nor less than the result of a group of people applying these precepts in each other's company: 'AMM is their sounds (as ignorant of them as one is about one's own nature)'.[15] What improvisation meant, then, was an activity as unforced and central to a musical life as respiration to organic life. His subsequent work on *The Great Learning* was an attempt to make this realization more available and accessible to those without years to invest in acquiring a 'musical state of being'.

During Cardew's Maoist years and the concentration on a social-realist idiom, the exhilarating but inevitably somewhat closed activity of free improvisation was discontinued in favour of music which could communicate its revolutionary message without the barrier to understanding created by the experimental ethos. In retrospect this can be seen as a temporary over-reaction, upon becoming belatedly aware of the 'irrelevance' of contemporary art music and its institutions in general; once again it wasn't temporary enough, and Cardew's projected reunion with AMM to perform *Treatise* in 1982 was prevented from taking place.

4 The Great Learning

I have mentioned above that one of Cardew's most important achievements in the field of experimental music is that of an appropriate mix of freedom and discipline in the compositions, such that, on the one hand, the performer is fruitfully involved in discovering his or her own musical resources, and on the other hand, the listener is presented with a definite and satisfying musical experience. *The Great Learning*, in its attempt to create such situations in the context of a larger performing body than was usual in experimental work previous to its conception (which is of course intimately related to that of the Scratch Orchestra and Cardew's class at Morley College), is intended as a model of quasi-social relationships between, in this case, performers (and between them and their audience).

Cardew had been interested in the Confucian writings for some years: the *Treatise Handbook* contains a reference dated March 1963 to Ezra Pound's translation of the *Ta Hsio* (i.e., the Great Learning),[16] and his eventual setting of its seven paragraphs, at least in its most familiar and published form, uses that translation. Pound was interested in making poetry out of the bare outlines supplied by the Chinese ideograms, and his translation contains numerous instances of an alternative figurative utterance alongside a more exact rendering: thus in paragraph 5, 'given the extreme knowable points, the inarticulate thoughts were defined with precision' is supplemented by 'the sun's lance coming to rest on the precise spot verbally'. This device of Pound's, to be found throughout his translations (as well as his original poetry) no doubt renders the text more amenable to the conception of musical settings or analogues: a more accurate translation of the above would be 'thoughts having been made sincere, minds were rectified'.[17] Pound was searching in Confucius for a world order based upon social discipline and a reverence for culture, which he eventually believed he had found in Mussolini's Fascism; Cardew's search for a model of collective responsibility (in music) also evolved through an absorption with Confucius, but one which at this stage critically ignored the reactionary social content of the *Ta Hsio*, seeing in it only his bourgeois ideal of order in, for example, the end of paragraph 5:

> Having attained this self-discipline, they set their own houses in order. Having order in their own homes, they brought good government to their own states. And when their states were well governed, the empire was brought into equilibrium.

His concern for 'equilibrium' caused him to ignore the importance and connotations (to Pound and to Confucius) of the word 'empire'.

Subsequent to Cardew's espousal of Communism, new translations of the texts were made (in 1972) which attempted to steer their emphasis towards populism; in paragraph 1, for instance, 'it [The Great Learning] is rooted in watching with affection the way people grow', becomes 'The Great Learning is rooted in love for the broad masses of the people', and so on. Cardew also stipulated that, in the 1972 Proms performance of parts of this version, banners bearing revolutionary slogans (e.g. 'A revolution is not a dinner party, it is an insurrection, an act of violence by which one class overthrows another') were to be displayed. Needless to say, this was prevented by the BBC: in any case, by the time Cardew wrote his critical essay on the piece in 1974,[18] his attitude towards it had changed once more. He now repudiated any attempt (e.g. by Pound, by Christian missionaries in China, by himself) to warp the Confucian text into a confirmation of 'pet ideas' and reverted to the original version, so that a performance would reveal its class character and ideological content intact and hold it up to be criticized, in the interests of enlightening its audience by disengagement, the realization that what is happening on stage (in *all* its aspects) is an exposé of techniques used by the ruling class for the purpose of institutional reaction. Whether or not one accepts the validity of this or any other mode of performance of the work, its stature as a musically successful large-scale composition, as it is, is difficult to deny. Moreover, it is fundamentally based around Pound's translation to the extent that to use any other ends up being inappropriate as well as compromising.

Example 5

The Great Learning is a summation of practically everything Cardew had learned about the workings of music. It is possible to see traces of the abstract serialist composer in the way it is organized around its text, not only in the sense of analogizing musical situations and processes from it, but also in that the text is, as it were, used economically in the generation of seemingly empirical material. Two examples: firstly, the graphic notations for whistles (paragraph 1 ; Ex. 5) and gueros (paragraph 4) are derived from the strokes of the Chinese characters making up that part of the text; secondly, the numbers of repetitions of words and phrases in paragraph 7 are the numbers of strokes used to form the characters of those words or phrases. There are many other examples of this arcane kind of derivation to be found in the score. The composer of 'inspirational' notations as in the *Two Books of Study*, and then *Treatise, Schooltime Compositions*, etc., is found in the organ parts of paragraphs 1 and 4, which invite the organist to elaborate imaginatively on a fairly sparse (staff-based) notation, and also the 'Number Score' and 'Action Score' of paragraph 5, which are points of departure for flights of irrationality (however 'disciplined'). The 'Ode Machines' of paragraph 5 and the vocal part of paragraph 2 also point forward to Cardew's later interest in an uncomplicated tonal idiom. The score as a whole, above all, is a frequently exuberant (and almost encyclopaedic) celebration of the possibilities inherent in a collective like the Scratch Orchestra, a theatre of action in which as many as a hundred performers are invited to discover and contribute (in a decisive manner) their personal and social musicality.

In paragraph 1, apart from an opening passage on clicking pebbles and an almost fully notated organ prelude (the most 'traditional' notation in the whole work), an alternation is set up between complete statements of the text by the speaking chorus, and interpretations by successive soloists of a passage in ideogram-derived notation, performed on a 'whistle' while those elsewhere in the batting order contribute to a chordal whistling drone. In the 1984 performance, as no doubt originally, the word 'whistle' was variously interpreted as a referee's whistle, swanee whistle, recorder mouthpiece, etc., which in the event gave quite an exhaustive view of what different renditions of the same notation are possible, from 'avant garde' virtuosity with multiphonics to perverse (and silent) slapstick. The austere repetitions of the text ('... clarifying the way wherein the intelligence increases through the process of looking straight into one's own heart and acting on the results...') produce Confucius's 'perfect equity' in their balance with such latitude.

Paragraph 2 sounds very different, and also involves the performers in a different way. The text is sung five times through by several groups of singers, each with a leader (to indicate their entries and provide the pitch) and a drummer. The volume generated by the drumming (of 26 repeated rhythmic cells, in an order left free to each drummer) creates an obstacle to the voices making themselves heard, especially as each repetition of the text transposes the sung (pentatonic) melody, each note occupying one long breath, up by a semitone so that the singers, by the end, not only have had to sustain maximum volume for around an hour, but also, to varying degrees, must reach for difficult high notes. Cardew in his instructions allows for octave transpositions in such cases, but it would seem appropriate in view of the explicitly challenging nature of the piece to 'attempt the impossible' or, in the words of the text, to 'keep one's head in moments of danger'. In his note for the commercial recording of paragraph 2, Cardew stresses the feeling of failure engendered by singing the piece, which is mirrored in the dissolution of coherence in the singing as the groups fall out of time with one another while at the end the drum rhythms are intended to move towards coherence once the singing has ended. Like most of *The Great Learning*, then, the situation created in this piece is defined in such a way as to negate any advantage in the possession (or lack) of musical training in its performers.

Paragraph 3 is more concerned with defining an overall sound than a performance attitude. The text ('things have root and branch...') is exemplified by a number of bass instruments (10 is suggested) playing slow ascending scales from a low A♭ which is returned to as a drone; Cardew suggests several examples of scales (A♭ major, ascending fourths, etc.) although instrumentalists are encouraged to invent their own. When this texture has been set up, the words are sung to any note of a three-note chord until this too has been established, whereupon the singers move individually to pitches they can hear (without transposition) from the ascending instrumental scales. This process occurs three times, each with a new chord: the chords are A major, E♭ minor, and C (no third). After this, a freer treatment of the material occurs for a duration determined only by the wishes of the vocalists (or a prearranged signal). The effect of these processes is not, as in paragraph 2, of dissolution but of a definite initial situation giving rise to a proliferating (harmonic) richness, as close to 'absolute' music as is attained in *The Great Learning*.

Paragraph 4, again, is more outgoing, and has the character of a ritual or processional. The organ part here is more schematic, and may also be realized in part by groups of homogeneous sounding instruments; its seven sections correspond to those of the text, which are set to a canon in which the vocalists shout the syllables singly in rhythmic unison while striking a cushion or similar object with a long 'wand'. The canon, each part one very slow beat (i.e. 5-10 seconds) behind the previous one, passes down a long line of seated vocalists which snakes through the performing space. With a sufficient number of performers the end of the line is a considerable time behind the beginning; not only does the text pass slowly down it (reflecting the logical train of thought in the text, on the subject of setting up 'good government'), but so do the graphic passages, this time interpreted on gueros, between sentences. This canonic verse/interlude structure is succeeded by a coda in which each vocalist, after finishing his or her part, recapitulates all seven guero passages without a break. The piece thus ends with the gradual thinning out of a chorus of gueros, its length dictated primarily by the number of performers, like paragraph 1. It seems to generate in performance just that quasi-mystical ambience that Cardew later criticized, which the optional improvised vocal solos do not do much to dispel. However, the difficulty of maintaining the extremely slow tempo, in the face of a great deal of interference from organ and gueros, certainly contributes to a suitably ceremonial, even funereal, attitude in performance, and eventually a feeling of great freedom and relief having come out at the other side, when the procession, of sounds rather than people, has vanished into the distance.

The idea of discipline followed by release is exploited more fully in paragraph 5, in which a complex juxtaposition and superimposition of more or less disciplined action is followed by a group improvisation of similar length with no instruction other than 'a dense forest that presents no obstacle to the mind or eye (or other sense)'. The improvisational situation here is a quite unique experience; although the heart of paragraph 5 is contained in the words 'they disciplined themselves' and the restrictions of the first half are intended as a preparatory action for it, the aforementioned release, could equally give rise to the opposite of discipline. I am not sure whether this did or did not happen in the 1984 performance, in which the improvisation was seemingly anarchic and contained much that had little to do with what had happened previously, or indeed with music. The conglomeration of a dumb show in sign language (laboriously memorized), improvised soloing, text recitations, the Action and Number scores, seven verbally-described 'compositions', and ten fully notated but unsynchronlzed vocal parts (the Ode Machines) seem to collapse the four days of isolated and silent preparation specified in 'Goldstaub' from Stockhausen's *Aus den sieben Tagen* (1968) into one hour (by no means isolated or silent): during the improvisation one is more aware of the freedom to do or play *anything* than the exhortation to act responsibly. Paragraph 5 is significantly described by Cardew as his 'view of the composition of the [Scratch] orchestra as it now exists [1971], with its high level of differentiation of actions and functions'[19] – also with its eventually destructive internal contradictions.

Paragraph 6 preserves the scheme of adjacent paragraphs contrasting with one another (although they were not conceived as being performed all together, for obvious reasons). In the instructions it is suggested that sound-sources used elsewhere in *The Great Learning* would be suitable: stones, whistles, speech, song, gueros, etc., but these are not individually specified. This piece requires intense listening by participants, of the kind that characterizes the ideal of free improvisation: they proceed independently through the piece but must frequently wait for (usually unconsciously-given) cues from the others, or from the environment. Some sounds, too, may be 'heard' rather than 'made'; thus any sound which occurs during performance is not only to be understood as part of it (as in Cage) but is drawn into each individual's performance. The element of 'discipline' is paramount here: it is seldom possible for anyone but the individual to tell where he or she is in the score, let alone whether it is being followed 'accurately' or not.

Example 6

The Great Learning, paragraph 7

NOTATION
→ The leader gives a signal and all enter concertedly at the same moment. The second of these signals is optional; those wishing to observe it should gather to the leader and choose a new note and enter just as at the beginning (see below).
"sing 9(f2) SWEPT AWAY" means: sing the words, "SWEPT AWAY" on a length-of-a-breath note (syllables freely disposed) nine times; The same note each time; of the nine notes two (any two) should be loud, the rest soft. After each note take in breath and sing again.
"hum 7" means: hum a length-of-a-breath note seven times; the same note each time; all soft.
"speak 1" means: speak the given words in steady tempo all together, in a low voice, once (follow the leader).

PROCEDURE
Each chorus member chooses his own note (silently) for the first line (IF eight times). All enter together on the leader's signal. For each subsequent line choose a note that you can hear being sung by a colleague. It may be necessary to move to within earshot of certain notes. The note, once chosen, must be carefully retained. Time may be taken over the choice. If there is no note, or only the note you have just been singing, or only a note or notes that you are unable to sing, choose your note for the next line freely. Do not sing the same note on two consecutive lines.
Each singer progresses through the text at his own speed. Remain stationary for the duration of a line; move around only between lines.
All must have completed "hum 3(f2)" before the signal for the last line is given. At the leader's discretion this last line may be omitted.

→ sing 8	IF
sing 5	THE ROOT
sing 13(f3)	BE IN CONFUSION
sing 6	NOTHING
sing 5 (f1)	WILL
sing 8	BE
sing 8	WELL
sing 7	GOVERNED
hum 7	
→ sing 8	THE SOLID
sing 8	CANNOT BE
sing 9(f2)	SWEPT AWAY
sing 8	AS
sing 17(f1)	TRIVIAL
sing 6	AND
sing 8	NOR
sing 8	CAN
sing 17(f1)	TRASH
sing 8	BE ESTABLISHED AS
sing 9 (f2)	SOLID
sing 5 (f1)	IT JUST
sing 4	DOES NOT
sing 6 (f1)	HAPPEN
hum 3 (f2)	
→ speak 1	MISTAKE NOT CLIFF FOR MORASS AND TREACHEROUS BRAMBLE

This is not true of paragraph 7 (Ex. 6 quotes the piece in full) which is an astonishing example of the minimum of instructions giving rise to music of strong identity and direction, although the process of harmonic attenuation from the initial dense dissonance (from all of the performers choosing a pitch randomly and independently) is much quicker, and a kind of equilibrium reached at a higher harmonic density, than might appear likely from the way the score describes it.[20] There seems to be an inherent tendency for the situation initially set up to produce a 'beautiful', diatonically based harmony from the short-lived chromatic/microtonal opening, even (or especially?) for those with untrained voices. For the listener to a complete performance (as well as a performer), paragraph 7 not only sums up, in its text, the philosophy of the whole work, but also finally reaches a 'point of rest' in its slow, enveloping, totally vocal music which forms an apt conclusion.

It would be difficult to accept paragraph 7, and much else in *The Great Learning*, in a spirit of alienation, whether participating or listening, however one may react to Cardew's own eventual appraisal of it as 'inflated rubbish'[21] and however ambivalent one may feel about its original philosophical aims. It is unfortunate that he did not feel able to use his abilities to organize music in this way in the service of more valid ideological goals, but he had his own reasons for this which I shall attempt to examine in the next and last section.

5 Socialist Music?

I have already touched upon the reasons why Cardew felt his embrace of revolutionary politics precluded any further pursuit of the many developments his music had undergone by 1971; a more important question remains – having accepted that all of a composer's actions are to be tested in the light of their relevance to the furtherance of socialism, and that it is not enough merely to change society gradually but necessary to plan for its overthrow, what is a composer to do next? I do not intend here to offer reasons why composers, or anyone else, should adopt such values; firstly for reasons of space, secondly because it could be and has been explained far more forcefully and succinctly than I would ever manage, and thirdly because the matter is to some degree at least self evident, and is becoming more so.

Reading Cardew's *Stockhausen Serves Imperialism*, as it grinds on through endless restatements of ideological rhetoric, however soundly based, eventually gives an impression of great bleakness, a dissonance with the optimistic aim of revolution and a new society. At the outset he states that not only is the avant garde and experimental music of his time worthless because its ideological influence (which is the true end product of an artist's work, as opposed to the artwork being in some way an end in itself) is irrelevant to the class struggle, but also that (therefore) the book itself is worthless, except in as much as it is a necessary exorcism for those like Tilbury and himself who, unlike the working class, have in the past been strongly influenced by artistic modernity.

It became obvious to Cardew that asking the question framed by Mao, 'whom do we serve, what class do we support?', produced the answer that his activity as a composer, as an improviser with AMM, and even as a member of the Scratch Orchestra, much as it may attempt a socialization of music, actually played into the hands of the ruling class and its cultural institutions, thus losing any radical impact it may have had in theory. The politicization of music must be rethought, the solution lying in integrating with the working class rather than either cheering it on from the sidelines or lecturing it from above, however one may thus cut oneself off from existing modes of dissemination. (It might be said that Cardew, having achieved some degree of public profile, was in an artificially good position to make this move.) The idea that music somehow stands outside the realities of the class system is an illusion; therefore the style of an engaged socialistic music should be one which is accessible, here and now, to the working people. But what style is that? Cardew's own background as a composer now begins to show itself when discussing the lack of criteria for criticizing modern music:

> By comparison with the effectiveness, wholesomeness, emotion, satisfaction, delight, inspiration and stimulus that we ... derive from Beethoven, Brahms and the rest, modern music (with very few exceptions) is footling, unwholesome, sensational, frustrating, offensive and depressing.

Although he adds in a footnote (written some time after the main text) that the attractions of bourgeois classical music will fade with the onset of revolution, it is clear that he is making certain assumptions regarding the accessibility of 'Beethoven, Brahms and the rest' to working-class people which might be contested. And if its attractions do fade (say they exist), will this not also be true of the compositions of Cardew and the rest which are in a similar style? And what will the world be left with then? Certainly not popular commercial music. And what are the 'few exceptions' in modern music which are effective, wholesome, and so on? Neither in 1974, when the book was published, nor at any time during the seven years remaining to him, did Cardew come near resolving these problems. The number of people whose political awareness and commitment were stirred by his later music must be very small, as must the number who actually had the opportunity of hearing any of it, in comparison with the size of its intended audience. Nevertheless, he continued to work in this direction with single-mindedness and even optimism, and it is my conviction that so must everyone else concerned with the production of music and its relationship with people (if it has none, then it is worthless by anyone's standards). Cardew's work begs a question to which there seems to be no answer, except the principle that musical problems are obviously not as important as political problems.

If working-class people are not in a position of awareness to accept any music in the service of socialism except the inevitable patronage offered by composers like the later Cardew, working in a deliberately simplified and banal idiom, then this is the fault of the processes of exploitation and stultification dealt out by the ruling classes to serve their interests. It is not good enough to assume that people who are expected to make rational and informed political decisions are at the same time incapable of being rational and informed about the culture of their projected society. It is unfortunate that most people are not in a position to come into contact, let alone sympathize, with radical musical ideas.

Notes

1. K. Stockhausen, programme note for *Carré*, in K. H. Wörmer, *Stockhausen, Life and Work*, tr. W. Hopkins (Faber, 1973).
2. C. Cardew, 'Report on Stockhausen's *Carré*', The Musical Times, cii, Sept. 1961, pp. 619, 698. [23-37]
3. R. de Beer, 'Interview with Stockhausen', *Key Notes*, xvii, 1983/1.
4. C. Cardew, *Treatise Handbook* (Peters, 1971). [107]
5. Latimer Press, 1974. [149-227]
6. Almeida Festival, London, June 1984; the performance was split over two evenings – paragraphs 1-4 and 5-7 – with a total duration of over 9 hours.
7. [Original article contained a discography not included here.]
8. C. Cardew, diary entry for 1 September 1964, quoted in J. Tilbury, The Music, in the programme of the Cardew Memorial Concert, Queen Elizabeth Hall, London, 16 May 1982.
9. C. Cardew, *Volo Solo*, preface to score (in *Treatise Handbook*).
10. Ibid.
11. *Treatise Handbook*. [97]
12. Ibid. [113]
13. J. Tilbury, 'Cornelius Cardew', Contact, xxvi, Spring 1983. [304]
14. *Treatise Handbook*. [125]
15. Ibid. [132]
16. Ibid. [99]
17. H. Gilonis, *The Ta Hsio of Confucius* (unpublished translation).
18. In connection with a performance of paragraphs 1 and 2 at the Berlin Philharmonic Hall in March 1974; the essay is included in *Stockhausen Serves Imperialism*. [202-212]
19. Sleeve note to Deutsche Grammophon recording of Paragraphs 2 and 7.
20. B. Eno, 'Generating and Organising Variety in the Arts', *Studio International*, Nov./Dec. 1976.
21. *Stockhausen Serves Imperialism*. [203, 210]

Editor's note: numbers shown in [ ] refer to pages in this book.

Cardew's *Treatise*

(mainly the visual aspects)

Brian Dennis

Tempo – No. 177 June 1991

Cornelius Cardew's 193 page *Treatise* is the longest and most elaborate piece of graphic music ever made. Although it was intended for improvisation and realization, using as many or as few pages as required, and with no fixed rules of interpretation, the piece can be regarded as a graphic construction inspired by music – and with 'music', in the broadest sense, as its subject matter. It was influenced by the philosophy of Frege and Wittgenstein, and in particular the latter's exhaustive *Tractatus Logico-Philosophicus*, which not only inspired the title but almost certainly the composer's economical approach to this endeavour and the rigorous development of his material. It was composed from 1963 to 1967.

Virtually all the pages of the score contain two fixed elements, one of which is more inviolable than the other: namely, a pair of staves at the bottom of each page and a central 'lifeline' or horizontal line which divides the page into two halves[1]. The two staves, which were intended for the convenience of a potential interpreter (for writing down his/her realization of a particular page of the score), are present throughout (although, as if to prove that anything is possible, one tiny violation does occur [on p.25] – a gesture typical of the composer!). However the lifeline is absent from a number of pages, is frequently obliterated, fragmented and generally incorporated into the overall effect of the design, as well as being used as a point of reference: either as a focal point or pivot, a 'ground' for objects to sit upon or a 'rail' from which they can hang.

Just as Wittgenstein tried to plot the limits of language by examining:

1. factual propositions, 2. 'pictures' of facts, and 3. elementary propositions as components of factual propositions (involving 'atomic' or key words) in an exhaustive and unified way, so Cardew limits his material to three basic elements, out of which a whole world of visual 'arguments' is constructed[2]:

1. **Numbers**   2. **Elements of Musical Notation**   3. **Abstract Shapes**

All three could be said to be present on almost every page, in the form of:

1. **Page numbers**   2. **The two lower staves** and 3. **The 'lifeline'**
(absent only from a few pages)

Page Numbers [3] speak for themselves (although with Cardew one can take nothing for granted) but **The two lower staves** have an influence which is profound; I will discuss this element first, using it at the same time as an introduction to the treatment of the **Elements of Musical Notation**. In a similar manner I will discuss **The Lifeline**, both for its own importance as a point of reference and as an introduction to the way in which other graphic materials are manipulated. A discussion of the **Numbers** will then be followed by a brief look at some of the complexities of both the treatment of the **Elements of Musical Notation** and the **Abstract Shapes** as a whole. As far as its structure is concerned, I will treat the work as if it were a conventional piece of music, reading it from left to right and from beginning to end. It is strongly apparent – whether one regards it as visual art, music or philosophical argument – that it was conceived in this way. Finally I will speculate a little on the links between the work and its influences, notably its connection with Wittgenstein's *Tractatus,* as well as attempting to place it in the context of English Experimental Music of the 1960s.

Example 1

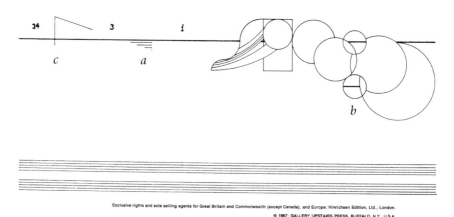

Exclusive rights and sole selling agents for Great Britain and Commonwealth (except Canada), and Europe: Hinrichsen Edition, Ltd., London.

© 1967: GALLERY UPSTAIRS PRESS, BUFFALO, N.Y., U.S.A.

The Two Lower Staves
The purpose of these staves is described above, but their relevance to the score is profound, I believe that not only are they there for the convenience of the reader/performer, but that they 'represent' the reader in an almost metaphysical manner. They symbolize the 'unknown' to whom the composer is trying to

communicate the incommunicable. This is not to do with any imperfections which might have arisen in the ruling of the staves, but in the fact that the staves are used as a major motif in the 'text' above. In other words the exact spacing and thickness of the two five-line staves occurs and reoccurs throughout the piece – quoted, half-quoted, looped, curved, convergent, divergent, aslant, in fact in every conceivable configuration. Many other thicknesses and spacings are also used to suggest staves, but the characteristics of the **lower staves** are particularly dominant. From the first tiny reference on p.1 (Ex. 1a), through many variants – the convergence on p.30, for example (Ex. 2) – through to the end of the work, they act as a major motif and, as if in valediction to the unknown reader/performer, the final 'cadence' of the piece consists of the composer providing two such staves of his own. On p.191 (Ex. 3) the 'lifeline' stops and after two beautifully drawn loop-designs (cf. Ex. 2), the staves emerge as shown: the top stave is hand-drawn (apart from line 2), the bottom is ruled (apart from line 2) and the process continues for two more pages of empty staves, identical except for the minute fluctuations of the composer's unguided hand. (NB. Straight lines, drawn without a ruler, have occurred three times in the piece already, thus preparing the reader/performer for the final 'cadence'.) Its uncanny emptiness cannot but remind one of the final sentence of Wittgenstein's *Tractatus*: 'What we cannot speak about we must pass over in silence'. The composer and performer, as it were, are united in this silence.

The Lifeline

This element is present in its central position for most of the score and although it is nearly obliterated many times (e.g. on p.133, at the 'climax' of the score, where large black circles virtually fill the page), some small portions usually survive. Only five pages are entirely without it, two of which I have already discussed (i.e. the last two pages). The others are pp. 115 – 6 and 141. Here the justification is almost certainly to prepare the reader/performer for *Treatise's*, climax and to signal its passing with silence (p.141 is entirely empty except for the lower staves). That *Treatise* has a climax, of a powerfully 'musical' kind, is obvious to anyone following it through. Black circles are used throughout the piece, often as crotchet heads, but the first of significant size occurs on p.113. The lifeline ceases on the following page and is absent for 2 3/8 pages as more black circles and their derivatives accumulate. It then returns, with what is at first a slow build-up, but grows powerfully, with fierce arrow like features rhythmically propelling the action forward until the circles reappear at p.130, swelling to the final climax on p.133, after which the circles diminish only slowly, until

Example 2

 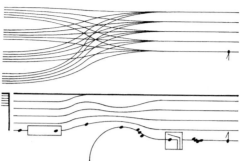

Example 3

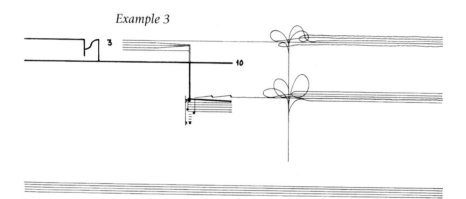

Example 4

Example 6

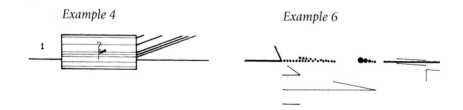

Example 5

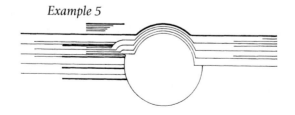

seemingly 'coming to rest' on p.140.[4] The 'silence' of p.141 not only provides a fitting contrast to the climax but also prepares us for the 'silence' of the final 'cadence'.

The involvement of the lifeline in the design is apparent from the very first page. Not only are shapes superimposed upon it, it is also frequently echoed (e.g. Ex. 1b). The thickness of the line helps to identify it, as indeed the thinness of the lower stave lines is important to *their* identity; these two pen widths are by far the commonest in the piece and Ex. 4 (from p.5) is just one of countless examples. The lifeline's frequent involvement with 'stave' systems can also be imagined from this example, as indeed in Ex. 5 (from p.17) where it is not only 'echoed' but briefly curved by a stencil as part of an implicit circle. The departure from its central position, either as a curve or as an oblique line, is often open-ended, leaving temporary lacunae. Sometimes it is broken quite savagely, as on p.126 (Ex. 6) or even 'hollowed out' as in Ex. 7 (from p.94). Ex. 8 (from p.183) is an excellent example of the lifeline being used as a pivot, and the extraordinary 'factory' on p.66 (Ex .9) illustrates the use of the lifeline as a 'ground'[5]. Finally it is worth mentioning that, in anticipation of the final cadence, the lifeline is 'hand-drawn' by the composer on pp. 169-171 and is virtually the only feature in a particularly sparse section.

The Numbers

Numbers play an important part in Cardew's *Octet' 61*. In fact its title refers to the numbers 1-8, which are featured liberally amongst the 'hieroglyphs' which make up the work (*Octet' 61* is, in fact, for any number of players, and is dedicated to the painter Jasper Johns, many of whose canvasses use numbers). In *Treatise*, numbers are scattered fairly sparsely throughout the score, although some sections are entirely without. At no point do they resemble musical symbols such as time signatures, tempo markings, etc. In fact the composer lays down strict rules which affect their appearance: 1. They are always hand-written with the same width of pen; 2. They are always the same size; and 3. They always sit 5 mm above the lifeline (or central plane if the lifeline is temporarily absent). Sometimes they act as markers: the long section which starts on p.23 is patently 'triggered' by a number 1, and after a powerful climax spread over three pages is terminated in like manner, with no other numbers coming between. Several examples of the 'triggering' or punctuating effect of numbers can be found elsewhere.

In this way, nine numbers are used in all: 1,2,3,4,5,6,8,10 & 34. (A tiny 7 appears once, but in a special context which I will discuss later). The vast bulk consist of 1s (96); the remainder diminish rapidly in number: 2 (27), 3 (19), 4

(9), **5** (7), **6** (1), **8** (1). The **34** begins the piece (Ex. 1c) . and the **10** marks the end of the lifeline before the final 'cadence' (Ex. 3). The **8** and the **6** are found very near to the beginning and end of the piece respectively (pp. 4 & 189): this may have a muted significance but it is far from coincidental. The tally of numbers and their hierarchic ratio (Cardew was still close to Stockhausen's thinking at the time) may well have been fixed at the onset, while the overwhelming dominance of the **1** suggests a more symbolic role (an atom, the first person singular or whatever). In any event there are entire sections, notably the climactic section (pp. 114-141), which have no numbers other than **1**.

As has been shown, Cardew makes rules but at some point usually breaks them. Indeed the 'number rules' remain unbroken for a very long time, and it is not until page 174 – where a set of seven tiny numbers appears inconspicuously near the bottom of the page (Ex. 10) – that the 'rules' begin to be broken. Then on p.182, five Letraset 1s (also arranged vertically) are placed above and below the lifeline (Ex. 11). These deviations play a significant part in bringing the piece to a close: the 'coda' which follows begins with a much quoted *tour de force* on p.183 (Ex. 12) while further violations of the 'number rules' occur on pp. 185 & 188-191 with hand-drawn numbers below the lifeline. The **10** which brings the lifeline to an end on p. 191 (Ex. 3) to my mind unites the dominant **1** with the circle which has been such a feature of the work as a whole, both graphically and as note-head. Indeed it could be said that here, in the plane of the lifeline, all three elements are unified in the final numbers.

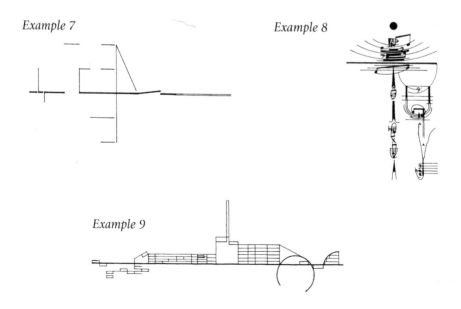

Example 7

Example 8

Example 9

Example 10

Example 11

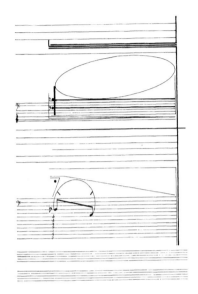

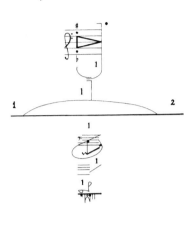

Example 12

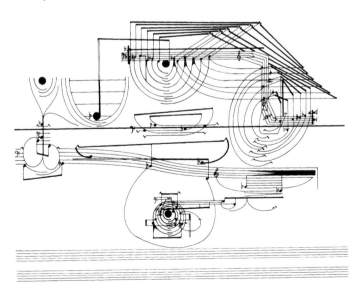

Elements of Musical Notation

Cardew is extremely economical with his choice of musical elements. Apart from the staves, which have already been discussed, note-heads are featured a great deal, both hand-drawn (i.e.. slightly oblique – see bottom of Ex. 2) or completely circular (as in Ex. 12, where there is a mixture). Minim heads occur just as frequently and are treated in the same way. Only occasionally do tails join up with the heads; they are most often featured headless but are alluded to constantly. The only rests I have found are dotted quaver and semi-quaver rests on page 156. Treble and bass clefs are used significantly, but no C clefs. Of the accidentals, flats are most frequent, sharps fairly common, whilst I can find only two naturals; again, the thinking seems to be hierarchical. All these elements are treated as part of the graphic process and are subject to every imaginable form of treatment: turned around, turned upside down, echoed, enlarged to the point where symbolism ends and abstraction begins, and so on. Like the **Numbers**, the hand-drawn aspect sets them apart, but here the composer substitutes graphic equivalents which are in turn distorted and recombined. In other words the treatment of the musical elements is extremely comprehensive, particularly considering the role of the staves already discussed.

Of the dynamics, only *p* and *f* are used, but to excellent effect, notably on pp. 23 – 29 where a large *f* dominates the beginning of the graphic section mentioned already (see **The Numbers** section). The most striking page of *p* and *f* motifs, however, is p.138. Here the subtleties of Cardew's art, as well as his way of 'arguing' shapes, are particularly apparent.

The Graphic Shapes

Curves, straight lines and areas of black are 'all that is the case', to paraphrase Wittgenstein (given that the composer is restricted to black ink and white paper)[6]. Shapes of various degrees of regularity, imperfection or, for that matter, recognisability, are formed from these elements. The circle has pride of place, the square is used with great significance, rectangles are fairly frequent, whilst the use of triangles is almost minimal. Up to p.46, it is as if the latter were being deliberately avoided. Again, the treatment is hierarchical. There is no attempt to create any feeling of depth; the whole work is as flat on the page as a Mondrian or Pollock, even though there is considerable use of overlay. Perspective, however, is quite absent.

Circles amongst shapes are as predominant as the 1s amongst the numbers, and regular portions of circles are also very frequent as, indeed, are regular portions of squares (i.e. $1/4$, $1/2$, & $3/4$ shapes) whilst the oval plays an important part towards the end (i.e. from p.144). If the piece is all but terminated by the **10** discussed earlier, it is also initiated by a similar combination, i.e.. **34** (see Ex. 1c)[7]. Given that *Tractatus'* final sentence ('What we cannot speak about we must pass over in silence') is dramatically the seventh and final premise/complex (in all its simplicity) of the entire work, *Treatise* 'begins' where words fail, and if the **34** is insufficient evidence for this (see footnote), then the horizontal 'graphic' seven (i.e. tilted through 90 degrees) which follows it (again Ex. 1c) should be ample proof of Cardew's intentions [8]. This, however, brings me to my final section.

Tractatus, Treatise and Experimental Music

As a work of graphic art, *Treatise* has undoubted highlights, and as a graphic work whose subject matter is music, it is second to none[9]. As the piece relates just as much to the Wittgenstein, there are many sections in the Cardew which strongly resemble exhaustive 'arguments' (albeit in graphic terms) and often austerely so: the 'coda' is one example while another section which particularly springs to mind (pp. 167-173), is very sparse indeed with its hand-drawn 'life-line' and very little else. Here one feels that the composer, like Wittgenstein, is trying to reduce an argument to its most basic components, while at other times there are whole complexes of multiple forms. This complexity, as well as the difficulty of making any single logical code of 'translation' from graphics to sound – especially as musical notation itself is part of the complicated interplay of forces – can thoroughly inhibit a musician such as myself from attempting to 'realize' even a small section of the piece (indeed Cardew himself, when he later turned against his experimental music, was most critical of the way in which in the 1960s, people imagined 'that anything could be turned into anything else'[10]. However, at the time, Cardew himself preferred *Treatise* to be performed by (to quote Michael Nyman[11]) 'people who by some fluke have (a) acquired a visual education, (b) escaped a musical education and (c) have nevertheless become musicians' (i.e. improvisers mainly of jazz, such as Keith Rowe and Eddie Prévost, who were the leading figures in AMM, a group to which Cardew belonged in the early 1960s.) My appreciation of the work, however, stems not from a regard for it as a piece of experimental music, but from a fascination with its visual dexterity and the author's attempt to create a large and entirely logical world of 'visual' musical imagery which seems to say everything 'about' music but none of which is music.

To describe the influence of Wittgenstein on Cardew and its relevance to English Experimental Music in general, we need to broaden our approach. On completing *Tractatus*, Wittgenstein felt he had said all that could be said in that particular field and turned away from philosophy altogether, initially to work as a school-master. Later, more dramatically, he denounced *Tractatus* altogether as, essentially, pursuing the wrong approach and proceeded to evolve an altogether different philosophy, arguably as influential as his earlier work had been. Without going into details, it is not difficult to see strong parallels with Cardew's own development after *Treatise*: the formation of the Scratch Orchestra with Cardew as its essential luminary, close in style to the way in which Wittgenstein taught at Cambridge, with its way of 'working out' ideas in situ with sudden insights, and significantly, with others (students, disciples or whatever); and then later, in 1971, Cardew's renunciation of virtually all former 'experimental' ideas in favour of a much more direct and practical kind of music (theoretically: 'music for the people' but rarely turning out as such). In fact this desire to say as much as possible in one highly complex direction (*Treatise*), to evolve ideas in a more social context (the Scratch Orchestra), and then to start afresh in a dangerously retrospective area (the re-application of tonality), is a tribute not only to the composer's strength of conviction but also to the courage with which he could repudiate his earlier work. I do know that Cardew was particularly fond of this quotation from Ezra Pound's 53rd Canto (at least at the time he wrote *The Great Learning*, but I suspect subsequently as well): 'Tching' (the great 18th century Chinese emperor, Tching Tang) 'prayed on the mountain and wrote MAKE IT NEW on his bath tub; Day by day make it new!' I suspect that Cardew found kindred spirits not only in old Chinese emperors (or for that matter, in Ezra Pound, whose translation of the Confucian *Great Learning* Cardew used in his settings), but especially in Wittgenstein whose intense desire to say 'everything and nothing' – and, in a sense, contain the world – was such an inspiration to the creator of *Treatise*.

I would like to thank Christopher Hobbs. who was a member of AMM for a time and took part in several 'realizations' of *Treatise*, as well as Virginia Anderson who is a leading authority on English Experimental Music, for stimulating many of the ideas of this article. Michael Parsons, who was particularly close to Cardew during the 'Scratch Orchestra' period, also made some helpful suggestions.

Notes

1. This was the composer's own expression (*Treatise Handbook* p.x). [113]
2. In his book *Wittgenstein* (Fontana, 1971), David Pears summarizes the aims of *Tractatus* in this way, denoting them X, Y & Z.
3. Like everything else, the page numbers are in Cardew's hand, but as they play no active part in the piece, I mention them only for completeness.
4. Richard Barrett draws particular attention to this section, quoting pp.130-133, in his excellent article on Cardew in *New Music '87* (OUP). [333-352]
5. Several designs in *Treatise*, intentionally or otherwise, resemble objects, a fact that was not lost on the players. Christopher Hobbs first drew my attention to the 'factory' and always referred to p.145 as the 'train-set' page.
6. *Tractatus* (here in the Pears/McGuinness translation) opens in a quasi-biblical way:
   1   The world is all that is the case.
   1.1   The world is the totality of facts, not of things etc.
7. On the **34** at the beginning, we have only the following cryptic remark by the composer to go on: 'It is a fact that there were 34 blank spaces before the first sign put in an appearance'. Whatever this means (34 attempts to begin the piece perhaps?), it does reinforce the significance of the upturned 7, which by definition is the first sign to appear after the 34 'blank spaces'.
8. This 'graphic' seven appears frequently throughout the score; most significantly perhaps on p.174 (Ex. 11) where it is to be found, this time in a vertical position, above the little string of numbers mentioned above.
9. Silvano Bussotti is, to my mind, closest to Cardew in artistic merit as a creator of graphic or near-graphic music. Many painters have, of course, also made music the subject matter of their work: Paul Klee's *Heroic Fiddling* (a homage to his friend, Adolph Busch) for example. Kandinsky's abstract canvasses also owe much to music, as is well known; indeed his choice of title frequently reflects this, e.g. *Composition No. 4, Improvisation No. 2*, etc.
10. From *Stockhausen Serves Imperialism and other articles* by Cornelius Cardew, (Latimer, 1974) p.83. [195]
11. From *Experimental Music: Cage and beyond* by Michael Nyman (Schirmer Books, 1974), p.100.

Editor's note: numbers shown in [ ] refer to pages in this book.

Briefly on Cornelius Cardew and John Cage
Christian Wolff

First published in Quaderni Perugini di musica contemporanea edited by Ulrike Brand and Alfonso Frattegiani-Bianchi, number 52-53 (A John Cage special issue), June, 1992. Then reprinted in Christian Wolff: Cues: *Writings & Conversations* MusikTexte, Zeitschrift für neue Musik, 1998.

Towards the end of the time when the newer European – Stockhausen, Kagel, Boulez, and others – and New York – Cage, and others – composers still maintained something of a lively exchange (say, about 1960), David Tudor and Cornelius Cardew (also Kurt Schwertsik and Frederic Rzewski) were notable for their involvement with both sides. Cardew had worked with Stockhausen, but then came to find the United States composers more congenial (he was also interested in current jazz, Thelonious Monk and Horace Silver, for instance). His performance (circa mid sixties) with Frederick Rzewski of Stockhausen's *Plus-Minus* in a Cagean spirit caused a scandal. Cardew's own work seems to me quite distinctive (including the later quasi-romantic political pieces), but from this time one could mention as close to United States work his *Memories of You, Octet 1961 for Jasper Johns* and *Solo with Accompaniment.*

This latter piece was written for the virtuoso and spectacular flutist Severino Gazzelloni and mischievously requires almost no exertion at all on the part of the soloist but has a very difficult accompanying part. This, as it happens – and I'm sure it's a coincidence – is exactly the case – plain and sober solo part, hard accompaniment – with Cage's 1987 flute and piano piece *Two.*

Cardew's pieces shortly after, like *The Tiger's Mind* or *Schooltime Compositions*, seem well removed from the world of Cage. In their ways they are highly indeterminate with respect to performance (but not at all with respect to their composition), and they are distinctively marked by (among other things) Blake, Cardew's fellow performers in the improvisation group AMM and Wittgenstein. Cage would appreciate the latter and probably Blake but he had no interest in improvisation. As far as I can remember, Cardew never showed interest in Zen or Indian philosophies. What both share is seriousness about the connections of moral issues and musical practices.

Though one could say that Cage's presence had transformed the musical landscape for him, Cardew was as much drawn to the then less known and in some ways more idiosyncratic figures like Feldman, La Monte Young, Terry Riley, George Brecht, Toshi Ichiyanagi and Takehisa Kosugi.

By the later sixties Cage was presented as a 'classic'. In the Draft Constitution of the Scratch Orchestra, published in 1969 in *The Musical Times* of London, the repertoire category of 'popular classics' included (playfully), along with Beethoven's *Pastoral Symphony* and Rachmaninov's *Second Piano Concerto*, Cage's *Concert for Piano and Orchestra*; though Cage was also represented in the list of current compositions by *Variations VI*.

Cardew's work with the Scratch Orchestra, social and musical, was remarkable. The orchestra's anarchic character was close to a practical realization of some of Cage's anarchic views, though its general flavor (until it was explicitly politicized to the far left) seemed milder, and its non-professional, folk-like and cottage industry character felt very English. Of the seven 'paragraphs' of Cardew's monumental *The Great Learning*, written for the Scratch, the second has something of the hard-edged force of certain Cage percussion pieces of 1939 to 1941, and the fifth is Cagean in its large collection of disparate, independent musical, theatrical and sound activities to be performed simultaneously.

By the early seventies Cardew had turned against the avant garde, criticizing sharply both Stockhausen and Cage (the latter at first somewhat more gently) from the Marxist-Leninist position to which he had come to devote himself. (Cage's interest in Mao did not move him.) Cardew's attack on what he regarded as Cage's apolitical formalism was strong, but oversimplified the relations between Cage's actual music and its reception (often still problematic for both audiences and sometimes performers) and Cage's articulate and challenging presence. Before long Cardew gave his main energies to political work and his own related cultural work, leaving behind polemics which had set some of us to thinking hard and which had done their task of freeing him up from the more esoteric and idiosyncratic strains – though they too have their value – of his cultural past.

Some Reflections on Cardew's 'John Cage: Ghost or Monster?'

John Tilbury

LMJ8 Contributors' Notes, *Leonardo Music Journal*, Vol. 8 (1998) pp. 66-68. Reprinted with permission.

Over a quarter of a century on, re-reading Cardew's seditious text, I can understand how what are now regarded as the 'archaisms' of the language can create barriers for the contemporary, and especially the contemporary young reader, many of whom were not born in 1972 when Cardew penned it. The unequivocal language of 'class warfare', which characterises the text throughout, the brutality of its sentiment may shock, even embarrass:

"Our music must be understood by our own people, it must arouse the masses, our friends, strike terror into our enemy, the bourgeoisie (i.e. because they can't understand it)."

The Condition of the Working Class in England was a work that Cardew studied in detail, and responded to. "The workers retain their humanity", Engels wrote, "only so long as they cherish a burning fury against the propertied classes."

"The main thing is to learn how to think crudely", Brecht insisted; and Walter Benjamin, (whom Cardew had read and quoted some years earlier but who, as 'arch-revisionist', was now, in 1972, beyond the revolutionary pale) had also recognised the necessity of crudeness: " Crude thoughts… should be part and parcel of dialectical thinking, because they are nothing but the referral of theory to practice." *Illuminations*, p.15. Thus: "I'm convinced", Cardew wrote, "that when a group of people get together and sing the *Internationale* this is a more complex, more subtle, a stronger and more musical experience than the whole of the avant garde put together. This is not pseudo-scientific fantasy but represents real people in the real world engaged in the most important struggle of all – the class struggle."

"There is only one lie, only one truth"; proletarian Art had to be tough, crude, it was meant to discompose and if necessary antagonise the left-liberal intelligentsia who, while bemoaning the capitalist system, would accommodate to it, use it to further their personal ambitions. They still hankered after commissions and fame within the bourgeois art establishment, at galleries and festivals, and would close off their minds when the intellectual going got tough, when the questions about Art became unanswerable because the answers were unthinkable.

But if Cardew's text is crude, I am also struck by its eminent reasonableness: for example, 'good' for Cardew means, indeed always meant, promoting desired change; that one's actions should be consequential – i.e. that it is no good wanting one thing and serving its opposite; that one should not practice self-delusion; that one should not accommodate evil; that it is necessary to stand up, if needs be, and be counted. And the most important of all these is the 'self-deception' from which many artists suffer abundantly, and especially, in Cardew's view, Cage. I, too, remember gasping at the naiveté of such accounts as when Cage, demonstrating the pervasiveness of 'chance' and its applicability in Art, recalls meeting Buckminster Fuller 'by accident' at Madrid airport – a felicitous example of the merely 'surface dynamism' which Cardew singles out for criticism in his article; the charm of contingency masks a deeper 'grand scheme' to which such 'contingencies' owe their existence. The overwhelming majority of the world's starving are unlikely ever to enjoy the luxury of such a chance meeting at Madrid airport.

In his diary Cardew wrote: "What Lenin does so well is to expose the reactionaries' capacity to pretend, and yet apparently seriously believe that they are not pretending. This is their puppet quality." Many of his friends believed that Cardew himself was practicing 'self-deception' at that time. But there was no question of pretence; Cardew dedicated himself to the cause body and soul; his commitment was awesome.

Cardew understood that too often the song is invalidated by the culture that sings it. So he drew a line and dared people to cross it; and few could: when he abandoned Western musical notation to join AMM; when he formed the Scratch Orchestra, in Michael Nyman's words "a successful experiment in social music-making, lived and died while Cage was still scratching his head," and finally, the politics. "The path of excess leads to the Palace of Wisdom," Blake wrote.

More recently, younger critics have warmed to Cardew's later music: referring to Cardew's later, much maligned political compositions. Ed Baxter wrote: "Cardew was right to take a stance... he was wise to stake out the social dimension to his music... His purpose was... to fight a corner and to express something human, faced with what Phil Ochs called 'the terrible heartless men' who still run our lives... Listening to them now I am overwhelmed, rendered inarticulate and revitalised. Great stuff. The newspaper is full of details of how long 'Starlight Express' has been running. It's all quite clear. 'There's only one lie, there's only one truth.' Whey hey hey!"

At the first performance of Paragraph 1 of *The Great Learning* at the Cheltenham Festival in 1968 the work created a furore; the public had split into two factions, participating through vocal approval or disapproval, to the extent that the music itself could hardly be heard. And I recall the broadcast talk in which Cardew's radical attitude towards music-making finds expression in his own reaction to the Cheltenham affair – and in his afterthoughts. Just as we should cultivate our own individual responsibility socially and politically, and only rely on our own judgement, so the audience at Cheltenham had every right, in Cardew's view, to act upon their judgement of a piece of music, and he applauds their lack of 'politeness'. The political dimension had already begun to emerge and in the vocabulary of his peremptory summing up of the affair there are overtones of violence which clearly foreshadow his later commitment to revolutionary politics: "When you find a certain situation intolerable you can attempt to change it, or terminate it."

Cardew had no time for the terrible compromises of real-politik. Hence, perhaps, the most constant themes in his work: Utopia and Failure. "Cardew – Utopista!" Cardew's teacher Petrassi exclaimed, with no hint of irony or dismissiveness in his words. "Fail, fail, try again, fail better", Beckett wrote. That this Utopia, or utopian nightmare some might say, could not be realised, and failed, does not in my view invalidate Cardew's political odyssey, any more than the 'failure' of the singers to be heard above the drumming in Paragraph 2 of *The Great Learning*, or of the Buddhist monks' chanting to be heard above the sound of the waterfall, should be the cause of embarrassment and humiliation; Cardew found nobility in failure. In a short broadcast talk Cardew expresses the antithesis to Western ambition and self-confidence in a way which I find strangely moving:

> Failure is an interesting topic; I read recently that one African tribe attributes the creation of the world to God's failure to hold everything together in one piece; his grip wasn't strong enough and it just whirled out of his hand. Then I read in the *Naked Ape* that such a tribe of so-called primitives is itself a failure; it has failed to evolve technologically. Another example: the American composer LaMonte Young says that if his music does not transport you to heaven he is failing. Everyone is failing; our entire experience is this side of perfection. Failure exists in relation to goals; Nature has no goals and so can't fail. Humans have goals and so they have to fail. Often the wonderful configurations produced by failure reveal the pettiness of the goals. Of course we have to go on striving for success, otherwise we could not genuinely fail. If Buster Keaton wasn't genuinely trying to put up his house it wouldn't be funny when it falls down on him.

People have spoken of the irrelevance, indeed the obscenity of artistic endeavour in the light of the unspeakable banalities of 20th century history. Tucked away in the back cover of Cardew's 1973/4 Journal is a sheet of notes on Hegel's *Aesthetics*. It ends:

> A question to be discussed: Art in the sense that it developed with the bourgeoisie to its great heights; will Art in this sense be carried over and developed by the Proletariat in its own interests. Or will the mode of Art associated with bourgeois philosophy (Hegel) pass away with the bourgeoisie? IMPORTANT.

In the *Critique of Judgement* Kant had called into question the primacy of the experience of Art in relation to the experience of nature; Cardew, too, had left "a chamber where are to be found those beauties that minister to vanity or to any social joys." But he did not turn to "the beautiful in nature in order to find, as it were, delight for his spirit…" Rather it was to the ill-formed, to the ugly, and to the temporal he turned; to the dispossessed, to the starving, to the victims against whose suffering and degradation no work of art, according to his own moral imperatives, could claim precedence. Cardew's Art was Life was Politics was… Art? Joyce's desiderata for an artist's life: silence, exile, cunning, was anathema to Cardew.

"Class stand. The artist should think to himself: do I really want the revolution to come? (Or is it simply an 'inspiring' possibility to juggle with?)" Cardew wrote. "Not criticism but revolution is the driving force of history," he read in the *German Ideology*.

Cornelius Cardew 1936-1981
Christopher Fox

CD notes – *Cornelius Cardew – chamber music 1955-64*
Apartment House
Matchless Recordings mrcd45, 2001

"Any direction modern music will take in England will come about only through Cardew, because of him, by way of him. If the new ideas in music are felt today as a movement in England, it's because he acts as a moral force, a moral centre." 'Conversations without Stravinsky', Morton Feldman, 1967

Cornelius Cardew was born in Gloucestershire in 1936. His mother was a painter, his father a potter, a pioneering figure in the English craft renaissance of the mid-20th century. After an archetypally English musical education (from cathedral chorister to the Royal Academy of Music to study piano, cello and composition), Cardew went to Cologne to study electronic music and within a year was Stockhausen's assistant, notably completing the score of *Carré* from Stockhausen's composition plans and later giving the premiere of *Plus-Minus*. More than any other English composer of his generation, he wholeheartedly absorbed the possibilities of the post-war avant garde, both European and American, into his compositional language, producing a series of strikingly original piano works including three sonatas (1955-8) and the *Two Books of Study for Pianists* (1958). By the early 1960s, however, his aesthetic sympathies were shifting from Stockhausen's determinism to the indeterminacy of John Cage. He returned to London, took a course in graphic design and was at the centre of radical music-making in Britain for the next decade.

In the succession of beautiful graphic scores which Cardew made during this period he explored different ways in which marks on paper could release musicians' creativity. *Octet '61* (1961), *Memories of You* (1964), *Solo with Accompaniment* (1964), *Schooltime Compositions* (1968) and, above all, *Treatise* (1963-7) all offer a fascinating mixture of more or less explicit instructions with visually beguiling notational designs – graphic and verbal riddles challenging their interpreters' imaginations. At the same time Cardew was becoming increasingly interested in free improvisation and in 1966 he became a member of the improvising group AMM. His activities as a composer continued but he turned from the enigmatic scores of the mid-'60s to something more straight-forwardly explicit, a setting of Ezra Pound's translation of Confucius, *The Great Learning* (1967-70) designed for performance by large groups of musicians and non-musicians alike. Each of the seven sections of *The Great Learning* is based on a 'Paragraph' from Confucius and, like the text, offers a model of collective responsibility articulated through different forms of musical interaction.

In May 1969 Cardew organised the first performance of the 'Second Paragraph', drawing together over fifty participants from a wide variety of backgrounds. Out of this gathering grew the Scratch Orchestra, a group that carried on working together only until 1972 but in that short time acquired legendary significance in the history of English experimental music. The Scratch Orchestra was as much a forum for the exchange of ideas as it was a performing group and in the intense ideological climate of the late-60s debate within the group became highly politicised, a process documented in Cardew's book *Stockhausen Serves Imperialism* (1974). In the Scratch Orchestra's performance of the first two paragraphs of *The Great Learning* at the 1972 Promenade concerts Cardew revised the Confucian texts to reflect his now Marxist-Leninist views on social responsibility and order. In the years that followed he went on to denounce not only this revision but all the music he had produced so far as the work of 'a politically backward composer wrapped up in the abstractions of the avant garde' and instead he concentrated on political activity, becoming a founder member of the Revolutionary Communist Party [of Britain (Marxist/Leninist)] in 1979. His musical output became avowedly functional: he wrote many songs for specific political campaigns and also returned to the piano, writing a series of rhapsodies and variations on popular tunes.

On December 13, 1981 Cornelius Cardew died, knocked down by a hit-and-run driver in Leyton, London. His killer has never been identified. The radical shift in idiom and aesthetic in Cardew's late music, together with his combative political stance, led to him being increasingly marginalised within the new music world. Since his death, however, his reputation has steadily grown, not only through the advocacy of his colleagues, students, family and friends, but also through the work of younger generations of musicians like those of Apartment House who have responded to the creative challenges offered in his scores and writings. We no longer have the chance to encounter Cardew's charismatic personality at first hand but we can still come to know it through the un-compromising imaginitive intensity of his music.

Cornelius Cardew – Early Works
Anton Lukoszevieze

notes from CD: *Cornelius Cardew – chamber music 1955-1964*
Apartment House, Matchless Recordings MRCD45, 2001

The works on this CD represent arguably the most experimental and radical music
to come out of Britain in the past 40 years. Cornelius Cardew's scores from the
early 1960's are notable for their elegant, original and precise notational design,
labyrinthine blueprints for realisation as totally new and original compositions.
They are open to ever new interpretations whose possibilities are restricted only
by the creativity of the performer. It is this responsibility laid at the feet of the
performer that contributes to their originality and beauty. Through performing
and organising these scores I am convinced that some of them only really 'live'
(notably *Octet '61* for Jasper Johns and *Solo with Accompaniment*) when the
interpreted material is welded together by the use of spontaneous improvisation.

Second String Trio and *Three Rhythmic Pieces for trumpet and piano* (1955)
These two early student works by Cardew are fascinating in their brevity and
Webernesque economy of execution. Subtly crafted, they have a fragmentary
elusiveness which seems to foreshadow the expressive disjointedness of the later
works on this recording.

Autumn '60 (1960)
In this work the conductor subverts his normal role: he can give clear beats or
vague beats, increase or decrease tempi, change the order of sections and even
stop conducting altogether. The players are also allowed the possibility of ignoring
or observing the written music and signs, as well as introducing their own material
into the performance. Cardew maintains a skeleton of his own pitch material
which will, by chance, remain just in and out of focus.

Octet '61 for Jasper Johns (1961)
The dedication to the American artist Jasper Johns reflects the obvious similarities
between the embedded numbers in the sixty graphic signs of Cardew's score and
Johns' number-overlaid drawings and paintings, which Cardew had seen at an
exhibition in Paris in 1960. In this version I have taken Cardew's use of overlaid
numbers as a starting point, so that we hear different parts of the sixty signs in
the score played simultaneously, overlaid in a multi-track recording. I have taken

Cardew's notation, realised it and doused it with my own spontaneity and improvisatory consciousness, adopting the use of a transistor radio at one point, in an attempt to get to what I perceive to be the heart of the matter.

Piece for Guitar (for Stella) (1961)

Much of Cardew's music developed out of his own activities as a performer and he had learned to play the guitar so that he could play in the British premiere of Boulez' *Le Marteau sans Maître*. The guitar piece (*for Stella*) (1961) contains music found in his earlier *First Movement for String Quartet* from 1961 and has a mobile form of 16 fragments, which the guitarist can play freely, repeat 'over and over', or even change.

Material (1964)

Material is just that, musical 'material' for any instruments capable of playing the dense chromatic chords in the score, which is a transcription of Cardew's *Third Orchestra Piece* (1960). The beginning is conducted briefly and then the musicians are left on their own to 'play', listen and wander about musically in a cool, hocketing and resonant indeterminate universe.

Solo with Accompaniment (1964)

This score could be read as a critique of Stockhausen's *Plus-Minus*, which Cardew premiered with Frederic Rzewski in 1964, and like *Plus-Minus* it consists of graphic matrices accompanied by an explanatory text and instructions. There the similarity ends. Few scores come anywhere near the ingenuity of *Solo with Accompaniment*, with its droll, ironic instrumental dialectic and subtle 'crossword' notation.

Memories of You (1964)

This is perhaps one of the strangest and most austere pieces on this CD. Memories of who? John Cage? The score offers nothing more than a series of circles, each of which contains the outline shape of a grand piano and a dot to represent an activity in, on or around the piano. The graphic symbol for the piano is similar to the dotted outline piano shapes found in Cage's *Concert for Piano and Orchestra* (1957-58) and Cardew, along with his pianist colleague, John Tilbury, was instrumental in introducing Cage's music into Britain. Sounds as themselves, floating in the acoustic space, like the music of another American, Morton Feldman.

Cornelius Cardew – Four Indeterminate Works
David Ryan

notes from CD: *Cornelius Cardew – chamber music 1955-1964*
Apartment House, Matchless Recordings MRCD45 2001 (amended October 2005)

It goes without saying that Cornelius Cardew was a major 'force' in British contemporary music. This would include his work on notation, his playing, his polemics, and also his active engagement in promoting experimental music. He was instrumental in making available works which otherwise would not have been heard in this country. I suspect his reputation as charismatic catalyst may have hindered his own works being taken as seriously as they deserved. This situation, of course, was exacerbated by Cardew's embrace – dramatically – of radical politics together with the public denunciation of his own earlier work. In the years immediately following his death it was this chasm between early and late work that was focused upon, which was endlessly talked about often at the expense of hearing the music. Those who consistently performed Cardew in those years (and still do), were predominantly his close associates: AMM and John Tilbury, who would characteristically turn out brilliant performances of *Treatise* or the early piano music. More recently the situation has changed, a wider net of performers are now engaged with Cardew's early work; and this is in tune with the nature of those pieces – with the increased possibility of a kind of maximum interpretative potential being realised.

What lies at the heart of Cardew's early work is his restlessness, a searching quality, and his tendency not to shy away from conundrums and contradictions. One such contradiction, which underpins many of his early works, is the relationship between pragmatism and idealism (perhaps a secret thread which links the earlier and later work). Cardew's own writings are energised by this duality. His attempts at addressing practical, concrete, performative problems and the consideration of more abstract philosophical issues characterised Cardew's approach to indeterminacy. This marks out Cardew's attitude as authentic interventions within the genre rather than – as with so many European composers at this time – a passing, almost decorative, fad. He had strong links, as friend, colleague, and performer, with other composers working in this way, most notably the Americans – Morton Feldman, Christian Wolff, and Earle Brown – all colleagues of John Cage. Each of these composers – Cardew included – developed their own solutions to the problems of 'Open Form' or Indeterminacy.

Four compositions which were originally published together by Universal

Edition in 1967 were presented with a prefatory note by the composer which proves a useful source for understanding his intentions: *Autumn 60, Solo with Accompaniment, Memories of You,* and *Material* are discussed together by Cardew, suggesting that "these pieces stand to one another in a relation of mutual support and enrichment; experienced gained from one is of vital importance in interpreting the others." He makes it clear that a very active participation is required by these pieces; the performer has to be an active interpreter, on a par, at times, with the composer: "Nobody" he says, "can be involved with this music in a merely professional capacity." Standing at the head of these compositions is *Autumn 60.* It is a brilliant exercise in persuading individual participation. It consists of a succession of various barred segments, in which each beat of every bar holds often contradictory performing instructions, potentially generating differing musical realisations of each event. As Cardew explains: "The musical potentialities of *Autumn 60* cannot be fully exploited in a single performance... the number of possible solutions for even a single beat far exceeds the number of musicians that can be got together for a performance..."

The implications of a piece like *Autumn 60* might parallel what Umberto Eco, writing in the early 1960s, referred to as a 'work-in-movement' – a work which is never 'closed', a performative event in which composer and performers unite in working within the piece's various limitations: "The 'work-in-movement' is the possibility of numerous different personal interventions, but it is not an amorphous invitation to indiscriminate participation. The invitation offers the performer the opportunity for an oriented insertion into something which always remains the world intended by the author."

What was the world intended by Cardew for *Autumn 60* ? Generally, the generated sound world has a fragmented, pointillistic atmosphere. Tying in with Eco's description, Cardew reminds us "The criterion of a good performance is not completeness (i.e. perfection) but rather the lucidity of its incompleteness." This holds true for *Autumn 60* and the other works in this set. *Material*, rather than exploring timbral discontinuities or interconnections, concentrates more on harmonic density and rhythmic flexibility, while *Solo with Accompaniment* on the other hand offers a reversal of the usual hierarchy associated with these designations: the accompaniment is highly complex, the solo is relatively simple. Here, in playing a steady long note, the soloist's breath or bow regulates the accompaniment, which is derived from a series of elaborate matrices. It is, however, *Memories of You* where the composer breaks almost completely with the traditional mould of notational practice: "More aggressive, tougher, simpler in conception" he suggests. The notation consists of various chains of circles each housing a diagrammatic outline of a grand piano. On each of these notations appear points which refer to the positions in space where a sound can either be initiated or concluded. Cardew suggests a choice (by the performer) of three objects to be utilised in making these sounds. It is a terse statement of interpretative freedom and the restraint of basic ground rules. Such a piece is difficult to pull off, and might end up as visual as it is aural.

These pieces create a coherent and cohesive statement of Cardew's approach to indeterminacy. They set in motion his dual attention to extreme pragmatism and philosophical, even utopian, ideals. They are subtle essays in how one might initiate a skeletal framework to be fleshed out, to be made corporeal, by future generations. Cardew referred to this as 'growth mechanisms': i.e. how changing performance practice and musical outlooks can be accommodated by compositional activity. It is a balance between 'cogent explicitness' and 'sufficient flexibility' rather than a fully notated 'self contained' piece:

> "The best guarantee for survival would be a completely self contained, closed logical system for each piece. Such systems might be rediscovered even after a lapse of thousands of years in a state of preservation comparable to Egyptian mummies. But however beautifully preserved they would nevertheless be dead, their language and meaning forgotten. So these little systems – these pieces – are not self contained; like seeds, they depend on the surrounding soil for nourishment, they are irremovably embedded in their environment which is the musical situation today."

Cardew's four indeterminate compositions have indeed proved their durability: not as 'closed systems', but as provocations for action, with all the attendant problems of judgement and ethics that this entails.

Index

Other books published by Copula

No Sound is Innocent
AMM and the Practice of Self-Invention, Meta-Musical Narratives
and other essays, Edwin Prévost 1995 ISBN 0-9525492-0-4

Minute Particulars
Meanings in music-making in the wake of hierarchial realignments
and other essays, Edwin Prévost 2004 ISBN 0-9525492-1-2

Forthcoming publication:

Cornelius Cardew: A Life Unfinished
A biography by John Tilbury
ISBN 0-9525492-3-9

Matchless Recordings and Publishing has a sizable catalogue of recordings
that feature many of the musics which inform and are discussed in the books
above. We also publish Cardew's score *The Great Learning*.

For details of these and other related items please write or go to:
www.matchlessrecordings.com